Hamlet Closely Observed

Hamlet
Closely Observed

MARTIN DODSWORTH

with a preface by
L.C. KNIGHTS

THE ATHLONE PRESS
London & Dover, New Hampshire

First published in 1985 by The Athlone Press Ltd
44 Bedford Row, London WC1R 4LY
and 51 Washington Street, Dover, New Hampshire 03820

British Library Cataloguing in Publication Data

Dodsworth, Martin
Hamlet closely observed.
1. Shakespeare, William. Hamlet
2. Shakespeare, William. King Lear
I. Title
823.3'3   PR2807

ISBN   0–485–11283–3

Library of Congress Cataloging in Publication Data

Dodsworth, Martin.
Hamlet closely observed.

Bibliography: p.
Includes index.
1. Shakespeare, William, 1564–1616. Hamlet.
2. Shakespeare, William, 1564–1616—Characters—Hamlet.
I. Title.
PR2807.D59   1985   822'.3'3   85–6151
ISBN 0–485–11283–3

Typeset by Inforum Ltd, Portsmouth
Printed in Great Britain at the
University Press, Cambridge

To my parents
with love

Contents

Preface

An American scholar has described *Hamlet* as 'the tragedy of an audience that cannot make up its mind', a verdict that would seem to be borne out by the voluminous and labyrinthine criticisms of the play. Martin Dodsworth does not offer a clew that will lead infallibly to 'the' meaning, but his very thorough 'close reading', backed by an impressive range of scholarship, is one of the most illuminating studies of the play that I have read.

His starting-point is the contemporary conception of 'honour', of the claims and duties by which those near the top of the social hierarchy asserted their place in society and established their sense of identity. In examining the meaning and implications of this he draws on the work of the anthropologist, Julian Pitt-Rivers, and on his own substantial knowledge of Renaissance history and literature. But as he says, he has 'tried to write a book about a play, not an idea in a play.'

Details of the particular code of honour that Martin Dodsworth finds implicit in *Hamlet* may be challenged by some Renaissance specialists. A careful reading of the book has certainly convinced me that the play is in fact permeated by a complex of ideas to which scholars have not so far given adequate attention. It does not much matter whether or not the reader gives unqualified assent to the formulations presented here. They are simply one way of pointing to the contemporary forms of those elusive assumptions of society against which at all times its more conscious members have to define what is most genuine for themselves. Hamlet is both a vividly delineated individual and a representative man: his fate is 'to be an examplar of human weakness despite and because of his attempted self-dedication to "honour" ' – or to whatever notions society upholds as static and unquestioned norms.

This bald account does not do justice to Mr Dodsworth's close and lively engagement with the text – text for a play that grips our interest in performance, and written text that we endlessly ponder. What makes the book both a pleasure to read and a stimulus to further thought is that the author works throughout in terms of a close engagement with all that most holds our attention in a powerful dramatic action, in the conflict and self-revelation of different characters, and in the ideas and evaluations that spring from that action. Scene after scene is brilliantly illuminated. Martin Dodsworth is a first-rate literary critic, as nimble as Empson, and as intelligently concerned with moral issues as James Smith. And with the ability to analyse the interaction of words in a medium as complex as Shakespeare's (the 'poetry'), he is also vividly aware of the play as theatre, where bodily movement, changing tempo and contrasting patterns of physical action are essential aspects of meaning. And his awareness of the moral issues provoked by the play is as firm as it is subtle and uncensorious: there is no question here of disparaging, or condescending to, the Prince. At a time when 'yet another book about *Hamlet*' seems to call for some justification, I would say simply that this book makes one – specialist or non-specialist – a better reader of Shakespeare.

Cambridge   L. C. Knights
King Edward VII Emeritus Professor of English
Literature, University of Cambridge

Acknowledgements

I would like to thank Joanna Dodsworth for suggesting that I read *Honour and Shame*; and Barbara Hardy, who made it possible for me to give much of my time to thinking about Shakespeare. Her encouragement has always been of great value to me. Royal Holloway College helped greatly by establishing and maintaining a scheme of sabbatical leave in difficult times. Elsie Dodsworth, who is much missed, and Slawek and Asia Rybicki all made it possible for me to give time to the writing of this book. I am thankful that I was able to discuss it in its early stages with James Smith, my former teacher, and with F. W. Bateson, my friend and neighbour. I am grateful to all those who read parts of this book as it was in the writing: John Barnard, F. W. Bateson, Francis Berry, Andrew Gibson, Barbara Hardy, Stephen Orgel and Christopher Ricks; and also to my later and necessarily anonymous readers. Finally, I thank all those writers whom I have consulted in thinking and writing about *Hamlet*, sometimes to agree, sometimes to disagree, but almost invariably with profit.

Brill, 1984

Introduction

Hamlet Closely Observed offers a 'close reading' of Shakespeare's play; that is, its primary concern is to elucidate the text by an interpretation of the words in which it is written, making use of historical and generic scholarship sparingly and only when the words themselves seem not to provide an adequate account of the imagined action of which they are part. It is not possible to dispense with such scholarship altogether, and indeed as far as concerns the idea of honour I have had to make intensive, though intermittent, reference to the work of historians and anthropologists as well as to that of literary scholars; yet simply in the interests of all those unlearned people who enjoy the works of Shakespeare and whose understanding is the basis for the esteem in which he is held even by scholars, it cannot be a bad thing every now and then to see what the play looks like when we use, as it were, the naked eye and not the spectacles of scholarship. In my own case, I find not that we can dispense with those spectacles altogether, but that we need to make rather less frequent use of them than our opticians suggest.

This is, nevertheless, a book that often refers to the work of other scholars, and necessarily so, given its aim. For the eye itself is rarely unprejudiced in what it sees. Our expectations condition sight; we look for the normal thing in the normal place, the hoped-for person where we would like that person to be. A 'close reading' must be at least partly corrective in its aim, striving to be alert to those moments when our own assumptions lead us to substitute, let us say, the normal thing for the extraordinary. I have found it helpful to throw these moments into relief by calling on the views of other twentieth-century critics, not merely because I disagree with them, but also because their assumptions, if they have not shaped those of my reader, can at least be taken as representative of them. This does not imply that the less recent, classical critics of Shakespeare—Johnson, Coleridge, Bradley—have nothing to offer us today, but merely that it has suited me in my corrective aim to think largely in terms of our own century. It is for the same reason that I have made such large use of the work of John Dover Wilson and Eleanor Prosser. What has made them so valuable to me in the course of my discussion is not that their views should be taken to represent those of a majority of scholars, but that they have both attempted relatively scrupulous readings of *Hamlet*. Their way of being close to Shakespeare's words has enabled me to advance a different and, I hope, better kind of closeness. In any case, I am grateful to them and to all their colleagues, and mine, whom I cite, sometimes to disagree with. Criticism is dialogue or, better, a conversation that continues through generations, reflecting, defining and even effecting historical change. Our differences of view are what enable us to take part in that enlivening conversation.

'Close readings' are, I fancy, a little out of fashion nowadays. They have little to do with the myth-based criticism of Northrop Frye or with the philosophical and theoretical style of writing about literature that has succeeded it. Nevertheless, I hope that no apology is needed for the close scrutiny to which in varying degree Shakespeare's text is here subjected. Shakespeare was a great dramatist by virtue of the way he wrote. Any interpretation of his plays, whether it is made in the study or the theatre, has to begin with the words Shakespeare wrote, though it may end far away from what those words imply. In this book there may be less generalization than some readers would like, but I hope that its particular comment contributes not merely to an understanding of this passage or that but to an overview of the play as a whole. There is a tendency in modern criticism to present *Hamlet* as inferior to the other three plays discussed by Bradley in his *Shakespearean Tragedy*, a tendency reinforced by the adverse judgement pronounced on the play by T. S. Eliot in his classic essay. I believe this to be a wrong tendency, and hope that I have been able to do justice to the profound ambiguity of the play, whilst at the same time showing it to develop in a consistent fashion without dissipation of dramatic or philosophical force and with an intensity of insight that does rival what we find in *King Lear*, *Othello* and *Macbeth*. However, this consistency has little to do with that very common interpretation of the play as the conflict between Hamlet and Claudius, 'two mighty opposites', and consequently I would reject valuations of the play based on it. Hamlet's fate has been, simply, to be misunderstood by spectators and readers. This misunderstanding reaches its furthest point in the belief that Hamlet's actions at the end of the play are justified by his being an agent of Providence—by his having, in this peculiar sense, his 'fate'. The rejection of this belief has critical implications with regard both to the play and to Shakespeare's tragedies in general.

'Close readers' of *Hamlet* are, however, slightly embarrassed by the question of what it is exactly that they are reading so closely. This is because there are three significant early printed texts of the play, disagreeing substantially one from another. I apologize for rehearsing once more their familiar differences, but they may not be familiar to all my readers. The First Quarto appeared in 1603 and offers a version of the play sometimes ludicrously incoherent; it is probably based on a reconstruction from memory made by an actor or actors who had at some time appeared in it, a reconstruction unwarranted by the owners of the copyright, who were, of course, the company of players to which Shakespeare belonged. The Second Quarto (1604–5) is almost twice as long as its predecessor and seems to bear a much closer relationship to the author's original manuscript; indeed, it may be a version in some way sanctioned by the copyright-holders. Nevertheless, the First Quarto, whose account of some scenes is in any case fundamentally different from that offered in the Second Quarto and the First Folio texts, sometimes offers readings superior to those of the 'better' texts. The First Folio text—that is, the version of the play printed in the posthumously collected and carefully prepared edition of Shakespeare's works of 1623–differs significantly in the matter of additions and omissions from the Second Quarto, as well as in hundreds of individual readings.

I have used the New Arden edition of *Hamlet*[1] as the basis of discussion in this book, occasionally considering alternative readings where they seem significantly to affect my interpretation. The text of this edition, in common with most other modern versions of the play, includes passages that are present in the Second Quarto but absent from the First Quarto, as well as passages present in the Folio text but absent from the Second Quarto. It is quite possible that nothing like this composite text was ever performed in Shakespeare's lifetime—or ever since, for that matter. Actors and producers have always been more interested in what works in the theatre than in respecting the author's every word. The question therefore arises as to what account a 'close reader' should take of the probable discrepancy between the text of *Hamlet* as generally presented by modern editors, the early printed texts of the play, and the successive versions of it that have been presented in the theatre.

Some writers take the view that it is in the nature of plays not to have a definitive text.[2] Plays are realized not on paper but in a succession of performances and productions in the theatre. However, poems are not realized on paper either, but in the minds of readers. In the case of *Hamlet*, as in the case of 'The Waste Land', there is a text and a performance, texts and performances. A literary critic is no more concerned with being 'definitive', in the sense of having the last word, than an actor is in rendering a part unplayable for ever more. The most that either can hope is to provide new criteria for the performances of others. Since 'definitive' interpretation is not the aim, we need not concern ourselves with the idea of a 'definitive text'. What is needed is a text which stand in a clearly defined relationship to what we believe the author designed for stage interpretation: Harold Jenkins's edition fulfils this criterion with distinction and adds to it much astute historical and interpretative commentary.

William Empson has suggested that when Shakespeare originally wrote *Hamlet*, on the basis of some older play, his version was so successful that he was led to capitalize on its success by making

> quite small additions and changes which screwed up the mystery [of Hamlet's nature] to the almost torturing point where we now have it—the sky was the limit now, not merely because the audiences wanted it, but because one needed only act so much of this 'shock troops' material as a particular audience seemed ripe for . . . in the big days of *Hamlet* they would decide how much, and which parts, of the full text to perform when they saw how a particular audience was shaping.[3]

Empson, then, thinks of the three significant early versions of *Hamlet* as reflecting the development of a text that was never entirely stable. He suggests that some passages were, as it were, optional— one or the other of them might be played on a given night. The differences between the Second Quarto and the First Folio texts might be accounted for if we suppose the optional passages elusive enough to be mislaid, some at one time, some at another. This seems very plausible, especially if we consider that allusions like those to the War of the Theatres in II.2, present in the First Folio but absent from the Second Quarto, would have been better suited to a London audience of the time than a provincial one ten years later.[4]

If we think of our composite text as made up of a core-*Hamlet* together with all the optional passages, the important question for the would-be 'close reader' becomes that of whether the optional passages conflict with one another in such a way that Option A implies one reading of the play and Option B another. In what follows I assume that there is no such conflict, though every optional passage (if that is what it is) has its own dramatic and poetic point to make, and I hope that this is borne out in the body of the book. If it is, then perhaps it may be allowed that in this one respect the reader in his study is more fortunate than the person in the audience at a performance of the play, for it is the reader whose experience of the play is more extensive.

That is not to say that the study has an invincible superiority over the theatre. Nothing can substitute for the immediacy and intensity of stage production. It does not follow that the critic's leisured contemplation of one speech, one line, or one word is somehow irrelevant to the play itself because it lacks the immediacy and intensity of the theatre. The actor's art is an art of subtlety and what he can suggest by one gesture may well take several pages to explicate—if it can be done at all—in rational prose. If we are curious about human nature and human institutions we cannot do without reasoning and explanation. The actor's glory may be to prompt such curiosity in us; the critic's, if he is lucky, to satisfy some of its demands and to further our understanding of ourselves and our history, in the mode of reason. This study aims to keep close to the established text of the play in the belief that it is primarily but not solely the words of the play that account for the excited admiration to which it gives rise, and not the story they tell, which another playwright might embody in other words (if, indeed, the 'story' can be distinguished so easily from the words in which it is told, something especially to be doubted in the case of this play, *Hamlet*).

It is no use pretending, however, that words exist in a void. They are inextricably linked to the context in which they are used. A 'close reading' of *Hamlet* cannot dispense altogether with discussion of Shakespeare's stagecraft as an element conditioning those words and conditioned by them. Nor can we avoid reference to historical scholarship: in some matters we have to put ourselves out to acquire knowledge which was apparently the natural possession of most if not all of Shakespeare's contemporary audience. In doing so, it is not of course necessary to abdicate all sense of ourselves as persons of our own time, making the judgements on the past that seem good to us. We do need, however, to be sure that our judgements are based on as full an understanding of the context in which the meaning of Shakespeare's words was grounded as is necessary.

As I have already suggested, to understand *Hamlet* part of the necessary knowledge of context has to do with honour. Shakespeare's art directs us always to the question of what Hamlet will do next and how we should feel about it. The question of what true honour is is quite subsidiary to this, yet not to be aware of what that question implies is to risk a misconception of what drives Hamlet to act as he does.

Anyone who wants to write about *Hamlet* from this point of view is, therefore, faced with a problem of balance. On the one hand, there must be no suggestion that 'honour' *tout court* is the focus of our interest in the play, but on the other the idea of honour needs to be developed enough for the reader to feel at home with it and to see the way in which it is relevant. My own solution is perhaps rather clumsy, but has the merit, I hope, of clarity. In my first chapter I discuss the role of honour in Elizabethan society, that is, as part of the historical context of Shakespeare's play, and go on to discuss the way in which ideas of honour figure in those parts of *Hamlet* that have to do with Polonius and his family. I do this partly in order to show some varieties of honour-behaviour, partly to show how these may be assimilated to a finely nuanced drama of individual choice and conflict, and partly because it seems to be Shakespeare's intention to make of the Polonius household fairly obvious and unperplexed adherents to the idea of honour who pointedly contrast with the perplexity and obliquity of Hamlet himself in this respect. However, once I have done with the Polonii, I turn my attention to Hamlet, following the action of the play through, with little general discussion, seeking in this way to give a faithful account of what its words suggest, and handling the topic of honour only in so far as this or that scene in the play seems to require it. In *Hamlet* 'honour' denotes a complex of ideas[5] always potential in the situation and the language of the play, part of the implied social context within which its words have meaning, but whose presence, though it is throughout a determining factor for interpretation, is not continuously realized in the text.

It may seem that the determining influence of honour in *Hamlet* must set an uncomfortable gap historically between us and the play, but I do not think that this is so, for a variety of reasons. In the first place, it must be questioned how far we are indeed imaginatively removed from the honour-behaviour reflected in the play. Neither duelling nor the self-conscious formulation of a sense of personal honour that goes beyond simple decency of conduct is part of civilized behaviour in the Western world, and indeed, though the word 'honourable' still has some force if used with care, the appeal to 'honour' is now pretty generally suspect. Furthermore, the fact that Renaissance honour is founded in the double standard of conduct for men and women puts it in opposition to the drive for equal treatment of the sexes which is basic to modern Western ideas of what is right. Nevertheless, and in general, it may be doubted whether society can altogether do without ideal forms of masculine and feminine conduct and the difficulties that must ensue when individuals, like Hamlet, feel themselves under pressure to conform to those ideals. Furthermore, although the forms and vocabulary of honour-behaviour may change, the underlying complex of ideas is resilient, and tends to appear—as an essay by Erving Goffman[6] suggests —in new forms. Sexual identity and the challenge of risk are both particulary pressing problems, not merely for the adolescent Hamlet but for the adolescent in general. Finally, Shakespeare himself, by not writing a play about honour in the way Beaumont and Fletcher were later to do, continually directs us to think about it in relation to its larger underlying concerns, such as the realization of individual identity within a given social matrix and the foundation of ethical ideas within a world which is perceived as in continual flux. These are not matters of remote historical interest to us. I hope that by adhering as closely as I have to the words of Shakespeare's play I may have been able to add to our understanding of just how subtly and forcefully these matters are presented in the play of *Hamlet*.

1 Honour and the Polonius Household

Prince Hamlet

Hamlet is a play about a prince. This is an even more important fact about it than that it is a play about a ghost or a play about revenge; but it is not a fact to which in recent years much emphasis has been given, in production or in criticism. It is not difficult to see why this should be so. Princeliness has little glamour for the twentieth century; or rather, what glamour it has is felt to be without substance. Hemingway's deflating comment on Scott Fitzgerald's 'The very rich are different from you and me' also sums up for our own time the predominant attitude to princes and princesses, lords and ladies: 'Yes—they have more money'. Scepticism of this kind does not leave much room for a sympathetic study of *Hamlet* as a play about a young man for whom his social rank is a crucial issue.

We like to see Hamlet as a kind of Everyman. Since Coleridge we have all found a smack of Hamlet in us, if, that is, we do not find him so reprehensibly odious as to present no possibility of identification at all; and certainly the former attitude is preferable to the latter. Yet it is this Everyman's specific social situation that enables the tragedy to come into being at all. A middle-class Hamlet would be very different from the one we have. The whole business of the Ghost, for example, would have to be handled differently. Its appearance could not be taken as a sign or portent for the state as a whole; its appearance to people other than the person it wants to speak with would seem odder; its association with archaic heroic encounter would be forced, if not impossible; its demand for justice might still be made powerfully, but its insistence on the insult to its own body and to family 'dignity' would be far more difficult to bring forward. The world of *Arden of Faversham* could not accommodate the Ghost from *Hamlet* with all its values unchanged. Indeed, the father's appeal to his son for revenge is aristocratic in essence, depending less on a sense that the law is inadequate to deal with the intricacies of this particular case than on the belief that the law is in some fashion at the son's bidding. There is therefore no need for the Ghost to mention justice, and it does not in fact do so. What Hamlet has to do is 'Remember me', that is, remember whose son he is, remember to what family he belongs, remember what membership of such a family entails. This appeal is essentially patrician. Faversham is a long way away.

That is not to say that *Hamlet* has no universal meaning. It is just that here, as in the other plays, such a meaning is mediated through the particulars of Shakespeare's time and place. One of these particulars which bulks large in *Hamlet* is the complex of ideas which cluster round Hamlet's princeliness, one which is easily designated in one word: 'honour'. A close reading of the play cannot ignore the significance of this term without in important ways distorting the work it tries to interpret.

This has been said before. Several earlier studies have set out to show the way in which honour determines major aspects of the action in *Hamlet*.[1] But these studies have not met with great success in modifying the view of the play generally taken by Shakespeare scholars. Harold Jenkins, for example, has little to say of it in his New Arden edition of the play; he cites none of the studies mentioned in my footnote. There seem to be two possible reasons for this indifference, apart from those which have to do with a reluctance to introduce class-based ideas into a play which is taken to have universal meaning. The first is that representations of what honour entailed in Elizabethan England are often rather implausible. The second is that very little work has been done on the record of aristocratic honour-based behaviour in England in Shakespeare's lifetime.

The implausibility is perhaps dependent on the small number of historical facts that are readily available. Accounts of Renaissance English honour almost inevitably base themselves on theory because so little is known about practice. In his large book on the subject, for example, Curtis Brown Watson has to rely largely on the writings of Aristotle and Cicero rather than on descriptions of how people actually behaved. He defends his manner of proceeding as follows:

It is enough to know that the English monarchs from Edward to Elizabeth made use of the *Nicomachean Ethics* as one of their principal works; that the numerous Italian dialogues on honour and the duel were directly indebted to Aristotle's definitions of honour, reputation, disgrace, injury and contempt; and that Cicero's *Offices* was the grammar school text-book on moral philosophy, for us to assign these two pagan philosophers a place of central significance. Even if Shakespeare's eyes were simply on the flesh-and-blood aristocrat, he could not have missed endless opportunities to witness the actual carrying-out of various cardinal aspects of the pagan-humanist ethics derived from these philosophers. The duelling scenes involving Romeo, Tybalt and Mercutio, and the duel between Hamlet and Laertes, are unmistakable reflections of the Renaissance code of honour and the duel, a code based on Aristotle.[2]

The facts of the first sentence are incontestable. However, it is wrong to assume that because the practice of honour was justified in Aristotelian terms, as it certainly was in Italy,[3] it was actually derived from Aristotle. On the contrary: the duel derived from the earlier trial by combat[4]—Aristotle's name was invoked merely in the cause of making it respectable. Whether we know this or not, it is hard to believe that Shakespeare, witnessing a challenge, would describe what he saw to himself as 'the actual carrying-out of various cardinal aspects of the pagan-humanist ethics' derived from Aristotle and Cicero. It is not impossible, but it is implausible, and all the more so since few of us have any idea at all of how often his eyes were on the flesh-and-blood aristocrat or of how often that aristocrat's behaviour might have been seen as reflecting specific aspects of honour.

Since Watson wrote, however, more work has been done both to grasp more clearly what ideas of honour have entailed at different times in different parts of Europe[5] and to document a little more fully the practice of honour in England in the following hundred years.[6] In both cases it appears that the concept of honour was changing in response to other social changes at the time *Hamlet* was written.

This gives new significance to the way the play is shaped. It begins, after all, with the recollection of a ceremonious and mortal exchange, in a military setting, between old Hamlet and old Fortinbras, the heroic qualitites of which are brought out by the appropriately archaic diction used. The play ends with another mortal encounter: but the setting is now domestic, the idiom is, however various, always contemporary in feeling and the heroism that may be evoked is a deeply suspect quality. The action of *Hamlet* is, as it were, suspended between these two honour-based encounters, one of them close to the older trial by combat, the other if not a duel, as Watson has it, then at least very like one. *Hamlet* is shaped as a passage from one conception of behaving honourably to another; this transition is not altogether that from one generation to another but has a wider significance within the play and in the world for which the play was written. It is therefore helpful to have some knowledge of the changing attitudes to honour in Renaissance England.

The containment of honour

Julio Caro Baroja quotes from a fifteenth-century Spanish chronicler who says of the feuds of which he writes that their underlying cause was the desire

> for greater worth [*mas valer*] as it was in ancient times throughout the whole world, among all the generations to this day, and those that are to come while the world endures.[7]

Baroja comments that the desire for 'this "prestige" or "*mas valer*" ' is 'an instinct arising in persons who live within social structures that are even older than Christianity or classical philosophy' and that it is connected with an idea of honour that is collective rather than individual, and based on a system of patrilineal clans. Families in this social system, which was common throughout Europe and all round the Mediterranean, were peculiarly sensitive to affronts to their honour, which effectively challenged their place in the social order. The characteristic response to such affronts took the form of the blood-feud. Trial by combat of the kind to be found in the first act of Shakespeare's own *Richard II* may be seen as an attempt by central authority–that is, the king– to contain the violent threat to stability inherent in clan-loyalty and the sense of collective honour, by bringing it within the rule of law and by focusing on individual action.

There can be no doubt of the relevance of this model for honour-behaviour to England, even in the early sixteenth century. Lawrence Stone has discussed the prevalence of aristocratic feuding in this period[8], and Mervyn James gives plenty of examples of the clan spirit at work in various of the rebellions against Tudor authority. 'Even in peace,' he remarks, 'the way of honour was the way of the sword, whose prestige was such that those who rose by other callings were often more than ready, given the opportunity, to take it. In an honour society violence, or the ever-present possibility of violence, was a way of life.'[9] Self-assertion, competitiveness and aggressivity were the mark of the man of honour of this kind, and James quotes *Troilus and Cressida* ('. . . honour travels in a strait so narrow/Where one but goes abreast . . . ' III.3.154–5) to make his point.

Evidently, the aggressive clannishness of this sort of honour-behaviour was a threat to royal authority, and continued to be so right into the century of Shakespeare's birth. James shows how the Tudor monarchs sought to contain the sense of honour by making it dependent on them. It was only in the sixteenth century that the English heralds were brought under the authority of the Crown itself, and the change was accompanied by a new insistence on service and obedience, not only in the concept of nobility promoted by the heralds themselves, but also in the new humanism of Sir Thomas Elyot's *The Boke named the Governour* (1531) and in what James refers to as 'the quietism and inner recollection which went with Lutheran "faith" '[10].

Baroja shows that there was a similar process of containment at work in Spain at this time.[11] In both countries the nobility were exhausted and demoralized by the internal conflicts of the previous century, and the monarchy asserted its authority as a source of honour, creating new honours (particularly, Baroja notes, individual honours, that is, ones that could not be passed on from generation to generation, so forming the basis for an enhanced sense of kin— compare Elizabeth I's knighthoods in England) and extending its jurisdiction over the existing nobility. But the results were not the same in either country. Mervyn James suggests correctly that Protestantism made a great deal of difference, creating a more urgent sense of the need for national unity as far as the Crown was concerned, and actively promoting an ethic of obedience to God's laws and His representatives on earth. One might add to this that not only Elizabeth's religion but also her sex helped to keep the old masculine ideas of honour in check. All her courtiers were her servants, and this use of a medieval convention was a further constraint on the jockeying for place and general aggressiveness that were, for example, commonplace in Spain. As James shows, honour simply fades away as a force in English politics in the latter part of the sixteenth century.

Yet it does not disappear. Elizabeth acted firmly to squash any conflicts which smacked of the point of honour, as we shall see in the next section; and her efforts were still needed in the 1590s. When James I came to the throne there was a new emphasis not only on the monarch as source of true nobility but also on the menace of duelling, against which James had to act more often than Elizabeth. Had Elizabeth been truly successful, this would hardly have been possible. It seems therefore that though she was able to control the sense of honour among her nobles, and even to modify it by introducing a stronger sense that there ought to be some relation between nobility and Christian ethics, she was not able to kill it. Shakespeare's *Hamlet* thrives, like other revenge plays, on the silent presence of an un-redeemed sense of honour which, though held in check, seemed still a fascinating and even frightening phenomenon in Elizabethan England. The question how much a man should or could take—the crucial one, once its collective aspect had been whittled away by state control—seems never quite to have been answered by the emphasis on Christian virtues of patience, fortitude and suffering, or by the more secular one of obedience to one's ruler.

The practice of honour

There is plenty of evidence for recognizable honour-based behaviour in the first decade or so of Elizabeth's reign. In 1559, for example, Sir William Pickering, a much-travelled man with a keen sense of dignity who had served as ambassador to France for Edward VI, received a challenge from the Earl of Bedford and is described as himself going about in such a way as to provoke a challenge from the Earl of Arundel. It is significant that Pickering—who, as a young man, had been a companion to the Earl of Surrey in breaking the windows of the citizens of London by shooting at them with crossbows—was at this time thought to be a suitable suitor for Elizabeth; Arundel is reported to have said he would take himself out of England if ever she should marry him.[12]

In the mid-sixties there was a whole succession of exchanges between Leicester and other parties. Again, the motivation seems to have been something to do with royal favour. On 31 March 1565 Thomas Randolph wrote to Sir Nicholas Throgmorton with a curious tale to tell about the Duke of Norfolk:

. . . The Duke's grace and my lord of Leicester were playing at tennis, the Queen beholding of them, and my lord Robert being hot and sweating took the Queen's napkin out of her hand and wiped his face, which the Duke seeing said that he was too saucy and swore that he would lay his racket upon his face; whereup rose a great trouble and the Queen offended sore with the Duke . . .

In modern terms the incident is trivial; what underlies it is rivalry not so much for the Queen's affections as for her favour. The public nature of Norfolk's gesture is essential to it; it is a claim of right, of what is his due. The Queen's anger does not reflect only her undoubted partiality for Leicester, but also her anxiety that the balance of power for which she worked among her courtiers should be maintained. She ordered the two rivals to make peace; but by the New Year the rivalry had broken out again. Leicester had got all his followers to put on blue stripes or laces; it was both a trial and a show of strength. Norfolk immediately put his people into yellow. This time both the principals got into hot water.[14]

Sir John Neale connects this incident with the feuding between Sussex and Leicester that was going on at court in the summer of 1565 and again in 1566, because Norfolk and Sussex were related. Sussex certainly had a grudge; Leicester had let it be known that he did not think much of the way his rival had conducted affairs in Ireland. The feud-response—fighting between retainers of the two households—is, of course, related to the show of strength by display of laces. Sussex, Norfolk and Leicester were all at this time single men and looking for advancement; their concern for their 'dignity' has little to do with the virtues of a Christian gentleman, much to do with that aggressive competitiveness which it was the monarch's task to curb. Also in 1566 Leicester found himself involved with another rival for the Queen's hand, Sir Thomas Heneage. Angered by his behaviour, Leicester threatened to have him beaten, appropriate treatment for an inferior (the assault on Dryden in Rose Alley more than a century later has always been attributed to the wrath of a nobleman). Heneage, a close friend of Pickering and known as a 'gentleman of reputation', answered that if Leicester came to him to insult him 'he would discover whether his sword could cut and thrust'. Once more the Queen intervened strongly and no duel took place.[15]

The Queen's action here is of a piece with her frustration of the attempt to revive the trial by combat in 1571, when a large crowd, gathered in Tothill Fields for the spectacle, were disappointed of the sight of blood, Elizabeth having persuaded the parties involved to compound their suit the previous day.[16] Honour-disputes, a threat to her political authority whatever their form (and the Tothill Fields affair was in fact entirely legal, approved by the Court of Common Pleas), had to be kept down.

This was something she was good at, but she never achieved such success that she could relax her grip, as the career of Robert Devereux, Earl of Essex, readily illustrates. His celebrated hot temper is best understood as the mark of an ambitious nobleman with a keenly developed sense of status—his own, that is, for he was very ready to 'forget' what was due to the Queen in the way of polite conduct. This forgetfulness smacks of a testing-out of his own power *vis-à-vis* hers. Early in his career he found himself fighting a duel with another young nobleman, Charles Blount; within the year he was to challenge Raleigh, though nothing came of it. Not too much importance should be attached to the fact that few challenges, as far as we can tell, emerged in actual combat; it was the public declaration of resentment that mattered, and the being ready to fight. In May 1589 Essex offered to fight any of the Spanish garrison at Lisbon in the name of his mistress Queen Elizabeth; in 1591 he angered the Queen by challenging the leader of the enemy French forces to single combat. In 1597, when Lord Howard of Effingham was made Earl of Nottingham as a consequence of his part in the Azores Voyage in which Essex, too, had distinguished himself, Essex demanded the right to trial by combat in order to vindicate himself; though it was not accorded him, the Queen reacted sympathetically and Essex was appointed Earl Marshal (with responsibility, therefore, for arbitration on affairs of honour).[17] This Cerberus was worthy of that sop.

In the end, it must be conceded, Essex did himself little good by this sort of behaviour, and his lack of political success could have indeed been used by Mervyn James to illustrate his thesis of the effective decline of the idea of honour in English politics as the sixteenth century turned to the seventeenth. At the same time his career illustrates the sense in which honour remained a live issue in Elizabeth's England. Above all the established nature of his reputation as a man of honour is worth noting, reflected in all manner of details: his receipt of the dedications of John Norden's *Mirror of Honour*

(1597) and of George Gyffard's *Treatise of True Fortitude* (1594), the latter a casuistical discussion of honour and its attributes; his arrogating to himself the right to create knights—twenty-one at a sitting in 1591, for which he was reprimanded by Burghley in the Queen's name (this did not stop his carrying on in this practice); his patronage of duellers like Southampton and Lord Bourgh;[18] and above all in his language. 'I am tied to my own reputation to use no tergiversation', he wrote at the beginning of his Irish expedition. 'Too ill success will be dangerous; let them fear that, who allow excuses, or can be content to overlive their honour.' The appeal to his own reputation, not to the Queen's wishes, is significant. '. . . Methinks it is the fairer choice to command armies than honours';[19] the man of honour determines what is of concern to him—no one else can.

Essex ended his career in 1601 on the scaffold. Harold Jenkins believes that some version of Shakespeare's *Hamlet* was being acted in 1600, or even at the end of 1599. There is no need to suggest that it is in some sense an 'Essex' play if we hold that some of the attitudes that fascinated Essex—marked concern for reputation, fierce resentment of wrong, above all insistence on the will alone as determining action— are reflected in *Hamlet*. Essex's career merely serves to show that there is nothing implausible in such a belief; that of Raleigh could be used just as well for the same purpose— there is, for example, the extraordinary story of Sir Francis Vere's attempt to get ahead of Raleigh in the first attack on Cadiz in 1596; Raleigh managed to overtake him but Vere attached a rope to Raleigh's ship so that he could draw level—all this as the battle started.[20] The thirst for honour, for acknowledgement of one's superiority, especially in such a masculine field of action as battle—this was, however much Elizabeth might strive against it, of importance in her lifetime; and it continued to be so once Elizabeth was gone and replaced by James.

What Elizabeth does seem to have done is to have squashed the tendency for families and households to feud. *Individual* resentment is the mark of the later years of her reign. This was greatly facilitated by the advent of the rapier, a light and handy weapon which was deadly only if used in single combat;[21] the first fencing-school opened in London in 1576, but it was not until the 1590s, when Vincentio Saviola and his brother opened their academy, that the duel seems to have caught on. According to Lawrence Stone, the number of duels and challenges mentioned in newsletters and correspondence jumps from five in the 1580s to nearly twenty in the next decade, to rise thereafter to a peak of thirty-three in the ten years 1610–19.[22]

The figures, of course, are meagre; they can be, and have been, [23] easily minimized. Thirty-three deaths in ten years is not a great many. But we have to remember on the one hand that only gentlemen of high rank were deemed fit to duel, and on the other that the duel as a possiblity was a potent fact of the imagination, if nothing else. Why otherwise was James so concerned to inveigh against it?[24] The reason surely lies in the dangerous fascination which the idea exercised; and that is more important than the statistic.

It is as a fact of the imagination, too, that Shakespeare treats honour in *Hamlet*. The play is not a demonstration of certain principles held unswervingly and applied directly to the fashioning of their lives by his characters. Shakespeare's treatment is dramatically persuasive because it shows characters whose grasp of themselves (and therefore of honour) is uncertain, modified by other aspects of their behaviour. This is true even of that part of the play where concern with honour is most emphatic—the part that has to do with Polonius and his family. Shakespeare is, of course, principally concerned with the new fashion of honour that had appeared in Europe in the hundred years or so before the writing of *Hamlet*— the honour that is the focus of individual rather than communal sentiment, and which has an important bearing on the idea of masculinity. This masculine element in the sentiment of English honour (which is also doubtless an English fantasy of honour) has to be explained by reference to a general account of honour which derives largely from Mediterranean models. It is interesting how well this works. Those who doubt the relevance of this material will need to consider on the one hand, for example, the congruence of attitudes such as those in the *charivari* throughout Europe, including England, in the Middle Ages and subsequently[25]—the *charivari* being a popular aspect of the essentially aristocratic cult of honour—and on the other the way in which these ideas of honour and masculinity are bound into the complex web of feeling and idea that is the drama of *Hamlet*. Once again, the point is made by a glance at Polonius and his children.

Polonius and the honour of the family

It is only a slight exaggeration to say that Laertes and Polonius talk about honour 'incessantly'.[26] When Laertes moralizes his farewell to Ophelia and Polonius his to Laertes, it is certainly the dominant idea. Laertes warns Ophelia not to be over-trusting in regard to Hamlet:

> . . . weigh what loss your honour may sustain
> If with too credent ear you list his songs,
> Or lose your heart, or your chaste treasure open
> To his unmaster'd importunity.   (I.3.29–32)

Laertes is concerned with honour as reputation; he is afraid that Ophelia will be credited with being too free in her behaviour, whether or not she has in fact lost her heart or given herself entirely to Hamlet. The greatest evil is what people will say. Polonius confirms her brother's advice. It might seem that he is more concerned for her moral welfare than for her reputation:

> I must tell you
> You do not understand yourself so clearly
> As it behoves my daughter and your honour.   (95–7)

But 'honour' as chastity in a woman has strong overtones of 'honour' as reputation here. What Polonius wants Ophelia to avoid is the outward sign of her relations with Hamlet:

> Tender yourself more dearly,
> Or—not to crack the wind of the poor phrase,
> Running it thus—you'll tender me a fool.   (107–9)

A baby would make fools of them all, as well as being a fool itself, because it would so completely devastate the family in the eyes of others. Polonius and Ophelia would be held equally incapable of preserving the honour of their family.

Polonius's concern for his family's reputation extends to his son. He sends his man Reynaldo to Paris expressly to discover what people are saying about him. But there is a difference in the kind of reputation he will tolerate in the case of his son. There must be no hint of sexual feeling or behaviour in what is said about Ophelia, but where Laertes is concerned, Reynaldo may

                                                 put on him
What forgeries you please—marry, none so rank
As may dishonour him—take heed of that—
But, sir, such wanton, wild, and usual slips
As are companions noted and most known
To youth and liberty.   (II.1.19–24)

The woman is expected to be vulnerable: special care must be taken
that her honour is not soiled. But the man is expected to have
vices—'gaming', 'drinking, fencing, swearing, Quarrelling, drabbing': these are acceptably manly. 'Liberty' is the natural companion
of a man's 'youth'; but Ophelia is chided for having been 'most free
and bounteous' in giving audience to Hamlet.

Pitt-Rivers has remarked that 'once the notion of reputation is
admitted as a constituent of honour, its value as a purely moral
concept faces ambiguities'[27] and this rapidly becomes clear in Shakespeare's depiction of the concern for good name and appearances in
the Polonius family. The double standard for men and women, the
faith in which Laertes shares with his father, is not exactly under
attack, but the inconsistencies and awkwardnesses to which it gives
rise are the basis for much that is strictly dramatic in, for example,
Laertes's advice to his sister.

There is much earnestness in his warning to her that she should
think of Hamlet's advances as

         a fashion and a toy in blood,
A violet in the youth of primy nature,
Forward, not permanent, sweet, not lasting . . .   (I.3.6–8)

but its force is weakened by his embarrassment at having to talk
about a person of high rank, Hamlet, whose behaviour seems to him
both right and wrong—right because young men of the nobility will
have their 'liberty' and wrong because he is putting his sister's
reputation at risk. His deference to the idea of rank is such that
Laertes is in constant difficulty when he refers to the undesirable
aspects of Hamlet's behaviour. His dismissal of the Prince's 'trifling'
manages to be less than censorious for this reason. It is 'a toy in
blood', an 'amorous sport of impulsive youth', says Harold Jenkins,
but the sense of 'blood' in association with high birth hovers about
the phrase: if Hamlet were not noble, this toying would not be
mitigated—indeed, it would not be a 'toy' at all. Hamlet's being a
youth of 'primy' nature does not only make of him a springlike

figure, but emphasizes his leading place in the hierarchy of rank. In such a nobleman only can such behaviour show as a violet. The moral that Ophelia might take from Laertes's lines here is that she would do well to gather rosebuds, or at least this violet, whilst she may. Hamlet offers her 'The perfume and suppliance of a minute' (9) and 'suppliance' suggests that she will be for him simply a means of relief or brief distraction; but—because within the freedoms of Shakespearean blank verse it can pun on the etymologically and usually accentually distinct 'súppliance'—also suggests the heady sensation of having such a high-blooded young aristocrat at one's inferior feet. No wonder Laertes concludes this opening speech 'No more'. The phrase means not only that Hamlet offers Ophelia no more than fleeting pleasure but also that Laertes is getting carried away and should say no more in this betraying vein.

Laertes subsequently tries not to insist too much on the promptings of Hamlet's body and to invoke reasons of state for the infidelity he expects him to show, but it all comes out wrong: he has to keep correcting the balance so that no disrespect is implied. It is just the same:

> For nature crescent does not grow alone
> In thews and bulk, but as this temple waxes,
> The inward service of the mind and soul
> Grows wide withal. (11–14)

First he tries to sanctify the body so powerfully invoked in 'thews and bulk' as a 'temple', then he tries to emphasize the overriding demands of 'the mind and soul'. The Riverside editors[28] gloss 'as this temple waxes' as follows: 'as the body develops, the powers of mind and spirit grow along with it', but of course that is flat contrary to the meaning of 'wide', which is to the effect that body and mind *part* company. There is more than a suggestion of 'wide of the mark', as if the body were too much for the mind to control, and perhaps a hint that the young prince offers service mentally at the feet of more than one young woman. Laertes has not expressed himself very well, though Shakespeare has, for his purposes, done so excellently.

> Perhaps he loves you now,
> And now no soil nor cautel doth besmirch
> The virtue of his will; but you must fear,
> His greatness weigh'd, his will is not his own.
> For he himself is subject to his birth . . . (14–18)

He begins again by attributing genuine 'love' to Hamlet, but his anxiety soon gets the better of him: 'the virtue of his will' manages to combine respect with the distrust Laertes is unwilling to express, since the phrase means both 'his virtuous intentions' and 'the strength of his desires'. The double strain continues in 'his will is not his own', which means both that Hamlet has to act as befits his position not as he pleases, so that, for example, he must leave himself open to the possibility of an advantageous marriage; and that, having youth and the liberty of 'greatness', his sexual feeling will inevitably get the better of him. He is 'subject to his birth'[29] and cannot help doing what his nature, his body, tells him to (but having responsibilities to his position in society, if Ophelia gets pregnant, he will not be able to do anything about it).

Conscious that what he has said is not quite so impressively respectful of the social order as his own insistence on 'honour' requires, Laertes tries again to elevate his tone:

> He may not, as unvalued persons do,
> Carve for himself, for on his choice depends
> The safety[30] and health of this whole state . . .   (19–21)

That is not bad, though 'carve for himself' may be a mite gross in this context, and he has perhaps exaggerated Hamlet's importance. Laertes ploughs on:

> And therefore must his choice be circumscrib'd
> Unto the voice and yielding of that body
> Whereof he is the head.   (22–4)

The last phrase is an attempt to regain balance after the awful capitulation to the undercurrent of his thought in 'yielding of that body': Laertes seems to be thinking of Ophelia yielding to Hamlet and Hamlet yielding to a body all too compliant to his 'will'. But thinking of Hamlet as 'head' to a body which has a 'voice' independent of the head only makes matters worse, suggesting total disorder. There is nothing for it: having got so far Laertes must make the best of things that he can. So:

> Then if he says he loves you,
> It fits your wisdom so far to believe it
> As he in his particular act and place[31]
> May give his saying deed . . .   (24–7)

The ambiguity bedevilling Laertes is still present. He is warning his sister not to expect more of Hamlet than of any other man whose superior rank makes marriage with her socially undesirable; at the same time he has a particular possible act of Hamlet's in mind, to be performed in a particular, that is, private place—the 'deed' that is all that Hamlet's saying has led up to. To banish that disgreeable picture and to make his meaning decent and respectful, therefore, he has to qualify the extent to which Hamlet *may* 'give his saying deed':

> which is no further
> Than the main voice of Denmark goes withal.   (27–8)

It is a characteristically Shakespearean speech in the completeness of its imagining of Laertes's mind, a completeness which avoids both crudity and caricature. The compromised moral position in the man who pursues honour in Laertes's fashion will, moreover, turn out to have an important bearing on Hamlet's own conduct.

Like his father, Laertes expects the young man of birth to be sexually aggressive. There is nothing unusual about that expectation. Pitt-Rivers observes of his Andalusian society that 'the ideal of the honourable man is expressed by the word *hombría*, "manliness" . . . Masculinity means courage whether it is employed for moral or immoral ends . . . the concept is expressed as the physical sexual quintessence of the male (*cojones*).' The increased importance attributed to individual honour in the case of noblemen as opposed to members of the inferior classes explains sufficiently the expectation that the honourable nobleman will be, like Don Juan, a sexual predator.[32]

Of course, we see little in Hamlet's behaviour that could justify the fears expressed by Laertes, apart from his faith in the relation between noble birth and young male conduct. He sees what his idea of honour leads him to expect. It is striking that a critic familiar with a society in which the manly ideal of honour still survives should have taken Laertes's view and, indeed, concluded that Hamlet had already seduced Ophelia before the opening of the play. His Spanish background rather than anything in what Hamlet says explains Salvador de Madariaga's strange conviction that a fully sexual relationship between Hamlet and Ophelia would have been more comprehensible and normal than the 'Jane Austenish coloured lithograph' that was what was usually made of this episode.[33]

It will appear from what has been said that the double standard of conduct for men and women to which Laertes subscribes is deeply rooted in the honour-behaviour of Western Europe:

> This division of labour in the aspects of honour . . . delegates the virtue expressed in sexual purity to the females and the duty of defending female virtue to the males. The honour of a man is involved therefore in the sexual purity of his mother, wife and daughters, and sisters, not in his own. *La mujer honrada, la pierna quebrada y en casa* (the honourable woman: locked in a house with a broken leg), the ancient and still popular saying goes, indicating the difficulties which male honour faces in this connection: for once the responsibility in this matter has been delegated the woman remains with her own responsibility alleviated. The frailty of women is the inevitable correlate of this conceptualization . . . [34]

Laertes and Polonius expect Hamlet to be sexually aggressive: they expect Ophelia to be weak, and they feel their own honour to be involved in hers.

Although acknowledging Hamlet's 'greatness' in respect to them, their sense of their own status is not small. Polonius's advice to his son is that he should behave as suits a young gentleman of standing. He must be seen to be a true member of his class; hence the importance attached to what Reynaldo can learn from people's gossip about Laertes—this is what the concern for reputation of this 'honourable' man comes down to. Laertes must attend to his dress,

> For the apparel oft proclaims the man.
> And they in France of the best rank and station
> Are of a most select and generous chief in that.
>
> (I.3. 72–4)

It is to be expected that he will 'quarrel'—that is, duel (the word itself was not yet in common use[35])—but he must be judicious about it. Indeed, if Polonius insists on self-examination as the basis for his son's behaviour ('to thine own self be true'), it appears that what he wants is a Laertes who checks his actions to see that they befit a man of his rank and class.

> Give thy thoughts no tongue,
> Nor any unproportion'd thought his act   (59–60)

combines advocacy of the Aristotelian mean with that of the reserve habitual to the man of good birth: 'Be thou familiar, but by no means vulgar . . . '(61) The word 'vulgar' retrospectively converts the universal morality of 'any unproportion'd thought' to a class basis. In *this* context, it means any thought unfitting a person of Laertes's standing in life, and indeed the sense of honour is customarily rooted in such a class feeling:

> Groups make certain that the conduct of their members will be appropriate through the establishment of a specific concept of honour, such as family honour, the honour of an officer, the reputation of a businessman for honest dealing. They do so especially with regard to those specific differences which mark them off from the broadest social group [the state].[36]

Laertes returns

At the beginning of the play, then, Polonius and Laertes are shown to be concerned about honour, in particular as it implies status, and status attributed to all the members of the family. This honour is felt to be vulnerable in so far as it is left in the hands of an unprotected woman, Ophelia; all the more so since both Laertes and Polonius seem to think it natural and in some measure reasonable for the young man of good birth to take advantage of the weakness of women who are socially inferior.

When Laertes returns from Paris, however, the emphasis is upon the obligation to restore the family honour when it has been disgraced. This is consistent with the way he behaves in the early scene with his father and sister, but shows a different aspect of the principles underlying that behaviour. Paul Siegel compares him to Tybalt in *Romeo and Juliet* because he has so thoroughly 'absorbed the Italian code of honour'[37]: this is to attribute too much to his stay abroad. He acts in a fashion that his father would approve. On the other hand, it *is* significant that he has been in France, because the French sense of honour had been notoriously acute since the 1560s (Chapman's *Bussy d'Ambois* is a fascinated study in French honour); France was just the place where Laertes would feel at home.[38]

Laertes feels as a bodily sensation the insult to his honour constituted by the unrevenged death and unceremonious burial of his father:

> That drop of blood that's calm proclaims me bastard,
> Cries cuckold to my father!   (IV.5.117–18)

The element of hyperbole should not be allowed to obstruct our view of the kind of feeling Laertes thinks he ought to have, and thinks he has. There is an intimate relation between honour and the physical person. Pitt-Rivers draws particular attention to the head as a focus for honorific ceremonial: the crowning of the monarch, the covering or uncovering of the head before respected persons, the right of a man of honour to be put to death by beheading (decapitation recognized that there was something worth chopping off). But there is nothing exclusive in the importance attached to the head. As we have seen in the previous section, the whole body, animated by the blood of distinguished ancestors, is a potent force for honour. And the underlying principle of the duel, the aristocratic extreme of honourable behaviour, is that offences to honour can be redeemed only by the letting of blood, that is, by an equivalent desecration of the physical person. '*La lessive de l'honneur ne se coule qu'au sang.*'[39]

Like his father, Laertes sets great store by the outward signs of status. He is therefore especially bitter about, and offended by, the failure to accord his father more than an 'obscure burial':

> No trophy, sword, nor hatchment o'er his bones,
> No noble rite nor formal ostentation   (IV.5.211–12)

The weight of his feeling attaches to that word 'noble', as so much of his father's did to the word 'vulgar' ('Be thou familiar, but by no means vulgar').

The 'honour' to which Laertes subscribes, and in which he has been instructed by his father, is one which requires essential worth to be reflected in outward forms. The idea is fundamental to the concept of honour in society:

> Honour is the value of a person in his own eyes, but also in the eyes of his society. It is his estimation of his own worth, his *claim* to pride, but it is also the acknowledgement of that claim, his excellence recognized by society, his *right* to pride.[40]

According to this view of honour, Laertes is right to resent the 'maimed rites' which are all that can be accorded the dead Ophelia, just as he is to resent the unceremonious burial of his father. The play does not, of course, ask us to take this view, but we need to have at least a sympathetic understanding of it if we are to respond to all that is present in the scene over Ophelia's grave. Laertes believes Hamlet to have deprived both his father and his sister of the 'ceremony' which was not simply *their* due but the whole family's. Laertes feels the dishonour acutely. Since honour is life, to be dishonoured is to be dead, at least in the spirit, and he despairingly asks for the process to be completed. He will be buried alive: 'Now pile your dust upon the quick and dead . . . ' (V.1.244). Hamlet is right to expose the frailty of Laertes's language by leaping into the grave with him. We know that Laertes does not really mean what he says; we have seen him plan for the future when Hamlet is to fall a victim to him, and we have other examples of grief with which to compare his and from which to conclude that his is vamped up. But in taking exception to his behaviour here, we are not expected necessarily, I think, to decry the idea of honour itself, or indeed the idea that external forms should complement intrinsic honour. Rather, we are made to feel that his conception of honour is not honourable enough.

A striking instance of this.—though it is not, of course, the only one—comes when Hamlet pleads madness in mitigation of any offence he may have caused Laertes, and receives the reply:

> I am satisfied in nature,
> Whose motive in this case should stir me most
> To my revenge; but in my terms of honour
> I stand aloof, and will no reconcilement
> Till by some elder masters of known honour
> I have a voice and precedent of peace
> To keep my name ungor'd. But till that time
> I do receive your offer'd love like love
> And will not wrong it. (V.2.240–8)

This is much worse than the moment when, egged on by Claudius to kill Hamlet, Laertes says that he is willing to 'cut his throat i' th' church', because here there is no egging on: he speaks quite deliberately. 'Love' and 'nature' stand opposed to 'honour', but he remains unshaken in his adherence to it (despite, for example, the belief that 'nature' prompts the man of honour to act as he does, which he expressed in his speech to Ophelia in I.3). 'Honour' is a kind of prop here, on which Laertes leans to justify his severance from human nature and his diminution of 'love' to something 'like love'. Twice 'honour' is at the limit of the line, filling it out and exhausting it, since in each case it sounds what it is, the feeblest—but the ultimate— justification of bad faith. How delicately Shakespeare does it! The narrowness of the point of view and the obstinacy with which it is maintained complement the youthful confused embarrassment of the warning to Ophelia against Lord Hamlet. Laertes is a young man; we see his immaturity harden into forms positively evil. The conclusion, however, is not that his devotion to a formal code of honour brings out the worst in him but that Claudius is able to make use of it to that end, thanks to Laertes's own immaturity and the openings which his concept of honour afford the king. We need to see how Claudius turns the sense of honour against itself.

His behaviour in regard to Laertes is certainly unorthodox. It is extraordinary that a king, law-maker and fount of all honours, should offer to submit himself to the judgement of others:

> Make choice of whom your wisest friends you will,
> And they shall hear and judge 'twixt you and me.
>
> (IV.5.201–2)

To be sure, the 'offence' he has in mind is not of the criminal variety; his offence would be one against honour, and in admitting the barest possibility of guilt he is careful to confine the context to that of offended honour:

>   Why, now you speak
> Like a good child and a true gentleman.
> That I am guiltless of your father's death . . .   (IV.5.147–9)

In the words 'child' and 'gentleman' he names the two respects in which Laertes might feel his honour touched. As his father's son he feels the slight to his father; as a man of honour in his own right he feels the slight to his father as one to himself also.

His offer to submit the matter to the adjudication of Laertes's peers is analogous to the use of the Earl Marshal's court in the reigns of Elizabeth I and James I as a means to settle disputes about honour— the practice was common throughout Europe. James, in fact, was to try to strengthen the authority of this court, though he effected little. 'Reputation, (which comes neerest to the life of a Generous and worthy minde)' should, he said, be determined either in the civil courts or by the 'Court of Honour . . . which was erected to no other end.'⁴¹ He well understood that the latter might be preferable to noblemen, since there they were subject to the judgement of their peers, whereas in the court of common law the verdict was determined by juries whose estimate of honour, as they were not themselves of noble birth, necessarily differed from that of noblemen. Claudius's offer, then, implies that in some sense, though the source of honours in Denmark, he may be on a par with Laertes. This is balm indeed to the young man's offended honour. It is plain that Claudius's only concern is to calm his rival's fury; the unprecedented offer (which is, in fact, purest flattery and is based upon Claudius's total indifference to the idea of honour upheld by Laertes) achieves its end.

Claudius is disturbed by the fact of Laertes's return because it is unadvertised: 'Her brother is in secret come from France' (IV.5.88). So long as he is not threatened by it himself, however, he is sympathetic to this need for secrecy, and when persuading Laertes to comply with his plan for Hamlet's despatch, he makes secrecy a prominent advantage of it:

> And for his death no wind of blame shall breathe,
> But even his mother shall uncharge the practice
> And call it accident. (IV.7.65–7)

Alice Shalvi has noted that 'such secrecy is not uncommon in the revenger',⁴² and this explains Claudius's anxiety at Laertes's return. The need for secrecy derives from the nature of honour itself. Since honour resides partly at least in status and reputation, it follows that loss of honour is accompained by loss of reputation. Secrecy in the time between the slighting of one's honour and the achievement of satisfaction in recompense for it is a means of protecting one's reputation when it is most vulnerable. Furthermore, a slight to honour is nothing if not a personal affront, and by the talion law that underlies honour-behaviour in this respect its purging must be personally sought by the victim, and by him alone:

> A man is . . . always the guardian and arbiter of his own honour, since it relates to his own consciousness and is too closely allied to his physical being, his will, and his judgement for anyone else to take responsibility for it.⁴³

Claudius understands the secrecy of Laertes's return as a sign that he

intends to redress the slight to his honour constituted by the extraordinary circumstances of his father's death and burial. There is no
need to regard this secrecy as particularly vile or Italianate, since it is
an intrinsic part of the structure of beliefs that is honour.[44]

On the other hand, Claudius's manipulation of Laertes is itself
derogatory to that honour which the young man is so concerned to
put right. Under the cover of secrecy, Laertes and Claudius are to
deprive Hamlet of all chance of life. He must face a rapier not merely
unbated but also poisoned and, if that should fail, a poisoned drink
will finish him off. Poisoning in England was abhorred,[45] but it is not
simply the sense of fair play that stands to be offended by the King's
plotting. Although in Spain the maxim held *a secreto agravio, secreta
venganza*, it certainly could not apply here, where the public offence
to his family requires public satisfaction for Laertes, but not merely
that. By allowing Claudius to make Hamlet's death doubly, even
trebly, sure Laertes makes certain that his honour can never be
vindicated against that of Hamlet; for the duel, like the judicial
combat, depends on putting the physical person in hazard under
conventionally defined conditions which imply a judgement of
destiny. He can hardly claim that his sacred honour has been upheld
by God if matters have been arranged so that God could intervene
only by a miracle. He should not, of course, have allowed Claudius
to propose the scheme to him; but it is Claudius who sees how the
'secrecy' traditionally associated with the affair of honour can tempt
him into the inherently wrongful revenge that he plans.

But of course Claudius is here also using the flattery which had
been so successful in calming Laertes on his arrival back in the court
of Denmark. The attraction of secrecy lies also in the fact that Laertes
is plotting *with the King* and with the King only, and so drawing out
into action the equality implied by Claudius in his willingness to
submit to the judgement of Laertes's 'wisest friends'. As we have
seen, his original secrecy in returning implied that he took sole
responsibility for the restoration of his family's honour; in accepting
the help of Claudius he puts that honour in question. Why does he do
so? Surely because of what it means to his offended feelings to have a
king address him in this way:

> Now must your conscience my acquittance seal,
> And you must put me in your heart for *friend*. . .   (IV.7.1–2)

Honour is a compound of the sense that one deserves respect for the righteousness of his ways and of the sense that one is owed respect by virtue of the position in society accorded him. Concentrating on the latter, Claudius induces Laertes—who is young and uncertain, despite his willingness to posture as someone totally committed—to lose contact with the former aspect altogether. The quest for virtue is swallowed up in the apparent gain of status.

Honour and contradiction

Laertes is the indubitable example of someone motivated by honour, and his behaviour illustrates important aspects of that principle. It also illustrates something else. In this play we are not to think of one code of honour played off against another, as is often suggested. Claudius plays on the immaturity of Laertes, but also upon contradictions inherent in the very idea of honour. Laertes interprets honour in a fashion that is consistent with the ideal view of it which he shares with his father but that also reflects on his own callow nature. This must be so. The individual's sense of himself is necessarily reflected in the behaviour towards him which he requires or is prepared to accept from others. The idea of a code presupposes the existence of a group which has established forms of conduct totally adequate to the sense of himself entertained by any one of its members. The ideal nature of such a group is too evident to need comment. The tendency to construct codes of honour manifested by the courtesy books is only testimony to the incurable longing for an impossible fixity of social forms. Shakespeare in his art respects the actual, not the ideal. The sense of honour, as he clearly sees and as he represents it here, is based on a set of rules liable to conflict among themselves and from which the individual makes his own selection, applying the rules only as and when he sees fit:[46]

> The notion of honour is something more than a means of expressing approval or disapproval. It possesses a general structure which is seen in the institutions and customary evaluations which are particular to a given culture. We might liken it to the concept of magic in the sense that, while its principles can be detected anywhere, they are clothed in conceptions which are not exactly equivalent from one place to another. Like magic also, it validates itself by an appeal to the facts (on which it imposes its own

interpretations) and becomes thereby involved in contradictions which reflect the conflicts of the social structure . . . [47]

I have tried to show how Claudius takes advantage of such a contradiction in his manipulation of Laertes. The confusions of Laertes's admonishment to Ophelia spring from another such contradiction—the necessity to respect Hamlet conflicts with the necessity of attributing to him motives that in others would be ignoble. The play thrives on such contradictions.

There is a good example in the scene between Polonius and his man, Reynaldo.

Acting tradition makes the part of Polonius a comic one, and of course the distinction which he draws between 'drabbing' and 'incontinency' is comic; but the humour lies not so much in the character of Polonius as in the principles of honourable conduct to which he subscribes. Though comic, there is nothing odd about these principles. Polonius says no more than a senior officer might do to a subaltern, explaining that it is all right for his visits to the brothel to be known but that if he wants to make advances to the CO's daughter he should be sure to do it in private. Reynaldo, being only a servant, subscribes to a different morality: Polonius understands that some people do, which is why he takes the trouble to say 'Drabbing—you may go so far'. It is not, even, that he disputes the immorality of drabbing: it is one of the *taints* of liberty, but such 'flash and outbreak' is the consequence of having 'a fiery mind', the natural expression of Laertes's manliness. Reynaldo's objection 'My Lord, that would dishonour him' could apply only to someone in whom the mind was not sufficiently fiery to excuse such taints; it is a naive contradiction of Polonius's 'What forgeries you please—marry, none so rank/As may dishonour him' ((II.1.20–1). Pitt-Rivers notices a difference in the extent to which honour permits sexual freedom between the classes in modern Andalusia. The smaller, the less urban and the poorer the community the more public opinion, the basis of reputation, 'recognizes virtue rather than precedence as the basis of honour'. Conversely, 'those whose claim to honour is greatest, and also most dependent upon lineal descent, are most careless of sexual honour.'[48] The exchange between Polonius and Reynaldo turns on the same paradox, to which the opposition of 'drabbing' and 'incontinency' draws our attention. It is magic indeed that keeps Polonius from a sense of contradiction, and it is a magic to which Reynaldo submits: he knows that his betters behave differently.

When Polonius attributes to Hamlet a 'larger tether within which he may walk' (I.3.125) he does no more than anticipate his linking of (noble male) 'youth and liberty' in the later scene. Freedom is, however, far from excusable a taint in Ophelia's conduct because, being a woman, she ought not to have a 'fiery mind':

> . . . you yourself
> Have of your audience been most free and bounteous.
> If it be so—as so 'tis put on me,
> And that in way of caution—I must tell you,
> You do not understand yourself so clearly
> As it behoves my daughter and your honour. (I.3.92–7)

When Ophelia protests that, after all, Hamlet has offered her love 'in honourable fashion' we have a conflict not unlike that between Polonius and Reynaldo. Because she is a woman, her understanding of Polonius's 'honour' is incomplete. She judges Hamlet in terms of his actions only, without reference to the social context, applying the simple, uncontaminated moral calculus of Reynaldo. She is, in the event, right to do so. Polonius expects Hamlet to conform to what he thinks of as the norm of courtly behaviour. Of course he will 'drab', like Laertes, and any woman of inferior class—and that includes Ophelia—is a potential 'drab' in respect of him.

These little squabbles about honour reflect not rival 'codes' but different points of view which are socially determined. This does not debar us from sympathizing with Ophelia and Reynaldo or from taking their side; but it does complicate the stand we take, since it inevitably involves us in an attitude to social organizations as a whole, and should be felt to do so. Yet Shakespeare is concerned as much with the individual's relation to individuals as with his implication in a social order; it is not merely convention that attributes inclusiveness of view to him—he actually has it. There is an implied difference of opinion between Polonius and Laertes as to which one ought to have the keeping of the family honour. They both agree, of course, that their honour is at stake in the conduct and reputation of Ophelia. But Laertes does not concede the simple point that as head of the family it is up to Polonius to talk to her about it. Ophelia's reply to her brother delicately suggests that he has spoken out of turn. She is able to turn the double standard against Laertes, daring

him to say that women are expected to obey a different morality
from men. (They are, but in a Christian society this has to remain
something largely understood in the social forms.) She challenges
the authority out of which he speaks, but not just his moral authority.
In suggesting that he may fail to keep his own advice she is remind-
ing him of the youth that makes his counselling her irregular within
the family situation:

> Do not, as some ungracious pastors do,
> Show me the steep and thorny way to heaven,
> Whiles like a puff'd and reckless libertine
> Himself the primrose path of dalliance treads,
> And recks not his own rede.   (I.3.47–51)

'Puff'd and reckless libertine' at once forestalls the conventional
palliation of trivial faults the young man might be bold enough to
offer, and also mocks his youth. (It could hardly be meant in its full
force—that would be quite out of keeping with Ophelia and her
relations to her family.)

The blessing which Polonius launches into immediately on enter-
ing confirms the audience's sense that Laertes *is* young and *does* lack
his father's authority—all the more in submitting to it readily. On
the other hand, Polonius's garrulity and his ready approval of what
Laertes has said ('Marry, well bethought' (90)) as well as the later
scene with Reynaldo which asserts authority but in a way which it is
hard to feel quite right—if Laertes is old enough to go to Paris, he is
old enough not to be put under surveillance there without cause—all
these things suggest the decay of authority which Laertes has anticipated with Ophelia.

The main point to be made about this ought to be simply the
supreme power of the dramatist who presents it so surely, so rightly,
and yet without undue emphasis. The relation of Laertes to Polonius
is offered with the imaginative realism that is the basis of Shakespeare's art, his observation of the interaction of individual with
individual. Yet even in this quite subordinate part of the play something of general importance is visible in the interplay of characters;
the close identification of Polonius and his family with concern for
honour of no very thoughtful kind does not preclude the possibility
for ambiguity and equivocation that the concept of honour entails.

Raising questions

By looking at the scenes most obviously concerned with Polonius and Laertes it is possible to identify clearly two aspects of their concern for honour. They think of honourable behaviour largely in terms of rank and reputation, and their notion of what is honourable is intimately linked with a double standard in conduct for men and women.

All this is quite clear and bears on Hamlet's own case; but it is not simple. Shakespeare's greatness as poet and dramatist is evident even in this relatively minor part of the play. He is not interested merely in tipping the wink to us that we should be thinking about Hamlet's dilemma as a dilemma of honour. The fluid nature of the concept itself interests him: and in presenting Laertes's self-entanglement in counselling Ophelia, and his entrapment at a later stage by the King's manipulation of ideas of honour, Shakespeare capitalizes upon this fluidity. *Hamlet* is a play of ambiguous and shifting values, and honour is one aspect of the ambiguous form of human existence that the play contemplates. Its value to Shakespeare lies in its serving to raise questions, not to settle them. In the next two chapters I shall show some of the ways in which the Laertes–Polonius matter relates to the first act of the play as a whole, and some of the questions that it raises.

2 Hamlet, body and soul

Dissatisfied spirit, unhappy body

The first two scenes of *Hamlet* are obviously and significantly contrasted. The obvious difference is that between the cold and dark
outside on the battlements of Elsinore and the smooth conduct of
business by day within, where only Hamlet's 'nighted colour' appears
to resist the 'cheer and comfort' of the new King's eye (I.2.68,116).
Coleridge finds a clear dramatic meaning in this contrast, speaking of
the 'relief' that is produced by the change from castle-platform to the
court indoors, which allows the character of Hamlet to present itself
without having 'to take up the leavings of exhaustion'.[1] What
Coleridge means, I think, is that the opening scene is so powerful in
its effect on the audience that to have introduced Hamlet in a scene
closely allied to that in tone (for example, by moving immediately
from Horatio's decision to go with his companions to tell the prince
about the Ghost's appearance to the latter part of scene 2 in which
they do so) would have been to introduce him unimpressively, all
our imaginative interest still being held by the Ghost and its mysteries.
But the word 'exhaustion' implies not merely that the opening scene
is powerful, but that it has a certain completeness. Even the characters
in the scene are aware of this: the coming of day, which they
describe so memorably and emphatically, signifies that the Ghost
can come no more for the time being, and that their business with it is
done. That is why the resolve to 'impart what we have seen tonight',
though giving forward impetus to the action, lacks urgency: the
dominant feeling at the end of the scene is that something is over.

This suggests that the contrast is not simply that between settings
but applies to the actions presented in them. This larger contrast is
emphasized by similarities between the two scenes. For example,
they both open with an emphasis on the normality of actions performed. Barnardo, meeting Francisco on the guard-platform, betrays
his anxiety by asking 'Who's there?'; Francisco corrects him—'Nay,
answer me'—and the routine change of guard is carried out in 'the
easy language of common life' so much admired by Coleridge. Then
comes mention of the Ghost, the language of the scene changes, and

normality is left behind. In the second scene the King's circumstances are unusual, but his effort, like Francisco's, is to see that routine matters are dealt with in the proper manner. Like Barnardo's question out of place, Claudius's opening reference to his predecessor's death only emphasizes the ease with which business then goes on as usual. The role of disturber of the peace this time is young Hamlet's.

Both scenes present a disturbance of normality; but the centres of disturbance are directly opposed. The Ghost comes from outside to walk the battlements of Elsinore; the court, on the other hand, is troubled by something within its own compass—by Hamlet's mourning, which marks him off from the rest of those on stage, and by the erratic force and savagery with which he treats the words addressed to him there. This motif of disturbance from within the second scene reaches its extreme form in the prince's soliloquy, when it appears that he is not himself the centre of disturbance in any simple sense, but that he is subject to a trouble that comes from within himself: 'Heaven and earth,/Must I remember?' He must: he has no choice. The order of his being is also broken.

However, the antithesis of disturbance from without and within can also be put in less general terms. The Ghost is a spirit almost possessed of a body. It is 'most like' the dead King:

> Such was the very armour he had on
> When he th'ambitious Norway combated.   (I.1.63–4)

It is seen to 'frown' and to 'stalk' in just the way old Hamlet used to—both operations being hard to conceive without imagining a body to perform them. Yet the Ghost has no body: ' 'Tis here.' ' 'Tis here.' ' 'Tis gone.'—'For it is as the air, invulnerable' (I.1.145–7, 150). Young Hamlet, on the other hand, has a body which is too much with him; he wants it to 'melt', to 'resolve itself into a dew'. 'Resolve' suggests not only dissolution into another form of being, but also the primitive sense of freedom, as in the *OED*'s citation from the Douay version of Daniel, 5.16: 'Thou canst interpret obscure thinges, and resolve thinges bound'. Hamlet wants to be free of all that is 'rank and gross in nature'. He wants to abandon the world to which the Ghost so insistently and, at this point in the play at least, ineffectually must return.

We might derive from this fundamental opposition of dissatisfied spirit and unhappy body an interpretation of the play something like

Stephen Booth's. He sees it in much the same way as he sees its first
scene—'insistently incoherent and just as insistently coherent':

> because it obviously makes sense and because it just as obviously
> cannot be made sense of [*Hamlet*] threatens our inevitable working
> assumption that there are no 'more things on earth' than can be
> understood in one philosophy.[2]

Such an interpretation does flatter, of course, a willingness in our
own time to push scepticism to the limits, but it also accords with an
element of scepticism in Renaissance thought, one which through
the *Essays* of Montaigne has been suggested as an influence on
Shakespeare's play.[3] Booth's arguments cannot be dismissed out of
hand, then. But the antithesis of spirit drawn to matter and matter
seeking to be spirit does not have to be seen in his terms; the play
itself, by its inclusion of the honour-concerned Polonius family
(who might be thought otherwise to be given an undue prominence
in the play's third scene) suggests a basis for interpretation in the idea
of honour. Such an interpretation, however, is not the straitjacket
'one philosophy' which, according to Booth, the play threatens; it
merely provides a dramatic, historic and human focus for the contradiction and paradox of his account.

For what the Polonius-family scenes show us is that the idea of
honour holds in precarious balance contrary notions of body and
spirit. The body is emphasized in the close relation between honour
and kinship, in the expected behaviour of young nobility ('unmaster'd
importunity'; 'A savageness in unreclaimed blood'; blood that, if
calm, would show Laertes not to be his father's son) and in the
entirely secular concern for Ophelia's virginity ('Tender yourself
more dearly/Or . . . you'll tender me a fool'). Yet the separation of a
concern for honour from the merely natural is just as important.
Polonius advises his son 'to thine own self be true', and the idea of
truth is a spiritual one: 'Thou canst not then be false to any man'.
Laertes is 'satisfied in nature' by Hamlet's apology, but not 'in
my terms of honour' (V.2.240,242). Laertes's first long speech to
Ophelia shows just how complicated the relation between spiritual
and physical qualities is in honour. He parallels the growth of the
body with that of the mind, but in such a way that these two aspects
of the human being seem to quarrel, rather then complement each
other:

For nature crescent does not grow alone
In thews and bulk, but as this temple waxes,
The inward service of the mind and soul
Grows wide withal.   (I.3.11–14)

The contrary impulses of the Ghost, who in some sense represents
old Hamlet, and of young Hamlet are illuminated in the tenacious
incoherence of young Laertes's address to his sister on the subject of
honour.

An old-fashioned hero

There is, after all, quite enough reference to matters of honour in the
first two scenes to make this connection with the Laertes speech
work, so that it might give a fleeting glimpse of one single thing that
might explain, if only it were not continually dissolving into other
things, the anxiety and tension building up in the play.

The Ghost, of course, is a heroic figure, 'fair and warlike', even
'majestical' in appearance, and the likeness of an admired warrior.
It gives rise to a peculiar form of speech opposed to the easy tones
in which the scene begins, and just as the Ghost itself comes, goes
and comes again, so does the way of speaking associated with it:
Nicholas Brooke writes accurately of an 'oscillation of tones' here.[4]
Reuben Brower identifies the idiom associated with the Ghost as
'epic' or 'heroic' in character;[5] it uses this idiom itself when at last it
speaks with Hamlet at the end of the act. Not every critic of the play
has liked this 'heroic' form of speech. H.A. Mason objects to the
'Double Dutch' of Marcellus's speech at I.1.72:

Good now, sit down, and tell me, he that knows,
Why this same strict and most observant watch
So nightly toils the subject of the land . . .

He writes of passages 'in a style so unpleasant that we might be inclined to suppose that Shakespeare did in fact approve of the style of
the player who so pleased Hamlet'.[6] It is possible that what he really
objects to is the ethic of honour that underlies this heroic style.

There cannot be much doubt that it is a heroic style, for it reflects
just those qualities demanded by Tasso in his *Discorsi del Poema Eroica*
(1594). For example, Tasso observes that 'the length of the members
and sentences, or clauses, as we may call them, gives greatness and

magnificence to speech': Marcellus's question following 'Good now sit down' stretches to more than eight lines, in striking contrast to what precedes it but fully in accord with Horatio's fashion of speaking right up to the Ghost's second entry. Tasso recommends repetition as 'an ornament that makes poetry rich and magnificent': Marcellus's speech is founded on a repeated 'why' and 'such'. Tasso recommends forms of syntactic and grammatical difficulty, like 'prolonged suspension of meaning',

> for the reader has an experience like that of someone who walks on a lonely road: the more deserted and uninhabited it is, the further off the inn seems, while a much longer road seems short when there are many places to stop and rest.[7]

Horatio's reply to Marcellus exemplifies this best, with its many parentheses and postponements, as here, where the subject, *king*, is kept apart from its verb, and the auxiliary of that verb, *was*, is held at a distance from its participle, *dar'd*:

> our last King
> Whose image even but now appear'd to us,
> Was, as you know by Fortinbras of Norway,
> Thereto prick'd on by a most emulate pride,
> Dar'd to the combat . . .   (I.1.83–6)

Tasso's ideal may be summed up as that of a 'roughness' evoking the 'great and magnificent' (it hardly needs explaining why this association should have been made at a time when masculine virtues were still identified with those of the warrior class). Shakespeare's diction in the 'heroic' passages of his opening scene contributes to this effect of 'roughness' by the mere fact of its idiosyncrasy—'emulate' as an adjective, 'competent' meaning 'equal', 'co-mart' (if that is indeed what Shakespeare wrote—Jenkins plausibly accepts the Folio reading 'cov'nant'), and the astonishing 'shark'd up'. The variety of resemblance between Shakespeare's practice in these passages and Tasso's precepts gives a pretty sure indication of the effect Shakespeare was seeking. It is one that can be justified dramatically in terms of a self-consciousness overtaking the men on guard who have seen the ghost (as they think) of the man they are talking about, as well as theoretically for its conformity to heroic norms.

Subject-matter matches style, of course, in these speeches. It is because the old king was heroic in his deeds that they induce a heroic style in his admirers. It is not merely his martial vigour, smiting sledded Polacks on the ice, that marks him out as heroic: it is also a quality of character, the aspect of him reflected in his challenge to Fortinbras. That challenge, after all, recalls Hector's in *Troilus and Cressida*: 'If there be one . . . /That holds his honour higher than his ease . . . : to him this challenge'– (I.3.264–71). It does not look back, however, only to a mythical past, but to an actual past in which such challenges had been issued and recorded, when the judicial combat, archaic by the middle of the sixteenth century in England, had been a customary recourse in the disputes of men of honour and their sovereign rulers:

> We read also that Princes themselves, contending for kingdomes, by that meane (to avoid effusion of blood) have determined their right: whereof we have ancient examples, as the combat of *Charles* Duke of *Anjoy* and *Peter* of *Arragon* contending for the Isle of *Sicil* . . . of the Duke of *Bohemia* and the Duke of *Lancaster* . . . [8]

At this point the heroism of Hamlet senior starts to take on the lineaments of honour, for the private duel (to which the fencing-match at the end of the play between Hamlet and Laertes stands in significant relation) derived historically from the judicial combat. Indeed the duel could be, and was, justified in the terms used by Sir William Segar in my quotation as justification for judicial encounters: 'to avoid effusion of blood'. Duelling was supposed to reduce the possibility of feuds. The combat between old Hamlet and old Fortinbras was, then, a proto-duel, and all the more so in that it was an affair of honour: Fortinbras was 'prick'd on by a most emulate pride'[9] and we are told (if we need to be told) that a man's honour is his 'right to pride'.[10] What makes this combat different from a duel, of course, is that its outcome was 'Well ratified by law and heraldry' (I.1.90). The old king is identified, then, with the triumphant fulfilment of an archaic code of honour, in accord with the laws of his realm and now under threat from young Fortinbras and his 'lawless resolutes'. Horatio assumes that it is the uproar caused by this young man that has brought the Ghost to Elsinore, 'prologue to the omen coming on', and when he questions it he imagines that its intention may be to see averted some event fateful for the country that had once been Hamlet senior's. In so far as the Ghost stands for old

Hamlet it stands for past certainties heroically practised and even, perhaps, for a heroic attempt to prevent their subversion in the present.

However, just as the Ghost cannot here be confidently identified
with Hamlet senior (it may be an illusion created by the Devil or
even something other than that), so do the certainties for which it
stands lose definition. It will emerge that Claudius called them in
question well before young Fortinbras, when he stole upon the
king's 'secure hour' (I.5.61) and poisoned him, 'Secure' implies a
touch of self-reproach on the Ghost's part, meaning 'careless' or
'over-confident' as well as 'carefree'. The honour for which it stands
is not necessarily to be regarded as the sum of all human virtues. Our
initial uncertainty about who or what the Ghost is blends in later
with our doubts about the validity of the honour with which it is
associated.

Ghostliness

Well over forty years ago John Dover Wilson proposed to clear up
the 'inconsistencies' which surround the Ghost in *Hamlet*.[11] Since
then his use of sixteenth-century texts on ghosts and demons has
been subject to a refining scholarship, notably by Robert H. West[12]
and Eleanor Prosser. The result has not been quite the thorough
mopping-up that Dover Wilson envisaged. Prosser writes engag-
ingly, at the end of her consideration of the first act:

> . . . in the fleeting perspective of the dramatic moment, we find
> only questions. If we could unequivocally pronounce the Ghost a
> demon and its command a damnable temptation, the tragedy
> would be destroyed. We cannot, and as a result are caught up in
> Hamlet's dilemma.[13]

Prosser's view of the play depends on a distinction between how it
looks to us whilst we are watching or reading it and how it looks
when we have got to the end of it and can cast our minds over the
whole action. By this means she is able forcibly to suggest that the
Ghost is indeed a demon, but that in performance or in reading we
tend not to credit its demonic character. Reading or seeing the play
is, then, for her an active experience in which we, like Hamlet,
though in imagination alone, wrestle with a devil who will not
declare himself unequivocally.

I think that this is fundamentally to misinterpret where the emphasis in *Hamlet* falls. The question whether or not the Ghost is what it seems, that is, Hamlet's father, creates dramatic suspense and an aura of doubt around the values with which it is associated, but in itself—and the fact is striking—it does not seem to matter very much to characters in the play whether it is a devil or not. It is alarming in itself because it is a ghost, not because it may be a devil. The latter idea figures in the play, but not very prominently. Horatio tries to stop Hamlet from following it:

> What if it tempt you toward the flood, my lord,
> Or to the dreadful summit of the cliff
> That beetles o'er his base into the sea . . .　　　　　(I.4.69–71)

It is plain that, though Horatio is thinking in terms of the traditional behaviour of devils-in-the-guise-of-ghosts, he is more concerned about what it might do than with what it is. He is more concerned that it will harm Hamlet than curious about its nature. Hamlet himself has already set that question on one side earlier in the scene:

> Be thou a spirit of health or goblin damn'd,
> Bring with thee airs from heaven or blasts from hell,
> Be thy intents wicked or charitable
> . . . I will speak to thee　　　　　(I.4.40–3,45)

Just as Horatio uses doubt about the Ghost's nature to rationalize his fear for Hamlet's safety, so Hamlet uses it to emphasize his determination to speak with it. In neither case does the possibility of the Ghost's being a devil arise as anything other than part of a general uncertainty governing relations with it. It is this understressed presentation of the possibility that the Ghost is a devil that makes Hamlet's later voicing of it—at the very end of the 'rogue and peasant slave' soliloquy, when he has already formulated his shaky plan to catch the conscience of the King—seem of secondary importance to the temporary respite from positive action that his plan will afford him.

We are uncertain about the Ghost, but not specifically uncertain as to whether it is or is not a devil. Rather we have to do with a general haze of doubts and anxiety surrounding it. Characters do not rush to identify it with Hamlet senior. It comes 'In the same figure like the King that's dead', says Barnardo, and 'Looks a not like the King?'

Marcellus echoes him: 'Is it not like the King?' Neither of them says it is the King. Horatio uses a similar reserve, decribing it to Hamlet as 'a figure like your father'. But of course the more the Ghost's likeness to the old king is stressed, the stronger we feel the possibility that it is he. This is brought out in the passage which prepares for Horatio's account of it to Hamlet. 'My father—methinks I see my father', says the prince:

> Where, my lord?
> > In my mind's eye, Horatio.   (I.2.184–5)

Horatio's question shows him to be thinking of the Ghost, as is natural, but of the Ghost as Hamlet's father. Hamlet's reply is an assurance that after all he is not really seeing his father, but there is an implication that he might have been doing so if he had been seeing the Ghost. Horatio's reminiscence 'I saw him once, a was a goodly king' is not simply an attempt to share Hamlet's backward look to his father's days but also tries to establish a simple sense of seeing, unconnected with ghosts and the supernatural. Hamlet concurs with this by putting the time when his father was to be seen into the past, and then Horatio finds himself unable to put off talking about the Ghost any longer. It is as though Hamlet's use of the word 'like' brings back to his mind the possibility he has tried to reject:

> A was a man, take him for all in all,
> I shall not look upon his like again.
> —My lord, I think I saw him yesternight.
> > > (I.2.187–9)

The possibility that matters is that the Ghost may be Hamlet's father, not that it may be the Devil, and this passage is entirely characteristic in its exploitation of the doubt which is also in some sense a hope.

It is not after all necessary to be able to say what a ghost might be if it is not the person it represents in order to feel doubtful about the sense in which it is that person. By their very nature, ghosts are things about which we cannot be certain, since they exist beyond the reach of human knowledge. Eleanor Prosser seems to suggest that because almost all learned commentary on ghosts in the sixteenth century took the line that ghosts were manifestations of the Devil the probability is that Shakespeare could rely on his audience giving this idea serious consideration from the start of the play.[14] This is to put greater store by the Christianization of belief than the evidence for the great mass of the population would seem to allow and also, and more importantly, to put the cart before the horse: learned commentary was preceded by the belief in ghosts and by the anxieties which the commentators sought to allay. The continuance of ghost-belief at a level unaffected by the works of Lavater and his sort is after all illustrated in the play itself. Hamlet suggests that his father's bones 'hearsed in death,/Have burst their cerements', in other words, that the Ghost is his father's corpse walking again. All the authorities, it seems, were positive that this never happened.[15] So much the worse for them: in this play the idea has life, just as it does in the ballad of 'The Wife of Usher's Well'. It has life because a ghost is an impossibility to which men give credence, and its denial of human categories cannot be argued away without arguing it out of existence itself.

Uncertainty about whether or in what sense the Ghost is Hamlet's father is integral to its presentation and to our recognition of it as a ghostlier ghost than the run of these creatures in Elizabethan drama—than, for example, the persistent ghost of Montferrers in *The Atheist's Tragedy* or the bustling ghost of the friar in *Bussy d'Ambois*. This uncertainty is reflected in the strange alternation of styles of speech in the opening scene which I have already noted, as well as in the doubts about the sense in which this ghost has a body, doubts to which I shall return in the next chapter. It does not merely serve, however, to make the Ghost truly ghostly, nor further to add to the suspense in characters' dealings with it; it reflects an ambiguous quality in the honour with which the Ghost is associated. This will appear more forcefully when I have considered the role of the young prince in the play's second scene.

Sullied flesh

Hamlet's attitude to Claudius and to his mother before he has heard the Ghost's story is that of a malcontent. What he has to say cannot be part of the ordinary discourse of the court at Elsinore now that his father is dead. His first words are spoken aside: they are ostentatiously not part of the business being transacted, just as he is separated from the rest of the court by his mourning dress. He speaks the ironic speech of the underdog, asserting his superiority by thinking it, and leaving it to others to see that this is what he is doing. His resentment

is plain; and it is equally plain that what he resents is his mother's
remarriage. Our understanding of this resentment depends on our
grasping Hamlet's own interpretation of his situation, as it appears in
the speech he makes after the King and company have withdrawn:

> O that this too too sullied flesh would melt,
> Thaw and resolve itself into a dew . . .

What reason has Hamlet to feel that his mother's remarriage has
sullied his flesh?

The answer to this question cannot lie simply in his dislike or
distrust of Claudius, nor can it altogether depend on Hamlet's grief
for his father and the feeling that his memory is undervalued by what
his mother has done. None of these would result in a sense that his
own flesh was sullied. Revulsion from sexual feeling might. His
mother's sexuality, presumed cause of her hasty remarriage and of
the slight upon the father he loved, might appear to her son so
loathsome now, that his own body, made out of that sexual appetite of hers, could seem tainted by it. His reaction here would
then anticipate the cruel treatment meted out to Ophelia by him
later on.[16]

Yet if we understand his feelings to be of this kind we risk viewing
the soliloquy as (in Eleanor Prosser's words—not that this is an
account to which she herself would subscribe) 'the tortured writhings
of an unbalanced neurotic who is over-reacting'.[17] The view does not
recommend itself, simple because it involves dramatic miscalculation.
To start the play at such a pitch leaves little room for development.
We need therefore to consider whether there is not an alternative
reason for Hamlet to feel that his flesh has been sullied.

One alternative, taken by Prosser, is to deny that it has been sullied
at all and to suppose that what Hamlet says is that his flesh is 'too too
solid'. This is the reading of the Folio; both the Quarto texts have
'sallied', which I take to be a variant of or misprint for 'sullied'. 'As
yet,' Prosser argues, 'Hamlet seems only shocked by her indecency
and repulsed by her grossness. There is no suggestion that he feels
himself corrupted. The wider implications come later.'[18] The fact
that Hamlet is considering suicide, however, does suggest that he
feels tainted by the world's being too much with him, and that his
'weary, stale, flat and unprofitable' feelings are a reflection of this.
We are willy-nilly thrust back upon the idea that Hamlet *does* feel his

flesh to have been sullied (we can still find a half-pun on 'solid', which the context also implies).

Gertrude's marriage to Claudius is, of course, incestuous, but it would be unwise to build too much on this as a basis for Hamlet's feelings—if, that is, it is agreed that an interpretation that does not present him as indulging a neurotic excess of feeling from the start is to be avoided. Hamlet and the Ghost are the only characters to remark on the incest, and this might imply that the others are partners in a conspiracy of silence not to name the shameful aspect of the royal passion; but they might also be understood not to question it at all. Neither Gertrude nor Claudius is troubled by the fact that their liaison is incestuous, though other things do waken guilt in them. It has been argued on historical grounds that, whatever the feelings expressed by characters, the audience was expected to be disgusted; Henry VIII divorced his first wife, Catherine of Aragon, on the grounds that she had been his brother's wife.[19] But this shows the ease with which an incestuous marriage could be entered into (that is, the weakness of the taboo) just as much as the revulsion it was supposed to engender. It is interesting that in Shakespeare's depiction of the divorce in *Henry VIII* he makes Henry's alienation from his Queen not a violent turn into abhorrence, but a gradual process. The word 'incest' with its associates is never used in that play. Historical argument, as so often, is not very helpful here. What the text itself suggest is that Hamlet and the Ghost both use the idea of incest merely to reinforce their horror at the sexual passion that sends Gertrude 'With such dexterity to incestuous sheets'. It is the dexterity that matters: the incest is a second thought. Similarly the Ghost deplores the transformation of his bed to 'A couch for luxury and damned incest': incest figures only as another way of speaking of her 'luxury'. Incest, then, takes a subordinate place to the indecent strength of Gertrude's desires as a motive for outrage for the Ghost and Hamlet. This would have seemed quite natural to anyone with a concern for honour.

The supposed dishonour to her kinsmen which follows when a widow remarries is a central concern in *The Duchess of Malfi*, and scholarship has demonstrated some of its manifestations in the life and literature of the times in illustration of that play.[20] The feeling that there was something wrong, excessive or shamefully comic about the widow who married again was apparently based in the view of sexual identity which 'delegates the virtue expressed in sexual purity to the females and the duty of defending female virtue to the males',[21] a principle to which both Polonius and Laertes, representatives of honour, subscribe. The widow who marries again threatens the division of the sexes necessary to the sense of honour by appropriating to herself the sexual aggressiveness which is supposed to be the property of the male. 'Once the sexual division of labour breaks down, women become men and where this occurs there can be neither honour nor shame.'[22] The speed with which Gertrude remarries only adds to the offence to honour which that marriage represents. In some countries at some times repugnance for hasty remarriage has been expressed in the laws themselves. In thirteenth-century Castile, for example, it was decreed that 'a woman who cohabits with a man less than a year after her widowhood' should incur infamy.[23] But the feeling exists at a level distinct from law in an honour-culture; Julio Caro Baroja says that the premature remarriage of widows was still, in 1965, regarded as a cause of dishonour in certain parts of Spain.[24]

There is, then, nothing extraordinary or pathological in Hamlet's feeling that his honour has been slighted by Gertrude's remarriage, since both the speed with which it took place and his own failure to prevent it when, after his father's death, he was head of his family and responsible for the protection of that weak and vulnerable woman, his mother, are aggravations of what would in the first place have been regarded as dishonouring. Hamlet feels this dishonour in his own body in just such a way as Laertes feels the effect of Polonius's death; only his repudiation of his 'flesh' reflects the fact of his past failure to maintain honour and a dispirited acceptance of the newly established *status quo*.

Hamlet's despondency would nevertheless alienate the whole-hearted subscriber to the values of honour; he ought to react in the forthright way of Laertes instead of moping about in conspicuous corners. The scene of Laertes's departure makes a very forceful point about a difference in temperament between the prince and the young nobleman. The obscurity that covers Hamlet's actions at the time when his mother's marriage was proposed (was he at Wittenberg or not?) does not make it easier for a reader or an audience to trust in his reactions now. Even for Horatio he is 'young Hamlet' (I.1.175)—the impression given by his first scene is that he is young absolutely, not merely in relation to his father. Was his failure to act over the marriage, then, the product of his youth rather than of a real deficiency of character? The question is not one which the dramatist presses us to answer, but it does put us at some distance from simple identification with Hamlet; and all the more so, of course, if we already have our reservations about the values associated with a dedication to honour. There is nothing historically implausible about such reservations. It can hardly be said, for example, that the three marriages of Bess of Hardwick earned her ignominy and dishonour; in its outcome *The Duchess of Malfi* surely does not endorse the view of Ferdinand and the Cardinal that the Duchess's marriage to Antonio was wrong (despite the official ecclesiastical line on remarriage, which was disapproving).[25] E. P. Thompson gives it as his impression that remarriage was less often the occasion for *charivari* in England than in France, and finds few literary references to it in sixteenth- and seventeenth-century literature.[26] This all suggests that Shakespeare intended Hamlet's situation to be recognizable within the honour tradition but that he was not relying on a specific view of the tradition to determine response to Hamlet at the opening of the play. Precisely because Hamlet is 'young', he may grow up in the course of dealing with his dilemma: however unfavourable or unsympathetic our original response, it is held in check by this consideration.

Hamlet has asked to go 'back to school in Wittenberg' and so to avoid Elsinore, the scene of his disgrace. It is equivalent to the wish to leave his sullied flesh behind him. He wants to creep away and forget ('Must I remember?' I.2.143). It is hardly surprising that he himself omits to mention his honour, since all his plans tend to the further diminishment of it. On the other hand we know, and he does not, that the Ghost has appeared. The merely hysterical energy of his soliloquy may be converted to action as the consequence of Horatio's news. Our interest in Hamlet's situation thus depends on both positive and negative feelings about it, and these feelings focus upon the matter of honour. Hamlet and the Ghost have this much in common.

Body, spirit, soul

The relation between the Ghost and young Hamlet is mysterious,

and is not clarified when the two meet. Doubts about the Ghost's
identity and the extent to which it is influencing Hamlet's behaviour
remain throughout the play, but their basis is not solely the interview
between the two on the platform of Elsinore. From the beginning of
the play's second scene, when we see Hamlet's mourning figure set
apart from the rest of the court, he stands in a questionable relationship to the Ghost. In *The Anatomy of Melancholy* Robert Burton states
the belief that melancholy persons are especially liable to 'diabolical
temptations and illusions'.[27] It is as though the Ghost, whether
diabolic or not, had been summoned up by Hamlet's troubled state
of mind.

Hamlet is not simply melancholy; he is a person who does not fit
in with his surroundings. His speech and his dress are equally out of
place where Claudius is trying to conduct business as usual. There
are other senses too in which he does not fit. He is the Queen's son,
but not the King's; he is 'Our chiefest courtier, cousin, and our son'
(these terms themselves come awkwardly together), yet he is treated
as a child, his wishes are overruled and the entire court leaves him to
sulk on his own. He is just the sort of person that in primitive society
is associated with witchcraft and demons. He is in what Mary
Douglas calls an 'interstitial' position in Elsinore society, uncomfortably poised between the old order and the new; and he is angry:
'The existence of any angry person in an interstitial position . . . is
dangerous, and this has nothing to do with the particular intentions
of the person.'[28] Knowing that the Ghost has appeared and respond-
ing to Hamlet at a primitive level, we recognize him as dangerous in
this way, despite his own sense of failure. The incalculable quality of
his relation to the Ghost, connecting our uncertainty as to the Ghost's
nature with our uncertainty as to the status of Hamlet's reaction to
his mother's remarriage, establishes him as a character of high
dramatic potential.

It is not unhelpful, in fact, to regard the Ghost as in some way a
manifestation to Hamlet of his own nature. The coincidence of
names between father and son and the conceptual affinity between
the centres of disturbance in scenes 1 and 2 suggest this. We would
only be regarding the Ghost in the same way as Montaigne considered
Socrates's *daimon* (presumably as referred to in the *Memorabilia* of
Xenophon and in Cicero):

The *Daemon* of *Socrates* was peradventure a certaine impulsion of

will, which without the advice of his discourse [E.J. Trechmann's
translation reads: 'without awaiting the consent of his reason']
presented it selfe unto him . . . Every man feeleth in himselfe some
image of such agitations, of a prompt, vehement and casuall
opinion.[29]

Is the Ghost an 'image of such agitations' as 'Every man feeleth in
himselfe'? Shakespeare's presentation hardly allows of a conclusive
answer, but does not forbid the possibility. It is worth noting because so much in this play has to do with an ambiguous realm
between body and soul, a realm of interaction where it becomes
unclear, as in the case of Hamlet in I.2, whether body affects soul
or vice versa, and where it would be quite appropriate for one
'perturbed spirit' (Hamlet) to call up another (the Ghost which bears
the semblance of Hamlet's Hamlet, his father).

The term 'spirit' is itself an interesting one. In the medical parlance
of the Renaissance it applied to a substance so much like soul as
perhaps not to be a substance at all:

Spirit is a most subtle vapour, which is expressed from the blood,
and the instrument of the soul, to perform all his actions; a common
tie or medium between the body and the soul, as some will have it;
or as Paracelsus, a fourth soul of itself.[30]

This usage only emphasizes an ambiguity inherent in the word
in general between 'spirit' as supernatural and 'spirit' as a natural
phenomenon of temperament. Shakespeare had already exploited
the possibilities of the term in *Julius Caesar*, where for example
Brutus, who has spoken of standing up 'against the spirit of Caesar',
is told by the ghost of Caesar that it is 'Thy evil spirit, Brutus'.

Just as 'spirit' in general spans the gap ambiguously between body
and soul, and as Caesar's 'spirit' does between Caesar and Brutus, so
the Ghost in *Hamlet* does between the sphere of Hamlet's body (his
melancholy condition) and that of soul, Hamlet's own soul—which
manifests itself in the sort of 'impulsions or will' of which Montaigne
speaks—and the soul of his father, with which the Ghost may or may
not be identified. The first two scenes of *Hamlet* do not merely
present us with a powerful fiction but link it with a philosophical
problem, the relation between body and spirit, which looms large in
the play and goes some way to account for the enduring tension of its
opening.

3 Hamlet and the Ghost

Heart and tongue

Somewhere between the overt dramatic power of the first two scenes and their perplexing and thoughtful undertones hovers the idea of honour, informing both. The play's third scene justifies its existence in part by focusing attention on this idea and implying its relevance to what has preceded it. The individual's share in a common family honour, the vulnerability of that honour when entrusted to an unprotected woman, the requirement that a man of honour should act in accordance with his place in society, and the identification of the sense of honour with qualities of the young nobleman's physical person—these all appear prominently in the exchanges of the Polonius household and have an obvious bearing on young Hamlet's situation.

The scene's function cannot, however, be altogether summed up as casting light in this simple fashion on the play's opening. In the overall poetic and dramatic effect, difference of tone counts just as much as similarity in ideas, for this third scene is quietly comic, and its comedy is provided at the expense of those who uphold the idea of honour, Laertes and Polonius.

Laertes's advice to his sister is given seriously, but not expertly. In my first chapter I have already discussed the tell-tale signs of embarrassment in it. Laertes ploughs on despite the fact that he becomes confused and awkward. Ophelia, by contrast, is self-possessed and says little. She acts in accord with the part Laertes has assigned her, of little sister, but does the minimum to give it credibility. The comedy is reinforced by her quiet dig at her brother about 'the primrose path of dalliance'. Laertes's cheerful reply to this, 'O, fear me not', shows him much too pleased with himself to feel that his own behaviour is touched in what Ophelia says. That seems to be the point which, for her own amusement, she is making.

Polonius is as complacent as his son, and his offered advice reflects the egoistic insensitivity manifest in Laertes's address to Ophelia, but hardened into a code of behaviour whose principal mark is a negative reserve. Laertes is not to say what he thinks, he is not to enter easily into friendship with anyone, he is not to rush into fights, but should act so that others are wary of him, and so on—these limitations on one's behaviour make being to one's own self true a sad, cold business. The comedy of Polonius's role is not here at its strongest, though the long speech to Laertes can, of course, be played for laughs, and is in any case founded on caricature. The subsequent interview with Ophelia is broader, thanks largely to the self-congratulatory punning in which he indulges; and it is more savage, since Polonius shows himself incapable of acting on the advice which he has so liberally given his son. Laertes was told to 'Take each man's censure, but reserve the judgment': Polonius has no reserve and refuses to take his daughter's views into account at all.

The upshot of this comedy is to distinguish clearly between the complacent and unenquiring dedication to honour of Polonius and his son and the problematic nature of honour as it is represented by the Ghost's 'fair and warlike form' and as it is experienced by Hamlet himself. Shakespeare's third scene makes the important point that what is to concern us in Hamlet's plight is not a matter simply of conforming to various external criteria of behaviour, but rather of defining the self to which he must be true. Polonius's first bit of advice to Laertes is this: 'Give thy thoughts no tongue': neither father nor son is troubled by it. But Hamlet's problem is summed up in his dissatisfaction with the role assigned him: 'But break, my heart, for I must hold my tongue' (I.2.159). He can either let himself break up, with his heart, or he can look for a new role, an honour consonant with the facts of his own nature. Hamlet's attempts to redefine his princely role become a search for his own identity in relation to the society of which he is a member. It is because the idea of honour is in the bulk of the play associated with this search that *Hamlet* continues to interest us as a great and absorbing study in fundamental processes of the human spirit. 'Codes' of behaviour, such as are often associated with his dilemma, do not deeply concern him until the end of the play where, having come to model himself on Laertes, he acquiesces in the plan to submit their dispute to the judgement of 'some elder masters of known honour' (V.2.244). For the rest of the play the idea of a 'code' is as irrelevant as it feels in the formulation offered to his son by Polonius. An understanding of the role of honour in *Hamlet* clears up many misunderstandings of what happens in the play, but is not the necessary one key to all that it contains.

Honour in the breach

Shakespeare abandons the confinement of Polonius's little household for the open air. The very first line of the next scene insists on
the change in atmosphere: 'The air bites shrewdly, it is very cold.'
Horatio calls it 'a nipping and an eager air': this emphasis suggests a
physical vulnerability, an awareness of the 'poor, bare fork'd animal'
that requires protection from the cold. We are a long way from the
comfortable point of view of Polonius. Hamlet's hostile description
of his stepfather's court, his malice barely subdued in 'swagg'ring
upspring', a term hardly conceivable in the previous scene of
worldly wisdom, only completes the antithesis.

Hamlet's disapproval of the King's drinking is possibly based less
on principle than on personal feeling, but he expresses his distaste in
absolute and impersonal terms: 'it is a custom/More honour'd in the
breach than the observance'. Besides scoring off his stepfather, these
words may be a covert justification for Hamlet's own failure to act
effectively so far, either to prevent his mother's second marriage or
to take himself away from Elsinore. It is better *not* to do some things:
Hamlet has wanted some things not done, and has not done others
himself. His judicious words lend him a stature that is not quite his.
They are an ominous prelude to the Ghost's appeal, for that is based
on custom and honour. It seems that it also is likely to be ignored by
Hamlet, and the consequences of that can hardly be happy. Indeed, in
the First Quarto and the Folio versions of the play the Ghost enters at
the word 'observance' as though to draw attention to the inauspicious
circumstances in which his appeal is to be made.

Only the Second Quarto, however, has the rest of Hamlet's
speech, as it appears in modern editions, and the Ghost does not enter
there until Hamlet has finished the twenty or so more lines allotted
him. Whatever the reason for their omission from the Folio, these
lines work poetically and dramatically to develop our awareness of
Hamlet's uncomfortable mode of existence at the beginning of the
play. In them Hamlet reflects first in particular on the damage done
the reputation of Denmark by the custom of 'heavy-headed revel':
'other nations . . . with swinish phrase/Soil our addition' ('addition'
here unites the two obsolete senses given by the *OED*, 'something
given to a man's name, to show his rank, occupation, or place of
residence, or otherwise to distinguish him' and 'something added to

a coat of arms, as a mark of honour'), and then goes on, in lines whose syntactical indiscipline recalls the want of control already shown in the first soliloquy, to some general considerations which are of particular interest as the words of someone who—'though I am native here/And to the manner born'—has in some sense been disclaiming part of his birthright. The dishonour accruing to the Danes from their custom of heavy drinking is like that derived from a man's circumstances of birth:

> So, oft it chances in particular men,
> That for some vicious mole of nature in them,
> As in their birth, wherein they are not guilty
> (Since nature cannot choose his origin),
> By their o'ergrowth of some complexion,
> Oft breaking down the pales and forts of reason,
> Or by some habit, that too much o'erleavens
> The form of plausive manners—that these men,
> Carrying, I say, the stamp of one defect,
> Being Nature's livery or Fortune's star,
> His virtues else, be they as pure as grace,
> As infinite as man may undergo,
> Shall in the general censure take corruption
> From that particular fault. The dram of evil
> Doth all the noble substance often dout
> To his own scandal.   (I.4.23–38)

The lack of control derives not so much from hysterical feeling, as in the first soliloquy, as from a going round and round the subject. Hamlet is rambling. What stands out is his concern with the advantages and disadvantages of birth. Though born a Dane he feels free to criticize Danish customs: Danes suffer in reputation for their drinking as a man may suffer in his from circumstances beyond his control—for example, his birth. Hamlet goes round and round this subject because it touches him nearly. He has allowed his birthright, his princely honour, to be impugned.

Granville-Barker sees that in this speech Hamlet refers to himself, but does not see how far it goes in this respect.[1] Hamlet does not merely refer to an 'o'ergrowth of some complexion' such as might be the cause of his own strange state. He hovers between exonerating a man from extrinsic defects, such as a 'habit', the gift as it might be of 'Fortune's star', and exonerating him also from intrinsic faults, the 'vicious mole' of one's 'birth'. It is characteristic that he should use the idea of physical defect metaphorically here ('mole'), since in association with the word 'nature' it makes it impossible to restrict the meaning of 'birth' to the social qualities accidentally associated with it. The consequence is that, by a blurring of categories, Hamlet manages to suggest that a man has little to be responsible for personally at all. The 'o'ergrowth of some complexion' illustrates this blurring in a single phrase, since 'complexion' may signify both a physical condition, a certain balance of the humours within the body, and a mental one, a habit of mind; this blurring effect is enhanced by Hamlet's speaking of 'their [particular men's] o'ergrowth of some complexion' because, by analogy with what the grammarians used to call the 'subjective' genitive, it might mean 'the o'ergrowth for which they are responsible' as well as 'the o'ergrowth in them'. The simultaneous presence of these two possible meanings tends to reduce the possibility of blame. The difference between extrinsic and intrinsic defect is lost; merely to be born the man one is is misfortune. If 'nature cannot choose his origin', then the opposition of 'Nature's livery or Fortune's star' is unreal.

These are not the thoughts of a Polonius or a Laertes. But the speech does not only reinforce our sense of Hamlet's awareness of himself as a mystery. He manipulates that awareness to satisfy the immediate ends of justifying his own inaction to himself.

This appears in two ways. First of all, it may be implied that cowardice is the 'dram of evil'[2] in Hamlet's own constitution. By the blurring of categories he has put himself beyond responsibility for it; and its significance is further minimized by the consideration that 'oft it chances' that people like himself 'in the general censure take corruption' for such things. The generality of men are far below the Hamlets of this world ('caviare to the general', II.2.434) and their censure may accordingly be set aside or made light of. The very word 'scandal' upon which the speech ends has a dying fall, given emphasis by its metrical irregularity, whether we scan 'To his own scándal' or 'To his own scándal', and by its loose syntactic connection with the rest of the sentence. The result is that the 'scandal' seems insignificant beside the robustly 'noble substance', locked in firmly in the preceding line:

the dram of evil
Doth all the noble substance often dout
To his own scandal.

Secondly, however, the speech may suggest that it is only the accident of birth that makes Hamlet feel his mother's remarriage so acutely. It may therefore be right to disown the consequences of being born her son, as it is right to disown Danish customs that are dishonouring. He may have acted more honourably 'in the breach than the observance' of what would conventionally be expected of him, and so be in a position to scorn the petty 'scandal' which the world might create about it. The nobility of his 'substance' may reside in his inaction.

None of this augurs a very warm welcome for the Ghost's summons to action. Hamlet speaks of the 'pales and forts of reason' as though reason itself were embattled, besieged, though reason too seems to be what is meant to warrant 'The pith and marrow of our attribute'. The Ghost enters as it were to attack this reason: it should stand to the prince to defend it. The tendency of his speech has been, however, to break down those distinctions that reason fosters. It may be, then, that he also will turn upon 'reason' itself. That might provide an opening for the Ghost; but what sort of opening, and how reliable, we cannot predict. Hamlet's world, unlike that of Laertes, is filled with ominous possibility—just such as Horatio envisages when he warns the prince that the Ghost may

assume some other horrible form
Which might deprive your sovereignty of reason
And draw you into madness . . .   (I.4.72–4)

Hamlet's Hamlet

When Hamlet sees the Ghost he looks upon a likeness of himself. The identity of names between father and son suggests that the father proposed himself as a model for his son. The Ghost, whatever it is, assumes the guise of that model.

Hamlet's speech now takes on the frozen and effortful quality of Horatio's when he spoke about Hamlet's father in the first scene. It is as though the Ghost compelled a response in keeping with the heroic virtues to which the old king could lay claim; and when it speaks it does so also in the constrained high style.

Hamlet regards the Ghost as eminently 'questionable' (43), that is, 'which invites questioning' as Jenkins has it, but more pertinently 'uncertain, doubtful'. The *OED* gives the first use of the word in this sense as Edward Topsell's in his *History of Four-Footed Beasts* (1607), but Shakespeare's context strongly implies it here by preceding the statement 'Thou com'st in such a questionable shape/That I will speak to thee' by a whole list of alternatives: 'Be thou a spirit of health or goblin damn'd', and so on. The Ghost's initial business is to provoke questions, and Hamlet formulates them: 'What may this mean. . . ? Say why is this? Wherefore? What should we do?' (51,57). These questions are characteristically associated by Hamlet with 'thoughts beyond the reaches of our souls', a phrase that captures completely the bafflement at the springs of human action underlying his speech about the 'dram of evil'. The Ghost *is* Hamlet in so far as Hamlet is, like it, a mystery to himself: the partial identification is made and qualified as he cries:

> I'll call thee Hamlet,
> King, father, royal Dane.   (44–5)

It is, of course, an imprudent, an over-hasty identification of the Ghost as his father anyway, as Horatio reminds him, and us. Yet it is perfectly comprehensible: Hamlet needs a foundation for his life, and the Ghost, in offering him a version of himself, a supernatural authentication for the model he is to follow, offers something like what is wanted. Beside this notion of a life filled with meaning from 'beyond the reaches of our souls' the mere life of the body, of the sullied flesh, does not signify:

> I do not set my life at a pin's fee,
> And for my soul, what can it do to that,
> Being a thing immortal as itself?   (65–7)

Theoretically at least the immortal soul may suffer eternal torment, and Hamlet should be concerned at that. His need for a Ghost capable of reflecting accurately the proper conditions of his own existence makes the Ghost answer his need at this point; Hamlet's manipulation of circumstance is made audible in his own bad logic, as well as by the Ghost's silence. It is, after all, Hamlet who is making all the noise when he declares 'My fate cries out'. Only he can hear it because only he has been listening for it.

Nature's nature

The Ghost's silence represents, in relation to the prince, the mystery of his own self, but in relation to old Hamlet it stands for a refusal to broadcast the disgrace of his treacherous murder until it can be revenged. Only Hamlet may be told of it: and his companions must swear to silence concerning the little they do know of the Ghost.

Its appeal to Hamlet, the 'noble youth' (I.5.38), is founded on the consanguinity of father and son. H.A. Mason, by objecting to the apparent humanity of the Ghost, draws attention to the strange pathos in this appeal. The Ghost, he says, 'is a spokesman for a rather mediocre human being not much better or worse than Hamlet himself'—can that be right?

> There is, too, a jarring grossness in all the complimentary self-references—a self too vividly aware of self—pitiful if it is an immortal spirit speaking from what ought to be the perspective of extra-temporality. What are we to make of the insistent account of the effects of the poison and in particular of (in *this* context) the phrase *All my smooth body*?[3]

What mitigates the 'grossness', surely, is the fact that the Ghost's expectation that Hamlet will do as he is told is based on the notion that his kinship makes it 'natural'. The idea of *natural* standards of behaviour is evoked in the repeated description of the murder as 'unnatural', and other phrases—'my days of nature', 'a wretch whose natural gifts were poor/To those of mine', 'The natural gates and alleys of the body'—drive home the appeal to Hamlet: 'If thou hast nature in thee, bear it not . . . ' (I.5.81).

It is as he is flesh of his flesh that Hamlet is bound (by 'nature') to act on his father's behalf. The Ghost's account of the transformation effected in the body of Hamlet senior by his brother's poison is anticipated in the lines which imagine the effect its words might have on Hamlet's physical person were it to speak of its own present sufferings:

> I could a tale unfold whose lightest word
> Would harrow up thy soul, freeze thy young blood,
> Make thy two eyes like stars start from their spheres,
> Thy knotted and combined locks to part,
> And each particular hair to stand on end,
> Like quills upon the fretful porpentine.   (I.5.15–20)

This imagined transformation which the Ghost declines to effect is answered by the account of one really effected in the body of Hamlet's father. The peculiar force of that lies not merely in the unsettling pathos of a spirit's lament for body but in its pertinence to the character addressed, who has felt his own flesh to be 'sullied' even before the Ghost's horrific account of his father's murder. Hamlet's flesh, as well as his soul, can be called 'prophetic', for the extent to which the family's dishonour is registered in physical reaction is not fully suggested until we hear the Ghost tell how

> a most instant tetter bark'd about,
> Most lazar-like, with vile and loathsome crust
> All my smooth body.

These words amplify the meaning of Hamlet's own 'sullied flesh'. They also increase the pressure on him.

It is, then, more important that the Ghost presents the aspect of a human being than that it may be of a 'rather mediocre' human being. There is, of course, a paradox in this. An 'immortal spirit' certainly should not be so much concerned with the time-bound world of Elsinore; but we are used to the idea of supernatural interest in the world of nature, and used to the obscurity in which it is shrouded. Furthermore, we are able to think of 'nature' as essential qualities underlying the appearance of things, as an ideal rather than a material phenomenon and in this way showing affinity with the metaphysical or supernatural. It is for such reasons that the Ghost's human attributes of emotion and exquisite delineation of sensation do not take away from its ghostliness.

Despite the equivocal wording of his own reflections on 'nature' in the 'to the manner born' speech, Hamlet capitulates to the Ghost's announcement that his father died by murder 'most foul, strange and unnatural'. But he does so in terms expressive of some reluctance, first in the structure of what is said ('Haste me to know't, *that* I . . . /May sweep to my revenge') and then in the similes used ('that I with wings as swift/As meditation, or the thoughts of love,/May sweep . . . '). It has often been remarked that these comparisons are oddly inappropriate. Yet 'thoughts of love' are precisely what the Ghost has sought to arouse—'love' of a specific, even jealous, kind—and the swiftness of Hamlet's own 'meditation' in the first soliloquy seemed to be just what prevented him from controlling it. What jars is not the similes themselves, but the word that ties them into the rest of the sentence—'sweep'; imagining so smooth a descent, so impossibly smooth we might say, upon the desired revenge. Hamlet's words strike a false note. The parenthesis which separates the subject, 'I', from its verb, 'sweep', makes the false note more prominent, but also explains its falsity—the parenthesis is a means of Hamlet's postponing for a moment saying what he intends to do. The unreal quality of the action at last proposed derives from the reluctance implicit in his use of the parenthesis.

A similar contradiction in feelings manifests itself in Hamlet's exclamation when the Ghost has left:

> O all you host of heaven! O earth! What else?
> And shall I couple hell? (I.5.92–3)

The questions are not purely rhetorical (it is not obvious in what sense the second one is meant to be answered), and that fact saps what positive quality there might be in the interjections. It strikes us as quite natural, therefore, that immediately something should weaken in him; it is the body:

> O fie! Hold, hold, my heart,
> And you my sinews grow not instant old,
> But bear me stiffly up. Remember thee?
> Ay, thou poor ghost, while memory holds a seat
> In this distracted globe. Remember thee?
> . . . Yes, by heaven! (93–7, 104)

The violence of his assertion that he *will* remember the Ghost hardly, in these circumstances, needs explaining, but is given a special significance by the previous weakening of his heart and sinews. 'I have sworn't—and so he must go through with it. But the firmness has been made to feel questionable.

This in its turn should influence our response to the ensuing scene of 'wild and whirling words'. Hamlet's behaviour may be explained in terms of the 'antic disposition' which, he tells Horatio, he may have to adopt at times in the future, but it is significant that the words to Horatio do not come before Hamlet's apparent fit of distraction but after it. The possibility that we should think him really out of his mind is in this way left open by Shakespeare. Furthermore, his behaviour looks distracted because it develops contradictory impulses

like those just considered. 'Would heart of man once think it'?—
Hamlet has 'wonderful news' and a secret to impart to the others;
this all implies the determination later voiced in his assurance that 'It
is an honest ghost, that let me tell you' (144). And yet he collapses into
feebleness:

> I hold it fit that we shake hands and part,
> You as your business and desire shall point you—
> For every man hath business and desire,
> Such as it is—and for my own poor part,
> I will go pray.   (I.5.134–8)

This feebleness, to be sure, is not without strength, since there is
plenty of irony in the lines at the expense of business and desire, as
well as prayer, and that implies no commitment to the abstention
from action which they suggest, though it does not imply either that
a course of action has been determined. On the other hand, there
is something weak even about the lines where Hamlet plainly is
contemplating action, since the honour which requires his act of
vengeance also requires that he should keep quiet about it unless
positively obliged to talk.

The business with the Ghost under the stage involves a similar
duality of effect. Eleanor Prosser thinks that it is devised in order that
the audience should notice that this ghost does behave like a devil.[4]
Yet it would be surprising if the Ghost, and not Hamlet—who is
actually on stage and in the presence of others with whom he is
attempting to deal—were to be at the centre of attention. Hamlet's
identification of the Ghost as devilish manages also to suggest that it
is harmless, an 'old mole'. It can be made the subject of irony without
fear of reprisal, it seems: 'boy . . . truepenny . . . this fellow in the
cellarage'. The effect is twofold; Hamlet suggests that the Ghost is of
no account, but he may be doing so because he is afraid or because he
wants to conceal his complicity with it from his companions. '*Hic et
ubique?*' he asks; according to Prosser this 'cannot refer to an "honest
ghost", for only God and the Devil can be both here and everywhere
at the same time'.[5] Hamlet's equivocal tone and difficult situation do,
however, create a context in which, ironically and with a range of
possible effects, he may be referring to what he believes to be an
'honest ghost' and to what might even be one.

The note struck by Shakespeare following the disappearance of the Ghost is one of uncertainty. The audience does not know quite what is going on in Hamlet's mind. It is not clear that Hamlet himself knows this. What he says is consistent with his having settled plans that he wants to conceal from his companions, but is not consistent solely with this; and the action is so devised as to allow the alternative, that his 'wild and whirling words' accurately reflect his state of mind, forcibly to suggest itself without receiving positive confirmation.

These doubts are reinforced by our uncertainty about the Ghost. The pattern of correspondence between the Ghost and Hamlet already touched on is continued in the relationship between the Ghost's doubtful status and the prince's ambiguous position in the court of Elsinore, an uncertainty intensifying the obscurity of his intentions in regard to the Ghost.

The sense of reciprocating uncertainties is reinforced by the refusal of either one of the two to speak of honour in the context of the Ghost's story. It is as though Hamlet's silence on the matter in I.2, made audible by the account of his father's actions in the first scene and by the concern for it in the Polonius family in the third, has its own positive effect on the Ghost, which is thrown back on the implicit pleas in its invocation of nature and the natural, and on the reiterated demands for revenge. The conceptual trinity of prestige, honour and revenge underlies what it says; Hamlet's sense of family honour is plainly under pressure. Nevertheless the pressure has its own obliquity. 'Revenge' is not exclusively associated with the obligations of kinship; in Shakespeare's time it might be used for 'punishment' or 'chastisement' without the least implication of personal animus. The Ghost speaks powerfully, but in such a way as to present its cause as one of justice in a general, as well as in the particular family, sense. Hamlet may choose to act out of a sense of what is owing to his nature, to his blood, his kin, or in accord with that proper order of things which may also be 'nature's', at least by intention.

The Ghost's appearance is, then, productive of tension not in the obvious sense only, in that it leaves us anxious about its own nature and the effect it may have upon Hamlet, but also because it continues that process of blurring distinctions already set in train in the prince's speech about the 'dram of evil'. Hamlet managed simultaneously to resent the diminution of honourable reputation and to suggest that it lay beyond a man's ability to answer for that diminution. Nature cannot choose his origin. The Ghost appeals to 'nature' but is itself an intrusion upon nature, and unnatural in its care for a 'smooth body' which can in no sense be a part of it, though it speaks with unnerving particularity of the poison 'swift as quicksilver' in its 'natural gates and alleys'. There is here suggested a conflict within nature itself, a conflict that finds expression in Hamlet's fear that his own body will not be strong enough to take the strain on it: 'Hold, hold, my heart!' Hamlet's mad behaviour subsequently may appear a diversion of this original physical strain into spiritual disorder. The diversion is all the more natural in that the heart is, in Burton's words, 'the seat and organ of all passions and affections'[6]—here the physical modulates to the spiritual as of right.

The Ghost's appeals to 'nature' in Hamlet, instead of leading us to condemn the momentary failing of his heart and sinews or the uncertain excitement that follows it, lead us to sympathize. Hamlet's body responds acutely to the sully of dishonour but Hamlet's body also rejects, it seems, and without his willing it to do so, the call to honour. Nature seems in this to be at war with itself, a fact which Hamlet discovers in his own experience when driven as hard as he is here. Later he prays 'O heart, lose not thy nature . . . /Let me be cruel, not unnatural' (III.2.384,386). Nature's cruelty, nature's order—the play calls these into question at the moment that the Ghost commands Hamlet as a father his son.

The heart of the mystery

In this play the body stands for an oppression of the spirit by the physical conditions in which it exists in this life; it stands for what binds men together in ties of love and duty; it stands for 'things rank and gross in nature merely'; and it stands for something so beautiful that even the dead may be imagined to mourn its loss—'all my smooth body'. It is, then, capable of inspiring the contradictory feelings already associated with 'nature'. Shakespeare's sense of the body, both of the consciousness of it which we may attribute to a character as well as of the uses to which it may be put by the actor, is crucial to the success of *Hamlet*. The body is given up to contradiction. Its noblest organ, vital, difficult of access, invisible and nevertheless vulnerable, is the heart. Hamlet's heart becomes a focus for the play's largest issues: it is one of the means by which they escape bloodlessness. The strain under which it labours following the interview with the Ghost is best understood in terms of this general function in the play.

When Hamlet reproaches Rosencrantz and Guildenstern: 'you would pluck out the heart of my mystery' (III.2.354–5) it is hard to limit the reference of that last word to the secret of what the Ghost told him. The word suggests that there is a mystery at Hamlet's heart as well as that it has a heart of its own. The word 'pluck' suggests that Rosencrantz and Guildenstern want to tear at Hamlet's heart as the eagle, for example, at Prometheus's liver. The musical context of the remark only reinforces the savagery implicit here. Hamlet seems to think of himself as a mystery, and perhaps as a mystery to himself, since it is very difficult to look into one's own heart (not easy, as Sidney suggested). And the mystery of himself ought to be the mystery of his honour, since one's honour is one's life. The difficulty, as I have tried to show, is that two views of honour are opposed deep within Hamlet—we might say, two conceptions of the man he should be. Is he to be his father's son? Or, in giving a meaning to Polonius's maxim 'To thine own self be true', must he repudiate the obligations which as his father's son, society puts upon him? It is this conflict that makes of Hamlet someone who is at once too much of a character for us to grasp and too little of one for us to feel him genuinely a whole person. And what we feel he seems to feel too: he associates his heart with the thought of depths opening up within him:

> Give me that man
> That is not passion's slave, and I will wear him
> In my heart's core, ay, in my heart of heart . . .
>
> (III.2.71–3)

It is as though his inmost being eludes him through an infinite recess of hearts within hearts. No wonder, then, that he cannot name the 'honour' which should be identical with all that he holds most precious in himself.

Yet it pains him that he cannot do so. The 'mystery' does not sit easy in his heart. It is as though he were suffering from an illness of the heart which he himself cannot diagnose. He tells Horatio 'Thou wouldst not think how ill all's here about my heart' (V.2.208–9) and we remember the earlier mention of that 'ill' in the account of his journey to England: 'Sir, in my heart there was a kind of fighting/ That would not let me sleep' (V.2.4–5). As so often in this play, acute bodily sensation is confused with spiritual distress. Hamlet's sense of 'The heart-ache and the thousand natural shocks/That flesh is heir to' (III.1.62–3) is the harbinger of this later acknowledgement of sickness in the heart; but he is anticipated by Claudius, for whom Hamlet's melancholy at the opening of the play shows 'A heart unfortified, or mind impatient':

> For what we know must be, and is as common
> As any the most vulgar thing to sense—
> Why should we in our peevish opposition
> Take it to heart? (I.2.96, 98–101)

His later diagnosis is not, then, to be taken as mere varnish to the rough treatment he prescribes in sending Hamlet to England:

> Haply the seas and countries different,
> With variable objects, shall expel
> This something settled matter in his heart . . .
>
> (III.1.173–5)

Indeed, it sends us back in mind to that moment when Hamlet reproaches himself:

> That I, the son of a dear father murder'd . . .
> Must like a whore unpack my heart with words . . .
>
> (II.2.579, 581)

Hamlet's sickness cannot be simply cured, because it consists in a conflict, 'a kind of fighting' *in* his heart. In this respect it is to be contrasted with that of Laertes. In both cases the heart is imperilled by the unsatisfactory condition of the honour associated with it, but for Laertes the cure is obvious and does good even when only in prospect:

> It warms the very sickness in my heart
> That I shall live and tell him to his teeth,
> 'Thus diest thou.' (IV.7.54–6)

The mystery of Hamlet's heart corresponds in one sense to the hole in the play's fabric about which William Empson talks in his brilliant study—surely the best essay on *Hamlet* ever written. He imagines what the problems were that faced Shakespeare when he decided to rehandle the story which was the basis of the now lost but once popular older version of *Hamlet*. He sees the chief difficulty as lying in this: that whilst the time was ripe for new plays dealing with revenge, the rhetoric of the old play, now worn thin, revealed the seemingly interminable quality in the delay in Hamlet's accomplishment of his revenge, which now looked merely ludicrous. Shakespeare's task, therefore, had to be 'to satisfy audiences who demanded a Revenge Play and then laughed when it was provided'. Empson suggests that Shakespeare worked out his answer along these lines:

> "The only way to shut this hole is to make it big. I shall make Hamlet walk up to the audience and tell them, again and again, 'I don't know why I'm delaying any more than you do; the motivation of this play is just as blank to me as it is to you; but I can't help it.' What is more I shall make it impossible for them to blame him. And *then* they daren't laugh." It turned out, of course, that this method, instead of reducing the old play to farce, made it thrillingly life-like and profound.[7]

In essence this is right, but Hamlet's inability to identify his motivation is complicated by its also being a refusal to acknowledge the area of concern that is responsible for his delay. Part of him is truly blank, without sophistication, but part of him is obstinately blank; and if *he* is a 'thrillingly life-like and profound' character, it is because the co-existence in him of these two attitudes is so well rendered by the playwright. Hamlet is *and is not* a mystery to himself.

Empson's brisk, de-mystifying tone makes a change from the reverence that often makes accounts of Shakespeare's tragedies less than perspicuous. But it does, I think, slight the quality of the play also.

Hamlet cannot name the honour at his heart, the honour which struggles within his body to identify itself. This reluctance or refusal to name what is in effect for him a vital principle is analogous to the custom whereby what is holy is not to be named or not to be given its proper name. Hamlet's sense of himself as a 'mystery' evokes this quasi-religious meaning with a religious association in the word 'mystery' itself (amply evidenced at this date). In so far as his 'honour' may be identified with that 'mystery', it acquires an association with

the God-given, or with the same order of things as the Ghost belongs
to. These possibilities are not mutually exclusive, but they do suggest
the two poles between which a man's honour may be located: loyalty
to God and the heart's independent moral imperatives, and loyalty to
the status derived from the family and maintained by the individual
following the imperatives of kin issuing from the heart which the
ancestors fashioned.[8] The opposition within his body of these two
ways of regarding honour underlies both beginning and end of the
play. Hamlet's first line, 'A little more than kin and less than kind,' is
an uncomfortable joke about kinship: it is less than natural ('kind')
that he should find himself closer kin of Claudius than has been the
case. This shift in the orientation of his world anticipates Hamlet's
discovery that it is in his own nature to 'let all sleep' (IV.4.59) despite
the claims of kin upon him. His last line is followed by Horatio's
testimony 'Now cracks a noble heart' (V.2.364). This suggests that
the prince dies not so much as a result of the poison on Laertes's foil
(though we must suppose this to be the efficient cause of death) as of
the 'kind of fighting' within his heart so much emphasized in the
play's last scene. Horatio's 'noble' plainly seeks to ennoble the circumstances of his friend's dying, but also promotes the thought that
this heart cracked because it was noble—had become so, or was so by
virtue of the 'kind of fighting' it had known. Characteristically, the
line refers us to the 'mystery' contained within Hamlet's body.

In the scene of Hamlet's meeting with the Ghost Hamlet imagines
that his heart is failing him, a physical weakness that is the preface to
the spiritual weakness and confusion of the rest of the scene. 'Would
heart of man once think it?' he asks a little later, when he seems about
to reveal what the Ghost has said to Horatio and Marcellus. There is
a reluctance in the heart to acknowledge not the revelation of
Claudius's treachery, for Hamlet had already guessed that and is
'sure' of it (I.5.109), but the claims laid upon it from 'beyond the
reaches of our souls'. This heart belongs to one of the 'fools of nature'
(I.4.54). The contrast with the Polonius household, where the heart
is a conventional symbol for Laertes ('Or lose your heart, or your
chaste treasure open' I.3.31) and a sure point of reference for Ophelia
('watchman to my heart' I.3.46), is complete. The play's next scene,
however, brings Ophelia's certainty face to face with Hamlet's
physical and spiritual disorder. In the next chapter I will consider the
significance of this development.

4   Hamlet's weakness

Hamlet's sigh

Hamlet's body enters into the substance of the play in such a way as to suggest the depth at which he is concerned with its issues. Honour is life, and is identified with the heart, difficult to get at, sensitive, mysterious. The play's many images of sickness and disease have a special painfulness when they are thought of in relation to the ideal untainted body of the man of honour—that body for which the Ghost yearns and which was disfigured by the poison administered by Claudius. Although adumbrated in the last scene of the first act, however, the full significance of the body in this play does not appear until Ophelia's description of the prince's disturbing visit to her in her 'closet'.

Hamlet says nothing to Ophelia. Reported speech is far more common in the theatre than reported silence, especially one reported in such detail: his failure or refusal to speak here is as noticeable as it was in I.2, and takes on an air of meaning from that similarity.[1] What it does mean, however, is obscure to Ophelia, as well as to the audience. It obviously recalls the Ghost's silence in the play's first scene as well as Hamlet's in the second scene, and dress and gesture accordingly assume the importance which attached to them there:

> with his doublet all unbrac'd,
> No hat upon his head, his stockings foul'd,
> Ungarter'd, and down-gyved to his ankle,
> Pale as his shirt, his knees knocking each other,
> And with a look so piteous in purport
> As if he had been loosed out of hell
> To speak of horrors . . .   (II.1.75–81)

Bridget Gellert Lyons has drawn attention to the way this account recalls the Ghost, and suggests that the effect is threefold: it draws attention to the 'implausibility or exaggeration' of Hamlet's pose of love-melancholy, it discredits the simple diagnosis based on that by Polonius, and it inclines us to see the Ghost as the real cause for

Hamlet's real melancholy.[2] I find it hard to agree that Hamlet is 'really' a melancholic in the sense proposed by Mrs Lyons; the whole topic will be dealt with a little further on in the argument. Surely the main point about this speech is that Ophelia's unconscious likening of Hamlet to the Ghost puts them both in the same category as mysteries. Hamlet's appearance to her is marvellous and strange, like the Ghost's to the watch: it is difficult to describe the motivation of either, and the mystery has something to do with the father–son relationship which puts them in a class apart. Ophelia's lines seem to confirm the assimilation of one to another which I have already discussed: it is as though the Ghost has taken possession of the prince's body. The fact that Ophelia knows nothing of the Ghost only makes her guileless testimony more forcible. Hamlet is made to seem more mysterious because of the extent to which he is himself called in doubt. The effect is reinforced as Ophelia amplifies her account.

The speech is one of intense pathos: Ophelia is frightened and cannot understand what has happened to Hamlet. She describes his actions in scrupulous detail because she cannot see beyond them, cannot find a meaning in them. Her incomprehension is matched by his; he is looking at her as intently as she must be looking at him, but he can only be taking note of externals, gazing at her face 'as a would draw it' but ignoring the distress he causes her as a person by his unexplained behaviour. It is like a grotesque parody of 'The Ecstasy': their eye-beams almost twisted, they remain obstinately distinct and unassimilated one to the other. Hamlet's sigh, which does not declare itself as a sigh for her, is a mark of this separation.

To this pathos of situation there is added a further twist—the pathos of Hamlet's own body, which is not only *blindly* expressive, but incompletely so:

> He took me by the wrist, and held me hard.
> Then goes he to the length of all his arm,
> And with his other hand thus o'er his brow
> He falls to such perusal of my face
> As a would draw it. Long stay'd he so.
> At last, a little shaking of mine arm,
> And thrice his head thus waving up and down,
> He rais'd a sign so piteous and profound

As it did seem to shatter all his bulk
And end his being.   (II.1.87–96)

This is extraordinary poetry. Ophelia observes Hamlet observing her and presents a full account, down to the 'little shaking of mine arm', but her very fullness is entangled with frustration; no meaningful detail seems to organize the rest. Arm, hand, brow and head do not appear to govern Hamlet's actions but to limit them. We can say of each line what part of the body is involved and what kind of movement, but we can say nothing more. The body weighs upon interpretation and inhibits it. 'He raised a sigh so piteous and profound'—'raise' means a good deal more here than the simple utterance of a sound suggested by the *OED*; it is, for a start, an effortful raising, one which is involved in and preluded by other gestures, the shaking of Ophelia's arm and the 'waving up and down' of Hamlet's head. The effort is that of raising something heavy from below—'profound' suggests a well of grief from which the sigh must laboriously be drawn, even though it represents a threat to Hamlet's very being—'it did seem to shatter all his bulk'.

In their suggestion of bodily anguish these lines anticipate the feeling 'how ill all's here' about the heart and the 'kind of fighting' in it of the play's last scene. In both the later instances Hamlet could be talking about the symptoms of physical illness—it would be perverse to interpret in this way, because the context presses a fuller meaning on one, yet the lines *would* permit the more restricted interpretation. Ophelia's lines, however, do not. Their function is to state a theme fully, that of the confusion of body and spirit. On the one hand she suggests that Hamlet participates in his body's acts: '*he* rais'd' the sigh. On the other hand, the sigh is a form of aggression on the body with which Hamlet's 'being' is identified. Acute awareness of the body and extreme indifference to it are both present, as in the speech 'O that this too, too sullied flesh . . . ' A question lurks within these lines: which part of Hamlet is really Hamlet, the body that suffers or the spirit that would escape, like the breath of a sigh, from its imprisonment, even at the price of utterly destroying the body it inhabits? The question could be phrased differently: is it Hamlet's spirit that raises the sigh or is it his body that forces the breath out of him? Does spirit rule the body or body the spirit? Ophelia is terrified because Hamlet is not like himself. The baffled point of view from

which she has to describe his actions presents him more like an
animated corpse, a zombie or a golem, than a person. It is as though
body had extinguished spirit altogether.

> That done, he lets me go,
> And with his head over his shoulder turn'd
> He seem'd to find his way without his eyes,
> For out o' doors he went without their helps,
> And to the last bended their light on me.   (II.1.96–100)

'He seem'd to find his way without his eyes' does not only make
Hamlet sound like an automaton; it also suggests his earlier speculation that the Ghost might be a body 'cast up again' from the grave
(I.4.51). There is a hint to the audience that if a spirit does rule this
body, then it is not necessarily Hamlet's. As Mrs Lyons points out,[3]
the lines also recall the Ghost's fixing its eyes 'most constantly' on
Horatio (I.2.234). In either case the autonomy of spirit, Hamlet's
freedom of the will, is put in doubt.

This is the further level of meaning to which the body and honour
refer in *Hamlet*. Honour involves the individual's will to a high
degree:

> even an oath which is not made freely is not binding, nor is a word
> of honour which is not intended as such. The attempt to use ritual
> to commit the honour of a man comes up against the difficulty that
> no man can commit his honour against his will, since his honour is
> what he wills and the attempt to oblige him to do so invites him to
> 'cross his fingers'. The ritual of the oath, like the rites of the
> church, is invalid without the intention of the participant.[4]

On the other hand, to the degree that honour is bound up with
membership of a particular group, a family or a class in society, it
overrides the claim of the individual:

> In both the family and the monarchy a single person symbolizes
> the group whose collective honour is vested in his person. The
> members owe obedience and respect of a kind which commits
> their individual honour without redress. Here intentions are
> irrelevant for, whatever his feelings about the matter, the indi-
> vidual is born a son and a subject, he does not compete or contract
> in order to become so.[5]

Whilst theoretically opposed in this fashion, these two ideas of honour tend in practice to become confused. Hamlet's flesh is sullied, whether he wills it or not, by the fact of his mother's marriage. But when Hamlet shows himself willing in the spirit to revenge his father but temporarily weak in the flesh, a question arises which of the two, spirit or flesh, reveals his true intention. The dilemma is compounded by the stress laid on the physical bond of kinship in the ideas of blood and nature, the latter of which is so heavily emphasized by the Ghost himself. In this fashion the problem of the will and its freedom, which the idea of honour almost inevitably entails, is identified with the problematic nature of Hamlet's own body and his relation to it. Ophelia's lines serve to make us conscious of the matter at the point in the drama when Hamlet's will comes particularly into question.

The relationship of body to spirit was—and is—problematic, of course, irrespective of the idea of honour. Contemporary medical thought put great emphasis on the body's influence on mind. Robert Burton glosses over the difficulties in the following passage, but they are obvious enough:

> For as the distraction of the mind, amongst other outward causes and perturbations, alters the temperature of the body, so the distraction and distemper of the body will cause a distemperature of the soul, and 'tis hard to decide which of these two do more harm to the other. Plato, Cyprian and some others . . . lay the greatest fault upon the soul, excusing the body; others again, accusing the body, excuse the soul, as a principal agent.[6]

When matters are so evenly balanced it is difficult to say which part of the person really determines his mode of existence. Burton concludes that 'so doth our soul perform all her actions, better or worse, as her organs [i.e. bodily organs] are disposed'; it is the natural consequence of humours-theory, but it dangerously restricts the freedom of the will. The habit of thinking metaphorically or analogically about the body only increases this restriction: Burton describes the heart as 'the sun of our body, the king and sole commander of it', and the lungs as 'the town-clerk or crier . . . the instrument of voice, as an orator to a king: annexed to the heart, to express his thoughts by voice'.[7] Metaphor is so much a part of the way of thinking that the heart's 'thoughts' seem to exist independently of the thoughts of the mind. And if they do, may not the heart

take precedence over the mind, body over spirit, temporarily if not
for long stretches of time?

The same way of thinking about the parts of the body obtains in
Hamlet as in *The Anatomy of Melancholy*, although here it is part of a
much more deeply sustained exploration of human nature and human
motive. Hamlet's 'heart of hearts' is but one example of the way in
which there may be confusion about the centre of authority within
the body. It is, of course, natural that a dilemma based on honour,
which is rooted in the body, should transform itself into questions of
the integrity of the person, and of the nature of human activity.
Since belief in honour, irrespective of individual concerns, tends to
oppose one set of values (those of a group) to another (those of
society as a whole), such questions have lurked beneath the surface of
the play since it began. When they become apparent, however, there
is a shift in the tone of the play and a change in the pace of events.

Polonius and Claudius: In the world of the everyday

Polonius, of course, does not find it difficult to say what is wrong
with Hamlet:

> This is the very ecstasy of love,
> Whose violent property fordoes itself
> And leads the will to desperate undertakings
> As oft as any passions under heaven
> That does afflict our natures.   (II.1.102–6)

Polonius has not, as we have, seen the Ghost with Hamlet; nor was
he present when the prince so distressed Ophelia. It is understandable,
therefore, that he should opt speedily for a consolingly obvious
explanation. It is not a stupid explanation, by any means. If we knew
nothing of the Ghost it might have been acceptable to us. As it is,
there are reasons why we should be drawn to it; for it does touch on
the areas of our special concern—the relations of body and soul. Love
has provoked an 'ecstasy' in Hamlet, a temporary separation of soul
from body (this was a more common meaning for the word than the
OED, unduly influenced, perhaps, by nineteenth-century rationalism,
is willing to admit); but whilst the hints of the Ghost's influence in
Ophelia's speech make the possibility disquieting, Polonius's formulation smoothes anxiety away. It is not 'being' itself that is threatened

with destruction (or self-destruction), it is only the 'violent property' of love that 'fordoes itself'. Nor is the will absent from Hamlet altogether—it has merely been led 'to desperate undertakings' and may presumably, at any moment, decline further leading. Polonius is a foolish old man, doubtless, but he is not a grotesque buffoon: his diagnosis has much to recommend it.

When he offers it to the King, however, he is ludicrously verbose and self-congratulatory. It would not be unreasonable to connect this with the mingled pleasure, fear and embarrassment caused him by the prospect of possible royal sanction for the pairing of Hamlet and Ophelia. But the effect is to take away reality from the diagnosis. The more he goes about it and about it, the less substantial his explanation seems. The stages of Hamlet's sickness, as he explicates them, have nothing much to do with Ophelia's terror at all, and very much to do with the old man's fantasies of his own wisdom and insight. His boast that

If circumstances lead me, I will find
Where truth is hid, though it were hid indeed
Within the centre   (II.2.157–9)

rings false because the 'art' which he puts on display tends to conceal nature instead of revealing it. Right from the start Hamlet speaks of 'that within that passes show' (I.2.85), and the ambiguous and unsatisfactory sigh described by Ophelia confirms our sense that what is within necessarily fails of expression. Because Polonius slights this element in our experience of Hamlet's condition his diagnosis, at first attractive, quickly loses plausibility.

And yet it establishes itself firmly in the action of the play. The result is to alienate us to some extent from that action. The plan of campaign which Polonius and Claudius agree upon must seem to us irrelevant to the end it is designed to meet. We are not any the less involved in what happens on stage, but our involvement takes the form of attending to lines of development other than those urged on us by the declared intentions of characters within the play. Our interest becomes that of the diagnostician; our aim is to identify the situation in which the characters (particularly Hamlet) are involved. How the situation develops ceases to be of paramount importance.

Understandably, critics and producers have been wary of interpreting the middle part of *Hamlet* in this fashion. The special quality

of the play's action after the first act is surely its sporadic and
haphazard nature. One event does not *entail* another in the way of
a well-made play. The interview with the Ghost does not entail
Hamlet's use of the players; the motive is forgotten and picked up
again only as it were by chance. The 'success' of the play-within-the
play should 'entail' the rapid despatch of Claudius: it does not.
Hamlet's mistaken killing of Polonius should entail the swift correc-
tion of that mistake in (once again) the death of Claudius: it does not.
Conversely, what Hamlet does is unprepared-for in conventional
terms. The decision to use the players, the killing of Polonius, and
the interview with Gertrude are all surprises for the audience. We
could have predicted Lear's treatment by his daughters; these actions
are unpredictable.

Because Claudius is shown consistently to follow plans in what he
does—because, that is, he acts as though one event entails another—
it can be tempting to explain the haphazard events of the middle part
by reference to his rationality. The text seems to deny importance to
the conventional ideal of action, but the expected emphasis can be
restored by representing Claudius as a consistent threat to which
Hamlet reacts with a brilliantly evasive display of the erratic—his
'antic disposition'. Such an interpretation is based on the assumption
that Claudius genuinely threatens Hamlet from at least the start of
the second act, seeing what follows as a kind of 'duel' between the
two 'mighty opposites' of whom Hamlet speaks only at the end of
the play (V.2.62).

It is worth emphasizing, therefore, that our sense of the irrelevance
of Polonius's diagnosis extends to the participation in it of the King.
What *he* does seems just as irrelevant as what Polonius does, because
following up Polonius's suggestion seems to be his main activity.
True, he does send for Rosencrantz and Guildenstern independently
of his counsellor, but in sending for Hamlet's friends he commits
himself to no more than the commonsense commonplace that someone who behaves oddly, as Hamlet does, will benefit from company
and distraction. 'Be not solitary, be not idle' is the sum of Burton's
advice in *The Anatomy of Melancholy*. There is nothing of menace
about Claudius's action here to make us attach more importance to it
than to his willingness to follow up Polonius's diagnosis of love-
melancholy. In the light of Hamlet's encounter with the Ghost, both
should strike us as irrelevant and unlikely to turn up much that will

interest us. We do not know certainly of Claudius's guilt until after the play-within-the-play, and his first genuinely threatening deed, the request to have Hamlet put to death in England, is not announced until IV.4. Hence, those who seek to strengthen the sense of action in the middle part of *Hamlet* by dwelling on the threat of Claudius distort the emphasis of the drama and slight its most original quality, the plunge into a series of events without relation according to the conventional logic of narrative and without motive according to the conventional view of body-mind relationships.

Hamlet's stability

I have described the kind of feeling that should be induced in the audience by the middle section of the play. It may seem that I am abandoning all notion of form in reading it in this way: in this section, by means of two rival accounts of II.2, the scene which most emphatically withholds the thread of action from us, I want to show the extent to which a design is nevertheless present in Shakespeare's text.

My view is close to that of Granville-Barker, except that I disagree with him when he loses nerve and interprets the bulk of the scene as 'preparation' for the final soliloquy:

> The scene . . . advances the action not a jot. But its dramatic significance lies just in this; in the casual (or so seeming) encounters and the evasively irrelevant talk, diluted at last into topical gossip of theatrical affairs . . . It is a sustained preparation for that outburst of self-reproach:
>
> O, what a rogue and peasant slave am I!
>
> which, when it comes, is by how much the more effective for the delay![8]

Later on Granville-Barker tells us that the effect of this soliloquy is of 'a most inconclusive summing-up', leaving us to feel that 'Hamlet is now at odds, not merely with the ills of this world, but within himself, and cannot but be impotent so.'[9] It is hard to see that this needs 'sustained preparation', since it is all of a piece with what we have seen already. It is only Granville-Barker's professional anxiety about the 'action' that leads him to impose the idea of 'preparation' on the accurately observed 'casualness' originally noted by him.

There is a human craving for order which, in its reduction of the individual to a type, distorts our relationship to reality more than it clarifies. The slight flaw introduced in Granville-Barker's account becomes an obscuring fault when notions of the 'duel' between Hamlet and Claudius are used to describe the coherence of II.2. Mark Rose is admirably clear, for example, but quite wrong, I think. (He has already characterized Claudius as 'dangerous' by virtue of 'his discipline, his self-control'):

> The sixth scene [i.e. II.2, Rose counting I.4 and 5 as one only] . . . is the longest in the play. As Alfred Harbage points out, it is unified by theme, beginning with Claudius, his mind focused on Hamlet, and ending with the prince, his mind focused on Claudius. The symmetrical organization encourages us to compare Claudius and Hamlet, for if Claudius is subtle and dangerous, Hamlet is even more so. The scene falls into three long segments: in the first, running 169 lines, Claudius prepares his instruments, Rosencrantz, Guildenstern and Polonius; in the middle, running 241 lines, Hamlet parries Claudius' indirect thrusts, meeting and defeating each of the spies; and in the final segment, running 181 lines, he prepares his own instruments, the actors.[10]

This account is *demonstrably* wrong. Certainly, the scene begins with the King's welcome to Rosencrantz and Guildenstern and his explanation why they are needed. But his mind is hardly 'focused' on Hamlet; his speech is followed by one from Gertrude, revealing her own concern and speaking for her husband ('such thanks/As fits a King's remembrance' 25–6). The suggestion is that husband and wife are equally worried, if not that Claudius is worried as much (or more) on his wife's account as on his own. Rosencrantz and Guildenstern figure not as *his* instruments but as *their* instruments. This may be Claudius's cunning, and the Ghost gives us ground to suspect that he *is* 'subtle and dangerous'. Nevertheless, the subtlety and danger are not unequivocally apparent, as Rose's account would require.

As for the preparation of Polonius as an 'instrument', Shakespeare conspicuously mingles his announcement of his diagnosis with state affairs—Claudius is seen to have other things to think about, and to think about them. He greets Polonius's news with keen interest, which may seem ominous ('O speak of that: that do I long to hear'(50)), but is quick to pass it on to Gertrude, so that not much can be built on the idea that his interest is peculiar and sinister. When

Polonius comes to his exposition Claudius speaks little, still consults with Gertrude and in concluding 'We will try it' (167) gives no sign of having more in mind than what Polonius proposes. These are hardly 'subtle and dangerous actions' and—as I have already suggested—in so far as they involve Claudius in concurrence with the unsubtle Polonius, tend to make of him a trifling rather than a mighty opposite for Hamlet. And with that not only does the balance of Rose's scheme disappear, but also the 'indirect thrusts' which for him make up the action of the scene and mask the casualness which Granville-Barker correctly observes.

The true meaning of that casualness surely lies in the way in which the accidental and coincidental nature of the action puts the emphasis on the one character to occupy the stage for the main part of the scene: Hamlet enters at line 168 and does not leave until the stage is cleared almost 450 lines later. He is the scene's most stable point, and this stability is significant as concerns Hamlet himself, the other characters, and the audience.

Hamlet *needs* to be presented with some element of stability. He is so much a mystery that without being submitted to the continuous examination of the other characters (and of us in the audience) he might seem to vapour away. His long exposure in this scene is a kind of guarantee of his really existing — or at least, of the problem he represents really existing. His stability is exclusively a stability of the body. He is changeable as a person in this scene, a creature of mood. His physical presence, unchanging despite the variations of mood and attitude in him, presents to our eyes a stage-image of the conflict and confusion in him of body and soul.

For the other characters he is the person to whom they address themselves. Momentarily he is the centre of their attention and activity—for Rosencrantz, Guildenstern and Polonius because he is a problem, a disturbance in the course of life; for the players because he is their superior and patron. Indeed, Hamlet is a problem because he is socially superior to almost everyone in the play; the two incentives to interest for the other characters coalesce in the view of Hamlet taken by us in the audience. (If he were not a prince, honour would not be so great an issue for him.) The presence of either Polonius or Rosencrantz and Guildenstern throughout the scene (except for the last fifty lines or so, of course) establishes Hamlet's substantiality as a problem: they represent the audience in their

desire to find out 'that within which passes show' and by having
Hamlet continuously before their eyes, keep his mystery continuously before ours.

From our point of view, however, Hamlet's stability in this long
scene has a further significance. For what is dramatic in this scene
inheres in the *presence* of the actor. It is not the action that counts, but
the fascination exerted by the character on other characters and by
the actor on the audience. This fascination was far from unknown to
the Elizabethan audience: Tamburlaine and Richard III both depend
upon it for their success, and so does Richard II. But in these cases
there is a considerable buttress of plot for the actor's exercise of his
personal art of fascination. In Hamlet the support is minimal. What
engrosses us is Hamlet's play *with* the other characters. It is an
exhibition of skill, like that of a fisherman who plays his line, like that
of an orator, or a clown, who plays with his audience. It lives in the
moment, it looks neither before nor after, it feels like improvisation,
and not least when Hamlet plunges into the recitation of a set speech:

> let me see, let me see:
> *The rugged Pyrrhus, like th' Hyrcanian beast—*
> 'Tis not so. It begins with Pyrrhus—
> *The rugged Pyrrhus, he whose sable arms . . .*
>
> (II.2.445–8)

What makes this more than a brilliantly defined actorial cadenza is
the actor's own admission that he does not understand its basis.
When its source is questioned, the spontaneous and improvisational
loses its spontaneity: it becomes problematic. The symmetries which
Rose discerns in this scene are important, because they place Hamlet's
encounter with Rosencrantz and Guildenstern at its very centre, and
at the centre of *that* comes Hamlet's confession that he cannot understand himself: 'I have of late, but wherefore I know not, lost all my
mirth . . . ' (295–6). It is this un-selfknowingness that integrates the
scene with the rest of the drama and establishes its depth. The actor's
physical presence takes on its fullest meaning only in relation to the
psychic depth here suggested.

The insistent quest for action, however, slights this quality of the
scene. Rose ignores the emphatically central speech and takes the
episode of Hamlet, Rosencrantz and Guildenstern to hinge on
Hamlet's 'direct thrust' at them 'Were you not sent for?' (274). By

such desperate means he presents us with a scene in which an illusory
initiative passes from Claudius to Hamlet.

As I hope I have shown, this exaggerates the quality of the King's
initiative at the beginning of the scene. And if the symmetry perceived
in the scene by Rose does anything *more* than lay emphasis on that
central speech of Hamlet's it tends to diminish the status of Hamlet's
initiative by making it a counterpart to that of Claudius. The
commonsense practicality of the King contrasts, perhaps, with the
rashness of Hamlet's decision. Neither promises much; both are
embedded in a world whose main concerns lie elsewhere, and both
result in decisions which look incidental, the King's made in con-
sultation with Gertrude and Polonius when the serious business of
government is done, Hamlet's made on the spur of the moment
('About, my brains. Hum . . . ' (588)) and when the scene is all but
over. The decisions that are made issue out of the ordinariness of
every day, however much that is heightened by our sense of the
underlying extraordinariness of Hamlet's own situation.

In the closet scene Hamlet describes his mother's remarriage as an
act that makes of 'sweet religion' 'A rhapsody of words' (III.4.47–8).
The word 'rhapsody' appears not to have taken on a musical sense
until the nineteenth century and the implication is, of course, pejorative, but when all allowance has been made for the formal elements I
have just discussed, 'rhapsody' would not be a bad description of
II.2. Ophelia describes gestures which do not explain themselves and
a gaze so deep she cannot plumb it. What ensues is a scene of
predominantly casual encounter (Rosencrantz and Guildenstern
arrive by chance following Hamlet's visit to Ophelia; they are not
instructed to find out anything in particular but to report what 'from
occasion' (16) they may glean, and so on)—but it is a scene where we
are held by Hamlet's gaze ('Man delights not me' (309)) and where
we hold *him* in our gaze and learn no more than did Ophelia. Her
narrative of Hamlet's dumb-show implies the form of the scene that
follows it.

The shape of melancholy

Critics who interpret the second act of *Hamlet* in terms of move and
countermove on the part of the King and his awkward stepson do so
partly because the essentially problematic nature of personal honour

is something not sufficiently allowed for or understood by them, partly because the rhapsodic quality of Act Two is better suited to twentieth-century dramatic practice—think of *Waiting for Godot* or *Endgame*— than to the Renaissance. Critics, therefore, try to clarify what in the play is obscure, for example, by describing the two courtiers as spies.[11] Yet as the sense of what the play is about is modified by more deliberate consideration of Hamlet's assumptions and his dilemma, so must our sense of how the play develops also be modified. Shakespeare's use of a rhapsodic form in the second act makes good sense in theatrical terms; indeed, it is the key to understanding his concept of the action in terms of stage movement.

The play begins with scenes of purposeful movement; the Ghost is sighted, Horatio informs the Prince, Hamlet sees the Ghost, speaks with it and excitedly disperses his companions. The general effect is only enhanced by the slower pace of the King's ceremonious despatch of business and Laertes's departure. At the beginning of Act Two the pace slows: both Polonius and Ophelia are concerned with persons who are not present on stage—it is as though action were being withheld from us. This sense of nothing being done is intensified in the next scene, prolific as it is in providing distractions for both Hamlet and the audience.

Plainly such a way of proceeding could not be carried on indefinitely. The contrast between the first two acts has a point: the call to honour is followed by a reaction into distress and self-doubt. But the action has to return, and in the third act it does. Its quality, however, is erratic. Hamlet's purpose in staging 'The Mousetrap' is not as firm as he would have it appear: similarly, his visit to his mother leaves motives in doubt. Action in the third act is not presented as the outcome of rational deliberation or a commitment of the whole person to what is being done. Act Three, then, offers something different in effect and feeling from its predecessor, but clearly consistent with it.

It is interesting that one can distinguish so clearly the character of individual acts. The significance of act-division for Shakespeare himself and for his theatre is elusive: it is even possible that it has no significance. In the case of *Hamlet* it must be remembered in any case that the Quartos published in his lifetime have no act-division, and that the Folio of 1623 distinguishes between Acts One and Two, but has no further division act from act. This leaves the limits of the third and fourth acts, if there be such, obscure; the fifth or last act has an obvious unity deriving from the surprise and implicit threat to the King of Hamlet's return and from the rivalry between Hamlet and Laertes, which there emerges as a matter of importance.

Do we need, then, to imagine that *Hamlet* has a five-act structure at all? Without committing myself to a view on the larger problems associated with act-division and the Elizabethan playwright, I find it helpful to think of *Hamlet* as composed of five acts; but there is something anomalous about the division between the third and fourth acts which relates to the rhapsodic character of Act Two.

Modern editions of the play give Act Three four scenes. There is something satisfactory about the sequence of events that allows the account of Hamlet's visit to Ophelia at the beginning of Act Two to be balanced by his visit to his mother at the end of the third act; it allows the continuity underlying the sporadic action of Act Three to be felt, as well as perceived, in the theatre as in the study. However, the earlier editions do not indicate a scene change or break in time between what we are used to calling III.4 and IV.1. Thus in the first Folio of 1623 Hamlet goes off tugging the body of Polonius, and Claudius immediately enters to Gertrude. This seems plausible as stage action, and is one reason why other commentators have suggested that Act Three does not really end until Hamlet has met Fortinbras on his way through Denmark (another accidental encounter). Hamlet's soliloquy on honour gives a strong ending to the act: 'O, from this time forth, / My thoughts be bloody, or be nothing worth!' Furthermore, this soliloquy parallels the closure of the second act also with a soliloquy; and as it arises out of a meeting and self-comparison with Fortinbras, it also anticipates and adds force to the conclusion of the play as a whole with Fortinbras's valediction of the dead Hamlet.[12]

This uncertainty about the shape of the action in *Hamlet* tends to confirm a *generally* rhapsodic quality in the middle section. Hamlet's precarious hold on things is reflected in the presentation of a reality that proposes alternative patternings of its own nature to anyone who contemplates it at all. New movements of possible significance begin at IV.1 and at IV.5; neither, in the end, contributes much at all to the solution of the dilemma with which the prince was presented in the first act. It is true that a new thread of purposive action begins with the return of Laertes in IV.5, and that by this means the play is given a new air, a new sense of direction. On the other hand, it can be argued that after the death of Polonius the reality of Hamlet's threat to Claudius is magnified, and the King's provision for his own safety requires that he should fulfil Hamlet's suspicions about the embassy to England (III.4.204–7) by making it the means of his nephew's death. It is possible, therefore, to discern a qualitative change in the play after III.4 as well as after IV.4. Like Orsino's mind, *Hamlet* is a 'very opal'.

Its opaline or rhapsodic quality evidently stands in a meaningful relationship to the nature of its protagonist. It matches his variousness, skittishness and want of determination. The point has not been missed by commentators.

The connection is made sensitively by Mrs Lyons, for example. She discusses Hamlet's 'variety of tones and styles' in relation to the 'antic disposition' which he says he may put on:

> A mixture of styles was particularly appropriate for the representation of melancholy, as Burton was also to show. Melancholy was a state that included violent opposites in feeling and behaviour, from total dejection and apathy to hysterical outbursts and frenzy, with swings from one to the other, as the Queen suggests in her descriptions of Hamlet's supposed 'fits' . . . The responses that melancholy engendered were not only various, but inappropriate since they were stimulated by internal disorders . . . For the representation of such a condition on the stage, the mixture of styles and moods of a performance that was labelled as 'antic' or grotesque, and that had some affinities with the satyr's antics (and therefore with rude satire), had a very obvious appropriateness.[13]

This is well put. It is consistent with the formal qualities which I have tried to describe, complies with the audience's disposition to regard Hamlet as a doctor might a particularly difficult case, and has behind it a long line of critics who have, perhaps with less knowledge, offered the same kind of diagnosis. In its account of the 'inappropriate' element in the melancholiac's response, it even explains how it is that this section of the play can survive the pejorative implications of 'rhapsody': 'In *Hamlet*', she says, 'the incongruities express Hamlet's discordant opposition to the tragic action and to his part in it'.[14]

Weakness and melancholy

When Claudius talks of Hamlet's 'transformation' he does not
necessarily have in mind something that has taken place since the
events of the first act; his words could equally well apply to a change
in the prince which took place at some time before the action of the
play had begun at all:

> Something have you heard
> Of Hamlet's transformation—so I call it,
> Sith nor th'exterior nor the inward man
> Resembles that it was. What it should be,
> More than his father's death, that thus hath put him
> So much from th'understanding of himself
> I cannot dream of.   (II.2.4–10)

The reference to change in the *exterior* man, however, sends us back
to Ophelia's speech, and so to the kind of diagnosis offered by
Polonius. It has often been remarked that Hamlet's appearance is
described by Ophelia as that of a melancholy lover. His dress
throughout the middle section of the play, as it was performed in
Shakespeare's time by his own company, suggested the disorder of
madness. Anthony Scoloker alludes to Shakespeare's play several
times in his poem *Daiphantus* (1604), and mentions the hero's dress:
'his shirt he onely weares, Much like mad-*Hamlet*'.[15] The very form
of the play's middle section conforms to the irregular motions of the
melancholiac, as we have seen; the information about dress only
confirms a diagnosis which can be made on quite other grounds.

The diagnosis is too simple, though. It does not properly account
for the variety of melancholy roles which Hamlet plays as disappointed lover, frustrated heir or offended son. Hamlet is not
merely changeable; what changes is the symptoms of his illness. The
symptoms do not cohere: this may be like life, but it is not much like
contemporary diagnostics, and makes them not very reliable as aids
to understanding. Mrs Lyons suggests that Hamlet feigns melancholy
but that he suffers from it too. Motivation of this order is certainly
consistent with the complication and ambiguity of the play as a
whole. Yet much of the case put forward by Mrs Lyons depends on
seeing Hamlet's actions in the last act as symptoms of a benign
melancholy influence. This is a view which I find unacceptable.

Furthermore, my own arguments about the organization of the first
act as centred on honour require one to show how Hamlet's motivation in the middle part of the play grows out of the earlier concern
for honour.

In one sense at least this does not seem a difficult task. Before
Hamlet starts acting strangely he warns his companions that

> I perchance hereafter shall think meet
> To put an antic disposition on . . .   (I.5.179–80)

After this declaration, anything odd in his behaviour can be referred
back to these lines, so that we can think, 'Although Hamlet is
behaving like a melancholiac or madman, he has told us that he was
going to do so; he is really in his right mind.' The changes in his
behaviour that can be put down to the melancholiac's erratic temperament can also be explained by the fact that Hamlet is merely *acting*
the part of a melancholiac and, like an actor, adjusts his role to each
different audience. When Claudius asks Rosencrantz and Guildenstern if they can

> Get from him why he puts on this confusion,
> Grating so harshly all his days of quiet
> With turbulent and dangerous lunacy   (III.1.2–4)

he expresses the natural distrust that such changes arouse in the
phrase 'puts on': Hamlet is like an actor assuming a part when he
goes on stage. (Equally naturally, however, he speaks of the 'turbulent and dangerous lunacy' as a real thing—Claudius is reluctant to
think the worst of Hamlet, as it were.) The motive for Hamlet's
'antic disposition' would be honour-based. Just as Laertes deems it
necessary to hide himself before he can move decisively to revenge
his father, so does Hamlet. His hiding-place is an assumed madness.

Yet this is another explanation that is too simple to fit the particular
case of Hamlet. For one thing, we are predisposed to discount
Hamlet's warning, first, because he is so plainly distracted—that is,
with his mind drawn in two directions at once—when he makes it,
and secondly because even before that moment he has struck us as
someone with the makings of a melancholiac. When, therefore,
Hamlet starts acting oddly, we are inclined to interpret his actions as
those of a sick man. The grief which cut him off from others and
which he would not alter was all too likely to end in seriously

disordered behaviour. If it were not for the actorial authority and the rapid change of significant roles displayed by Hamlet we would certainly opt for the pseudo-medical explanation altogether. As it is, we hover between one explanation and another, at one moment drawn to think of him as a melancholiac, at the next suspecting him of cunning and control.

The result is something like the over-determination of motive which may also be associated with the Ghost. Just as it does not need both the appearance of the Ghost *and* the nature of Hamlet himself to explain his desire for revenge, so it does not need *both* Hamlet's sensitivity to honour *and* his melancholy to explain the delay. This over-determination contributes largely to our sense of Hamlet as a mystery, since it sets up contradictory forms of motivation in rivalry—the control of the resolute prince in search of restored honour and the want of control of the melancholiac.

In the last act of the play Hamlet himself interprets his actions as those of a madman:

> What I have done
> That might your nature, honour, and exception
> Roughly awake, I here proclaim was madness.
>
> (V.2.226–8)

The occasion is of the kind that Hamlet would take seriously, since it involves his honour. His words do not settle the matter, any more than does the earlier suggestion to his mother that really he is not mad at all, only 'mad in craft' (III.4.190). But they do look back to the moment at the end of Act Two when Hamlet tells himself that the Devil could be taking advantage of 'my weakness and my melancholy' (II.2.597). *There* at least he admits there is something wrong with him. I suggest that he even shadowily presents us with the over-determined nature of his sickness, which on the one hand derives from melancholy or madness, and on the other reflects the consequences for honour and the body of the man of honour when 'weakness', physical or moral, prevents him from securing satisfaction.

It is in keeping with the play as a whole that over-determination is only ambiguously present in the line. 'Weakness' is at once synonymous with 'melancholy' and distinguished from it; the effect is similar to that discussed by Empson with regard to Shakespeare's use of *and* in conjunction with *of*.[16] Polonius uses the word 'weakness' in the medical context when he is offering his diagnosis to Claudius:

> . . . he, repell'd—a short tale to make—
> Fell into a sadness, then into a fast,
> Thence to a watch, thence into a weakness,
> Thence to a lightness, and, by this declension,
> Into the madness wherein now he raves,
> And all we mourn for.   (II.2.146–51)

According to Dover Wilson,[17] Polonius is using a precise medical vocabulary here. He is listing Hamlet's symptoms—dejection ('sadness'), distaste for food ('fast'), insomnia ('watch'), crazy behaviour ('weakness') and fits of delirium ('lightness'). The last distinction is a fine one, of course; and in fact the examples of usage with which Dover Wilson seeks to enforce his interpretation 'crazy behaviour', all drawn from Shakespeare, are not very convincing. The *OED* seems nearer the mark in suggesting that Polonius refers to 'a weakened condition of body; an attack of faintness'. Indeed all the passages which it cites indicate that 'weakness' without qualification would be taken to mean *physical* weakness: the first example for the sense 'defect of character' is dated c.1645. If Polonius, then, refers primarily to physical weakness (Jenkins suggests that he means general debility), so, probably, does Hamlet. On the one hand, his weakness—that is, his inability to act (the word is certainly moving *towards* the meaning 'defect of character')—is a result of his melancholy condition; on the other it is distinct from it; it is the weakness of his sinews following the Ghost's departure, and the sign of his body's incomplete participation in the idea of honour adhered to by his father. 'It cannot be/But I am pigeon-liver'd' (II.2.572–3) says Hamlet of himself; thirty lines later, when he talks of his 'weakness', the word connects with that self-accusation as well as with the exculpatory 'melancholy'. The phrase combines Hamlet's sense of the mystery which is himself with the over-determination which contributes to *our* sense of the same mystery.

But it also relates to the question of mind and body which I discussed in the first section of this chapter. 'Weakness' is and is not a physical condition; 'melancholy' is possessed of a similar ambiguity, partly because, as Burton observed, it was hard to tell whether the body was the cause of mental defect or the mind a cause of bodily defect, and partly because the whole psychology of the humours was based on a view of bodily function that was more theoretical than concrete. The process whereby a humour became 'adust' and so induced a melancholy condition was supposed to be a physical one, but it was a physical process that could not be observed. It was physical but it was without a *full* physicality, since its material basis could only be imagined. In the theory of humours, therefore, mental and bodily merge, and as they merge the question of the individual's responsibility for his actions becomes more acute. Thus the idea of honour—which had been the dominant idea in the first act, and which regains dominance in the last act of the play, following the return of Laertes—is in the middle section of the play put on the same level as, and even confused with, the ideas of melancholy and of an inability to act meaningfully as motivating forces in Hamlet's behaviour. The two latter ideas, however, derive from that of honour through the significance of the body in honour-belief; and the soliloquies at the end of II.2 and IV.4, significantly placed as they are, maintain a dramatic continuity between the first and last acts by the emphasis which they place on honour.

In what follows I intend to look at some aspects of the dramatic presentation of honour in the middle section of *Hamlet*. I hope that the reader will bear in mind, however, the sense in which its role there is qualified by an awareness of the other ideas just mentioned. As for the dramatic benefits which accrue to Shakespeare by the complication of form, motive and point of view which has been discussed in this chapter, I hope that they will appear more and more clearly as my argument develops.

5 Hamlet and his inferiors

The rogue and peasant slave

Hamlet's soliloquy at the end of the second act is one of the two focal points in the play's middle section for his and our concern for honour. Accounts of this speech tend to give it an orderliness which it does not in fact possess, even if they allow, as does Eleanor Prosser's,[1] that Hamlet momentarily loses control in it.

The self-reproach with which it opens—'O what a rogue and peasant slave am I!'—immediately establishes honour as the subject of the speech. Hamlet accuses himself of having put himself outside the class to which he properly belongs and which is the visible sign of his consanguinity with his father. The note is aristocratic in the extreme; we have heard nothing like it in the first act. 'Rogue', 'peasant', 'slave': the words are vehicles for self-contempt, as later 'dull and muddy-mettled rascal', 'John-a-dreams', 'whore' and 'very drab'. The implication is consistently one of class-betrayal. The obligations of rank are those of honour: in failing to act on behalf of the family honour Hamlet has to all intents and purposes deprived himself of rank.

It is monstrous that the player can 'force his soul so to his own conceit' when Hamlet is unable to do so, because the player is, after all, little better than 'a rogue and peasant slave'; by comparing himself with such a man Hamlet seeks to force *his* soul to *his* conceit. He expects the aristocrat in himself to affirm itself and to remove the shame that makes him inferior even to a player.

He is intent on the outward signs of the actor's art, on the fact that he can command his body and its features, not on the means he may employ to do this; and so his description breaks up into a list of appearances huddled one upon another and with slight syntactic relation to the rest of the sentence. It is especially noticeable that 'wann'd', which is formally an intransitive verb, comes to feel adjectival as the list which follows it is prolonged:

Is it not monstrous that this player here . . .
Could force his soul so to his own conceit

That from her working all his visage wann'd,
Tears in his eyes, distraction in his aspect,
A broken voice, and his whole function suiting
With forms to his conceit? (545–51)[2]

The 'whole function' of Hamlet's body should spontaneously suit
itself to his 'conceit' of vengeance for his father, but he cannot even
force his soul to work upon his body in such a way as to make action
possible. The deadlock of his own body and soul, summed up in the
picture of himself as quite inert ('I/A dull and muddy-mettled rascal,
peak/Like John-a-dreams') stands in powerful contrast both to the
working of the player's visage (for that 'wanning' of the face is a
positive act) and to its effect upon its imagined audience, cleaving
'the general ear', amazing 'The very faculties of eyes and ears'.

As before, the idea of honour is linked with that of the responsive
body. So long as Hamlet's body refuses to respond to the call of his
soul, Hamlet will remain dishonoured.

So far the speech has a clear logical structure. Hamlet compares
himself with the player and finds that he is in practice outclassed even
by him. It would seem that, by dwelling on the comparison, he
hopes to secure a reaction in himself—an affirmation of the aristocratic values to which the Ghost appealed. The speech is complicated
in several ways. First, the more Hamlet insists upon the comparison
without a reaction's taking place, the more he vituperatively confirms
his own weakness. Second, in making the actor the basis of his
self-reproach he chooses a treacherous model. The actor is superior
to Hamlet only in the control he exercises over his body. Hamlet
does not imagine him as using that body to effect revenge.

What would he do
Had he the motive and the cue for passion
That I have? He would drown the stage with tears . . .

(554–6)

but he would not act, it seems, anywhere else than upon the stage; it
would still be as though all he did was 'in a fiction, in a dream of
passion'. Far from being a spur to action for Hamlet, therefore, the
player provides him with a means of evading contemplation of the
necessity for action. And so the antithesis of Hamlet and the player
breaks down—as Hamlet comes near the end of his comparison a

dawning likeness between the two can be discerned. Both are creatures of dream: Hamlet is

> Like John-a-dreams, unpregnant of my cause,
> And can say nothing . . .   (563–4)

The dreams have such a powerful hold on him that he is rendered
speechless; he is like an unpractised actor so taken up in the illusion of
which he is a part that he cannot pronounce his words. The distinction
between the player and Hamlet is not eradicated by these lines, but it
is considerably reduced. It is now not far to go before the idea will
occur that the player who 'can cleave the general ear with horrid
speech' must once have been a speechless neophyte like Hamlet.

Perhaps for this reason Hamlet turns from his comparison to
contemplation of the causes he has for taking action, in a volte-face
designed to fill his 'nothing' with *something*:

> . . . can say nothing—no, not for a king
> Upon whose property and most dear life
> A damn'd defeat was made.   (564–6)

The strong emphasis in rhythm and alliteration by contrast with
what precedes suggests a corrective forcing of his soul to its task by
Hamlet. 'Am *I* a coward?' The answer plainly should be 'no'. But it
has to be wrung from him by his imagining a series of insults of the
grossest kind, such as one would expect, in a Laertes, would lead to a
challenge and satisfaction one way or the other. The insults are, of
course, insults to the body or ones that are felt *in* the body, and the
strong, succinct verbs imagine actions quick, firm and assured in
their contempt— 'breaks', 'plucks', 'blows', 'tweaks':

> Who calls me villain, breaks my pate across,
> Plucks off my beard, and blows it in my face,
> Tweaks me by the nose, gives me the lie i' th' throat
> As deep as to the lungs—who does me this?   (567–70)

The trouble with such imagining is that it has an accustomizing
force. Imagining such things, one realizes an imaginative acqui-
escence in them. This is the fate that overcomes Hamlet. 'Am *I* a
coward?' The emphasis asserts that such a thing is unthinkable. But
he has no secure hold upon its unthinkability. The emphasis is gone
in 'Who calls me *villain*', it is gone in '*Tweaks* me', it is gone in '*gives*

me'. He *can* conceive of his own cowardice, even if such conceiving is itself a kind of betrayal of his father and the claims of blood.

Consequently he has to turn upon himself yet again in order to invoke the will to revenge:

> I am pigeon-liver'd, and lack gall
> To make oppression bitter, or ere this
> I should ha' fatted all the region kites
> With this slave's offal. Bloody, bawdy villain!
> Remorseless, treacherous, lecherous, kindless villain!

(573–7)

The 'bloody, bawdy villain' is obviously Claudius; Hamlet is once again soliciting his own honourable emotions, this time by contemplating the villainy of the man he must challenge. Nevertheless it is curious that when he calls Claudius a 'slave' he uses of him a term which at the opening of the soliloquy he used of himself, because there is something of a pattern behind it. Hamlet talks of Claudius's 'offal', for example, only three lines after describing himself as 'pigeon-liver'd'; liver is offal. It is Claudius who is 'kindless' now, but Hamlet's very first words in the play told us that *he* was 'less than kind'. Only one word here clearly distinguishes Claudius from Hamlet; Claudius is 'bloody', for he has killed a man. Hamlet has not, nor does he seem at this point likely to. He could, however, see himself as 'remorseless', that is, without pity for the father whose death he has not avenged; and 'lecherous', too, making a fool of himself in Ophelia's chamber. In other words, it looks as though in exclaiming against Claudius Hamlet is making him a scapegoat for his own sins. Even his outburst against the 'bloody' Claudius is mere adaptation of his frustrated rage with himself, and the label 'bloody' is the single important token of the attempt to escape his self-division. The more he has talked, the more he has said nothing—the nothing that his 'weakness', or his virtuously honourable revulsion from the revenge demanded from him by formal honour, makes of him.

The emphasis of his own words and their consequent ineffectiveness at last strike even Hamlet. He returns to the very beginning of the speech by likening himself to someone at the very bottom of the class-structure—'a whore', 'a very drab, A scullion'.[3] The only way out of the vicious circle of words is to devise a plan on the spot. Once he has a rational plan of action upon foot, Hamlet will have no cause for such internal conflict as the soliloquy has so far revealed. A plan, any plan, will show that he can act for honour, and so that he is no peasant but his father's son. 'About, my brains. Hum . . . '

The plan, however, is not much. Hamlet has already asked the players if they can do 'The Murther of Gonzago' for him, and has already suggested the insertion of new material (530–8). All that is new about the plan, then, is that the performance of 'The Murther' shall be a *test*. Hamlet intends to act just as he was going to act before the soliloquy began. This raises the question what in the first place the audience was to make of the arrangements with the first player about 'The Mousetrap'; it cannot be supposed that Hamlet is merely gratifying his authorial pretensions in adding to the text of the players' little drama, and even without precise knowledge of the affairs of the Gonzaga the nature of the play is clearly indicated (Italianate assassination). Given the sequence of feeling in the soliloquy, we have to suppose that previously Hamlet had merely intended giving Claudius a *mauvais quart d'heure*. If we imagine him to have had more than this in mind, the soliloquy loses its dramatic coherence. By converting the maliciously intended performance into a test, Hamlet makes the essentially purposeless play-within-a-play purposeful and makes himself, not an idle John-a-dreams, but one whose action is that of a loyal son and true aristocrat.

The path of honour is not so easily followed. Even if the argument which I have just advanced is not acceptable to the reader, it should be plain that Hamlet's resolve is encumbered by suggestions of what earlier in the speech he has been trying to shake off. A truly aristocratic honour sorts ill with the theatre. The notion that Claudius will betray himself by his looks is naive[4] and seems more so when we recall the self-directed rhetoric of the earlier line 'Make mad the guilty, and appal the free'. 'If a do blench, I know my course' implies what has not been suggested before, that Hamlet doubts whether Claudius is guilty or not. This doubt is justified by a further one. The Ghost may be a devil. And then again Hamlet *is* ill and perhaps does not quite measure up to his father's standard.

Hamlet just manages to stop the new succession of misgivings in time:

> the play's the thing
> Wherein I'll catch the conscience of the King.

He may succeed in *that*, but it hardly looks as though he will be able to do more. To pluck bright honour from the pale-faced moon would be no easy leap for Hamlet.

The dramatic quality of the soliloquy lies in the sense of struggle which it generates. Harry Levin, quoting 'Am I a coward? Who calls me villain?', suggests that 'Hamlet's monologues are character- istically devoted to the most rigorous self-examination'[5]; in that case, this one is uncharacteristic. It consists of a series of attempts to arouse the man of honour in Hamlet, first by telling himself that he is inferior even to the player; second by telling himself that he is a coward prepared to put up with the most blatant insult; third by contemplating the villainy of Claudius. None is successful, and the 'plan' which Hamlet finally devises, though it redirects his attention (and ours) to action, is very thin in promise. The unstated motivation of the speech, which is nevertheless very fully expressed in it, is a kind of deadlock between revulsion at the demands of formal honour and acknowledgement of their binding force on Hamlet. The most significant action which this deadlock will permit is the kind of oscillation exemplified by the soliloquy—which derives from a con- flict in himself which Hamlet cannot analyse. Indeed, the furthest that the reader can get in analysis is to outline the opposing forces of 'honour' that are involved, and to note the association of this conflict with the problem of body–mind relations at the opening of the speech and with 'melancholy' at its conclusion. He cannot, I think, get further at the precipitating cause of the conflict because such conflict is inherent in honour-belief, as it is in judgements about body–mind relations or the boundaries of reason and insanity.

The Prince and the Player

But how does this soliloquy relate to the drama as a whole? Harry Levin's interpretation depends heavily on the idea that it stands in a complementary relation to the player's speech. It will be seen how radically different the speech can look in this light:

> . . . the soliloquy is the mirror-opposite of the speech. Both passages are very nearly of the same length, and seem to be subdivided into three movements which run somewhat parallel. But where the speech proceeds from the slayer to the slain, and from the royal victim to the queenly mourner, the soliloquy

moves from that suggestive figure to another king and finally toward another villain. And where the speech leads from action to passion, the soliloquy reverses this direction. Where the Player's diction is heavily external, underlining the fundamental discrepancy between words and deeds, Hamlet's words are by convention his thoughts, directing inward their jabs of self-accusation. Midway, where the Player curses Fortune as a strumpet, Hamlet falls 'a-cursing like a very drab'. Well may he hesitate, 'like a neutral to his will and matter', at the very point where even the rugged Pyrrhus paused and did nothing . . . we may cite the precedent as a justification—if further justification still be needed—for Hamlet's often criticized delay. While he must hold his tongue, so long as he 'cannot speak' his genuine sentiments, the Player is vocal on his behalf.[6]

There are signs of a forcing of the argument here. If we include the part of it spoken by Hamlet, it is true that the player's speech is barely four lines longer than the soliloquy. But its interruptions make it significantly longer—and make it feel longer too. The fact that Hamlet himself speaks the first fourteen lines about Pyrrhus tends to reduce the symmetry of the speeches (an external consideration anyway) and makes the similarity of his situation to that of Pyrrhus obvious even before the player has uttered a word. The confusion about where the player's speech begins makes the positioning of the allusions to strumpet and drab relatively uncertain, and the division of both speeches into three parts has little practical meaning. Even when Priam the victim is mentioned we look at him from the point of view of Pyrrhus, and do not look long, or in the same way as we do at Pyrrhus or Hecuba. In the soliloquy Hecuba is not given prominence, the king is mentioned twice (564–6 and 579) and in neither case is held before our eyes or Hamlet's more than fleetingly, and the last part of what Hamlet has to say is concerned as much with the Ghost as with the villain Claudius. Levin is really on very shaky ground in discerning a formal parallelism, as he is in asserting that the player speaks on Hamlet's behalf. Hamlet speaks for himself the most pertinent lines of 'the player's speech'.

The points of interest obviously established about the speech are that it superimposes the image of Pyrrhus as revenger upon that of the revenger-designate, by having Hamlet himself start it off, and that it tends to show the revenger in a bad light, culminating with the pathetic description of Hecuba's suffering. It cannot be supposed that Hamlet misses the similarity between himself and Pyrrhus. It follows that by calling more and more upon the audience for sympathy with the victims of revenge rather than with its agent, the speech more and more reflects adversely upon the determination to be like Pyrrhus which at first seemed implicit in Hamlet's choice of this description for recitation. The speech as a whole reflects his inability to sustain the role of avenger, and so *anticipates* the soliloquy. At the same time, the stage image of the prince silent before the vagabond player prepares us piquantly for Hamlet's struggle to reassert class-feeling in himself in the soliloquy. Finally, the archaic diction of the speech associates itself with the heroic attributes of the Ghost, simultaneously proclaiming the *power* of its honour-based images and their remoteness from the scene in which Hamlet himself is an actor, establishing in the minds of the audience a kind of oscillatory movement which is transformed in the various calls to honour and relapses from it in the soliloquy itself.

The relationship between the player's speech and the final soliloquy is, then, almost entirely anticipatory. But that is true not only of the player's speech but of the scene as a whole in so far as it concerns Hamlet. His soliloquy takes into itself, as it were, discrete elements of II.2 and identifies him as their sum. The different roles which he has adopted in regard to Polonius, to Rosencrantz and Guildenstern, and to the players are transformed into the different forms of persuasion he seeks to use upon himself to 'force' his soul, conceit and body into agreement; and the unexplained and quasi-inexplicable movements of the speech, which convert the persuasive rhetoric of formal honour into a collusive rhetoric tending to justify and naturalize the cowardice which by another name is virtue, correspond to the merely accidental basis of the encounters in the body of the scene. Furthermore, because the oscillatory movement of the soliloquy in a sense repeats the arbitrary movement of the scene as a whole, it tends to confirm the sense of Hamlet as stable in his instability (irritatingly stable, one might say) which I have already argued is the basic idea for the scene's dramatic structure. The soliloquy looks forward to the third act *only* in its last fifteen or so lines, when Hamlet's tenuous 'plan' is formulated. The bridge between Act Two and Act Three is the slightest imaginable but, because it is the only hope for the drama—which cannot remain locked in stasis for ever—it must, and does, carry the most intense expectations of the audience with it into this third act.

Hamlet as honest man

If there is anything novel in what I am saying, then it derives partly from my interpretation of Hamlet's 'plan'. Critics accept—too readily, to my mind—Hamlet's words with the player following line 530 as according completely with the announcement at the end of the soliloquy. But 'About my brains' implies some addition to whatever he had in his mind at line 530. The actor has to make sense of this implication, and I have tried to supply that sense.

I think also that the emphasis I am placing on class is comparatively unusual. It is a subject from which critics at the best of times are apt to turn away. Only one critic really grasps the nettle in *Hamlet*, and that is William Empson:

> One reason . . . why [Hamlet] could be made so baffling without his character becoming confused was that it made him give a tremendous display of top-class behaviour, even in his secret mind as expressed in soliloquy . . . the paradoxical chivalry towards Laertes . . . really belongs, I think, to the situation of continuing to claim a peculiar status as an aristocrat after the practical status has been lost . . .
>
> The curious indifference of Hamlet to the facts does make him what we call egotistical, but this would be viewed as part of his lordliness . . . [7]

More recently S.P. Zitner[8] has argued that Hamlet's situation is intrinsically a class-situation; the question of what to do about affronted honour was meaningful only for the members of an aristocracy whose authority was being undermined as new ideas about their place in the social hierarchy established themselves. Zitner does not show how deeply Hamlet's feelings also are formed by ideas of class; how natural it is for him to find himself in a typical class-situation. By contrast Empson's comments, though brief, go far into the 'mystery' of Hamlet's character. If my argument about honour is right, this is as it should be. The link between honour and kinship, reputation and status, makes Hamlet's class-membership as mysterious as his obligations to the sense of honour which the Ghost apparently regards as 'natural'. It is this link which binds together the oscillating dubieties of the soliloquy 'O what a rogue and peasant slave am I' and the sequence of encounters leading up to it.

Hamlet's first exchange is with Polonius. As we should expect, Polonius extends his class-consciousness into the forms of address which he uses. Claudius is 'my lord' or 'my liege', Gertrude is 'my dear Majesty' and when it is necessary to speak of Hamlet's madness the news is softened by respect; 'Your *noble* son is mad' (II.2.43,86, 135,92). But this hardly prepares us for the extreme formality which he uses with Hamlet. Polonius uses the honorific in every speech addressed to the prince until their dialogue concludes at line 219:

> How does my good Lord Hamlet?
> *Ham.* Well, God-a-mercy.
> *Pol.* Do you know me, my lord?   (II.2.171–3)

And so on.

This sudden splattering of honorifics can be explained in three different ways. First, by reference to Polonius: he believes Hamlet to be mad and the repeated honorific is a sign of the distance between the two, and implicitly an invocation of it; further, the prospect of a union between Hamlet and Ophelia may make Polonius more than ordinarily aware of the young man's rank. Second, by reference to Hamlet: he may by his manner impose a consciousness of rank upon Polonius. Third, by reference to the author: it may be his aim to draw the audience's attention to class-attitudes in the scene as a whole. These explanations are not mutually exclusive, and all apply to the exchange. It is Hamlet's attitude that needs close examination.

He is contemptuous of Polonius and builds his contempt upon the deference shown him. The old man's question 'Do you know me, my lord?' maintains the conventional social hierarchy whilst implying that one of the two is well-nigh imbecilic. If it is Hamlet, then the honour which is accorded him is questionable; if it is Polonius, then his maintenance of the conventions is. Hamlet's reply, 'Excellent well. You are a fishmonger', whatever its exact meaning, is undoubtedly a gross insult to a man of Polonius's standing, of his age, and of his honour-consciousness. Whether a 'fishmonger' is a go-between (there is no solid evidence for this), a fornicator, or a man with fish to sell, in the sense of a daughter to marry, the primary sense draws attention to the insult to *class*: a fishmonger and a Lord Chamberlain are miles apart socially. Hamlet's reply is in this way an attack upon the deference shown him. But there is a sense in which it accepts that deference. Polonius's humility is what makes it possible for Hamlet to insult him so easily; the prince is using (or abusing) the privileges of his station. In reply to the exaggerated respect which is shown him he affects an exaggerated loftiness. Polonius accepts the bad treatment meted out to him as that of a man who is out of his mind—'How say you by that? Still harping on my daughter. Yet he knew me not at first; a said I was a fishmonger. A is far gone' (II.2.187–9)—but also as explicable in terms of aristocratic behaviour, 'the flash and outbreak of a fiery mind' (II.1.33)—'And truly in my youth I suffered much extremity for love, very near this' (II.2.189–90). Our doubts about the reality or extent of Hamlet's sanity ironically reflect on this extraordinary display of court manners. The mirror of art distances us from our own nature, but it remains recognizably ours. The scene must have been deeply disturbing to the original audience, but it is hardly less so today. Using the rules to break the rules must always be shocking and must always raise questions about the meaning and value of social behaviour in general.

Hamlet is in the middle of these questions, not on the outside formulating them in a spirit of calm assurance or of dangerous experiment. His attitude to the rules remains ambiguous: he does not simply want to be rid of them, but to base them on honour as virtue rather than honour as precedence. He wants rules, but he wants different rules. He yearns for a world where 'honesty' is the dominant motive:

> . . . You are a fishmonger.
> *Pol.* Not I, my lord.
> *Ham.* Then I would you were so honest a man.
> *Pol.* Honest, my lord?
> *Ham.* Ay sir. To be honest, as this world goes, is to be one man
>   picked out of ten thousand.   (II.2.174–9)

The man who is 'honest' follows virtues without respect to rank: the word is related to 'honour' but is not equivalent to it. Hamlet's use of it marks a significant stage in his living-out of the problem set him by the Ghost.

William Empson has some extremely acute pages on the development of meaning in the word 'honest', the central point in his
argument being that somewhere in the middle of the sixteenth
century ' "not lying, not stealing, keeping promises" becomes the
head sense instead of "deserving and receiving social honour" '. He
thinks of the new use of the word as signifying 'general praise among
friends, on a good fellow basis . . . cut . . . off from the feeling of
moral approval'. He does not offer an extended account of the
word's relation to 'honour' but his view on the matter is clear:

> . . . it was because 'honourable' was in reach when required that
> the word for the more social and less solemn aspects of honour [i.e.
> 'honest'] was free to develop on its own; on the other hand, the
> connection of the two words, the possible antithesis between
> them, would tend to keep alive in *honest* a sort of shrubbery of
> ideas about honour.[9]

I think that Empson's new use of the word 'honest' with the sense
'not lying, not stealing, keeping promises' reflects the gradual
debasement of the word as it was associated with honour at the lower
levels of society. 'Honesty' seems to have been in some ways identical with 'honour', or so some of the proverbial and quasi-proverbial
sayings of Shakespeare's day and earlier would suggest. It was
identical with the individual's sense of himself and with the sense of
virtue, for example: 'He that loses his honesty has nothing else to
lose'. It was a kind of minimal honour—honour without respect to
social status: 'Honesty is no pride'.[10] It thus corresponds to the
honour of the *pueblo* described by Pitt-Rivers: 'In the *pueblo* the ideal
of equality in honour reigns and precedence deriving from birth and
associated with status is missing'.[11] Empson's examples make it plain
that the word 'honesty' could easily be emptied of moral significance, but the proverbial uses show that moral values remained
latent in the word. Its non-aristocratic affinities are made clear if the
two sayings already quoted are contrasted with the sententious
'Great honours are great burdens' and the potentially ironic 'The
more rich the more honour'.[12]

Hamlet's use of the word 'honest' is not, then, incompatible with
his being a man of honour, but it sets up a context in which moral
values considered absolutely are likely to outweigh any supposed
necessity of maintaining the existing social order and *its* values. It

permits Hamlet to criticise the social order to which he belongs without placing him outside that order, and this explains how he can be recognizably a gentleman and yet, as Empson says, maintain 'a curious appeal for the lower classes in the audience as a satirist on the upper class'.[13]

Polonius asks Hamlet what he is reading; the answer is 'Slanders, sir, for the satirical rogue says here that old men have gray beards, that their faces are wrinkled', and so on:

> All which, sir, though I most powerfully and potently believe, yet I hold it not honesty to have it thus set down. For yourself, sir, shall grow old as I am—if like a crab you could go backward.
> (II.2.200–04)

Hamlet pretends now to be looking at the idea of 'honesty' from Polonius's point of view; he implies that simple truths, such as fishmongers are willing to face, are not acceptable to him. What is 'honest' is not now to be settled by reference to a universal code of right and wrong but by consulting the opinions of those to whom we defer, our elders. To do so, however, is to turn the natural order of things upside-down, to go backward like a crab. As before, the word 'honesty' implies Hamlet's disenchantment with the social imperative that such a man as he should get satisfaction for honour; but as before it is used in a context where thanks to Hamlet's rank, the deference shown him by Polonius and the possibility that he is not in full possession of his wits, such criticism as the word contains does not entail absolute repudiation by Hamlet of his social role.

Francis Fergusson sees the action of this play as alternating between the ritual and the improvisational. The latter word, at least, is well chosen, though Fergusson's idea that the play's meaning is revealed in alternating scenes of ritual and improvisation seems to me un-supported either by the text or by the diagram which he himself supplies.[14] With Polonius, Hamlet *improvises*— that is, he speaks as though he has no mind made up, no plan of action. At one level, he just wants Polonius to go away. At another, he is fully taken up with the honour whose obligation weighs on him; he explores both its limits simultaneously: as status, in the way he treats Polonius, and as virtue, in his reflections on honesty. At neither level is there any sign of an overall strategy. He seems still not to know what to do about the Ghost. Although the memory of what he has said about an 'antic disposition' encourages us to suppose that he may be concealing his intentions by feigning to have none, the more he treats status and virtue as he does here the less likely will it seem that that is the case. In particular, his fascination with a rank-indifferent 'honesty' augurs ill for any project, such as revenge, which is based on birth and status rather than on universal morality.

Rosencrantz and Guildenstern are welcome to Hamlet because with them he can forget the burden of rank which Polonius makes especially heavy for him. They enter with expressions of respect— 'My honoured lord', 'My most dear lord'—but are quickly set right by Hamlet:

> My excellent good friends. How dost thou, Guildenstern?
> Ah, Rosencrantz. Good lads, how do you both?
> *Ros.* As the indifferent children of the earth.
> *Guil.* Happy in that we are not over-happy; on Fortune's cap we are
> not the very button.   (II.2.224–9)

They grasp the roles which have been allotted them by Hamlet perfectly; in declaring their own indifference to rank, they merely comply with Hamlet's distaste for his own rank and what that entails. The joke that they are Fortune's 'privates' manages to link them with the socially levelling force of sex and at the same time to suggest that whatever social distinction is one's lot is meaningless, because only the gift of a strumpet. Many of the senses and feelings associated with the word 'honest' by Empson are suggested in the tone of this exchange. There is a touch of 'frank, going out of one's way to tell the truth', of 'faithful to friends, employers, etc.' , of 'indifferent to money, taking it for granted', of 'having manly vigour, bluff', of 'not deceiving himself, or those to whom he is intelligible by sympathy, about his own desires or emotions', and perhaps of 'always recognizable as a gentleman', in the way either one of them speaks. It is not surprising, therefore, that the word 'honest' should pop up in their speech, since it is so answerable to the part they impersonate and the mood which Hamlet generates:

Ham. . . . What news?
Ros. None, my lord, but the world's grown honest.
Ham. Then is doomsday near. But your news is not true.

(II.2.236–8)

Hamlet is thinking of a personal doomsday for Claudius, not just the scriptural one. If the world were grown honest, then it would be his duty to challenge his uncle; fortunately, affairs have not reached that state. In this speech, he reaches the limit of honour as virtue; putting all the weight on 'honesty' and none on 'honour' still leads him to the point of action. He turns back from it with relief. The idea that the world is hopelessly corrupt is comforting because it puts his inability to act in the best light possible. (Hamlet's meaning could only be allowed to appear in a joke in this way, of course: he cannot contemplate his dilemma directly.)

Hamlet now takes another tack. The world is a prison, or a series of prisons, of which Demark is one. The prisoners it contains are held on the authority of Fortune. This is tantamount to denying any human freedom to act; the suggestion that man's physical destiny is settled by arbitrary 'Fortune' is complemented by the notion that all value is settled by reference to an arbitrary subjectivism: 'there is nothing good or bad, but thinking makes it so. To me it [Denmark] is a prison' (II.2.249–51). Either doctrine is comforting to a man seeking to evade the obligation that he feels.

It would be tedious to continue this detailed commentary on the scene. The conversation with Rosencrantz and Guildenstern goes on to the subject of ambition and the conclusion that it is a dream:

> Then are our beggars bodies, and our monarchs and outstretched heroes the beggars' shadows. Shall we to th'court? For by my fay, I cannot reason. (II.2. 263–5)

Hamlet has swiftly returned to the idea that class is meaningless, and that the hierarchy established by the court is one of unreason. He rejects the offer of his friends to wait upon him, not just because he is 'most dreadfully attended' and therefore unable to offer them the hospitality that he should, but also because, so long as they are not in his service, he can speak to them as an equal, 'like an honest man' (268). It is this relationship that he seeks to preserve when he conjures them to be direct with him

> by the rights of our fellowship, by the consonancy of our youth, by the obligation of our ever-preserved love and by what more dear a better proposer can charge you withal . . . (284–7)

The appeal is an appeal to the rights of honesty, though the idea of 'virtue' is no longer apparent, since the thought of 'doomsday' is too disquieting. But their calculated telling of the truth excludes them from such fellowship because it *is* calculated. Hamlet immediately moves into the central speech of the scene, which declares him a mystery to himself as well as them; the possibility of being open recedes. Indeed, Hamlet now acts the lord with them turning upon Rosencrantz like a schoolmaster on a naughty child:

> Man delights not me—nor woman neither, though by your smiling you seem to say so.
> *Ros.* My lord, there was no such stuff in my thoughts.   (309–11)

But no sooner has the idyll of 'honesty' with Rosencrantz and Guildenstern been broken than the announcement of the players' approach is made. Hamlet welcomes them first just because they *are* players, the implication being that nobody is really the person he seems to be at Elsinore. Then (326–7) they are identified as the players in whom he was personally interested. Like him, they have suffered 'inhibition' thanks to the 'late innovation'—the dialogue establishes grounds for Hamlet's sympathy with them, and the remark on the war of the theatres that after all the children will be adults themselves one day, and so are constrained now to 'exclaim against their own succession' (349), establishes Hamlet's conception of the community of actors as an 'honest' one, that is, one that is founded on principles of unity, not principles of rank, however inverted. (Since the child actors are associated with a hierarchy turned mad, being 'most tyrannically clapped' and so berattling 'the common stages' 'that many wearing rapiers are afraid of goosequills and dare scarce come thither' (338–42), it is natural that Polonius should on his second appearance be described as 'that great baby you see there . . . not yet out of his swaddling-clouts' (382–3).) Thus, as far as Hamlet is concerned, the scene consists in oscillation between the attitude of great lord and that of 'honest man'. With Polonius he freezes; but to Rosencrantz and Guildenstern he warms—until, that is, their essential dishonesty is revealed to him: they are replaced by the players as embodiment of the fellowship with others which allows Hamlet to forget his rank.

But Hamlet's relation with the players, however much he chaffs with them or pretends to equality—'Welcome, good friends', and so on—is essentially that of a master to servants. The fellowship is illusion: they do not chaff him back, and the first player is notably reserved in his words to the prince, as well he might be—officially rogues and vagabonds, some actors at least were businessmen of no little standing, and Shakespeare himself took the matter of rank seriously.[15] More to the point, Hamlet himself knows that his relationship with the players is constrained: it is no more real than what he had imagined with Rosencrantz and Guildenstern, though the acting-out of it can be turned into a kind of rebuke to them:

> Gentlemen, you are welcome to Elsinore. Your hands, come then. Th'appurtenance of welcome is fashion and ceremony. Let me comply with you in this garb—lest my extent to the players, which I tell you must show fairly outwards, should more appear like entertainment than yours.   (367–71)

Thus there is a progressive quality to the scene: Hamlet's situation becomes more pathetic because it becomes plainer that the simple way of 'honesty' is not open to him. The apparent freedom and the undeniable elegance of his prose are belied by this gradual revelation and make the transition into tumultuous verse in the soliloquy a form of relief, as well as the climax of the scene.

Much more could be said about the players in this scene, and especially about the player's imitation of a man of rank, Aeneas. But enough has been said, I hope, to show how the soliloquy takes into itself the matter of the scene as a whole, and how this in turn relates to what I have already argued about the play. It is time now to take up the thread of action cast at the end of the scene and to see what happens in the third act.

6 Hamlet's being

Detachment and theatricality

The third act opens with some necessary reminders of plot. The King wants to know why the prince 'puts on this confusion', and there is a hint—if only a hint—in this formulation that he suspects the confusion to be merely assumed. His cry of pain when Polonius's words 'lash' his conscience links with this. It does not positively confirm the Ghost's revelations, should we happen to doubt them, since he does not name the 'deed' whose consequence is a 'heavy burden'; but it does tend to mark him out as a guilty creature. On the other hand, it also draws attention to a tender conscience which may not tolerate further burdens. Our interest in Claudius is quickened, then, because he is on the brink of action, but also on the brink of moral choice of an important kind. At the same time, the announcement by Rosencrantz and Guildenstern of the evening's theatricals advances Hamlet's 'plan': two lines of action seem about to converge.

Our sense that Hamlet had entered upon a course of action at the end of II.2 may have been tenuous, but a good deal is done to reinforce it in these opening lines of the third act. Nor is it a matter of screwing us up for the coming court performance only; more immediately we are promised the scene to be played between Hamlet and Ophelia for the benefit of Claudius and Polonius. This 'scene' is just as much prepared for as the play-within-the-play; like that, it is *set into* the action of the play as a whole. Such in-setting seems to reflect Shakespeare's solution to the problem of moving on from the relative plotlessness of Act Two without allowing the audience's attention to be deflected from the mystery of 'that within'. The mystery is presented, in Hamlet's encounter with Ophelia and in the play-within-the-play, *within* the action of the tragedy.

With the current of action running so briskly, and with everything set for the meeting between the prince and his supposed love, it is surprising that Shakespeare does not get on with it. But no: the famous soliloquy intervenes, and whilst Hamlet debates *his* question, that other one, 'If't be th'affliction of his love or no/That thus he

suffers for' (III.1.36–7), recedes in our minds. The effect is discon-
certing, but dramatic in the extreme. In the first Quarto of the play
Hamlet's encounter with Ophelia comes at the equivalent of II.2.169–
70, but it is still preceded by the soliloquy. Whoever was responsible
for that arrangement seems already to have appreciated the force
with which we register the supplanting of one question by another.

Yet, coming in the place where we are used to find it, the soliloquy
has more power to disconcert. If we have responded fully to the air of
purposeful activity with which the third act begins and by means of
which it seems to substantiate the reasonableness of Hamlet's 'plan',
we do not expect the prince now to enter debating with himself what
is 'nobler' as a course of action. We may not have thought, but surely
we felt, that he had made up his mind. If there are questions still to be
asked they relate to the execution and the consequences of his 'plan',
which by the time we arrive at his third-act entry we are disposed to
think of simply as a *plan*. What will Hamlet do if he is persuaded,
after the performance, that Claudius is indeed guilty of his father's
murder? More interesting: what will he do if the King's guilt is *not*
confirmed? The question that ought to be foremost in our minds—
and surely it is only our own familiarity with the text in its entirety,
and the uncertain grasp of pace in stage production, that obscure
this—is 'revenge or not revenge?'. 'To be or not to be' is *not* the
question.[1]

The speech offers a kind of 'still centre' to the play; that has been
said often enough, but its stillness is for the audience inseparable
from sensations of surprise and bafflement. This needs to be kept in
mind when critics speak of its detachment (according to William
Empson, its 'utter detachment'[2]—another critic describes its tone as
'academic',[3] thus carrying the description into absurdity). We do not
regard it with detachment.

Hamlet's detachment is, perhaps, another matter. Harry Levin,
who finds the soliloquy to be 'quietly meditative', remarks on the
relationship between Hamlet and the audience which it establishes:

> The convention of the soliloquy, treating his speech as if it were
> unheard by the other actors, isolates him from them and brings
> him closer to us.[4]

Hamlet's fierce engagement in the casual encounters of the second
act is gone, but it is replaced by a new intimacy with the audience, a

vibrancy that makes this still centre less than still. The speech is detached, it seems to me, only in relation to the preceding moments of the play. Levin, on the other hand, says that *in tone* it is 'so detached that the whole episode [that is, Hamlet's encounter with Ophelia] has been misplaced in the First Quarto'. This is not very plausible; it is not its tone, but its enigmatic relation to the action in its accepted place that makes Levin's argument possible. But, in any case, Empson's suggestion that Shakespeare himself originally put the soliloquy, and what ensues, into the second act and then transferred them to the third for greater dramatic effect seems more attractive. Empson argues that the new position had the advantage of bringing to the fore 'problems about whether he [Hamlet] is very theatrical or very sincere'.[5] It is these problems which make the word 'detachment' less than appropriate to a description of the speech, and which justify one in using the term 'vibrancy' to suggest the fluctuation not only of our feelings but those of Hamlet also.

There is one sense in which Hamlet's speech is undoubtedly theatrical, and that is in its presentation. As he speaks, he is being watched by others on stage, and their focusing of their attention upon him creates, as it were, a stage-within-the-stage. The result is curiously incongruous with what we expect of Hamlet at this point. At the moment when we think that he is at last going to be frank with himself and with us (because the apparent solution to his dilemma, the 'plan', frees him from the necessity of further posturing), he is put in the position of an actor playing for the benefit of an audience. It may be that we can trust him no more than we would a player who

Could force his soul so to his own conceit
That from her working all the visage wann'd . . .

(II.2.547–8)

At any rate, the feeling that Hamlet is speaking in a theatrical context—though one of which we must take him to be unaware—undercuts, even if slightly, the directness of his address. The dramatist raises the possibility for us of Hamlet's being no more sincere, no more direct, than a player, the false relation between whose speech and reality has already been brought to our attention in the play.

The idea of theatricality bears with it a pejorative implication, the merest ghost of which is suggested by Hamlet's speaking his soliloquy on the stage-within-the-stage, the full force of which the dramatist indicates by other means. Although Hamlet's theatricality here does not present him in a good light, however, it does not lose him our sympathy. The reason is that theatrical gestures have an equivocal force; they are products of detachment and of excessive self-identification, so that we never quite know where we stand in relation to them. Because Hamlet's speech takes full advantage of this fluctuating nature of our response to theatricality, it is worth looking briefly at what the term 'theatrical' entails. The *OED* suggests, among other definitions, 'artificial, affected, assumed' and 'calculated for display, showy, spectacular'. The element of detachment is clearly visible in these words; the theatrical person, it is implied, stands apart and puts on, assumes, his theatricality; it is calculated. On the other hand, it may be 'extravagantly or irrelevantly histrionic', and now the stress falls on exaggeration and excess, both terms implying the possibility of a reduction in consciousness and a failure to calculate. Exploiting the ambiguity of 'theatrical' gesture to the full, Hamlet's soliloquy evokes almost simultaneously disbelief ('He is putting all this on') and pathos ('How he suffers!').

Claudius and Polonius set the stage appropriately for the strange performance that is 'To be or not to be'. But that is not all they do for it. Their presence behind the arras is a reminder that Hamlet's fate is not entirely within his own hands, although he speaks as though it is. Whether his speech strikes us as detached or impassioned, it must be felt by us as not altogether adequate to the situation actually obtaining for him; it is tainted by irrelevance. And where it is 'irrelevantly histrionic', it is theatrical.

But of course it is the speech itself, not its context, that most certainly establishes the theatricality, most evidently in its quality of being 'calculated for display, showy, spectacular'. The soliloquy puts 'thought' on display; but it is a thought without substance. It *sounds* like thought. 'To be or not to be, that is the question': it is *the* question, the one which remains as essential when all other possibilites have been canvassed. The assurance with which Hamlet opens the speech implies a long process of thought behind it; the formulation of *the* question cannot be an easy matter. Hamlet's assurance, however, is not soundly based. Doubts multiply as the implications of his question are set forth: one can either be or not be; if being, one can suffer or take arms; if taking arms, one can end one's troubles or oneself; ending oneself, one may sleep peacefully or dream dreams as awful as the sufferings of daily life.[6] One might expect Hamlet's assurance, in the face of this, to crumble away, but it does not do so. As Harry Levin has remarked, there is an underlying circularity to the structure of the opening sentence of the speech which brings Hamlet round to the same point as that with which he began—the point that suicide is only doubtfully desirable. The sentence has a stability that bolsters up his assurance quite as much as its syntactic shiftiness works to diminish it. Furthermore, its circularity is evasive, permitting Hamlet the illusion of thought without allowing the momentous 'question' to present itself steadily as an object of that thought. Its show of thought effectively protects him from real thinking. As the rest of the speech demonstrates, Hamlet derives satisfaction from this show: it is the comfort of theatrical gesture.

Thanks to the vibrant quality of the gesture, however, we are not deprived of a moment of special intimacy with Hamlet in the soliloquy. But it is a *special* intimacy; it only lets us penetrate more deeply the web of argument and feeling with which he obscures his dilemma. Upon that, the speech casts no light; instead, it passes various elements of the dilemma under review, putting them in new combinations, subjecting them to new processes of investigation and categorization. We have already encountered the feeling that his own body is the vessel of family honour, for example, and that his heart is *locus* for that honour. The feeling recurs in the poignant reference to 'The heart-ache and the thousand natural shocks/That flesh is heir to'. The very choice of metaphor suggests the ambivalence with which he regards his inheritance. Again, he broaches the topic of his cowardice, but in a context that makes it excusable. The native hue of resolution, presumably his father's contribution, is 'sicklied o'er with the pale cast of thought'. Here we have a variant of the theory that what is wrong with him is only melancholy, but one that nevertheless raises all the imponderables associated with mind–body relations. (The idea has already been suggested in the phrase 'take arms against a sea of troubles', with its hint of a mad battle with the waves.) The appearance of such topics in a speech which fails to look any of them in the face creates the illusion of thought (illusory because there is no consistent intellectual content). It evades the issues, it comforts Hamlet because it evades, and comforts him further because it can then be made yet another scapegoat for his inadequacy to the demands of honour; 'the pale cast of thought' is to blame. Yet the speech is never *merely* theatrical, because at every point it reminds us, if not Hamlet, of the reality of his situation: and that excites our deepest interest and sympathy. There is no question of our being detached from that. As for the speech itself, we may say that its detachment is spurious in so far as it is controlled by Hamlet's determination to evade the issue which confronts him, but genuine in so far as he is unconscious of his own motivation. Shakespeare makes use of the tension between these aspects of the personality in the speech in masterly fashion. The point is worth illustrating further.

Nobility and suicide

Hamlet asks himself which of two alternatives is 'nobler in the mind'; it is as though he were asking himself in what true nobility might consist. This was exactly the sort of question which appealed to Shakespeare's contemporaries; it is discussed, for example, by William Segar in his *Honor Military and Civill* (1602), where he sums the issue up concisely in this fashion:

> men may be reputed Noble by three means. First by nature or descent of Ancestors, which is the vulgar opinion. Secondly, for vertue onely, which the Philosophers affirme. Thirdly, by mixture of Auncient Noble blood with vertue, which is indeed the true and most commendable kind of Nobilitie.[7]

The distinction between nobility of birth and nobility of virtue underlies Hamlet's use of the word but does not appear in it. His question is not, simply, what course of action is more fitting to the mind of a nobleman. The word 'mind' itself puts the emphasis on the nobility that has nothing to do with birth (though here we ought to remember the equivocal relations between mind and body already hinted at in the play). Yet the emphasis is not so strong that the meaning 'noble by birth' can be banished from our interpretation. What is plain in Segar is not really so in Hamlet.

Hamlet's language tells us that the options are still open for him: he has not yet made up his mind in what sense he is noble. That surely is the point of the metaphors which he goes on to use:

Whether 'tis nobler in the mind to suffer
The slings and arrows of outrageous fortune,

Or to take arms against a sea of troubles,
And by opposing, end them. (III.1.57–60)

Nigel Alexander's commentary strikes just the wrong note:

> The militaristic imagery in which the choice of existence is
> expressed gives an immediate expression of how violent, and how
> desperate, is the struggle within Hamlet's own mind. The lines
> present a military situation in which final defeat is inevitable.[8]

I think that one can call the lines 'violent' only if one is prepared to
say also that they are dreamlike and undisturbed. The imagery
manages simultaneously to preserve two different ideas of honour:
the active honour of the soldier—especially deferred to in Shakespeare's own time, and loosely associated with Segar's nobility 'of
nature'—and the philosopher's honour, here that of the Stoic suicide.
The lines connote indecison and posturing. The force of any violence
implied is diminished—first, by the selective form of its imagining,
'slings and arrows' giving us the hurly-burly of war without the least
sense of the vulnerable bodies that are ultimately its object (the same
selectivity is, of course, at work in the line following) and second, by
the obscurity which veils the motive for this activity.

Hamlet's next sentence suggests an attempt to clarify his thought
and to commit himself firmly to the Stoic version of right action. He
has thought of ending his troubles by opposing them. The phrasing
is ambiguous, as has often been remarked, since the troubles may
come to an end either because they have ceased to exist or because he
has. Hamlet now apparently resolves the ambiguity by taking up the
latter meaning only;

            to die—to sleep
No more; and by a sleep to say we end
The heartache and the thousand natural shocks
That flesh is heir to; 'tis a consummation
Devoutly to be wish'd (III.1.60–4)

But Hamlet by no means commits himself to suicide as a means of
overcoming the troubles of life. He does not even momentarily do
so. He does not say: 'and by a sleep to end/The heartache . . . '; he
says: 'and by a sleep *to say* we end/The heartache . . . '. The idea

remains an idea for him; it does not become a belief. The hazy syntax makes it possible for us to understand (and for him to mean) either that *death*, being a sleep, is devoutly to be wish'd, or that *saying* (and being able to say) *that death is an end to heartache* is the consummation so earnestly desired. The syntax can also imply, of course, a state of mind in which the speaker refuses to choose between these alternatives, either through unwillingness or through inability, and it leaves it open to us to understand that Hamlet does not even see that he is evading a choice. I think that we have to interpret it in this last way to explain the power of the lines, which seem to advance an argument without themselves progressing and to clarify whilst leaving everything as indeterminate as it was.

Roman thoughts

Suicide was the supreme act of Roman courage: Horatio, offering to kill himself, declares, 'I am more an antique Roman than a Dane' (V.2.346). In Shakespeare's plays it is generally taken as a mark of Roman nobility that a man contemplates or commits suicide. Antony, asking Eros to kill him, has a 'noble countenance'; and when Eros kills himself rather than his master, Antony laments that his follower has by his suicide, like Cleopatra, 'got upon me/A nobleness in record' (*Antony and Cleopatra*, IV.14.85, 98–9). Similarly, after Brutus has asked Dardanius to kill him, he is described as a 'noble vessel full of grief'. Antony may be right to call him 'the noblest Roman of them all'; his death, by which he alone 'hath honour', certainly accords with such a judgment (*Julius Caesar*, V.5.13, 68, 57). When Hamlet asks what is nobler in the mind he is asking a potentially Roman question, and Roman principles are latent in his speech.

Indeed, in 'To be or not to be' we are presented with a clear example of something which T.S. Eliot found in Shakespeare to be derived ultimately from Seneca—'the attitude of self-dramatization assumed by some of Shakespeare's heroes at moments of tragic intensity'. Eliot's own example is Othello's last speech. Much of what he says of that might be applied to this soliloquy of Hamlet:

> What Othello seems to me to be doing in making this speech is *cheering himself up*. He is endeavouring to escape reality, he has ceased to think about Desdemona, and is thinking about himself. Humility is the most difficult of all virtues to achieve; nothing dies

harder than the desire to think well of oneself. Othello succeeds in turning himself into a pathetic figure, by adopting an *aesthetic* rather than a moral attitude, dramatising himself against his environment. He takes in the spectator, but the human motive is primarily to take in himself. I do not believe that any writer has ever exposed this *bovarysme*, the human will to see things as they are not, more clearly than Shakespeare.[9]

The function of Hamlet's thinking that is not real thinking is likewise to cheer himself up. He too is endeavouring to escape reality, has ceased to think about Claudius, and is thinking about himself. Yet Hamlet would not deserve the harsh treatment given to Othello by Eliot. For one thing, he is not laying claim to the virtue of humility; and for another, we can only sympathize with his attempts to think well of himself, since they are a reaction to the Ghost's plea that he should act in a way that might give him cause to think ill of himself. Nor does Hamlet need, as Othello does, to turn himself into a pathetic figure; his very situation commands our pity and anxiety on his behalf. We may regret his failure to face the issues before him in a positive fashion, but any tendency to blame him is moderated by reflection on the very complex and forbidding nature of those issues. Othello's *bovarysme* may be presented for censure; Hamlet's is designed to provoke a response more complicated than that.

Does he, for example, 'take himself in'? If he does so, then it is not altogether willingly. I have already pointed out the apparent effort to clarify his thought which comes in 'To die—to sleep'; such an effort works counter to any easy settlement in self-deluding rhetoric. Empson's isolation of the problem of the speech as being one of determining the *extent* of its theatricality is a further reminder that we would be unwise to plump for a simple answer. If Hamlet evades reality by striking a Stoic pose, it may be that he is deluded not so much by himself as by Stoicism; or it may be that we are unable to say in what proportion he is to blame and in what Seneca.

No more than did Eliot do I wish to establish the influence of Seneca, rather than of his stoicism, on Shakespeare. Nor do I wish to be caught in the trap of thinking that the Stoics were the only Romans to praise suicide. Yet I think that the parallels between Hamlet's speech and what may be found in Seneca are striking. They do not establish Seneca as the one unquestionable source for the thought-processes of Hamlet's soliloquy, but they do bring out clearly its 'Roman' quality and the sense in which Hamlet may be considered deluded by 'philosophy' rather than self-deluding.[10]

Hamlet's question is one for which a base might be found in Seneca: although the Roman philosopher held that death should be regarded as a thing indifferent, he did not find every occasion proper for suicide: 'we need to be warned and strengthened in *both* directions—not to love or to hate life overmuch'. It follows that the case for suicide must always be made with respect to particular circumstances. Death is not likened by Seneca to a sleep, but he does say that it need not be painful or a cause of grief: Marcellinus, who took his own life, 'passed away, not without a feeling of pleasure, as he himself remarked,—such a feeling as a slow dissolution is wont to give' (Seneca compares it to fainting). Like Hamlet, he admired the endurance of people with none of the signs of outward honour—barbarians, sailors, farmers and soldiers. And he acknowledged that it was natural to fear death ('the fear of going to the underworld is equalled by the fear of going nowhere'), although he insistently pointed out how readily available were the means of death ('a tiny blade will sever the sutures of the neck').[11]

It is not the fact of these parallels so much as the affinity which they imply between Hamlet's ambiguities and Seneca's that I find interesting. In creating Hamlet's anxious meditation upon death Shakespeare exploits contradictions of the same order as those in Seneca's thought. In contemplating suicide his hero strikes Roman attitudes, but since those attitudes are themselves uncertain it is hardly surprising that he derives no firmness of purpose from them. For Seneca seeks to combine two different attitudes to life, one which sees the soul as superior to all that surrounds it, affirming its superiority in the act of suicide, the other which advocates a *via media* in life, the philosopher demanding of it neither too much nor too little. There is no necessary conflict between these two views, but they do nevertheless conflict in Seneca's writings, since he never establishes the conditions under which a suicide might be regarded as unsatisfactory or which might make the pursuit of a *via media* impracticable. In consequence the extremism of his advocacy of suicide jars with his recommendation of the austerely carefree life of the Stoic philosopher.

His attitude to the life of his day reflects the uncertainties inherent in this conflict. Just as we can distinguish between Hamlet's interest in 'honesty' and in 'honour', so we can between Seneca's in 'honestum' and 'honor'. The former word seems consistently to denote virtue and admirable qualities, [12] the latter generally signifies external honours, such as the consulship or other public office, and is accompanied by feelings of indifference or contempt. But Seneca does not always use 'honor' in this fashion—sometimes he uses it respectfully. [13] There is an analogy with Hamlet here. Although 'honestum' does not have the class-associations that go with 'honest' in England ('honest fellow', and so on), Seneca's admiration for the virtue that is 'honestum' leads him to praise hardy barbarians and suchlike, as I have already noted; he even speaks of the world as one great republic ('hac magna republica') in a way that suggests democratic feeling. [14] The effect, however, is much like that of Hamlet's gestures towards the 'honest' life: such passages only confirm the prevailing aristocratic tone of contempt for such folk as the 'huntsman and peasant' of *De Constantia* (II.2). Compare the lines in Hamlet's soliloquy:

> For who would bear the whips and scorns of time,
> Th'oppressor's wrong, the proud man's contumely,
> The pangs of dispriz'd love, the law's delay,
> The insolence of office, and the spurns
> That patient merit of th'unworthy takes,
> When he himself might his quietus make
> With a bare bodkin? Who would fardels bear,
> To grunt and sweat under a weary life . . .   (III.1.70–7)

The amplitude of this passage suggest a Hamlet who luxuriates in the thought of 'patient merit'. The misfortunes catalogued at such length are not his own—they belong to a man or men of far lower rank. These can be distinguished by name, at length; his own cannot. By imagining the lesser, nameable sufferings of others Hamlet is able to relieve himself deviously of his own feelings. The isolated phrase 'a bare bodkin' insists on not only the availability but the lowliness of the instrument of death; its bareness has to be borne, as the curious arrangement of the line suggests: 'With a *bare* bodkin? Who would fardels *bear* . . . ' There is an air of relish about this, quite consistent with Hamlet's dwelling on the thought of grunting and sweating one's way through life. But the relish derives from the sense in which such imagining is, for Hamlet, fantasy. He is expected, and expects himself, *not* to grunt and sweat at all.

This might seem to invite the simple verdict that Hamlet is self-deluding. But the lines are based on a dramatic tension between Hamlet's continuing anxiety and the devious relief from it to be had in contemplating the endurance of 'simple' men, a tension responsible for both the changes in direction and the non-progressive quality of 'thought' in the speech. It is the continuous presence of that tension that makes 'self-deluding' at once too dogmatic and too unsympathetic properly to describe the effect of the soliloquy.

As for the Roman element in it, plainly the speech is very different from anything to be found in Seneca *because* we feel a tension to underlie it. The contradictions resting laxly in the bulk of *his* spurious philosophizing are brought into uncomfortable relationship under the pressure of Hamlet's need. Shakespeare's character seeks comfort in Roman thoughts, he may even want to be deluded by them; but they provide him neither a solid prop nor a shield behind which to take shelter. No one, properly speaking, is taken in.

First person plural

Hamlet considers suicide but rejects it. He does so, as we have seen, by contemplating the example of endurance that is offered him by people far below his standing in class. The example was one admired also by Seneca, although his admiration for endurance marries ill with his advocacy of suicide. Hamlet defeats one Roman thought (suicide) by another (endurance). He goes on, in the wavering fashion of this speech, to reassert his aristocratic status by pleading that he is *forced* to identify with his noble savage:

> who would fardels bear . . .
> *But that* the dread of something after death,
> The undiscover'd country, from whose bourn
> No traveller returns, puzzles the will,
> And *makes* us rather bear those ills we have
> Than fly to others that we know not of?

The obliquity of these lines rests in the force of the pronoun 'we'. By and large Hamlet uses this in a plural sense, but not always so. Occasionally he uses it as a royal form of the first person singular, as when he replies to the message brought by Rosencrantz after the play-within-the-play:

Ros. She desires to speak with you in her closet ere you go to bed.
Ham. We shall obey, were she ten times our mother. Have you any
further trade with us? (III.2.322–5)

Because the first person plural can have this singular, class-based meaning, there is something ambiguous about the dread that makes *us* bear those ills *we* have.

Hamlet speaks of the way in which this dread 'puzzles the will'; we can hardly believe that he is not implying here that he has himself experienced that puzzling of the will. He is, then, at least partly talking about himself, and 'us' and 'we' have an aura of the royal usage about them—the usage is especially significant in the light it casts on Hamlet's momentary sympathy for (may we not even say 'identification with'?) 'patient merit'. For if 'the ills we have to bear' are simply the ills that royal Hamlet may suffer, then it may be that one of the things he has to put up with is the necessity, felt to be degrading, of bearing fardels, or their equivalent in the moral life, like any rogue or peasant slave.

The first person plural here suggests a movement in Hamlet's mind to dissociate himself from simple honesty, suggests a clinging to the aristocratic consciousness which is always possible for him. But it does not confirm it. 'We' is not certainly Hamlet in his royalty; it may well be Hamlet and all other men: 'conscience does make cowards of us all'.

The pronoun here is very slippery, but is for that reason serviceable to Hamlet, since it contains within itself the contradiction between noble savage and noble prince which he is unable to resolve; it enables him to speak as if the contradiction did not exist, and so to give his soliloquy its curious dreamlike, untroubled quality, and yet to vent his feelings fully in the strain of ambiguity that underlies its surface.

Hamlet himself is to play ironically with the contradiction inherent in the pronoun in the next scene, when he is commenting on 'The Mousetrap':

'Tis a knavish piece of work, but what o' that? Your Majesty, and
we that have free souls, it touches us not. Let the galled jade wince,
our withers are unwrung. (III.2.235–8)

The irony lies in speaking so that the listener cannot decide whether 'Your Majesty, and we that have free souls' establishes a distinction or not. Editors generally assume that it does, glossing 'free' as 'guiltless': the implication is that the King's soul is not free. But Hamlet's 'we' may be another example of the royal use, staking a claim by kinship in his stepfather's majesty, and suggesting that the pair of them are above feeling that the message of a mere play could be aimed at them. The speech is plausible, I think, only if we suppose Claudius to be obliged to take it in this latter fashion.[15]

Seneca and the slipperiness of Stoicism

> Shakespeare was a much finer instrument for transformations than any of his contemporaries, finer perhaps even than Dante. He also needed less contact in order to be able to absorb all that he required. The element of Seneca is the most completely absorbed and transmogrified, because it was already the most diffused throughout Shakespeare's world.[16]

Bearing in mind these words of Eliot, we should not be surprised to find the mark of Stoicism, and of Seneca in particular, engraved deep in the character of Hamlet. But it is worth emphasizing that Shakespeare uses Seneca in a deeply critical and highly dramatic way. He exploits the *slippery* nature of his thought, much as he exploits that of the first person plural. Let us look, then, at the slipperiness of Seneca's Stoicism.

In the eighty-second letter to Lucilius, Seneca accepts that

> it is natural to fear the world of shades, whither death is supposed to lead. Therefore, though death is something indifferent, it is nevertheless not a thing we can easily ignore.

He argues that the glory of overcoming this fear arises from its being a *natural* fear that we triumph over; suicide is a victory for the human will, since logic and philosophical maxims are both equally unfit to defeat the terror with which men are inspired by death. 'Do you propose to construct catchwords for me, or to string together petty syllogisms? It takes great weapons to strike down great monsters.'[17]

This rejection of logic and philosophy is at odds with Seneca's usual respect for reason as the governing principle in human life. But when he considers the afterlife, Seneca does abandon reason.

Although he dismisses belief in the conventional classical afterworld as ill-founded, he bases his own faith in the immortality of the soul on the merest assertion. The criteria by which other people's beliefs are judged are quickly dropped where his own are concerned:

> The soul's homeland is the whole space that encircles the height and breadth of the firmament, the whole rounded dome within which lie land and sea, within which the upper air that sunders the human from the divine also unites them, and where all the sentinel stars are taking their turn on duty . . . the soul will not put up with a narrow span of existence.[18]

What he knows of the soul in its relation to the divine is based largely, it appears, on sentimental and ultimately self-regarding reverie in picturesque circumstances:

> If ever you have come upon a grove that is full of ancient trees which have grown to an unusual height, shutting out a view of the sky by a veil of pleached and intertwining branches, then the loftiness of the forest, the seclusion of the spot, and your marvel at the thick unbroken shade in the midst of the open spaces, will prove to you the presence of deity.[19]

His exhortations to abandon beliefs in the afterlife that rival his own consequently fail to convince.

There is another reason why Seneca is unconvincing on this point. It is natural to fear death; but 'by no wisdom can natural weaknesses of the body be removed . . . nature exerts her own power and through such a weakness makes her presence known to the strongest.' Indeed, this applies to defects of the soul as well as of the body:

> Whatever is assigned to us by the terms of our birth and the blend in our constitutions will stick with us, no matter how hard or how long the soul may have tried to master itself. And we cannot forbid these feelings any more than we can summon them.[20]

Thus, inability to overcome the fear of death can hardly be held against a man. Indeed, man's dependence on nature would almost seem to render otiose Seneca's endeavours to point out to him a path of virtue at all.

Although Hamlet might seem to turn his back on Senecan posturing when he rejects the idea of suicide, this is not really the case.

Seneca's own view of nature was large enough to include contradictions, and this is certainly true of what he has to say about natural
weakness. It is not surprising, then, that the *tone* of Hamlet's soliloquy
should remain unchanged, despite the apparently momentous rejection of the possibility broached at its beginning. Hamlet is equally
'philosophical'—at least, according to the bad example of Seneca—
when he contemplates suicide and when he rejects it. What legitimizes
the refusal to commit suicide, despite its Senecan credentials, is
something else of which Seneca approved—the admirable endurance
of 'patient merit', Hamlet's consideration of which is coloured, like
Seneca's, by aristocratic sentimentalism.

Hamlet declines to commit suicide because the available information on the afterlife is uncertain; did not even Seneca, reflecting on
the soul's supposed immortality, describe himself as a 'dreamer of
dreams'?[21] Considering the slippery foundations of Seneca's own
arguments, Hamlet quite reasonably fears the dreams that may
follow death. Yet this it not how he puts it himself. Hamlet simply
affirms the fear of death as a natural condition: 'conscience does
make cowards of us all'. In the very next line, however, he speaks of
'the native hue of resolution' as though that were a necessary part of
human nature too. Well—human nature probably does embody
contradiction and conflict of such an order, but if it does Hamlet
should really take notice of the fact, not speak on as though there
were no conflict to mention at all. May we not put it down to 'the
element of Seneca . . . the most diffused throughout Shakespeare's
world' that he does so?

In the conclusion to the soliloquy it is the conjunction 'and' that
has most work to do in concealing, at least from Hamlet's inner ear,
the contradiction and conflict underlying what he says. Its function is
to bind clauses together without revealing why they do go together
in that way ('And thus . . . ', '*And* enterprises . . . '):

> Thus conscience does make cowards of us all.
> And thus the native hue of resolution
> Is sicklied o'er with the pale cast of thought . . .

(III.1.83–5)

'*And* thus' suggests that phenomena identical in respect to their
universality are being compared, but this cannot be so. It may be true
that we are all cowards when faced by the thought of dying; it is

certainly not true that we would all regard it with 'resolution' were it not for 'thought'. It is only by thinking that we realize that resolution is needed.

Why, then, are these two propositions falsely linked together? The natural explanation, surely, is that Hamlet has moved from the idea of facing suicide to that of an encounter with Claudius. 'Thought' may well inhibit 'the native hue of resolution' in that respect; *'native hue'* seems to show Hamlet recalling the *natural* quality of the obligation placed on him by the Ghost, as if to bolster up his resolution; and 'conscience' takes on retrospectively its modern meaning of 'moral sense' rather than 'consciousness', which strikes one at first as most applicable. Since an encounter with Claudius of the kind Hamlet has in mind is potentially suicidal, the progression is not too abrupt to be plausible—on the contrary; it even returns us to something said earlier in the soliloquy, to taking arms against a sea of troubles and by opposing, ending them.

Indeed, Hamlet can be felt to continue thinking simultaneously about his own death *and* that of Claudius:

> And enterprises of great pitch and moment
> With this regard their currents turn awry
> And lose the name of action.   (III.1.85–7)

Once again, the conjunction 'and' suggests that the enterprises turning awry are identical with the process just described, of the native hue being sicklied o'er. And once again this is not really the case. The opposition of 'thought' to 'resolution' is at least frank, but it gives way here to something more slippery still. Two nouns ('enterprises' and 'currents') precede the verb in a construction which makes it impossible to say which is subject, which is object, or whether the verb is transitive or intransitive (since 'enterprises of great pitch and moment . . . their currents' would be a possible genitive form.)[22] The 'nature' of the syntax itself here tends to dissipate the possibility of fixing responsibility for Hamlet's inability to act positively on any single cause; the enterprise may be misconceived or the current it seeks to ride may be adverse—the words themselves make no distinction. The sentence drifts to rest with another ambiguous conjunction and the reduction of the issues so momentously proposed ('To be or not to be') to a matter of words: 'And lose the name of action'.

Just so do enterprises of great pitch and moment their currents
turn awry:

> Soft you now,
> The fair Ophelia!

The dramatic tension depends on Hamlet's naming a generalized
kind of deflection from greatness with a semblance of determination
at the same time as he allows himself to be deflected from thoughts of
his own great enterprises. The flat contradictions of Seneca and his
kind take on an individual urgency in the labyrinthine intricacy and
equivocation of Hamlet's Roman thoughts.

Dreaming

Hamlet reflects on what he says, as though he were two persons, not
one. 'To die—to sleep, / No more . . .'. He explains to himself the
meaning of what he has just said, picks up his own words, listens to
himself carefully: 'To die, to sleep; / To sleep, perchance to dream
. . . '. Perhaps this is part of the effect of detachment which critics
have noticed: there is a *hint* of the lecture-room, of the lecturer
glossing a familiar text. Equally there is a hint of the actor whose
speech is being judged as he speaks, whose next move is already
being predicted by his audience. As Hamlet speaks he is watched by
Claudius and Polonius; but he is also watched by himself. The effect
is to suggest that the reality of Hamlet's thoughts, and of Hamlet
himself, is suspect. It needs looking into. The very subject of his
thought at this point is insubstantial—dreams. Hamlet's physical
presence on the stage is belied by the variety of possible illusions it
may import.

> 'To sleep—perchance to dream.' If the discontents of this life are
> bad dreams, as he has averred to Rosencrantz and Guildenstern,
> those of the next may be worse; and who shall say which are more
> real?[23]

For Hamlet, at least, whatever he looks at can be dissolved into
illusion. What troubles him? 'Bad dreams.' Doubtless he means that
ironically, to be interpreted as it is interpreted by Guildenstern:
'Which dreams indeed are ambition' (II.2.257), but the phrase
suggests also a feeling that the Ghost was not real—not really his

father, or even—though this can hardly be—not really there in Elsinore at all.[24] In the mouth of a man in Hamlet's situation the words have something wishful, as well as ironic, about them; and the wishfulness can be felt strongly because what is wished is so very unspecific. Those 'bad dreams' may be anything that gets in the way of Hamlet's being simply the thing he is, anything that requires he should act not just honestly but with honour, anything that makes him representative of the family and a class. Whatever it is, it is a bad dream, a dream because ideal, and because existing in addition to the moral imperatives of one's solitary and individual being, which *is* reality; bad because in conflict with those imperatives, or because a threat to the self which is identified with them. The satisfaction of naming what troubles him as 'bad dreams' is that it affirms Hamlet's own reality as the individual who is subject to them and is thus linked with his confident, even arrogant, bearing toward them.

In 'To be or not to be' there is no confidence and no arrogance. What troubles Hamlet now is 'the dread of something after death', 'what dreams may come,/When we have shuffled off this mortal coil', a denigratory phrase for his own bodily existence. 'Coil' is usually glossed as 'turmoil': it suggests both the ruthlessness of Hamlet's own being and the meaningless scurry of other people as seen by him. We are close to 'life's fitful fever' as seen and experienced by Macbeth. To die is to 'shuffle off' this coil: it is felt to be ludicrous, if not disreputable, and in either case, therefore, as shameful to the man of honour. All that dying can achieve is 'dreams'. What Hamlet wants is oblivion, a sleep without dreams, where the Ghost's imperative, revenge, cannot reach him. But

> what dreams *may* come,
> When we have shuffled off this mortal coil,
> Must give us pause—there's the respect
> That makes calamity of so long life . . .   (III.1.66–9)

The Ghost's imperative is matched by another, the property of dreams that *must* give us pause. Neither on this side nor that of the grave can Hamlet be sure of himself in himself; in either place he is subject to forces that menace his self-sufficiency, his self, narrowly conceived.

The transition from *may* to *must* in these lines is worth dwelling on. In the first place, it has a general significance for Hamlet; he aspires to be free, but *must* has obtruded into his life, and will not be shaken off. He has tried; he has said that he could count himself a thing of infinite space and be content, were it not for his bad dreams, like the ghosts of troubled dead Kings, 'most dreadfully' attending on him. In his conversation with Rosencrantz and Guildenstern, nevertheless, he is able to dismiss these dreams—'A dream itself is but a shadow'—and though it is only by false reasoning that he does so ('by my fay, I cannot reason') his posture is that of a free man. But in 'To be or not to be' his freedom is subject to a double necessity, the Ghost's requirement of revenge and then the dreams that must give us pause (—all of us, or just the one of us, royal Hamlet? Once again, Shakespeare exploits the ambiguous pronoun). The dreams that will trouble Hamlet in death may or may not be specifically reminders of a royal father unrevenged; the pronoun suggests his wishfully evading thoughts of the imperative specifically addressed to him from outside human life by merging them indistinguishably with the painful consciousness of all that will have been left by him, on his death, undone that should have been done. These evasive tactics cannot, however, really be said to do Hamlet any good, because instead of cancelling out the hateful necessity of revenge they merely supplement it with another, that of suffering in the afterlife.

But is that a necessity? He speaks only of 'what dreams *may* come'; but the following *must* weighs more heavily in our minds and his, not just because *must* is stronger than *may*, but because its strength is realized for us and him in giving him pause, now, at the moment he speaks, even as the dreams will give him pause after he has died. The demonstration is not logical, but Hamlet obviously feels its strength. The pause is at once part of the future and in the present: it is what Hamlet will experience and what he does experience. The essentially static nature of the soliloquy realizes itself in this identity of tenses, and poignantly conveys the pressure upon Hamlet of both forms of necessity. It is the thought that even his own death cannot protect him from the consequences of his encounter with the Ghost that makes him pause. Now and in the future, he is subject to necessity: his whole life and afterlife are to be lived out under that sign.

And so 'there's the respect/That makes calamity of so long life' refers also to both his present and his future life; the consideration that we may in some way suffer further for our pains after death makes us endure the pains we have for as long as life permits us. This is the interpretation of the words which editors prefer; there is, however, another which is possible. Calamity may be of so long life because it is not terminated by death, but continues in the sufferings of the afterlife. The second interpretation is at odds with the first, of course; editors perhaps have plumped for the comforting straightforwardness of the first because it *is* comforting, and because they want to keep back firmly a third interpretation which seems quite nonsensical—'the consideration of suffering after death makes it calamitous to live long'. This third sense is not, however, so nonsensical as all that. Indeed, it begs for our attention because it suggests that death is at least an end to the calamity of not knowing under what conditions life is lived—a calamity well instanced by the contradiction between the first and second interpretations advanced. The phrase which gives rise to all three meanings—which are in conflict with themselves and which advance rival versions of reality —expresses, then, as finely and as fully as one can imagine, the horrific vision of life which Hamlet entertains.

Hamlet's habitation with shadows, his unnerving communication with dreams, may be compared with the nihilism of Macbeth. *That* has a certain magnificence, in that Macbeth is able to represent it clearly to himself:

> Life's but a walking shadow; a poor player,
> That struts and frets his hour upon the stage,
> And then is heard no more: it is a tale
> Told by an idiot, full of sound and fury,
> Signifying nothing.   (*Macbeth*, V.5.24–8)

Macbeth has thought that he could cheat the witches, and that his interpretation of the impossibility of their prophecies must be validated. He recognizes himself as an idiot, one who has told himself a story whose signification was nothing. Birnam Wood came to Dunsinane after all. But he sticks to the only sort of meaning he can imagine, even in the hour that he knows it to be false:

> Blow, wind! come, wrack!
> At least we'll die with harness on our back.   (V.5.51–2)

His final going out to meet the army of Malcolm and Macduff is a desperate, sometimes giddy defence of what he has made of his life. It is indefensible: we know it to be so, but we feel also the rightness that is almost there in his wanting to defend it. We recognize in him simultaneously a fearfully human likeness to us and an encroaching self-constraint which we must for our salvation reject—a self-constraint culminating in the iron words 'no more' and 'nothing' of the speech 'tomorrow and tomorrow'.

Macbeth, like Hamlet, evokes in us no simple response, yet it is his determining himself, his hardening himself and holding himself to conclusions (suicide is not a conclusion, it has no meaning, and so he refuses to 'play the Roman fool') that is responsible for our complicated feelings about him. In the case of Hamlet, it is his inability to reach conclusions that is to move us. The point may be made by comparing Macbeth's death, which he goes out to meet, with Hamlet's, which comes to him as it were in a passage of by-play. But we may say that even by the middle of the play all conclusions melt and disappear for him. We cannot attribute this to some bent of scepticism which is his property as a 'thinker'; it is felt as something deeper than that, suggestive of a whole stance to life, as Macbeth's growing rigidity is. 'To die—to sleep,/No more': there is nothing of the strength of iron about Hamlet's 'no more', which is characteristically ambiguous, and evokes ambiguous feeling in us.

To distinguish this feeling from that evoked by Macbeth, one has to say that Hamlet calls far more deeply on our sympathy. The movements of consciousness evident in the soliloquy only confirm its fundamentally static nature; they reflect the twisting and turning of someone caught in a trap. Macbeth describes his situation falsely, thus defining it with the clarity and solidity he hopes to impose on life:

> They have tied me to a stake: I cannot fly,
> But, bear-like, I must fight the course. (V.7.1–2)

Neither the witches nor any one else, save himself, tied Macbeth to his stake: the trap was of his own creating and here he is trying to shift the responsibility off himself. But Hamlet really is in a trap not of his own making: his dilemma is one which is presented him by circumstance, by his being the son of a certain father in a certain society. We are all so born into situations not of our own choosing; it is to be hoped that we do not all regard ourselves as trapped in our ways as Hamlet is in his. Hamlet is unlucky, because his situation makes peculiarly difficult demands on him, demands that make it difficult for us to be hard on him when he recoils from them. Our own experience, and a frank acknowledgement of the real difficulty of Hamlet's situation, draw us very close to him in his agonies of indecision, even as we are saddened or repelled (but not, surely, from the man himself) by all that desperate, inconclusive toying with the Roman foolery of Stoic suicide and endurance.

It is because Hamlet's speech is very much the speech of a man in a particular situation that, for all its play with dream, illusion and ambiguity, it makes a direct impression of substance upon us. Because it has elements of theatricality in it and about it, one is tempted to invoke the related paradigms 'All the world's a stage' and 'life is a dream' in order to account for the power of Hamlet's soliloquy.[25] The play as a whole does draw life from these commonplaces. Yet it does so not in order to make of them some kind of doctrine which it has to impart to us, but in order to place them within another view of things—the view of Hamlet which the play in its entirety affords us. Even by this point in the drama, Hamlet's twisting and turning about the theme of illusion and reality cannot but strike us as inadequate to the situation in which he finds himself. But if it does so strike us, it does not follow either that Hamlet loses our sympathy or that he loses substance as a consequence of his 'habitation with shadows'. He appears to us often as an actor, acting in a world of his own dreaming; we remain aware, however, of a person who is not an actor and who is Hamlet, whose concern is not to dream but to be; and before I leave this soliloquy, I want to say something of this person.

Being

'To be or not to be' is a difficult speech to explicate, full of ambiguous words and phrases, evoking similarly ambiguous feelings. There are still many readers, let alone playgoers, who dislike such delving into meaning; they feel that the play of multiple meaning can be hostile to Shakespeare's dramatic intention, distracting us from the action and presenting the actor with an impossible task— for to convey so much in a single performance seems not to be done. The character whom it is the actor's job to impersonate dies beneath the weight of explication imposed upon his speech. Such readers, it might be said, misunderstand what it is that the explicator sets out to do, which is above all to bring into the range of consciousness meanings of which, though unconscious, we may still feel the effects. The difficulty here, however, is that the effects are so contradictory —theatrical and genuine, violent and dreamlike, and so on—that it is hard to name a quality that should be uppermost in consciousness, with others subordinate to it and related to less important meanings of which we remain unconscious. It does not create difficulty for the actor that the speech lays movements of thought over its essentially static nature—on the contrary, he is aided by this contrast. But that the stasis should be the product of a tension between such extremes as I have already outlined—that surely is too much for the actor to present.

Consider the opening phrase. The tension characterizing the speech as a whole is evident from the start in the contrast between the question's large frame of reference and the small words in which it is couched. The conflict of possible meanings merely adds to our sense of strain. I have taken the question to be one about suicide, but the interpretation is not exclusive, nor is it even necessarily first in order of importance. Dr Johnson supposed that Hamlet's question was whether, 'after our present state, we are *to be or not to be*', and he produced a perfectly coherent account of the speech on this basis, though conceding that, 'bursting from a man distracted with contrariety of desires, and overwhelmed with the magnitude of his own purposes', it 'is connected rather in the speaker's mind than on his tongue'. (This consideration, I take it, may be supposed to legitimate the rather strained ellipsis with which Johnson's interpretation requires the speech to begin.) L. C. Knights, with equal plausibility, has argued that 'Hamlet's deep underlying concern is with essential being':

> What it seems to me that Hamlet is saying at the opening of the soliloquy is that what it means to be is the question of all questions; 'and this is so,' he goes on, 'whether we believe with Boethius that the blows of Fortune must be endured, or whether we think it better actively to combat evil—which, in my case, is likely to result in my own death' . . . [26]

There are three things at least which need to be said about these three conflicting meanings of 'the question'. The first is that however tolerable ambiguity may be in lyric and philosophic poetry it is not so easily accommodated to dramatic poetry, where speech should bear the impress of character or of a vital principle which may take the place of what conventionally we consider as character. Such an impress necessarily limits the range of what can be said: ambiguity must accommodate itself to the nature of the speaker. The question is, then, whether these three meanings of *to be* can be referred to a single principle embodied in Hamlet.

The second point follows from this. They can. All three meanings meet in a fourth, which is close to the one proposed by Knights—'What it means to be', in the society with which the play *Hamlet* presents us, is 'to be with honour'. A man's honour is his and his alone: 'it relates to his own consciousness and is too closely allied to his physical being, his will and his judgement for anyone else to take responsibility for it'. It is particularly identified with one's being as an expression of the truth of that being: 'a man commits his honour only through his *sincere* intentions'. This is so far true that honour takes precedence over morality; a man is not dishonoured by lying in itself—he is dishonoured only by lying when he has bound himself, on his honour, not to. Honour is a reflection of the individual's place in a divine hierarchy, and consequently is to be identified not merely with his mortal life: partaking of the sacred, it may stand for the immortal soul itself.[27] To be with honour is, then, to be assured of being in this life as well as in the next; it is to be assured of being, in the large sense which Knights would attribute to it.

The third point is that if this fourth sense of *to be* does not quite *reconcile* the other three meanings, even if it does subsume them, that is only to be expected—for we have already seen that the concept of honour always brings with it contradiction and strain. The merit of the suggestion lies not in annihilating altogether the stress of meaning laid upon the opening words of the soliloquy, but in referring it to a principle which we have already seen embodied in the situation and character of Hamlet.

And in this too there is perhaps a hint of how the actor should bear himself in the soliloquy. The stoic posturing, the hesitancy and the ambiguity all belong very much to the mind. We hear the words; we sense behind them a pressure of meanings which cannot entirely be grasped. But honour, the honour which in one form or another they debate, is as much an affair of the body as of the mind. It is especially in the physical person that honour is felt to be affronted, and it is by putting the physical person at risk that honour is satisfied. The thought of that risk is certainly one element in the soliloquy itself; and the risk is something of which we in the audience may be more pressingly aware than Hamlet himself; for we see him at risk at the very moment he speaks, under the judgement of Claudius and Polonius. It is not only that the elusive complexity of his thought draws attention to his bodily presence, as something that is different from all that; Claudius and Polonius watching make evident to us the vulnerability of that body, a vulnerability which gives pathos not only to the opening question about 'being', but also to such a line as 'Thus conscience does make cowards of us all'. Conscience, as I have said, means both 'consciousness' and 'moral sense': it is an aspect of honour. But its special pathos derives from our witnessing the limitations of Hamlet's consciousness. He does not know that he is being watched. Perhaps it is this sense of vulnerability and threat that makes us most aware of Hamlet's individual *being* within that threat.

7 Hamlet and Ophelia

Depths

There is a sense in which III.1 is perfectly symmetrical. The interview between Hamlet and Ophelia is suspended between a soliloquy by Hamlet at its beginning and one by Ophelia at its end; the whole is introduced by a scene of court life in which Claudius and Polonius set up the interview and terminated by a complementary scene in which Claudius and Polonius conclude what they may from what they have seen: 'Love? his affections do not that way tend . . . ' and 'yet I do believe/The origin and commencement of his grief/Sprung from neglected love'.

This 'perfect' symmetry is, however, qualified in a number of ways, most obviously in a disproportion of parts, since just as Hamlet's soliloquy is longer than Ophelia's, so is the introductory Claudius matter in relation to that at the end. The scene opens with a crowded stage, and it closes with only two persons left in view.

Nevertheless, a producer might feel that there is sufficient symmetry here to justify treating the whole scene as a single unit of action, playing down the traditional emphasis on Hamlet's soliloquy and determinedly keeping in play the mood of action restored at the end of II.2. Naturally such a long-drawn-out account of the soliloquy as I have offered would seem irrelevant to someone intent in this manner on conventional dramatic values.

The dramatic values in Hamlet are not, however, conventional. In this case, what matters dramatically is the sense of strain created in a scene which is symmetrically conceived from the point of view of Claudius, but which is not so as far as Hamlet is concerned. The symmetry expresses an action which Claudius, the observer and deviser, believes he has under his control; the elements in the scene that reduce its symmetry—Hamlet's unexpectedly long soliloquy, the brevity and inconclusiveness of the dialogue between Claudius and Polonius at its end—express an action that is not perfectly controlled either by its devisers or by its agents.

Mark Rose writes modestly of 'To be or not to be' that its 'precise psychological function . . . that is, why Hamlet is considering suicide —is uncertain' and goes on:

> But its dramatic function is not: the speech, however we interpret it, is conspicuously 'deep' and it establishes the prince as more thoughtful than those around him.[1]

There is much that needs to be added to this, for whilst the 'depth' of the soliloquy, understood in psychological terms, is not to be disputed, it is not clear that it could *establish* Hamlet's 'thoughtfulness', since the disposition to think (or at least, to withdraw from action into the mind) has been evident in him from the beginning. Surely the point has to do with the contrast between the kind of depth exhibited by Hamlet and that which we see in Claudius and Polonius? They trust to their ability to 'frankly judge', and might consider themselves 'deep' both because they have that ability and because they have succeeded in arranging for Hamlet unsuspectingly to offer himself to that judgement. The psychological depth of the prince's soliloquy—for however inconclusive, however evasive, depth *is* there, though it is a depth of need, a cry for rescue, rather than expression of deep self-knowledge—stands in contrast to the assurance and cunning of the King and his counsellor, whose superficiality is only stressed by Polonius's moralizing:

> We are oft to blame in this,
> 'Tis too much prov'd, that with devotion's visage
> And pious action we do sugar o'er
> The devil himself.   (III.1.45–8)

It is plain that it does not occur to Polonius that this might be an occasion when he *is* to blame. 'Oft' is a conveniently unspecific escape clause which allows him to impose inauthenticity of action upon Ophelia without questioning himself and yet without denying himself the luxury of faith in his own probity. There is a suggestion here of one kind of depth, in the idea of the Devil himself sugared o'er 'with devotion's visage/And pious action', but Polonius's eye is on the surface only, and our eye is upon his. It is for this reason that Claudius's muffled exclamation of guilt so dramatically takes us by surprise:

> O, 'tis too true.
> How smart a lash that speech doth give my conscience.
> The harlot's cheek, beautied with plast'ring art,
> Is not more ugly to the thing that helps it
> Than is my deed to my most painted word.
> O heavy burden! (III.1.49–54)

This speech reveals to us real depth, by comparison with that from which Polonius averts his eye. Its reality is the subjective reality of guilt which exists for the individual alone. How intensely it exists for him is suggested by its registering Polonius's indifferent platitude as a lash to the conscience, and a 'smart' lash at that. Polonius speaks of how 'we do sugar o'er the devil himself' as though the right hand might not know what the left were doing—'sugaring o'er' is an act without inherent moral quality. But Claudius, with his guilt, exists in a world permeated by moral value. The 'harlot's cheek' is 'ugly to the thing that helps it'; that is, editors tell us, is ugly compared to the paint that makes it look beautiful; but the form of expression chosen by the poet has a force that such a paraphrase must miss, for it suggests that the cheek's ugliness is ugliness in the eyes of, in the mind of, 'the thing that helps it'. The word 'helps', having about it something of human generosity, humanizes the mere 'thing' as it were, and so Claudius's phrase is made to evoke a willing/unwilling human partnership in the relation of paint to cheek, the evocation being the stronger for 'plast'ring art's' hint of the physician and his promise of healing the sick body.[2] Indeed, the very notion of the harlot's cheek as *beautied* with paint is one that must arouse equivocal feeling, because it is one of beauty that is morally tainted. We are drawn to the one, repelled by the other. Claudius describes his speech as 'painted': in this aside, the complex emotions of guilt in possession show more than another surface beneath the paint. They show the moral life.

Depth upon depth: Hamlet's soliloquy reveals something deeper than Claudius's aside, for it goes further. Claudius opens up a moral space defined by two terms, the beauty he would possess and the sense that it is after all the deceptive, even unwholesome, beauty of the harlot, from which he would turn away, and in so far as his lines suggest movement it is a perpetual exchange between these two terms. But in Hamlet's soliloquy the terms themselves are equivocal and dissolve; one form of greatness turns to another; being itself is in question. He opens up a moral space without limit, or rather one in which the limits are only apparent, for they are equivocal. The contrast is most evident between Claudius's 'conscience' that can feel a smart lash—can feel, that is, sharply—and Hamlet's, which 'does make cowards of us all' but in a manner which is morally beyond definition.

From Polonius to Claudius to Hamlet there is a progression inherently dramatic, but not of a kind we can easily imagine the author to have planned; dramatic but not expressing itself in any exterior action clearly to be demanded, though the gifted actor, the gifted producer, will find a means of suggesting what goes on here—the opening up of spiritual gulfs. These gulfs are not to be accommodated within the symmetry of the scene.

A shift in weight

At first it seems that Ophelia's entry is to call Hamlet back from the depths of himself. He holds himself back from his potentially endless course of speculation: 'Soft you now'. Ophelia comes as a representative of that definite world with which Polonius is so familiar (and in which endless speculation is transformed to the pseudo-certainties of the Chamberlain's account of the growth of Hamlet's sickness). That world categorizes the individual and defines him in terms of relationship: Hamlet is the Queen's son and consequently in problematic relation to the King; Ophelia is Polonius's daughter and problematic to the extent that she seeks to act for herself and in her own right. Hamlet now categorizes Ophelia in terms of her relationship to the world at large: 'The fair Ophelia'. The phrase implies that Hamlet has put himself in relation to this world (and has to that extent withdrawn himself from the gulf of himself) but that he has done so at the price of denying Ophelia's individual existence as a person. 'The fair Ophelia' looks at her from outside and sets a distance between her and the speaker which is maintained in what follows: 'Nymph, in thy orisons/Be all my sins remember'd'. The main effect here is the contrast between the innocence, if not the semi-divinity, of the nymph, and Hamlet's sinfulness; but the artificiality of the distance between the two of them that the prince by this means creates is brought home by contrasting it with the specific guilt for sin to which the King testified immediately before the soliloquy. In its turn, this artificiality suggests the tenuousness of Hamlet's hold on the categories of Polonius's world; he is far gone still, and Ophelia will have much to do if she is to call him back to the shared life of the human individual which lies on the far side of her father's conception of things.

'Good my lord,/How does your honour for this many a day?' seems straightforward enough; surely *this* will help Hamlet to relocate himself in space and time? But though it is part of Ophelia's guilelessness to use the honorifics by which her father and his society set such store, it is part of Hamlet's difficulty that he has become unusually sensitive to them: 'I humbly thank you, well, well, well' mocks, deprecates and attempts to reject this title by which she addresses him, and is ominously big with the meanings of his soliloquy, an assumption of 'honesty' that is nevertheless dependent on the self-conscious superiority of the aristocrat.

Hamlet disclaims the forms of honour, but acts out of a sense of their privileges here; but Ophelia, who outwardly observes them ('My lord, I have remembrances of yours'), presses upon Hamlet in a manner effectually to deny them—she insists on her individual and personal existence. Harold Jenkins, who has written of the relationship between Ophelia and the prince with great tact and insight, has remarked on the way in which, in this scene, 'the expected roles of the lovers are reversed':

> Ophelia, to be sure, has denied Hamlet access to her, but it is she, not he, who speaks of the 'many a day' since they have met. And though she returns Hamlet's gifts, it is not she but he who now repudiates their loves.[3]

To this one might add that the pattern of reversal is completed in the way in which Ophelia's return of Hamlet's gifts becomes a kind of aggression, a threat from the order of reality in which he needs to re-establish himself. His denial of the gifts is a denial of existence at the level where Ophelia can in this manner attack him: 'No, not I, I never gave you aught'. The words have been variously construed, to the effect that the remembrances were given to another Ophelia than this,[4] or that they amounted to nothing in Hamlet's estimation;[5] but the significant point seems to me, as it does to Jenkins, to be Hamlet's denial that *he* gave them to her: 'No, not I. I never . . . '. What is at issue for him is his concept of himself, and his will to determine that for himself. We are close upon the gulfs of the soliloquy again.

For the audience, then, there is a pathetic quality in the unknowingness with which Ophelia applies herself to her task: her speech has meaning enough in itself, but in its context the meaning is greater than we can imagine her perceiving:

> My honour'd lord, you know right well you did,
> And with them words of so sweet breath compos'd
> As made the things more rich. Their perfume lost,
> Take these again; for to the noble mind
> Rich gifts wax poor when givers prove unkind.
> There, my lord.   (III.1.97–102)

Harold Jenkins notes the ironic echo here of Laertes's description of Hamlet's love as to be esteemed a 'violet' with 'perfume' 'sweet not lasting', but there are echoes of what has more recently been heard too. Ophelia's account of Hamlet's words as making 'more rich' the gifts he gave her recalls and contrasts with Claudius's reference to his 'painted word' helping his 'deed' to beauty with its 'plast'ring art'. More strikingly, Ophelia's allusion to the 'noble mind' takes us back directly to the second line of Hamlet's soliloquy and the painfully inconclusive survey of 'nobility' that ensues.

In Hamlet's reply to her the soliloquy reaches its conclusion: 'Ha, ha! are you honest?' In these words Hamlet does not reconcile honesty to nobility, though that might seem to have been the conclusion towards which 'To be or not to be', in its erratic way, was striving; instead he uses his nobility as rank to give him the means of disparaging honesty as virtue. The moment is decisive: the indefiniteness of the soliloquy turns into the destructive force of Hamlet's passion concentrated upon Ophelia. The name of action re-enters Hamlet's life: and it is action to ward off the offered intimacy from Ophelia, action that is entirely negative, and that in its negativity constitutes Hamlet's first step into the universe of evil.

If up to this point the scene has struck one as overweighted, that is, too full of implication, it is at this moment, when the dialogue swings from verse to prose in the emphatically disruptive rhythm of Hamlet's exclamation, that the weight is justified: we have to feel it shift as Hamlet's own 'heavy burden' (III.1.54) is cast off him and on to Ophelia. And it is because she is so unfairly victimized by this gesture of his that we recognize now in Hamlet not a commitment to wrong, but the first realization in his actions of the potential wrong stored up in his apprehension of honour.

The weight does shift

In this century it has become commonplace to think of Hamlet as a source of corruption as well as one who is infected by it. Wilson Knight, H.D.F. Kitto and L.C.Knights have all contributed to the establishment of this view, which finds sophisticated expression in Professor Knights's book on the play: 'Hamlet, in his confrontation of this world [of evil, in the play], feels himself paralysed because an exclusive concentration on evil, or—say—something in the manner of the concentration is itself corrupting.' Knights lays great emphasis on Hamlet's promise to 'remember' the Ghost:

> he commits himself to a passion that has all the exclusiveness of an infatuation . . . Hamlet's exclusive concentration upon things rank and gross and his consequent recoil from life determine his attitude to death . . . he is fascinated by it, fascinated not merely by 'the dread of something after death', but by the whole process of earthly corruption, as in the long brooding on the skulls in the churchyard . . . these attitudes of fascinated revulsion combine with a regressive longing for the death that, from another point of view, appears so repulsive.[6]

Does all this really follow from Hamlet's promise to the Ghost that 'thy commandment all alone shall live/Within the book and volume of my brain' (I.5.102–3)? I cannot believe that it does. Professor Knights makes no allowance for the extraordinary equivocal note of that scene, which hardly suggests the quality of dedication found by him in Hamlet's subsequent action. Indeed, the play's second act pointedly *refuses* to show us a Hamlet given over to 'remembering' the Ghost. If that is what he is doing there, we have to deduce it from noticeably unforthcoming dialogue.

Whether Professor Knights thinks that Hamlet's treatment of Ophelia stems from his 'exclusive concentration on evil' or not is uncertain, but the odds are that he does, since 'To be or not to be', which precedes the crucial scene with her, is a central document in his case against Hamlet. Yet he hops about the play so in his analysis of Hamlet's 'self-disgust, his spreading sexual nausea, and his con-demnation of others' that it is not easy to say how he thinks the play *develops* (though that is of concern in the study as much as in the theatre). He certainly disapproves of Hamlet's behaviour to Ophelia, but so do I: the question is whether the shift of weight in this scene is as dramatic, as natural and surprising as I have suggested or whether it is rooted in a nature we have already seen to be corrupt.

It can, of course, be said that Hamlet's consciousness from the start is a poisoned one:

> How weary, stale, flat and unprofitable
> Seem to me all the uses of this world!   (I.2.133–4)

But Professor Knights is surely right not to make too much of this, even without referring to the idea of the taint of honour felt in the flesh: 'This sense of being tainted is both explicable and natural . . . '. That is something different from what we find in III.1:

> The disgust with the self that we must all at some time feel, for whatever cause, changes its quality when it is used to shock and damage, as Hamlet uses it to damage his dawning relationship with Ophelia.[7]

But if Hamlet's corruption is not evident in his earlier expressions of self-disgust or in an entire self-dedication to the Ghost's 'com-mandment', where is it? My reading of 'To be or not to be', whilst to some extent it confirms Professor Knights's view of it as showing 'that the set of Hamlet's consciousness is towards a region where no resolution is possible',[8] does not really allow us to think of that consciousness as corrupted so much as caught in a social and ethical web stronger than the consciousness itself. The problem is weakness, not corruption, and a weakness for which it is hard not to feel sympathy, as it belongs to someone unformed and untried. (It is not right to observe that Hamlet, at the age of thirty, ought in this respect to be formed: the point of his having until recently been a student is not to suggest the powerful qualities of his mind, for some students are lacking in intellectual distinction, but to explain his unprepared-ness when found by the Ghost's call to honour. Scholars are not much concerned with such matters.)[9]

Professor Jenkins is a better exponent of the corruption in Hamlet. His account of the meeting with Ophelia sees it as something preluded already in the labelling of Polonius as a 'fishmonger' in II.2 and the subsequent remarks about Jephthah's daughter. For a 'fishmonger' was not simply a whoremonger: besides this cant term there existed the idea that a fishmonger's daughter would be particularly prone to breed. In thinking of Ophelia as a 'fishmonger's' daughter, Hamlet thinks of her especially in her sexual and reproductive role. However, when later in the same scene (II.2.403ff.) Hamlet associates her with Jephthah's daughter—'O Jephthah, judge of Israel, what a treasure hadst thou!'—he thinks of her as someone loved spiritually and without reference to the body, since it was her father that loved Jephthah's daughter, and as someone without sexual knowledge, since she died a virgin. These two ways of considering Ophelia, then, stand in an antithetical relationship. Jenkins concludes:

> What [Hamlet] is recoiling from is sexuality and generation, all that goes to the breeding of sinners. He sees Ophelia confronted with a choice between being a fishmonger's daughter or Jephthah's, and he makes the choice for her himself when he bids her get her to a nunnery and declares there shall be no more marriage.[10]

That is all well and good; but Professor Jenkins hitches this reading on to the more generalized one of Hamlet's being a man obsessed. It is not necessarily a false reaction to this play to say that 'Hamlet's inability to meet life's challenge, his reluctance to act out the part that life requires of him is shown not least in his recoil from mating and procreation, his abhorrence of conception and breeding', though it would be charitable to reflect that life makes an unusually heavy demand on him, and prudent to note that this recoil does not manifest itself until the play's third act. But Professor Jenkins is surely wrong in what he has to say of the earlier encounter with Polonius:

> Hamlet recognizes in him the father of the woman he might marry, and it is an imagination that dwells on her as a potential mate, all too liable to conceive and breed, that sees her father as a fishmonger. An association of ideas is clear; but it is not one that 'reason and sanity' determine. It has the character of obsession. Whether we think of Hamlet as mad, or only seeming or affecting to be mad, will ultimately make no difference.[11]

What is wrong here is that Jenkins ignores the logic whereby Hamlet should wish to insult Polonius's status as a nobleman by calling him a low-class tradesman, and as a person of gravity and wisdom who upholds the social order by calling him a whoremonger. The suggestion that Ophelia might 'conceive' follows as a further, quite gratuitous insult suggested by the connotation of fishmongers' daughters. It may evidence a callousness to Ophelia on Hamlet's part, willed or unwilled, but 'obsession' seems to be going too far. His remarks, after all, are addressed to Polonius and, if we bear in mind what Laertes in accord with his father had to say to Ophelia of Hamlet's 'unmaster'd importunity' (I.3.32) they may strike us as not without aptness.

As for Jephthah's daughter, the reference is at some distance from the fishmonger passage, so that the antithesis which Professor Jenkins offers has about it something slightly strained. In any case Hamlet's point, as far as it may be construed, is one about Jephthah. Polonius says: 'If you call me Jephthah, my lord, I have a daughter that I love passing well' (II.2.407ff.), but Hamlet denies that this follows, since Jephthah, according to the story in Judges xi, allowed his daughter to be sacrificed. The implication is, ironically, that Polonius's love is not like that; but it is. We have seen him sacrifice Ophelia's feelings to the family pride.

Thus, despite the acuteness of much that he has to say, it does not seem to me that Professor Jenkins is really able to show us that II.2 is vital to an understanding of Hamlet's subsequent rejection of Ophelia, though he may have helped to show Shakespeare's procedure with regard to our unconscious expectations. When Hamlet turns on Ophelia we are shocked,[12] but not because we see him as a man obsessed with the flesh and its taint. The weight really does shift, and Hamlet really does at this moment *become* guilty of a positively wrong action.

Surface and depth

Up to the point of Hamlet's attack on Ophelia, he has held our sympathy—or at least it has remained evenly balanced. But as he abuses the girl who loves him and whom he is supposed to have loved it becomes impossible for us not to feel that he is behaving wrongly, and for discreditable reasons, since the whole display is so evidently a means of distracting himself from his own inability to meet the demands laid on him by the Ghost. It is because this consideration bulks so large that the possibility that his bitterness to her arises from the stifling of a genuine affection does not enter seriously into our reponse to the scene. Though we cannot approve him or his actions here, however, it does not follow that Hamlet will never be able to regain our sympathy. He acts wrongly towards Ophelia; but this opens up for him possibilities of guilt and repentance—possibilities of which, since Claudius's exclamation preceding the soliloquy, we must be painfully aware. Hamlet has not, by this wrong action, passed beyond the limits either of understanding or of fellow-feeling. Quite the reverse is true: he has moved from the abstraction and remoteness of a process of speculation which could have been endless, into the world of human relationships where ends and beginnings ceaselessly renew themselves in the creation of actualities. Consequently, with Hamlet's vicious turning upon Ophelia, the whole quality of movement in the play changes. It cannot feel again as it did in the deceptively random exchanges of the second act. The emphasis is now on action—but action of a distinctive kind.

As I have suggested, Hamlet is not acting in any positive fashion when he turns on Ophelia. He has no end in view: the point is made dramatically by his offering to go twice before he actually does go. The tirade fascinates him in itself, not for anything that it may achieve. An 'explanation' of his vehemence on the lines that Hamlet knows that Ophelia's father is behind the arras not only lacks the necessary support from the text: it misses the truth of Shakespeare's depiction in Hamlet of the devious satisfaction of a thwarted desire. Our attention in this scene is divided between the violence with which Hamlet urges the nunnery on Ophelia and the sense that this violence is not properly connected to its cause, Hamlet's bafflement at the task imposed on him by the Ghost. In an important way, the action here must be regarded as superficial: it attempts to deny the depth, the infinitude of speculation revealed by the soliloquy, but, as it does nothing but raise the *possibility* of Hamlet's understanding where he is (in a world of vulnerable human beings to whom one may act rightly or wrongly, in regard to whom one may feel love, pity, guilt and remorse), it succeeds only in keeping present, in the mind's eye, the abyss of speculation it would cover over.

This quality of the superficial in the action continues well beyond the 'nunnery' scene:[13] I shall argue that it characterizes Hamlet's behaviour up to the moment of his departure for England. It is an important point to argue, because if it is accepted it becomes impossible to interpret the play in terms of the famous conflict of two 'mighty opposites'. Hamlet does not show himself 'mighty' in the threat he represents to Claudius (it is not Hamlet's 'rebellion' which looks 'giant-like' to him, but that of Laertes (IV.5.122)), or in the slight action he takes.

This superficiality in Hamlet's action now becomes the important clue to follow; but in doing so, it must be remembered that what lends it that quality is the sense that Hamlet is evading the problems raised for him by the Ghost. We do not, therefore, leave questions of honour behind us; but we do find them to be present in a different fashion from before.

To begin with, of course, Hamlet's concern with 'honesty' reflects his own internal debate. Ophelia's innocent question 'Could beauty, my Lord, have better commerce than with honesty?' is infuriating because it treats what perplexes Hamlet as though it were a simple matter. Hamlet's reply turns on the idea of honesty's malleability; it is a reproof to her guilelessness:

> . . . the power of beauty will sooner transform honesty from what it is to a bawd than the force of honesty can translate beauty into his likeness. This was sometime a paradox, but now the time gives it proof. I did love you once.   (III.1.111–5)

This follows on in straightforward fashion from Hamlet's sarcastically satiric observation that 'if you be honest and fair, your honesty should admit no discourse to your beauty'. Its basis is the commonplace of woman's frailty fundamental to the double standard in honour-behaviour. A beautiful woman should avoid the world if she wants to remain 'honest', because in the world honesty more often than not proves vulnerable.

However, somewhere in the speech just quoted Hamlet stops thinking about Ophelia and starts thinking about himself. It comes to rest on 'I did love you once,' not 'you did love me'. If time has proved the paradox that virtue has less force than a corrupting beauty, Hamlet suggests that it has been proved on him. How can this be? We know of no rival for Ophelia in his affections.

One answer to the question is to turn to the 'antic disposition' theory and suppose that Hamlet's self-accusation is part of his campaign to get himself labelled as mad. But that is hardly convincing. The harshness of his address to Ophelia is, in its lack of motivation, quite sufficient to maintain and even extend any existing aura of craziness. The 'antic disposition' cannot, in any case, account for the drift from thinking about Ophelia to thinking about himself in the speech in question.

Another way of dealing with the problem would be to suggest that it does not signify, that in so far as the 'drift' disturbs us it is the effect of a momentary ineptitude on Shakespeare's part which we would do well to overlook. This solution puts too high a premium on clarity: it supposes that there would be no value in obscurity which, though it might be possible to explicate only at length, makes its point precisely by a ruffling of the feelings whose cause we cannot identify so long as we are caught up, as surely we are, in the action of the scene.

What effects this disturbance is an ambiguity in expression when Hamlet imagines the odds against 'the force of honesty' translating 'beauty into his likeness'. Noticeably the phrase does not, as we would expect, exactly balance the preceding clause. It is furthermore a puzzling phrase: if honesty is beautiful already, the exercise of 'translation' is redundant, but if honesty is ugly something is wrong in Hamlet's implied valuation of it. Hamlet, however, is someone who has been concerned with honesty distinctively throughout the play—who has, indeed, just been speaking of 'patient merit' as though its sufferings were his own; it seems natural, therefore, that his mind should drift from Ophelia's honesty to his own. Its appeal for him has been as an alternative to honour: he has used the pose of honest man to make his 'weakness' a virtue and not weakness at all. He has tried the strength of honesty to make his inaction and indecisiveness look beautiful to him, to give him a beautiful 'likeness'— that is, appearance—but, as the circularities of 'To be or not to be' imply, he has failed. The suggestion that illegitimate force has been applied works in all three meanings for the phrase that have a bearing on Hamlet himself: where '*his* likeness' is Hamlet's own appearance, the idea is that he has not been able to make himself look beautiful to himself; where 'his likeness' is beauty's appearance, the suggestion is that his pose as honest man has not been able to make its basic meanness look better than it is; where 'his likeness' is honesty's, the sense is that the force of his pose was not strong enough to make beautiful in practice what was theoretically so—a life of simple good-fellowship and virtue, putting up with the whips and scorns of time, for example the scorn which is one's due for not avenging one's dead father. All these meanings lie as it were just beneath the surface of consciousness, for Hamlet and for us, motivating and naturalizing the shift in emphasis within the speech from Ophelia to Hamlet himself.

It is worth noting also that the elusiveness of Hamlet's meaning here has a dramatic point too: it puts more force on the idea of translation—that is, change—because at this point language itself seems to be in flux, and on appearance because the quickness of delivery deceives the ear. The words convey a sense of the world's continuous change, a context in which Hamlet can conceal from himself the wrongfulness of his behaviour to Ophelia. He is inconstant, the words might suggest, because inconstancy is the way of the world:

> I am myself indifferent honest, but yet I could accuse me of such things that it were better my mother had not borne me. I am very proud, revengeful, ambitious, with more offences at my beck than I have thoughts to put them in, imagination to give them shape, or time to act them in.   (III.1.122–7)

Glossing the passage on 'the power of beauty' in the old Arden edition, Dowden found that in it Hamlet was referring to himself ('his own honesty represented as a wanton passion for beauty'); and he notes in this speech also self-reference: 'Hamlet brings general accusations against manhood and womanhood; but these particular vices are ironically named as those of which he has been suspected or calumniously accused . . .'. But Dowden does not go far enough in either case. In the first speech Hamlet's talk of transformation, and of honesty transformed, must surely send us back to the changing attitudes of 'To be or not to be' and the transformation of the native hue of resolution dwelt on at its end. *His* honesty is nothing fixed; the most honest, the most beautiful, attitudes that he can strike somehow transform themselves into their opposites. He appears to blame Ophelia for the instability of his intentions when he talks of the power of beauty transforming honesty, and we have to imagine his deriving satisfaction from the unjustified accusations yet we know that it is unjustified, and have seen for ourselves the way in which his attempt at honesty has been thwarted by a narcissistic theatricalism. He ought, then, to accuse himself, not Ophelia; but experience has shown it not to be worth while ('the time gives it proof'). Transformation being now the rule, he may act out his passion without reference to the old certainties ('I did love you once').

The second speech also takes its force from this deep self-dishonesty. Hamlet depicts himself as a walking paradox. He is 'indifferent honest' but also 'very proud, revengeful, ambitious', and so on. His nature includes more vices than can be expressed. Indeed, there is not *time* enough for them to realize themselves in acts. The impression given is of pressure on the person from the passions within him, not of the 'indifferent honest' person's exercising, or being able to exercise, any control on them. Professor Jenkins says that Hamlet is here speaking of 'his own sins',[14] but what is striking is that he speaks of them not *as* sins, but as forces of nature. The idea of responsibility is lacking. He is to himself a monster, but not a moral monster. He says that he is an 'arrant knave', but it is obviously just a cant phrase, designed to warn Ophelia off:

> What should such fellows as I do crawling between earth and heaven? We are arrant knaves all, believe none of us. Go thy ways to a nunnery. (III.1.128–30)

His honesty is only in the frankness with which he unleashes the tempestuous contradictions of his nature on Ophelia. It has no substance. We may dimly discern here a consciousness of Hamlet's sinfulness; we may think that in Ophelia 'he sees the image of his mother';[15] but the important thing is to grasp the manner in which Hamlet, whilst applying the moral lash to himself and others, shields himself from its effects by depicting himself as one so largely subject to paradox and self-contradiction that moral terms have no meaning in regard to him. 'You should not have believed me, for virtue cannot so inoculate our old stock but we shall relish of it' (III.1.117–19) does refer to the idea of original sin, but in such a way that it has no moral or religious force. To use this doctrine as Hamlet does use it, to *justify* wrong conduct, is to deny it meaning of any kind.

Don Juanism

In this scene, Hamlet presents the repulsive face of a figure who was
destined to become popular in the seventeenth century: the inconstant lover. Elizabethan poetry treats extensively of woman's
inconstancy and the pains of her lover, but in the works of later
poets—Donne, Carew, Suckling, for example—the subject is
handled ironically, sometimes even savagely. If woman can be inconstant, so can man; and he can even pride himself on it, and justify
his behaviour by reference to nature at large, as in Cowley's poem on
the subject:

> You might as well this *Day* inconstant name,
> Because the *Weather* is not still the same,
> That it was yesterday: or blame the *Year*,
> Cause the *Spring, Flowers*; and *Autumn, Fruit* does bear.
> The *World's* a *Scene* of *Changes,* and to be
> *Constant,* in *Nature* were *Inconstancy.*[16]

This English development is only a reflection of what had already
occurred on the Continent.[17] The high tone of Elizabethan literature
was inimical to its appearance in public in the 1590s, however,
though there is an interesting song on the subject of inconstancy,
attributed to Robert Devereux, Earl of Essex ('Change thy mind
since she doth change').[18] So one has not got much to go on if one
wants to argue that Hamlet's pose is to be interpreted by the audience
as modelled on that of the inconstant lover justifying himself by
reference to the mutability of all things. All that one can say is that
there was a classical model available in Ovid's *Amores*, II.iv, and
Englished with spirit by Marlowe:

> A young wench pleaseth, and an old is good;
> This for her looks, that for her womanhood.
> Nay what is she that any Roman loves
> But my ambitious ranging mind approves?

that there was a plentiful literature of worldly mutability, and that
Donne was writing the *Songs and Sonets* about the time Shakespeare's
play was written.

   And yet . . . and yet we *can* add one thing more, and that is that
male brutality to women of the kind we see in Hamlet could actually

be sanctioned by some versions of honour-conduct. The extreme case is that of Don Juan:

> The figure of Don Juan, in its more elaborate forms, is the quint-essence of the punctilious, fiery man, always ready to challenge another; who, to demonstrate his superiority in all aspects of a young man's disorderly life has to be not only the one who risks his life most, kills most, gambles most, spends most, wears the most elegant clothes, but also the one who conquers the greatest number of women, and who brings the greatest ingenuity to their seduction. For since the honour or shame of the female sex was a matter of such concern to their families, the demonstration of personal supremacy in this constituted one of the remarkable triumphs. [19]

One might, then, go so far as to say that Don Juan represents himself to the stone guest as a man of honour not so much *despite* his behaviour to the women he has abandoned as on account of it. Julian Pitt-Rivers remarks:

> Don Juan is a protagonist of the 'pecking-order theory of honour'. He is an affronter of other men, a humiliator and deceiver by design of both men and women . . . but not a voluptuary and not, be it noted, an adulterer: his four female victims are presumed virgins; he is not a man to grant precedence to another even in this. [20]

Now Don Juan is an extreme case: but his case derives quite straight-forwardly from the twin aspects of honour as 'manliness' (with a sexual implication) and honour as status. It may be that in a particular representation of the Don Juan story, such as Tirso de Molina's *El Burlador de Sevilla*, the motivation of the central figure is complicated, so that sexual inadequacy or whatever has to be seen at the bottom of his behaviour; in that case one would say that his actions were not derived from, but rationalized according to, the aspects of honour just mentioned. (I do not in fact believe that this is necessary as far as Tirso de Molina is concerned.) Whether honour rationalizes or originates the gentleman-lover's inconstancy does not matter here: the point is that honour as status and defiant inconstancy have a natural relationship that could realize itself without reference to literary models such as Don Juan would provide. I have already noted that Hamlet makes illegitimate use of his status in abusing Ophelia. Whilst claiming to be 'indifferent honest', whilst speaking with the supposed frankness of 'honesty', he is nevertheless aristocratically overbearing. He does not reject the honorifics used by Ophelia, her repeated 'my lord's, 'your lordship's and so on: he exploits the abasement in her that they imply.

This is not unlike the behaviour of Don Juan: only Don Juan is a seducer, Hamlet is not. The fact makes Hamlet's exhibition of proud inconstancy more repulsive, not less, because the love he entertained for Ophelia was not the mere collector's greed of the Spaniard. The love letter that Polonius reads to the King and Queen is at once ludicrous and pathetic—it must follow that Hamlet is not the libertine that Laertes supposed him to be, but really feels for Ophelia and really is incapable of expressing his feelings with fluency or grace: he is in the same class as the young men in *Love's Labour's Lost*. It is all the more shocking, then, that he should here assume the tones of a rake: 'We are arrant knaves, believe none of us. Go thy ways to a nunnery.' One kind of honour, embodied in the true feeling and propriety of his conduct with Ophelia, has been replaced by another, the *hauteur* of one who stands upon his rank, and yet who uses that rank to claim 'honesty' for himself and to abuse Ophelia and, through her, all women. The effect is very complicated: William Empson is probably right to suggest too that there is sympathy for Hamlet here as a satirist of court-vice, and as a madman whose insanity in some sense authenticates the general truth of what he has to say about women.[21] To hold all this in mind at once cannot be easy for actor or reader. But our sense that Hamlet's behaviour here *is* complex, that it is multifaceted, and that it is a transformation, reinforces the general impression of a great deal of behaviour on his part covering up the abyss which in the soliloquy had been revealed. For this reason, despite the difficulty of saying what exactly Hamlet is up to, the scene is intensely dramatic.

> You jig and amble, and you lisp, you nickname God's creatures, and make your wantonness your ignorance. Go to, I'll no more on't, it hath made me mad. I say we will have no mo marriage.
> (III.1.146–9)

Hamlet's rejection of marriage is a rejection of the possibility of union and harmony. He describes women's behaviour in terms of its diversity and its restlessness, its appearance and its incoherence: their wantonness does not connect with knowledge or conscience. But his own behaviour in this very scene may be described in similar terms. His violence of speech is all that holds together the fragmentary reflections of this or that kind of person: the cynic, the honest fellow, the nobleman, the Donne-ish inconstant, the madman, the schemer— their images shine out from the turbulent waters of his harangue and disappear. They come and go, as Hamlet comes and goes, offering to leave and returning, leaving once more and returning once more. God hath given him one face and he makes himself another and another and another, each face a mask, eggshell-thin, a bubble thrown up from the maelstrom.

Ophelia

Ophelia's soliloquy closes the episode, then, with a profound aptness. Against his incoherence and complexity stand her simplicity and order. She evokes another Hamlet, whose various activities did cohere in the unity of being of the Renaissance gentleman, and do cohere in the formality of her language:

> O, what a noble mind is here o'erthrown!
> The courtier's, soldier's, scholar's, eye, tongue, sword,
> Th'expectancy and rose of the fair state,
> The glass of fashion and the mould of form,
> Th'observ'd of all observers, quite, quite down!

Hamlet's mind may be o'erthrown, but it has not lost its nobility: instead the nobility it has retained has been that of the man who maintains status at the expense of virtue. That man has made of himself a composite of images that do not quite hang together; Ophelia recalls a composite whose various aspects, distinctly named, nevertheless do join together: the eye is the organ of the scholar as well as the courtier, the tongue also distinguishes them both, and the tongue is the courtier's sword, as the sword is the soldier's tongue. The line suggests a complexity antithetical to that with which Hamlet presents us, yet it does so with a cleanliness and neatness of expression pointedly different from either his language to Ophelia or that in the soliloquy which this one balances.

It is because Ophelia's soliloquy is in this way woven into the

poetic and dramatic texture of the play that it is wrong to read it as
the product of her fantasy. The speech gives a most precise account
of what Hamlet now is not, and at the same time, by dwelling on the
idea of nobility ('that noble and most sovereign reason'), suggests
how one kind of nobility might have been exchanged for or transformed to another. In addition, Ophelia's own grief is given expression all the more moving because it shows her, almost as soon as she
has mentioned her own wretchedness, in a most un-Hamlet-like
gesture, turning from it to generous thoughts of the man who is its
cause:

> And I, of ladies most deject and wretched,
> That suck'd the honey of his music vows,
> Now see that noble and most sovereign reason
> Like sweet bells jangled out of tune and harsh,
> That unmatch'd form and feature of blown youth
> Blasted with ecstasy.   (III.1.157–62)

Of course, there is irony here: Laertes had warned his sister that

>   in the morn and liquid dew of youth
> Contagious blastments are most imminent   (I.3.41–2)

—but because her sentence has turned away from herself to dwell on
Hamlet, it would be hard to imagine her as conscious of the irony.
This unconsciousness, then, looks lovely by the side of his: hers
triumphs over her own misfortune, but his is one that allows him to
overlook the pain he causes her, making his wantonness his ignorance:

>   O, woe is me
> T'have seen what I have seen, see what I see   (III.1.162–3)

allows Ophelia one further instance of her own simplicity, one
further irony: her eye is clear, his had been dulled, in her regard as
well as in that of the watcher behind the arras. Again, the point lies in
her unconsciousness: she does not say a word about Claudius and her
father because all her mind is on the prince. The whole speech has
about it the depth of commitment to life in the form of another
person that Hamlet's own soliloquy lacked but, by testifying to the
original worth of the man we have seen to behave so detestably, commands our sympathy for him even as it points to his disintegration.

8 Hamlet's theatre

The storm

Hamlet's mercurial quality derives from instability. Since it is an instability of situation which, in the fashion and for the reasons which I have already given, he internalizes, it is possible to regard him with sympathy and at the same time with blame—sympathy in so far as his situation imposes uncertainty of mind and act upon him, blame in so far as he consciously and willingly amplifies these uncertainties into irresponsibility. Since we can only deduce a degree of consciousness in Hamlet's deplorable behaviour towards Ophelia, it is not possible to draw up an accurate account of the balance of sympathies. Hamlet frustrates us by refusing a thorough exploration of the abyss that is his heart. It is important to understand this because the conventional opposition between the man of sincerity and the play-actor seems to work very much against him in an age conditioned to think in terms of sincerity and authenticity. It would not be surprising to discover that Shakespeare thought of the actor not as a hypocrite, someone who advances opinions other than his own, but as a divaricator, someone who reticently holds back his true feelings, which are nevertheless partly revealed in the impersonation of his roles. It seems to me, at any rate, that this is the light in which we should regard Hamlet in the 'Mousetrap' scene.

One of the obstacles to a clear understanding of this scene is the interlude with the players which Shakespeare uses to introduce it, for its purpose is by no means obvious. It is often used to give us Shakespeare's own conception of the art of acting. 'Speak the speech, I pray you, as I pronounced it to you, trippingly on the tongue; but if you mouth it as many of your players do, I had as lief the town-crier spoke my lines.' The advice is sound, as any frequent visitor to amateur and professional performances of Shakespeare can confirm. It is easy to stretch Hamlet's first-person in 'my lines' to include his author speaking through him. Yet if we do so we are quickly sidetracked from the immediate business of this episode, which is to emphasize the equivocal difference between Hamlet and the actors he addresses.

He makes that emphasis himself in the very sentence with which the new scene begins, and which I have already quoted. He speaks as an aristocrat, one to whom plebeian town-criers are offensive, and he warns the actors that they will incur similar odium if they make a hash of saying *his* lines. To begin with, certainly, one might think that he is speaking here as a special kind of aristocrat, that is, as an artist, and that the offensive quality of what he says, as it might be felt by the actors themselves, is instigated by this. One might think that there is even a hint of solidarity amongst artists—the creator on one side, the interpreters on the other. But by the time he has got to the end of his speech this notion can hardly be sustained. Hamlet holds himself distinctly apart from the actors whom he addresses and if his remark 'I would have such a fellow whipt for o'erdoing Termagant. It out-Herods Herod. Pray you avoid it', cannot fairly be presented as a veiled threat to the players, nevertheless it leaves one in no doubt as to the class-feeling that underlies his downrightness, and which the courtesy of 'pray you avoid' does nothing to qualify as a self-consciously erected barrier between him and the poor folk before him. *They* are 'your players'—in other words, our good friends our inferiors. No wonder this encounter shows them to be so subdued. Whether or no Hamlet speaks good sense, he speaks it in the tone of a harangue. The players can do little but shuffle their feet and offer the placatory responses such a tirade requests: 'I warrant your honour' (15) and 'I hope we have reformed that indifferently with us, sir'[1] (36–7). By so doing, of course, they confirm the aristocrat in the necessity and the hopelessness of his instructions to them that they should speak and act as he does.

The terms in which Hamlet speaks are ones with which we are by now familiar and which characterize his relations with those beneath him in rank. 'O, it offends me to the soul', he says, 'to hear a robustious perwig-pated fellow tear a passion to tatters, to very rags, to split the ears of the groundlings, who for the most part are capable of nothing but inexplicable dumb-shows and noise.' The 'robustious perwig-pated fellow' is colleague to the one who made Hamlet himself feel 'A rogue and peasant slave'—now he returns the opprobrium. As for his contempt for the 'groundlings', it is of a piece with his earlier remark about 'caviare to the general'. Lest we react to this by citing Sidney's aristocratic stance in order to render Hamlet orthodox, we should remember that there is a difference between the production of such sentiments in a prose treatise imitating the Italian and their appearance in a play where the speaker's relations with his society as a whole are very much in question. Furthermore we should recall that Hamlet's literary taste is naive compared with Sidney's: 'Come give us a taste of your quality. Come a passionate speech' (II.2. 427–8)—whatever he may say in justification of his preferences it is the *passionate* qualities of drama only that seem to attract him, 'passion' being a prominent word here in his address to the players, as it was when he considered the player 'in a fiction, in a dream of passion'. This simple preference is at odds with any elaborated theory of aristocratic discrimination and accords only too well with the innocently ludicrous sophistication of his love letter to Ophelia.

But 'passion', of course, is what Hamlet has to envy in the players. The point of his soliloquy at the end of the second act was that he could not get himself worked up even to the pitch of an actor who had merely to imagine causes for passion which for Hamlet were real. It is not hard to feel that both the aristocratic stance and the intensity of his address to the players derive from a similar mixture of envy and fellow-feeling, a fellow-feeling which, of course, must be denied. In the 'rogue and peasant slave' soliloquy the actor mysteriously acquired the heroic qualities which properly belonged to Hamlet, whilst Hamlet felt himself become 'a dull and muddy-mettled rascal'. The vehemence of his address now makes any identification with the players he is haranguing impossible—but further suggests that the 'impossibility' is nevertheless much on his mind.

His hankering after some different way of regarding the society whose conventional expectations prove so hard on him does come through in his insistence on the importance of acting in accordance with 'nature'. The players should 'o'erstep not the modesty of nature'; they 'hold as 'twere the mirror up to nature. Here 'nature' seems to stand for a level of existence before specifically social individuation has set in. The reference to 'modesty' as a quality of 'nature' puts it squarely on the side of 'honesty' in its opposition to 'honour'.

Not all nature is modest, however. Having laid bare to Hamlet the true situation underlying Claudius's reign, the Ghost exhorted him

'If thou hast nature in thee, bear it not' (I.5.81). This appeal to nature was made to pride in blood, not modesty. It is because he is unable altogether to deny the legitimacy of the Ghost's appeal that Hamlet seeks to escape it by construing 'nature' in a different sense. The enterprise is hardly likely to succeed, and it does not. From the vision of a 'modest' nature Hamlet soon passes to that of one where class-division and the contempt which it makes possible are the norm:

O, there be players that I have seen play . . . that, neither having th'accent of Christians, nor the gait of Christian, pagan nor man, have so strutted and bellowed that I have thought some of Nature's journeymen had made men, and not made them well, they imitated humanity so abominably. (III.2.28–35)

Nature's journeymen! Of course *they* could not be expected to do their job well. In reverting to this way of thinking, Hamlet once more declares himself his father's son. The little play of meaning here is one reflection of that mercurial quality that belongs to Hamlet's own fragmented nature.

The instability in him is 'naturally' associated with his addiction to 'passion'. Etymologically, the word refers to passive suffering, but for Hamlet it has the qualities of action—'the very torrent, tempest, and, as I may say, whirlwind of your passion'. To be in a passion is, for him, to act, so that he can blind himself to the difference between play-acting and acting in earnest when he wishes to; but it is also to be in the power of nature. Passion is like weather and the rushing streams which are the product of weather: you can be swept away by it. To be in a passion, then, is not only to act: it is to be acted upon. Passion is at once action and inaction: it is that state of incoherent yet effective irresponsibility which we have already seen at work in the exchange with Ophelia, and of which the address to the players, though so different in tone, is another example. The players bow to the storm—and we may be confident that they will remain unaffected when it is past.

The calm

The exchange with Horatio which follows soon after the players

have disappeared to make ready is complementary to the advice
Hamlet has just given. The same topics appear, but handled differently. 'Passion' is explicitly what Hamlet talks about; the word
'nature' does not appear, but the vaguely Stoic idea of a virtuous
poverty, 'a man that Fortune's buffets and rewards/Hast ta'en with
equal thanks', substitutes for it, the two being associated through the
idea of a golden age without hierarchical distinctions—an idea
which, though it does not surface in the text, is nevertheless important to it. Whilst the players drove Hamlet to a response which
denied him the identification with them to which we know him
covertly drawn, Horatio produces the necessary reaction whereby
the prince is able to demonstrate his superiority to the mob by
choosing to make a 'poor man' his ideal.

'Why should the poor be flatter'd?', he asks, as though no reason
could be adduced for such flattery; but one reason certainly exists—
that it may flatter the rich that they can transcend their own prejudice
in pretending to admire those who are below them in fortune.
Horatio, it should be noted, is not too far below Hamlet to find
difficulty in moving about the palace-world of Elsinore.

It may seem cruel to take this speech of noble sentiment in a sense
discreditable to the speaker. Can it really be that we are not to
respond wholeheartedly to these lines?

> Give me that man
> That is not passion's slave, and I will wear him
> In my heart's core, ay, in my heart of heart,
> As I do thee.
>
> (71–4)

Hamlet's elaboration of 'heart's core' as 'heart of heart' is a
reminder to us that the heart is indeed an abyss; it is a touch of
self-consciousness that asks us in some sense to put ourselves at a
distance from what is said as, a moment later, appears in the near-
apology of 'Something too much of this'. What seems an example of
classic English reticence is not really that, or at any rate it does not
sanction any certain element of the genuine to be attributed to
Hamlet here. The lines have the self-regarding quality of the sentimental. 'Give me that man . . . ' Hamlet is conducting a reverie in
company, and only at the last moment does his sentence swoop into
the actuality of his setting: 'As I do thee' registers his recalling

himself to where he is, and 'Something too much of that' his consciousness of the gap between his last clause and all the rest, where he
had not had Horatio in mind at all, but himself—himself as he wished
he might be.

This is so, I think, even when he apparently speaks most directly of
and to Horatio:

> Since my dear soul was mistress of her[2] choice
> And could of men distinguish her election,
> Sh'ath seal'd thee for herself. . .   (63–5)

This, from a man whose name has always been associated—and
rightly—with the inability to make up his mind, is surely significant.
Hamlet's declaration to Horatio allows him the luxury of seeing
himself as decisive, an ethically strong if unconventional aristocrat,
no 'John-a-dreams'; and consequently someone who *uses* drama, is
not simply caught up by the whirlwind of its passions. It is because
the idea of choice is so weighted by meaning for him that Hamlet
dwells on it here.

Hamlet takes note of Horatio briefly, as it were, by declaring that
his soul has 'seal'd *thee* for herself', but the sense of a person being
addressed is not sustained in the rest of the sentence:

> . . . for thou hast been
> As one, suff'ring all, that suffers nothing,
> A man that Fortune's buffets and rewards
> Hast ta'en with equal thanks; and blest are those
> Whose blood and judgement are so well co-meddled
> That they are not a pipe for Fortune's finger
> To sound what stop she please.   (65–71)

The grammatical shift from 'thou hast been' to 'blest are those' only
confirms our awareness that Hamlet is not really talking about or to
Horatio; he is himself the man buffeted by 'the slings and arrows of
outrageous fortune', or at least under attack from them; 'patient
merit' and the nobility of suffering in the mind are rehearsed again
here, and again for his own doubtful benefit. The speech anticipates
later references to himself by the prince: the 'co-meddled' 'blood and
judgement' look ahead to the mingled 'excitements of my reason and
my blood' (IV.4.58) of 'How all occasions . . . ' and the 'pipe for
Fortune's finger' turns up again at the end of the scene when Hamlet

demands of Guildenstern ' 'Sblood, do you think I am easier to be played on than a pipe?' Given that Fortune is a 'strumpet' (II.2.489) and that her finger is an instrument of pleasure, a suggestion of Hamlet's susceptibility to 'unmanly' sex in which he is himself passive, 'passion's slave', appears in the lines also, hinting at personal motives of inadequacy that drive the prince to the idealization in this speech. 'Give me that man/That is not passion's slave' implies some continuing sense in Hamlet himself that he is, *au fond*, 'a rogue and peasant slave', a sense that it is the object of this speech to exorcise.

And indeed it does succeed in this. Invulnerable to the lure of passion, Hamlet is able briskly to expound his plan to Horatio with a confidence that holds at bay the possibility that Hamlet himself is already poisoned within:

> If his occulted guilt
> Do not itself unkennel in one speech,
> It is a damned ghost that we have seen,
> And my imaginations are as foul
> As Vulcan's stithy. (80–84)

Whatever the outcome of 'The Mousetrap', we know enough by now to say that Hamlet's imaginations are indeed 'foul' and to feel that, despite this, no simple judgement can be passed on them. The complex relations of body and spirit, of social structure and the individual, of honour and virtue, forbid it.

A necessary question

The relation between Hamlet's advice to the players and his commendation of Horatio is largely thematic and antithetical. In the first he comments on the art of simulation and its kinship with 'nature' truthfully displayed; in the second he speaks in theatrical tones about what he expects to strike his listener as having only the simple truth that should go with 'nature'. In both episodes he speaks as an aristocrat—in the first as one so used to giving orders that are carried out that his tone is more conspiratorial than imperious (the players, however, understand that they are not to reply as equals to the prince); in the second as one whose aristocracy reveals itself as a matter of the spirit as well as one of material circumstance, overlooking the fact of Horatio's poverty in order to honour him (and incidentally to establish himself as a source of true honour).

Although the thematic and antithetical qualities of the two episodes explain why they belong together and show their appropriateness to the play in general terms, they do not account for their being placed at this point in the play. Neither episode contributes significantly to the plot of *Hamlet*. From the point of view of a developing action the advice to the players is frankly an excrescence, and if it is claimed that it was necessary for the dramatist to establish further Horatio's position as confidant to the prince, one could reasonably argue that this is done quite adequately by the exchange following the abandonment of 'The Mousetrap'. It rather looks as though Shakespeare is back to the trick he used in the previous act of offering us action which is frustratingly not a furtherance of the matter most urgently in hand. Of course, this could work on stage; we are impatient for some movement as far as the staging of 'The Mousetrap' is concerned, and our impatience is increased by the appearance of irrelevant material at the very moment we are drawn to anticipate that staging —we see the players, we learn that the King and Queen will shortly arrive to see the play. This could work: but surely it is not the most important aspect of Shakespeare's management of theatrical art here.

What is striking is the contrast with Act II Scene 2. There Shakespeare presented us with a mere congeries of happenings, Hamlet's role being a passive one in relation to them. Here, on the other hand, Hamlet is an agent or, more properly, *the* agent. He brings into being the encounters we observe. If he gives the players advice, we are to understand it is because he wishes to do so. His aggressiveness here is not like that which he showed in talking to Polonius or Rosencrantz and Guildenstern in the second act; that has to be provoked from him, this comes at his own bidding. Dramatically, therefore, the most striking line in the morsel of the play-scene which I am considering here is the one in which Hamlet summons Horatio. It emphasizes the arbitrary quality of his appearance, but makes that arbitrariness dependent on the will of Hamlet himself: 'What ho, Horatio!' This quality is not diminished by any sense we may have that Hamlet has been planning to speak with Horatio. ('Since Hamlet has just given Rosencrantz and Guildenstern a plain hint that they should leave him, we are to believe that he had some indication of Horatio's arrival, and wants to be alone with him.')[3] Hamlet reveals no reason for talking to Horatio now rather than previously about the motives for staging 'The Mousetrap', nor does he mention the fact that Horatio is being let into the secret rather late. Indeed, Hamlet's words to Horatio seem so much designed to contribute to his own notion of himself as a decisive agent that the request to Horatio to help him by watching Claudius closely may strike us as being as much a surprise for Hamlet as for his friend.[4] The difference between Hamlet's role in the second act and here lies in our no longer wondering *when* he will do something, but *what* he will do when he does act. It thus reinforces the sense of a decisive change in the quality of the action from the moment when Hamlet turned on Ophelia, even whilst it directs our interest to the superficial level of the action where what matters most is the outcome of his confrontation with Claudius.

The advice to the players and the commendation of Horatio function naturally, therefore, as a development of what the scene with Ophelia revealed about Hamlet; and the nervously antithetical quality they have in relation to each other and, in particular, the speed with which the prince moves from one kind of address to another emphasize the instability of his position, ethically and psychologically, at the moment he is about to embark on the doubtful 'action' that is 'The Mousetrap'. This in its turn increases the pressure under which we, as an audience, are put, by giving us a good deal more than the outcome of the play-scene to think about: for Hamlet himself is now 'a necessary question of the play . . . to be considered'.

At the entrance of the King and Queen, Hamlet remarks: 'They are coming to the play. I must be idle . . . ' The line has a very different force here from what it would have had if all that precedes it in the scene had been omitted. The *OED* says that 'idle' here means 'void of meaning or sense; foolish, silly, incoherent; . . . light-headed, out of one's mind, delirious'. Bearing in mind Hamlet's role as a decisive agent in the lines before this, however, I find it difficult not also to read the word as W. W. Greg did in 1919[5] as meaning simply 'not engaged in work', meaning 'I must present myself as having no aim in view in the presentation of this play'. But enforced idleness *is* a kind of work, and Hamlet's first words of simulated madness strike us as, if not laboured, at least a good job of work: the contrast between the unconsidered easiness of the King's question and the unexpected force of Hamlet's reply draws attention to this:

—How fares our cousin Hamlet?
—Excellent, i'faith, of the chameleon's dish: I eat the air, promise-
cramm'd. You cannot feed capons so.   (92–4)

The conspicuously concise aggressiveness of this aims at an effect of
'idleness' by being so disjointedly obscure as to seem crazy. The
contrast of Hamlet's style of speaking here with that of his address to
Horatio and, again, with the advice to the players makes us conscious
of the degree to which this 'idleness' is the product of work, specifically the work of the actor with whom Hamlet is so reluctant to
identify himself. Finally, the rapidity with which Hamlet moves
from one style to another and then to this third brings to mind the
instability of the self which has embarked on the business of 'acting'
for the benefit of others. We await the beginning of 'The Mousetrap'
not merely divided in our interest between the outcome of Hamlet's
'plan' and the resolution of his ethical and psychological crisis, but
uncertain as to which line of interest is to dominate in what follows.
The suspension of this anxiety is one element in the success of the
play-within-the-play; its intensification in what follows another of
those shocks upon which the greatness of *Hamlet* immovably rests.

Dumb-show and speech

Hamlet presents a play at the court of Elsinore. His object in doing
this is to find some indication of the King's guilt and confirmation of
the Ghost's story in some word or gesture it may wring from
Claudius. I have tried to show how little we may attribute fixity of
resolve to Hamlet at the moment when he formulates his 'plan'.
Excellent reasons may be adduced for thinking that this plan would
seem as doubtful in its essence at the time of the play's first performance as it does now.[6] Furthermore, in the interval between striking
off his idea and realizing it, Hamlet has been presented to us as
significantly unsure of himself, unstable to an extent which once
more calls in question his sanity and also leads us to doubt his ability
to see clearly an ethical issue, such as that which has been posed him
by the Ghost. In these circumstances it is hardly possible for us to
regard his 'plan' apart from the general question of the crisis in his
own nature which has to do with identity, right conduct ('honour')
and the individual's relation to his kin. Hamlet's own equivocal

stance towards the play-within-the-play is symbolized in the competing interest two kinds of acting have for us in this scene—the action of the players and Hamlet's 'acting' of idleness. In both cases the interest is intensified—and with it our sense of its being a competing interest—by the question of the degree to which truth underlines the mere performance: does 'The Mousetrap' tell the truth about the death of old Hamlet? Is Hamlet really mad as well as pretending to be mad?

These reflections have a bearing on any interpretation of the play-scene. In the first place it is not possible to regard the play-within-the-play as a weapon in that duel between 'mighty opposites' which Hamlet conjures up at the end of the play and which is so convenient a way of making the play discussable in short space. Hamlet's motives and the play's status as a weapon are both questionable. Secondly, I think that we can afford to be frank about Shakespeare's failure in the play-scene to manage perfectly all the material he has to hand, and to mitigate this frankness by confessing that a proper understanding of the complexity of this material and its superbly dramatic qualities helps us also to see why the mismanagement of it in some respects does not very much matter.

I have in mind here two of the oldest problems of *Hamlet* criticism, the duplication of material in 'The Mousetrap' and the dumb-show that precedes it, and the long delay in Claudius's reaction which, one might reasonably feel, the dumb-show was quite enough to set off. Did he see it?

These questions have recently been rehearsed in some detail by W. W. Robson, and the care with which he has surveyed various possibilities will help me to deal with the matter more summarily. Robson's reading seems to me to have one serious defect—he subscribes to the 'mighty opposites' theory and therefore speaks of 'the duel between Hamlet and the King'. Naturally, then, he believes that the King should be the focus of our attention as well as Hamlet's; at this moment in the 'duel' it is the King's response that, in his opinion, matters:

> If the elaborate preparation for the Play Scene has any point, then it seems clear that the King will be the central figure of the Play Scene; so that his reactions throughout are of the greatest interest.[7]

From this point of view the dumb-show is an embarrassment. If our attention is on the King, we will naturally wonder why it is that he does not react to the silent enactment of the murder of Hamlet's father, the crime which gained him the throne; but does react when the play, going over the same ground, comes to the second version of the poisoning.

> So far as the action is concerned—and on the usual assumption it is the action which alone is significant—the spoken play adds nothing whatsoever. Consequently, if this assumption is correct, either the King must have betrayed himself over the dumb-show, or there is no imaginable reason why he should betray himself at all.[8]

I think that we have to abandon our 'usual assumptions' in order to understand this scene, and that even then we have to reconcile ourselves to a degree of imperfection in it.

First of all, we have to imagine what Shakespeare's motives in having both dumb-show and play might have been. Robson's suggestion, very delicately made, seems to be that Shakespeare wanted to put into his play the idea of relative points of view. He quotes a saying of Wittgenstein: 'The world of the happy man is a different one from that of the unhappy man'. The dumb-show, then, would offer us the King's reaction as it would appear in the world of the happy man; the play itself would produce the reaction visible in the unhappy man. It is certainly arguable that *Hamlet* contains within itself the seeds of some disturbing philosophical relativism, so that there is no inherent implausibility about this suggestion so far as its effect on the whole play is concerned. On the other hand, though it could certainly be made to work in the modern theatre—by the use of different kinds of lighting, for example—it is not clear that it could have worked in Shakespeare's theatre. There does not seem to be enough in the text to have put the audience on to what the poet is supposed to have been up to. Consequently Robson's suggestion does not seem to be on a much better footing than one he rejects, and which he ascribes to those who look at Shakespeare's plays as 'poems'. Their line about the dumb-show, he says, would be like this:

> No doubt the *producer* has a problem here, in deciding what the King should do. Perhaps he was just not paying attention: or perhaps he was firmly controlling himself. It doesn't matter. The play scene is not an episode from real life, dramatically transcribed.

The King does not betray himself at the point when, in real life, it would be natural for him to do so, but at the point when it suits Shakespeare's theatrical purposes. Shakespeare has good *dramatic* reasons for including both the dumb-show and the spoken playlet. He used the dumb-show to remind the audience of the Ghost's story, and to heighten the tension while we watch the spoken playlet. He added the spoken playlet to give the opportunity for Hamlet to make his barbed comments and mutter his cryptic jests. In short, the word *convention* is invoked: and for some readers, and perhaps, some play-goers, that, nowadays, may be enough to settle the question.[9]

The idea of 'convention' is, I think, a red herring here, and Professor Robson's own objection, that this interpretation draws attention away from Claudius, does not seem acceptable. What, then, are the merits and demerits of this interpretation? Is it a merit that we are 'reminded of the Ghost's story? Is it a merit that the spoken playlet has its tension heightened by our consciousness of the content of the dumb-show?

I doubt if we do need to be reminded of the Ghost's story: it makes a vivid impression in the first act and we are unlikely to have forgotten it. It may be true that it leads us to anticipate the events in the spoken play so that we are impatient with its verbiage, and tension is consequently increased; but it is not clear that this effect is needed, and certainly anticipation could have the reverse effect of diminishing our interest in what the Player King and Queen have to say. On the other hand the silence in which the dumb-show is enacted has an undeniable thematic value, and enhances the sense of a contrast between the murderer's effective action and Hamlet's own wordy inaction. Indeed, it reflects very strongly indeed in his lavish dispensation of bitter jokes at the moment the play is performed, so that his 'idleness' does seem something more than assumed.

Furthermore the dumb-show works powerfully as an intrusion of the past into the present: the fact that we do not know at this point whether or not it is an accurate representation of the past is irrelevant to this effect—what matters is that the present is in the grip of the past, and that Hamlet's independence as an agent, the role established for or by him at the opening of the scene, is in this way diminished though not destroyed. The dumb-show, because it is dumb, makes the present problematic as well as the past, and reflects on Hamlet as well as on the King. Because the playlet establishes its speakers firmly as belonging to the realm of fiction—for example, by having them speak in couplets—the effect of the past, the actual past of the play's own characters, weighing on the present is to be achieved only by the dumb-show.

But why should the playlet be so elaborate? Why should it be part of the play at all? Having shown reasons why Shakespeare might want a dumb-show, I should go on to show what different purposes could be served by words and, if possible, to show that they are indeed realized in what Shakespeare wrote.

Wormwood

Claudius breaks up Hamlet's theatrical entertainment by rising to his feet at the moment he hears this line: 'On wholesome life usurps immediately' (254). We are not to suppose, I think, that Claudius waits for the player to finish his sentence, or that Shakespeare was so taken up with the force of what Lucianus had to say that he determined to postpone the King's interruption until Lucianus had finished his speech. We may reasonably ask, then, why Claudius is made to object at this point rather than any other to a play which, as his question to Hamlet 'is there no offence in't?' shows, has made him uncomfortable even before the murderer enters. The answer lies in the wording of the line I have quoted: what sets Claudius off is the challenge to his authority in the word *usurp*. The challenge is one that he imputes to the player's words; it is not implied by the words themselves. The King's guilt declares itself in his reaction, just as Hamlet had hoped that it would. This is an effect that could have been produced only by using words.

'Lucianus, nephew to the King' speaks six lines before the play in which he figures is interrupted and abandoned. But those six lines are preceded by a whole 'scene' from 'The Mousetrap', a scene of seventy-two lines in length—that is, somewhat longer than, for example, IV.4, where Hamlet meets with Fortinbras's Captain, and soliloquizes on the nature of honour. In order to understand what Shakespeare is up to here, we surely have to account for the emphasis he lays on this part of 'The Mousetrap'—all the more so in that nothing in it seems to derive from the Ghost's story. Like Claudius, Lucianus is a kinsman of the man he murders; like Claudius in the

Ghost's story, he poisons his victim through the ear. But we have no reason to believe either that Hamlet senior, growing old, encouraged his wife to think of a second marriage or that Gertrude swore as vehemently as the Player Queen not to remarry. We have no reason to think that remarriage was even a subject of discussion between her and her first husband.

One explanation for the scene's inclusion in 'The Mousetrap' may be that it shows Hamlet accusing Gertrude of complicity in her husband's death. The Player Queen declares emphatically that she will not remarry:

> In second husband let me be accurst;
> None wed the second but who kill'd the first.
>
> (174–5)

Despite the context, in which the Player King urges the naturalness of remarriage for women in a world governed by mutability, these lines must be offensive to Gertrude, especially since the idea that remarriage goes with husband-murder is repeated only a few lines later, and before the King has been able to launch into his long speech:

> A second time I kill my husband dead,
> When second husband kisses me in bed.
>
> (179–80)

Yet Gertrude at this point says nothing and does nothing that Shakespeare felt it necessary that we should know about. It is not until the scene is over that Hamlet asks her what she thinks of the play and she replies that 'The lady doth protest too much, methinks'.

What are we to make of this? Are we to think Gertrude so thick-skinned as not to have felt the attack on her behaviour? Surely not: neither in the closet scene nor earlier in the play is Gertrude shown as stupid in this fashion. Is she turning upon Hamlet his own sardonic humour, treating him as he might treat Polonius or Rosencrantz and Guildenstern? Only those who see Shakespeare as a seventeenth-century Zola, dispassionately observing the laws of evolution as they work themselves out in hereditary traits, are likely to be attracted by this idea; and in any case Hamlet's reply 'O, but she'll keep her word' is quite unflustered. The Queen has missed her aim, as he never does. No: Gertrude's remark is understated not, surely, in the way of irony, but with the control of someone under pressure. Primarily the pressure comes from Hamlet's mad behaviour in choosing to use the play to slander her. The question of her possible complicity in the murder must be subordinate to this; the Ghost's failure to suggest any responsibility on her part and its tenderness towards her make it unlikely that she was involved. The question comes, then, independently from Hamlet, and is all too plausibly explained by the anti-woman bias of the scene with Ophelia and of his first soliloquy. Gertrude's reply to Hamlet implies forbearance, a willingness to humour him, but not so far as to admit guilt either for her first husband's death or for her second marriage.

In the First Quarto version of the closet scene (III.4) she explicitly denies any part in the murder—'I never knew of this most horride murder'—and her reaction to the news of Claudius's attempt to dispose of Hamlet, in the First Quarto equivalent for IV.6, tends to confirm this, for she says there of her husband:

> Then I perceive there's treason in his lookes
> That seem'd to sugar o're his villanie . . .

William Empson has suggested that the First Quarto represents a first draft for the play and that these two scenes were subsequently altered to make the Queen's relation to the murder more obscure, and so to enhance the play's general ambiguity.[10] As I interpret Gertrude's response here, it preserves the possibility of Empson's interpretation but reduces its likelihood. An effect, then, of the first scene of 'The Mousetrap' is to show the tolerance of the Queen towards her son. Shakespeare's purpose, however, seems to be to reflect more on Hamlet than on his mother, by showing him to launch a sudden attack on her, quite unexpectedly and unauthorized by the Ghost's narrative. The Ghost had said: 'Taint not thy mind, nor let thy soul contrive/Against thy mother aught' (I.5.85–6); Hamlet, having contrived something against his mother, is treated by her as someone whose mind is tainted, that is, unstable.

The dramatic strategy underlying the scene of the Player King and Queen therefore seems to me to be directed largely at Hamlet; at the very moment that his 'plan' is being realized, there is a reflection on his sanity. The 'idle words' (*Lucrece* 1016) of this scene call in question the extent to which Hamlet himself is 'idle' in pretending to be 'idle', and refer us from the stage upon the stage to the stage upon

which it is uncertain whether Hamlet is feigning or not. 'That's
wormwood!' he exclaims, but the play is wormwood for himself as
much as for his mother, and in a rather different and certainly more
terrible sense.

A knavish piece of work

The scene does not reflect on Hamlet merely as it is his instrument
for a purpose which may be attributed to sickness. What is said in the
scene itself also has a bearing on his situation, but in a negative way.
Whilst the Player Queen asserts more and more fiercely the fidelity
which the dumb-show leads us to think she will speedily abandon,
the Player King speaks impressively for an acceptance of human
nature in its weakness and its fallibility. The style is, of course,
designed to be heard as conspicuously 'theatrical': no one else in the
play of *Hamlet* speaks in the couplets that belong to 'The Mousetrap',
but they are not couplets to which we can afford to condescend:

> I do believe you think what now you speak;
> But what we do determine, oft we break.
> Purpose is but the slave to memory,
> Of violent birth, but poor validity,
> Which now, the fruit unripe, sticks on the tree,
> But fall unshaken when they mellow be.
> Most necessary 'tis that we forget
> To pay ourselves what to ourselves is debt.   (181–8)

The monosyllables of the first line are associated with an effort to be
direct where directness is difficult, since we do not always speak
what we think, and since our understanding of others must be based
on belief, not certainty—a belief realized perhaps at a tangent to what
is actually told us. The second line reverses the normal order of
subject and object in order to enact an ending (a termination, something determined) that is not the end; *break* has a melancholy and
violent quality, reflecting both on the destruction of her husband
with which the Player Queen's determination to marry his murderer
is equated, and also on the breakdown which seems to be Hamlet's
lot as a consequence of his effort to come to a decision about the
Ghost. This violence emerges by name in the second couplet as a
'violent birth', the birth being that of a purpose that is of its nature to

be broken. The polysyllabic cadence of the rhymes here harmonizes
with the mood of the first couplet ('memory', 'validity'—the lines
terminate uncertainly, in a murmur) so that the sententiousness
strikes one as a natural extension of the earnestness with which
the speech begins, and permits the speaker a move back into self-
reference again, by means of the commonplace idea that 'ripeness is
all'. The Player King will fall inevitably, whether the tree is shaken or
not, for it is not in the nature of things on earth to endure. In a world
where all is change, it is foolish to expect stability for oneself.
Necessity must be accepted, must be recognized; and this recognition
implies a large sense on the part of the person who carries it out. It
may be necessary to forget, but forgetting cannot be willed: it would
seem therefore that there is a fundamental opposition of the human
individual to the necessity which imposes on him. And what we
have to forget is something which it is in the first place difficult to
grasp. We must forget 'To pay ourselves what to ourselves is debt'.
The Riverside Shakespeare glosses the couplet in this way: 'such
resolutions are debts we owe to ourselves, and it would be foolish to
pay such debts'.[11] This gloss brings out the narrow sense of 'self' that
we are requested here to overcome. Ordinarily what is owing to
oneself is a motive for action ('I owe it to myself to . . .'): it is basic to
the sentiment of honour. And in a society which esteems personal
wealth, as in one whose religion is expressed in mercantile terms, the
notion of a debt that doesn't need paying is exceptionally shocking.
What the Riverside gloss does not note, of course, is that the second
line is functionally ambiguous, so that it also means: 'it is not for us to
pay the debt we have ourselves incurred', this sense putting an
emphasis on redemption by another, that is, Christ. The ambiguity
is important because is manages to combine deep religious feeling of
the most humane kind with a sense of the violation to our everyday
selves that such a genuine religious feeling must entail. It is the force
with which such feeling is recognized in the individual life that
answers and checks the violence with which the 'mere' individual
formulates his purposes.

   These packed lines are, in a characteristically Shakespearean way,
great poetry. It might be objected that there is more in them than can
be grasped in the theatre but the objection cannot be sustained; the
lines work powerfully enough if they only suggest the Player King's
awareness of the difficulty of what he proposes. Change may be

inherent to the world's nature, but it goes against the grain to acknowledge the fact.

The relevance of all this to Hamlet's own situation should be clear. At the most superficial level the Player King is saying, with some variation, what was said to Hamlet in the play's second scene:

> Thou know'st 'tis common; all that lives must die,
> Passing through nature to eternity. (I.2.72–3)

But here there is a proper acknowledgement of the difficulty human kind has in accepting this truth.

At another level the Player King is talking about honour. He is arguing against that exaggerated sense of honour which leads Hamlet to suppose his flesh 'sullied' by his mother's remarriage, and which in Chapman's play *The Widow's Tears* is made the stuff of comedy, as it is of tragedy in Webster's *Duchess of Malfi*. (In my opinion both these plays are hostile to the aspect of 'honour' with which they deal, a hostility which is not without significance for a reading of *Hamlet*.) Consequently, at its heart the scene contains a powerful plea against the honour-motivation which is apparent in Hamlet's thoughts—he is not like Hieronymo in *The Spanish Tragedy*, for whom the cry is always 'Justice'. Hamlet says of 'The Mousetrap':

> Your Majesty, and we that have free souls, it touches us not. Let
> the galled jade wince, our withers are unwrung. (III.2.236–8)

But the play is adapted to touch him just as well as it touches the King.

The pertinence of what the Player King has to say to the situation in which Hamlet finds himself increases, for he now starts to discuss a topic of peculiar interest to the prince—'passion':

> What to ourselves in passion we propose,
> The passion ending, doth the purpose lose.
> The violence of either grief or joy
> Their own enactures with themselves destroy.
> Where joy most revels grief doth most lament;
> Grief joys, joy grieves, on slender accident. (189–94)

The 'passion' here is the passionate feeling which Hamlet admired in the player's speech about Troy, and the passion of suffering which is what we are aware of in 'To be or not to be'. But it is the later speech which has most to do with what the Player King says, for it is a speech of lost purpose, the consequence of Hamlet's earlier rapture at the player. The paradox of grief or joy destroying itself even as it is given expression, so that joy contains grief and grief joy, is close to Hamlet's sense that

> the native hue of resolution
> Is sicklied o'er with the pale cast of thought.

The speech in which Hamlet comes to formulate his 'plan' and that in which he betrays his own theatrical stance to that 'plan' are both reflected in the word 'enactures', since 'enact' has a positive theatrical association ('I did enact Julius Caesar', says Polonius earlier in the scene): and the notion of self-destruction looks back to the suicidal nature of 'To be or not to be'. The Folio reads 'ennactors' for the Second Quarto's 'ennactures', and this suggests a pun: excessive passion destroys itself by destroying whoever acts it out. This takes up into the speech the paradoxical relationship of mind and body raised most noticeably in Ophelia's account of the prince's visit to her chamber. (It is worth noting that the thirty lines of this speech are only six in the First Quarto and that those now under discussion are absent there. If the idea of the Second Quarto as a revised text can in any way be accepted, we might accept it here in lines which poetically and dramatically do so much for the text.)

Shakespeare's complete mastery of tone must be remarked on somehow: the last couplet of those quoted enacts a destruction of harmony, in the jingling opposition of joy and grief, the last phrase, 'on slender accident', dangling unhappily at the end of the sentence and of the line, but leading perfectly into the subject-matter of the next two lines, stated with the simplicity of a popular saying:

> This world is not for aye, nor 'tis not strange
> That even our loves should with our fortunes change . . .

The lines that follow, on the vicissitudes of fortune and the relative status of poor man and great, maintain this simplicity with something of an air of rebuke for the Stoic posturing of 'To be or not to be' and Hamlet's lugubrious commendation of Horatio:

> But orderly to end where I begun,
> Our wills and fates do so contrary run,

That our devices still are overthrown:
Our thoughts are ours, their ends none of our own.

Like 'passion', the word 'thoughts' has special relevance for Hamlet, a 'fool of nature' whose disposition shakes 'With thoughts beyond the reaches of our souls' (I.4.54–6) and for whom 'there is nothing either good or bad, but thinking makes it so' (II.2.249–50). The Player King suggests at once the fundamental nature of thought (it is here associated with the will itself) and its importance; and he calls in question the value of the 'device' in which on Hamlet's behalf he plays a part.

The spoken part of 'The Mousetrap' is, then, full of meaning. Hamlet calls it 'a knavish piece of work', and its rhymes and artful simplicities are certainly meant to suggest a form of popular theatre. Stylistically it is very different from the player's speech about Pyrrhus. Its knavishness has something to do with the treatment of the aspect of honour raised by remarriage: it speaks wisely about this through a figure whom we are necessarily to find sympathetic, and rebukes the prince in his uncertain grasp of the world and of his place in it. Furthermore, by suggesting that Hamlet's mind is indeed tainted, and showing Gertrude and Claudius exercising tolerance towards him under the most trying circumstances, 'The Mousetrap' manages to run counter to the underlying assumptions of Hamlet's 'device'.

I think it is now possible to return to the question of the dumb-show and the verse-play. I have tried to show that they fulfil different functions in the play of *Hamlet*. It remains to see how far these functions can be reconciled. I think they plainly can. Although the dumb-show is an oddity among dumb-shows, in that it simply anticipates the action of the 'play' which it precedes, its effect on us is not diminished. It does two things: it produces an interval of intense silence which contrasts strongly with the ambiguous language all about it, and it represents graphically an action from the past still potent in the present—indeed, its potency may be said to make Hamlet incapable of action. The King and Queen watch the dumb-show uncomfortably in silence; but their silence is legitimized for the court as an expression of the tolerance extended to the sick prince. Furthermore, the very exceptional nature of the dumb-show permits us to see it as less easy for them to interpret than might otherwise be the case. The King is silent because he cannot betray his criminality.

He is silent, therefore, until the word *usurp* enables him to react as though he were politically under threat.

Nevertheless, 'The Mousetrap' and its dumb-show are to some extent unsatisfactory elements in the play. The Player King's long speech is commanding poetry, and its dramatic function properly understood enables us to dispense with the gratuitous emphasis on the figure of Lucianus placed by those commentators who would have him made up to look like Hamlet.[12] On the other hand its length makes the Queen's tolerance less real to us. Whilst one dramatic point is made another is neglected, and it is the discomfort arising from this which has led to so much furious discussion of the dumb-show.

The quick-change artist

Despite all this, 'The Mousetrap' ought to work on stage (it is usually severely cut). It presents the producer with problems but they are capable of solution, however imperfect that solution may be from the point of view of a reader. The spectator's attention is divided pretty clearly between the play-within-the-play and Hamlet, its presenter. The division of interest, like the distinction of styles, is an outward sign of our mixed feelings about Hamlet's 'plan' as possibly useful but apparently crazy and about his crazy behaviour, apparently assumed but all too possibly genuine. The simple narrative tension which is brought about by our waiting to see how the King will respond to the play is complicated and heightened by these other forms of anxiety which the scene provokes in us.

The tension resolves itself brilliantly by a surprise, followed by the fulfilment of our worst fears about Hamlet. The surprise is the King's exit. Ten lines after Lucianus has poured poison in the ear of the sleeping Player King, Hamlet is alone with Horatio. The action which his play provokes is withdrawal, a kind of rout. But Hamlet himself seems not to notice this. Ophelia is the person who remarks upon the King's rising: Hamlet is talking, and so even at the moment of his 'victory' the audience's attention is distracted. In listening to Hamlet, they may well miss the significant action—and the implication is that Hamlet may, too. Admittedly, it is not a necessary conclusion that he will. Hamlet's eyes may be on Claudius even as he prattles about Gonzago and the story 'in very choice Italian'. But in any case the effect of distraction holds.

It is a surprise that Claudius so promptly retreats; it is not so surprising to find that Hamlet is unable to break out of the theatre in which he has been indulging:

> Would not this, sir, and a forest of feathers, if the rest of my fortunes turn Turk with me, with Provincial roses on my razed shoes, get me a fellowship in a cry of players?   (269–72)

'I'll take the Ghost's word for a thousand pound'—very well, then, the time for action has come. Hamlet does not immediately act; that need not be held against him, though he ought to have had some notion of what followed on his plan's fulfilment. But what is disturbing is his failure to change his tone significantly from that of the 'idle' Hamlet playing his part as the actors played theirs. His extravagant quotation from unknown ballads (could they derive in fact from plays?) is in the same key as 'For O, for O, the hobby-horse is forgot' (133). This should be disturbing.

When 'The Mousetrap' is over, Hamlet shows the same instability as he did in the encounters with the players and Horatio that immediately preceded it. The mercurial changes in tone depend here, as they did there, upon a sensitivity to status and the expectations attendant on it. With Horatio Hamlet clowns in the accent of the people, though his talk of a 'cry of players' is enough to indicate the distance at which he remains from really assuming an identity with the common view of common people. But with Rosencrantz and Guildenstern he plays the aristocrat, using the royal 'we' to hold them off from him—'Have you any further trade with us?'. Guildenstern very soon observes, correctly, that 'this courtesy is not of the right breed' (306–7): and its wrongness is increased by the elaboration of Hamlet's manners: 'But is there no sequel at the heels of this mother's admiration? Impart.'

It is true that Rosencrantz and Guildenstern, since they are in the confidence of the King, may be regarded by Hamlet as enemies. But his contempt is misplaced, since there is no reason to suppose they are not acting in good faith. Rosencrantz reminds Hamlet of their former friendship:

> —My lord, you once did love me.
> —And do still, by these pickers and stealers.

Hamlet's droll oath is a repudiation of the fact of love: men don't have hands, they have pickers and stealers constantly at the ready to take advantage of their fellows' weakness. In the previous scene, Ophelia's soliloquy stood as a powerful reminder of the falsity of such a view. Here Rosencrantz, by his directness, exposes the prince's attitudinizing for what it is:

> Good my lord, what is your cause of distemper? You do surely bar the door upon your own liberty if you deny your griefs to your friend.   (328–30)

Although Hamlet seems to take this for a threat, replying with a tight brevity strikingly in contrast with the open construction of what Rosencrantz says, it is hard to agree with him. His extravagant behaviour, which is now capable of a political interpretation, must lead to trouble unless he can give even Claudius's men a palliative line to work on. He might himself, in his present uncertainty—it is worth noting that he is back to his second-act role of being acted on, by being summoned to his mother—find it useful to provide the Court with reasons for humouring him more. But no: 'Sir, I lack advancement' is a remark unlikely to win him the breathing-space he needs.

There follows the marvellous passage in which Hamlet turns upon Guildenstern, asserting his theatrical command of the situation. The aftermath of 'The Mousetrap' needs just this kind of animation on the surface of the narrative to keep the play from drifting quietly away. Such another reversal of expectation occurs when Polonius enters to repeat the courtiers' message:

> —My lord, the Queen would speak with you, and presently.
> —Do you see yonder cloud that's almost in shape of a camel?

As with Guildenstern, Hamlet is here asserting his command; but in both cases what he says reflects on him and calls in doubt the real nature of that command. For the cloud that is 'like a camel', 'back'd like a weasel' and 'very like a whale' is only like Hamlet himself, mobile and without a fixed identity. This is the most pathetic appeal to 'nature' in the play. Similarly, when Hamlet tells Guildenstern that, 'though you fret me, you cannot play upon me', he invites the response that when he himself is playing a part with such vigour, this is doubtless true. He is still unable to emerge from the fictive world of 'The Mousetrap'; he is playing comedy for the King (286) and he does so with the players' instruments. His command, then, will last only so long as he remains within the imaginary world in which he can indefinitely change roles, from prince to peasant and back again.

'They fool me to the top of my bent'—'They compel me to play the fool till I can endure to do it no longer' says Dr Johnson, and Dover Wilson adds: 'Hamlet's nerves are giving out.'[13] Jenkins glosses 'the top of my bent' rather differently: 'the height of my capacity, the utmost limit I can go to'. In either case there seems to be an excessive concern to protect the prince from an imputation to which his behaviour certainly gives rise: that he *wants* to play the fool. It is not only his behaviour that suggests this, either. The natural interpretation of *bent* is not offered by Johnson or Jenkins. *Bent* must mean 'inclination'[14] unless there are good reasons in the context to put the idea on one side. Hamlet is saying: 'They are treating me as a fool to the complete satisfaction of my wishes'. It is disturbing, but quite consistent with all that he has so far said and done, that he does not think that it may be folly to be taken for a fool: but plainly Dr Johnson and Harold Jenkins took the point.

It is reinforced by the last of his quick-changes in this scene, his lapse into the posturing of his soliloquy ' 'Tis now the very witching time of night . . ' Eleanor Prosser's blood, it seems, runs cold at these lines, but not because they are so evidently play-acting—these are the 'damnable faces' (247) Hamlet saw in Lucianus—but because she believes Hamlet really to mean what he says.[15] 'Now could I drink hot blood . . . ' The shifts and changes of Hamlet's mood since the King left the stage are surely designed to make such a response implausible. It springs from the assumption that all we are concerned with in *Hamlet* is what the prince will do. But we are equally concerned with what he is, with the issues of social and individual identity. 'O heart, lose not thy nature' (384); but 'nature', like his heart, is a mystery. The scene ends, then, with a Hamlet whose relation to either strikes one as fragile and, held by this fragility, the play's action seems big with possibility, the world of Denmark alarmingly open to the random incursions of violence and madness.

9 Claudius and Gertrude

Abstraction

The act and scene-divisions of the modern text of *Hamlet* have slight authority except in so far as they persuade us they are right. By and large—I shall deal with a possible exception later—they do so. The first act is of one kind, the second of another; the first develops action, the second presents inaction and fosters the impatience which that naturally breeds in us. The third act, too, has its own integrity. It is devoted to a peculiar kind of theatre, to action which belies its own intensity. The meeting of Hamlet and Ophelia staged by Polonius, the play staged by Hamlet, the histrionics of the closet scene, for which Gertrude is the intended audience—these scenes may advance the story but they move within the restricted area of theatricality. Scene 3 is no exception to this rule: it shows another actor, this time Claudius, and his 'audience', Hamlet. However, the scene is devised so that our recognition of its theatrical quality will shock us. Claudius, after all, is trying *not* to act in the soliloquy which precedes his prayer and which, as it were, explicates the prayer for us. Furthermore, at the opening of the scene he appears to be a man whose words give direct expression to his thoughts. It seems that there is no need for this man to play a part. By the end of the scene we are brought to acknowledge that nevertheless this is what he has to do.

He is presented to us initially as a frank, brisk realist, unafraid to speak his mind in uncomplicated English:

> I like him not, nor stands it safe with us
> To let his madness range. Therefore prepare you.
>
> (III.3.1–2)

The assurance of these lines is all the more marked because they follow on immediately from the mad giggle and posturing of Hamlet in the previous scene. They restore confidence in the play's narrative, and suggest for the first time that Claudius has it in him not merely to oppose Hamlet, but to do it mightily:

The terms of our estate may not endure
Hazard so near us as doth hourly grow
Out of his brows.   (5–7)

The forms of expression is compact and masculine. *The terms of our estate* with judicious emphasis includes Claudius's fear for his nation, a noble sentiment, and his fear for himself, an ignoble one concealed with determination; the *hazard* that grows out of Hamlet's *brows* is both the madness that is visible in his eyes and the ambition to place a crown upon his head that Claudius apparently suspects in him.[1]

The prominence which is now given to Rosencrantz and Guildenstern may seem odd; what they say contributes nothing to the narrative, and does little in the way of providing them with definite characters. What, then, is the reason for the relative leisure with which they speak of all the lives that depend upon the single life of a king?

Some interpreters portray Rosencrantz and Guildenstern as sycophants, and their willingness to elaborate upon the theme they have set themselves here may seem to justify this. In picking up the acceptable idea that the King fears Hamlet because Hamlet puts the nation in danger, they tacitly reject the idea that the King fears for himself. It is not clear, however, that they have even grasped this implication in what Claudius says. If we grant that what they say here can be taken, even so, as flattery and time-serving, we are presented with a difficulty that really is not easily solved. Claudius is not especially susceptible to flattery. Though he does not express impatience at the attempted courtliness of Polonius, as Gertrude does, he is always brisk and to the point in his questioning of him and he sets his opinion on one side without hesitation. He is represented as businesslike in his dealings with other men. It is hard, therefore, to believe that he would accept flattery from Rosencrantz and Guildenstern—flattery that is recognizable as such to us—with complacency.

To understand this passage we need a hypothesis about the King's behaviour, not that of Rosencrantz and Guildenstern. That is to say that the important thing to note is not how much the two courtiers have to say, but how long the King remains silent before he brings the interview to an end: 'Arm you, I pray you, to this speedy voyage . . . '

There is an obvious reason why the King should be abstracted: it lies in the emotions which 'The Mousetrap' may be supposed to have aroused in him but which he cannot voice even to those nearest him. His silence here anticipates, that is, what is expressed in soliloquy once he is left alone.

As for Rosencrantz and Guildenstern, it is a mistake to bring them close to comedy, I think. The text yields no positive evidence that they act in anything other than good faith towards Hamlet, nor does it give grounds for attributing extraordinary foolishness to them for acting in the way they do. It is unnecessary for them to say here what they do say, but we do not have to see them as driven to speak by stupidity. Claudius's lapse into silence would be sufficient motive for a courteous effort not to notice it. Any weakness in what Guildenstern says is more than made up for in the strength of Rosencrantz's lines.

These reflect powerfully on the action of the play as a whole and upon Claudius's situation in particular; the Ghost in the play's very first scene was interpreted by Horatio as a 'spirit upon whose weal depends and rests/The lives of many' and it is the pressure of past events associated with the Ghost which we may detect in the ominous abstraction of the King. There is, then, an eerie quality in the observation that

> The cess of majesty
> Dies not alone, but like a gulf doth draw
> What's near it with it.   (15–17)

Though nominally this is to be applied to Claudius, the words in which it is couched refer us to the Ghost, with whom the idea of a 'strong' majesty is firmly associated—'the majesty of buried Denmark', 'so majestical' (I.1.51,148). Claudius was near that majesty in that he was then the King's brother; the lines that, if he hears them, should assure him of his importance can instead suggest that he will be swept away in the undertow of old Hamlet's death. The 'gulf' that draws 'what's near it with it' evokes the sea outside the castle. Horatio feared that the Ghost might tempt young Hamlet 'toward the flood':

> Or to the dreadful summit of the cliff
> That beetles o'er his base into the sea . . .   (I.4.69–71)

Rosencrantz's words evoke a fleeting glimpse of the death of Claudius ensuing upon that of old Hamlet, as young Hamlet might have disappeared into the sea's gulf upon the track of the Ghost.

This 'gulf' may also be associated with madness. Gertrude later describes her son as 'Mad as the sea and wind', so that an allusion to the young Hamlet may in some fashion hover behind what Rosencrantz says. His madness, involved as it is in the eyes of Claudius and, we may assume, the court with a claim to 'majesty', may cause not only his death but that of the King. Horatio thought the Ghost might 'draw' Hamlet 'into madness', so that there is half an echo of a previous speech here. Madness is further coupled with the sea in Hamlet's 'sea of troubles': Rosencrantz suggests a growing strain upon Claudius's majesty that derives from the very first scene of the play.

I concede, of course, that what I am saying depends on picking up very slight suggestions, but their slightness does not invalidate the point that what Rosencrantz says here summons up a special *frisson* which has to do specifically with the words he uses. No essential point is being made by him that we need to grasp in order to follow the play's narrative; nor is it necessary that the actor should consciously articulate the factors contributing to the effect that he can create. On the other hand, it does help anyone who believes that profundity as well as intensity characterizes the play to see that the effect is not gratuitous, but is organically related to the whole drama.

It would, indeed, be possible to go further in a consideration of this 'gulf' referring it both to that blankness about the play's motivation which Empson[2] imputes to its author's consciousness and to the metaphysical question of what lies beyond consciousness and the relations of this world with the undiscovered country from whose bourn some travellers may, or may not, return. In this scene, however, the most important association of this 'gulf' is with those unuttered thoughts which have drawn the King's attention away from Rosencrantz and Guildenstern, which hold him silent, and which brand him as an actor, a divided person whose words do not cleave to his thoughts, when next he speaks: 'Arm you, I pray you . . .'

The defeat of intellect

The King's soliloquy is prepared for as the self-communing of a man who seeks to regain an integrity of being which we feel should 'naturally' be his: it is the speech of an actor who is trying to put acting on one side. His attempt is not successful, but it is nevertheless impressive in its earnestness when compared with the twists and turns of Hamlet's mind in soliloquy. This contrast is urged upon us not only by the juxtaposition of Claudius in soliloquy with Hamlet also speaking to himself, but by echoes in what he says of Hamlet's own words and also references to Hamlet-associated material. The King's prologue to prayer is one of the most remarkable passages in the play, and I cannot agree with Howard Jacobson that 'the idea of Claudius having a troubled conscience does not appear to excite Shakespeare greatly and he presents it to us in indifferent verse'.[3] Although it lacks the peculiar kind of excitement that we associate with Hamlet's soliloquies, this speech nevertheless does consummately what is required of it. To see how it does this, and how it contributes to the play from which it derives, is to understand that its verse is not 'indifferent' and that poetic drama allows of a greater variety of tone than Howard Jacobson imagines.

The essential quality of the speech is its concentration—not in the sense that it packs a great many meanings into a relatively small space, as is so often the case in *Hamlet*, but in that it expresses the King's attempt to focus upon one object to the exclusion of others: his guilt.

> O, my offence is rank, it smells to heaven;
> It hath the primal eldest curse upon't—
> A brother's murder.　　　　　　　　　　　　　　　(36–8)

When the pronoun of the first person singular enters this speech, it enters as it were reluctantly only because the verb 'pray' must have a subject, and that subject must be 'I': 'Pray can I not'. The grudging quality of this first mention of himself is reinforced by the conditional clause which follows, expressed with an impersonality which would be pathetic were it not (in its sharpness) so painful: 'Though inclination be as sharp as will'. The simple diction and primitively pure sentence-structure are equally expressive of the King's resolve not to be caught up in the sort of sophistry which underlies Hamlet's soliloquies. Indeed, Hamlet's lines on discovering the King at prayer seem deliberately to contrast with the mood of Claudius's speech in the restlessness with which they shift from first person to third and back again, and in the incongruous colloquialism of their diction. There is no concentration here:

> Now might I do it pat, now a is a-praying.
> And now I'll do't.
> > And so a goes to heaven;
> And so am I reveng'd. (73–6)

The abbreviated third-person pronoun is a token of that self-centredness we have seen so often in him.

Claudius is reluctant to speak of himself, rather than of his guilt. He appeals to principles ('Whereto serves mercy . . . '); he talks about himself as though what happens in him is distinct from the self it happens to ('My stronger guilt defeats my strong intent'); he distances himself from himself by simile ('Like a man to double business bound'). All this is a reaction to that abstraction, that loss of himself in himself, at the beginning of the scene.

It is very noticeable that Claudius is here ordering his thoughts. The prominent structure of what he says is not a reflection of Shakespeare's lack of engagement but of the King's struggle to bend 'will' to 'inclination'. We should be conscious of the mind's determination to control its operations that is evidenced in the plain precision of 'double business' or 'twofold force' or the careful counting out of 'those effects for which I did the murder :/My crown, mine own ambition, and my queen'. Macbeth similarly attempts to order his thoughts, though in his case it is to defend himself from the full consciousness of guilt which, a little later, breaks in and defeats his attempt at method: 'He's here in double trust: First, as I am his kinsman and his subject . . . ' (*Macbeth*, I.7.12ff.). Claudius, however, has his imagination on a much tighter rein—hence the simile drained of colour, 'white as snow'—Shakespeare's interest in him is of a different kind. The more Claudius concentrates himself on the promise of redemption that lies beyond his self, the more inevitably he is thrown back upon himself. Macbeth's soliloquy dramatizes the triumph of a guilty imagination; Claudius's is about the defeat of intellect.

This defeat is expressed in the grammatical structure of what he has to say. Despite the simplicity of diction, the lucid syntax and the effort to order and control what is said, the speech is characterized by anxious movement, a movement which derives largely from the exchange of statement and question in the most part of the passage. The statements themselves are not so firm as they seem because they anticipate an assurance that does not come ('O, my offence is rank . . . That can not be . . . 'tis not so above'); they imply the questions which follow them, and which fly in all directions:

> What then? What rests?
> Try what repentance can. What can it not?
> Yet what can it, when one can not repent?
>
> (64–6)

Here, as earlier, when the questions apparently produce an offer of certainty, it proves illusory:

> . . . what's in prayer but this twofold force,
> To be forestalled ere we come to fall,
> Or pardon'd being down? Then I'll look up.
> My fault is past—but O, what form of prayer
> Can serve my turn?   (48–52)

The King's clarity of expression, which is associated with the effort of his intellect to coerce his will, only exposes the conflict inherent to his situation, the depth of guilt from which he cannot free himself, which sits in judgement on him and makes his every action that of an actor. If his speech resolves itself in a series of exclamations it is because the exclamation is initially a verbless form, and cannot command criticism as spurious 'action'; where there is no verb there is no action:

> O wretched state! O bosom black as death!
> O limed soul, that struggling to be free
> Art more engag'd!   (67–9)

Language, as it is a means of communication, is by habit connected with something done—the transfer of information—and the verb is indispensably part of this doing. Claudius's exclamations soon modulate, therefore, first to an imperative addressed beyond him and then to imperatives which are addressed to parts of himself considered as though they were separate from himself:

Help, angels! Make assay.
Bow, stubborn knees; and heart with strings of steel,
Be soft as sinews of the new-born babe. (69–71)

These last commands return us to a problem familiar elsewhere in
the play—that of the relations between mind, soul and body—and
at the same time, graphically representing the interior division of
Claudius, comment on the actorial inauthenticity of the words with
which he falls to his prayer: 'All may be well'.

God's actors

At one point in his soliloquy Claudius becomes eloquent not in his
own desperate fashion, but in that of Hamlet:

In the corrupted currents of this world
Offence's gilded hand may shove by justice,
And oft 'tis seen the wicked prize itself
Buys out the law. But 'tis not so above:
There is no shuffling, there the action lies
In his true nature, and we ourselves compell'd
Even to the teeth and forehead of our faults
To give in evidence. (57–64)

This passage associates itself with 'To be or not to be':

enterprises of great pitch and moment
With this regard their currents turn awry
And lose the name of action.

Currents corrupted are currents turned awry; they falsify the nature
of action which has its name properly only somewhere other than
where the speaker is. 'Shove'[4] belongs with the vocabulary of
physical gesture of which Hamlet is master ('Plucks off my beard
and blows it in my face,/Tweaks me by the nose . . . ' (II.2.568–9);
'crook and pregnant hinges of the knee' (III.2.61); 'Popp'd in between
th' election and my hopes' (V.2.65)) and quickly converts to one
from the soliloquy in question: 'shuffled off this mortal coil'. Beyond
this the attitude to public life, seen as hopelessly corrupt, corresponds
to that part of the speech where Hamlet condemns

> the law's delay,
> The insolence of office, and the spurns
> That patient merit of th'unworthy takes . . .

This is not the only place in this scene where Claudius recalls Hamlet. The most obvious is that where he sees himself to 'stand in pause where first I shall begin', which looks back to 'Pyrrhus' pause' in the player's speech and Hamlet's application of it to himself. We may already have been put in mind of this passage by Rosencrantz's likening of the King to a 'massy wheel', which suggests 'the spokes and fellies' of Fortune's wheel bowling 'down the hill of heaven', invoked by the player following the death of Priam.

The point of these references is not simply ironic. The scene does indeed present us Hamlet at a pause facing Claudius at a pause, both recalling the moment of unheroic pathos in the heroic narrative of Troy; but it leaves us to reflect a good deal more than that life frustrates us in this manner. Hamlet and Claudius are opposites: what happens here is that the opposites both find their likeness in the seemingly authentic and actually inauthentic gestures of an actor. In a play so much concerned with ethical issues on the one hand (revenge, the question of second marriage) and with problems of identity on the other (the question of what it means to Hamlet that he is his father's son), this blurring of opposites must be very disturbing indeed.

It is an unexpected turn in events, and its consequence is just as unexpected. It increases one's sympathy for Hamlet at a point where it seemed that he might forfeit it altogether.

Critics often assume that Hamlet reaches his nadir in this scene. He rejects the opportunity of killing Claudius because he is at prayer and so ready to die; Hamlet wants him to be as unprepared for death as his father was, and to be damned as well as to die. This devotion to revenge is so thoroughgoing as to chill the blood, it is argued. Revenge is an unchristian act; invoking religion in order to intensify the act of revenge makes it more shocking still. One might add to this that Hamlet himself speaks quite cheerfully about the whole matter:

> Then trip him, that his heels may kick at heaven
> And that his soul may be as damn'd and black
> As hell, whereto it goes. My mother stays . . .

(93–5)

The grotesque image of Claudius thrown upside-down is memorably nasty; but it is hardly a convincing sign of Hamlet's unwavering desire for vengeance. On the contrary: by making a joke of the matter it deflects attention from what revenge must entail. It is not the understatement of English sang-froid which would appropriately find the subject of a joke in the idea of postponing an inevitable death. It is more like the bravado with which, later, Hamlet tries to pass off the deaths of Rosencrantz and Guildenstern, a twist to the nature of things that make his precarious poise a little more secure.

In any case, Hamlet's soliloquy is plainly in the mould of 'O what a rogue and peasant slave . . . ', an attempt yet again to give himself the strength to kill Claudius (but not yet, O Lord, not yet). He plays upon himself as he did in calling Claudius names. 'Bloody, bawdy villain!/Remorseless, treacherous, lecherous, kindless villain' is translated to the imagining of the King 'drunk asleep, or in his rage,/Or in th'incestuous pleasure of his bed . . .' It has no more to do with the performance of an act of revenge in the one case than in the other. Hamlet, like the victim he proposes, is merely acting.

This is not by any means a pretty thing to contemplate. Hamlet does not win our sympathy by what he says here, but by the fact that his histrionics are equated with those of Claudius. Authenticity of utterance is achieved by neither Hamlet nor the King; both of them are caught in the trap of wanting to act with absolute commitment to the act, but not to do so at the moment. The inability of Claudius to be master of his own deeds pleads for Hamlet's inability even to identify the deeds which properly he should intend. The idea of the *theatrum mundi*, that 'All the world's a stage', on which men act for the inscrutable benefit of God, is often associated with the play of *Hamlet*, although the possible allusions to it are not many. The persistence with which it appears reflects accurately the force of this scene in which two of God's actors, neither in possession of his part, are shown to us side by side in all the pathos of their ignorance, a pathos fully expressed in the King's concluding couplet:

My words fly up, my thoughts remain below.
Words without thoughts never to heaven go.

These lines apply not only to the King's prayer but to both the scene's soliloquies. Hamlet and Claudius are actors who feel unable to reach their audience, which is simultaneously God and themselves.

A tableau

As the third act of *Hamlet* develops, the meaning which attaches to its characteristic theatricality intensifies as its form changes. We begin with the private drama of Hamlet's great soliloquy and the deflection which that semi-spurious meditation produces in his behaviour to Ophelia, a process held sharply in focus by the scene's framing device. In the 'Mousetrap' scene, however, two forms of theatre compete for our attention, the players' on the one hand, Hamlet's on the other: these two forms are contrasted, the former avowing its own theatricality, but realized by players who are in their public capacity instruments of a private 'plan'; the latter ambiguous in its nature so that we question the extent to which Hamlet is simulating madness rather than suffering it. This contrast checks any possibility of universalizing the idea of theatre; but the spectacle in the following scene of the two opposites, Hamlet and the King, both incapable of authentic utterance or action, forces the point upon us.

In all these scenes, the idea of honour is also important. There is a natural relationship between the life of honour and the theatrical mode, because honour entails a separation of the act from its intent ('a physical affront is a dishonour, regardless of the moral issues involved') and of intention from the act ('To show dishonourable intentions is to be dishonoured regardless of the result'[5]): it cultivates a consciousness of self which turns the events of everyday life into a drama where the actions of others derive their prime significance from what they imply about the status of the person observing, and where that person's actions seek above all to impose upon others his own conception of his status. Shakespeare, however, does not leave us merely to deduce this relationship between honour and theatricality; he makes honour a central concern of the characters in the third act, and allows our view of it to develop in parallel with our understanding of the element of theatre in it.

It should be evident, by now, how he does this in the first two scenes. To begin with, we are encouraged to consider the conflict within Hamlet between the related concepts of honour and honesty; the second scene, however, establishes a rather different conflict between the 'natural' honour of the Player King (the allusions to the seasonal cycle are important in establishing the quality of this concept, as is the union in one figure of a man at once humble, morally and socially, and royal) and the cultivated honour of the revenger, significantly embodied in a man whose own sanity is in doubt. The theme of honour, then, is here enlarged by taking it beyond represent-ation as a conflict within the individual and locating the conflict to which it gives rise explicitly within society and in nature. The third scene adds to this consideration a metaphysical dimension.

God and the individual consciousness are the twin poles of honour. The King rules by the grace of God; he is the fount of honour and upon him depends the social hierarchy which is expressed in varying degrees of ceremonial:

> We can see the hierarchy of honour stretching from its source in God, through a King whose legitimacy depends upon divine sanction, through the ranks of the social structure down to those who had no honour at all, the heretics and the infamous.[6]

God might in a more direct fashion validate a person's honour: Pitt-Rivers reminds us that 'the judicial combats of the Middle Ages and later the duel settled affairs of honour by submitting them to the judgement of Destiny',[7] the last word being mere periphrasis. The attempted extension and consolidation of monarchic privilege in sixteenth-century Europe led, however, as we know, to the dis-appearance of trial by combat and the symbolic outlawry of duelling, and a new emphasis on the 'divinity doth hedge a king' later invoked by Claudius (IV.5.123). Hamlet's uncle conceives of himself, cor-rectly, as in some special relationship to God. He has the outward honour which goes with kingship—crown, queen, and power—but the inward aspect of honour, which we may term indifferently virtue, or the self's approval of its acts, is not there to validate it.

Because there is an outward form of honour, however, the indivi-dual must watch carefully to see that he receives his due and that his own actions do not diminish the degree of honour which he may legitimately claim. Consciousness of honour heightens self-consciousness: a man has to be alert on three fronts at once—the possibility of insult to the physical being requires extreme watchful-ness, the possibility of insult to the spiritual being demands that the judgement also should be in continual play, and in either case the will must be exercised in positive assertion of status.[8] All three aspects of honour as it is focused on the individual are exemplified in Hamlet, the inveterate self-communer and questioner of his will; and the tendency to exclusiveness in the self-consciousness fostered by them appears in the guilelessness with which, in excusing himself from killing the King, he invokes the idea of damnation for Claudius but not for himself.

In the third scene of his third act Shakespeare, then, presents a tableau on the theme of honour, in which neither the God to whom Claudius prays nor the sense of a self claiming satisfaction to which Hamlet appeals can validate the honour apparently within their grasp. This conclusion is as desolating as the earlier one, that neither seemed capable of authentic utterance or action. 'In Calderon's plays the heroes invoke their honour with a standard phrase, *Soy quién soy*, I am who I am',[9] says Pitt-Rivers once more. Neither Claudius nor Hamlet can say that, though they both wish they could. To lack honour is to be without authenticity, to exist only in the fictive world of the actor. The strength of that world is what is to be tested in the following scene.

Sense apoplex'd

Surprisingly, it shows the world of 'theatre' to have more strength than the world of domestic concern and natural affection, as that is represented by the Queen. In the prayer scene a spurious quality emerges from within the King to sap the force of what he says: as he speaks he discovers his own bad faith. In the closet scene the Queen speaks throughout in good faith: she has the authenticity of utterance which Claudius seeks but cannot find. Yet she is overcome by the inauthentic speeches of her son. In this section I shall try to show how this is brought about, and what in this context 'inauthentic' means.

But first it is necessary to show in what way one popular interpretation of the scene's opening is unsatisfactory. This is how Eleanor Prosser represents Hamlet's appearance before his mother and the lines leading up to the death of Polonius:

> . . . he enters the chamber in a mood that Gertrude immediately recognises as murderous. At first, she is merely indignant and adopts the role of scolding parent, but the violence under his sardonic taunts suddenly warns her that she is not safe alone. As she moves to the door to seek help, he drops all pretence and seizes

her roughly, revealing the rage that is seething within him. Gertrude has good reason to believe he is going to kill her and cries out in terror.[10]

The passage can, of course, be played in this manner. Yet the attention paid to staging here is of a fundamentally wrong kind. Prosser describes a scene which is quite consistent with her acceptance of 'Now might I do it pat' at face value. But she achieves this consistency by inventing stage effects that are no necessary implication of the text. Gertrude, for instance, says nothing to suggest that she 'immediately' recognizes her son's mood as 'murderous'. An actress can make us understand that there has been such a recognition by her physical gestures—but the text does not ask her to do so. It is only Eleanor Prosser, with her determination to take Hamlet's words 'at face value', who requires this overlay to the Shakepearean text. In fact the first twenty lines or so of Hamlet's interview with Gertrude are designed to show Hamlet's words—which are, as so often, chosen to define a role—overcoming those of the Queen, which we can indeed take 'at face value', her surfaces revealing completely her depths.

Polonius has told her to 'lay home' to her son, to 'be round with him', and this is just what she does in her first words to Hamlet: 'Hamlet, thou hast thy father much offended'. This is not an anxious line. Hamlet comes to her room in answer to her command, which has a double force as that of a parent and a queen. She feels herself to have the upper hand, and her reproach for that reason may be quite majestically administered. Hamlet's reply is insolently to reproach her: 'Mother, you have my father much offended'.

The form of what Hamlet says here is important. We can describe what he does in two ways, either as appropriating his mother's words to his own use, or as turning them back against her. In either case what matters is his refusal to acknowledge that they share a language. 'Hamlet's father' means one thing to Gertrude, another to Hamlet, and he is intent on maintaining that this makes communication from her to him impossible. He denies that, things being as they are, Gertrude *can* 'be round with him.'

She has reason now to feel indignant, and her indignation is reflected in her words: 'Come, come, you answer with an idle tongue'. She talks as though impatient with a child; Hamlet's tongue is 'idle'—he is merely playing with words, childishly seeking to avert the force of what she says. In her way she is right, but Hamlet adds to his childishness an adult will, which cannot be cowed, as she is trying here to do. He persists in his strategy of appropriation and rejection, this time taking over the form of her line but inverting its content, as a sign of the absolute opposition he maintains to exist between the two of them: 'Go, go, you question with a wicked tongue'.

Is there a 'violence under his sardonic taunts?' The absoluteness of his denying community with Gertrude certainly makes 'violence' a reasonable word to apply here. Whether it is yet of a kind to threaten her physically may be doubted. Certainly it will emerge as a threat in a moment, but it will appear more terrifying as it is sudden. For the time being Hamlet is feigning indifference, denying his mother's authority but not declaring the basis of that denial.

> —Why, how now, Hamlet?
> —What's the matter now?
> —Have you forgot me?   (12–13)

Forgetting is precisely what Hamlet's uneasy state of mind and his failure to act in exorcism of the Ghost's presence will not permit him, and so this question provokes an answer different in quality to the rest:

> No, by the rood, not so.
> You are the Queen, your husband's brother's wife,
> And would it were not so, you are my mother.   (13–15)

One person is both her 'husband's brother's wife' and 'my mother'. The complete distinction that he wants to exist between his language and his mother's breaks down here. In his system he wants only 'so many *things* . . . in equal number of words', but in acknowledging the Queen to be his mother he acknowledges that this is not possible, that the division between them is something that does not really exist.

The Queen thinks that he is at the same game of playing with language, however: she feels defeated by him, and makes to go for others 'that can speak' to him. She moves because, though Hamlet deprives her of a voice, she is not willing to abdicate authority over him, an authority which his 'pranks' so far in the scene will incline her to enforce. There is no hint that she fears for her life. But her action prompts a corresponding move on his part—he seizes her and imposes his own will on hers: 'You go not . . . ' At the same time he intends to assert himself over the language they share, by turning it into a mirror, 'a glass/Where you may see the inmost part of you'. His phrase recalls the 'mirror up to nature' and warns us that words are no less ambiguous for being used by someone who is an actor, choosing here the role of tutor to his own mother.

Indeed, at the moment he proposes to make words mere reflectors of the 'truth' about his mother, Hamlet by his action reveals himself as a person, as a *subject*, whose objectivity may be questioned—first by the speech with which he asserts his power over his mother, and then by the immediacy with which he answers Polonius's cry with a thrust through the arras. Surely the effect intended here is one of contrast with the previous assumed indifference, Hamlet jumping to an erratic and dangerous life, dangerous because erratic. 'There seems no reason to doubt that he believes he is stabbing the King',[11] writes Eleanor Prosser, but the reverse is true. 'Nay, I know not. Is it the King?' gives us every reason for this doubt. The act by which he kills Polonius is indeed 'rash' ('Hasty, impetuous, reckless, acting without due consideration or regard for consequences', says the *OED*), and 'I know not' says as much. The thought that it might be the King could come after the event as a means of giving it meaning which it really lacks, or it could be imagined, as Prosser imagines it, really informing the deed. The doubt is important because once again we recognize an underlying question about mind-body relations: was it Hamlet who killed Polonius, or was it merely his body acting in dissociation from his mind?

From this point on in the scene we are, I think, uncertain whether there is a person called Hamlet who can authenticate what he says as 'really' felt by him. At the same time, this uncertainty leaves Gertrude without a son to admonish in the straightforward way she had planned: she becomes his audience and a spectator trying to make sense of the show he puts forward—'Alas, he's mad.' (106). It is a frightening show and one that truly chastens its witness, but if Hamlet's words are like daggers to her, they are so not merely for what they say about her relations with Claudius but for what they imply that she has done to Hamlet in consequence of those relations. 'O Hamlet, thou hast cleft my heart in twain' (158)—one half is his, the other belongs to Claudius, and she now concedes, too late, the impracticality of such an arrangement. Indeed, it was not merely impractical—it was wrong:

Thou turn'st my eyes into my very soul,
And there I see such black and grained spots
As will not leave their tinct.   (89–91)

Though Hamlet wants her guilt to arise solely from the fact of her remarriage, this is not the guilt she admits to feeling. Nowhere in this scene does she disown her marriage to Claudius, and we think she does so only if we see a Hamlet more like Eleanor Prosser's than Shakespeare's. Her guilt is at once more comprehensive and more particular than that, provoked by the thought of the weakness which is common to all men and which in her has brought about this decline in her son, and by the 'madness' which he demonstrates before her and which never ceases to be her concern throughout the scene. In her guilt, the world of 'theatre' defeats the world of domestic concern. Hamlet defeats Gertrude, because his speech is mere 'rhapsody' and sense cannot make sense of nonsense. At the same time, Gertrude does have responsibility for her son's condition, and it is her recognition of this responsibility that makes her helpless to act. Furthermore, the cause of all her troubles lies indeed in 'sense', the physical fulfilment of her love for Claudius. That love's ambiguous nature, its vulnerability to interpretation as lust, its elusiveness, its inseparable link with human frailty as well as strength, lies behind Hamlet's assertion that 'sure that sense Is apoplex'd', accounts for the paralysis (apoplexy) of the Queen's good sense here, and calls back our sympathy for the tormented Hamlet at the moment he needs it most. A moral paralysis—but also physical as far as the killing of the King is concerned—is, after all, the prince's special mark in this play.

True colour

A critical moment in the history of Hamlet's moral paralysis is recorded in 'To be or not to be'. The violence with which he turns upon Ophelia in the same scene comes as a sort of relief to his frustration, just as here the manhandling of his mother and the murder of Polonius strike one primarily as a means of relieving the tension in himself arising from his failure to kill Claudius. His treatment of his mother in what ensues parallels his behaviour to Ophelia, and suggests that Hamlet's antifeminism has a specific meaning for him: it is not merely what characterizes an assumed role. Our consciousness that Hamlet is satisfying two very different impulses in what he says to Gertrude heightens our sense of it as inauthentic speech. I shall consider it first in the light of dramatic role devised with Gertrude in mind. In the next section I look at the private satisfactions available in it for Hamlet.

It is certainly the speech of an actor. This is made clear to us in many ways. For one thing, he shouts. The Queen remarks on the noise he makes. Hamlet, it seems, 'roars . . . and thunders' mouthing his speech 'as many of our players do'. Hamlet is in effect tearing 'a passion to tatters, to very rags'. Johnson's gloss on Hamlet's description of his own conduct as 'laps'd in time and passion' at line 108 as 'having suffered time to slip and passion to cool' misses the theatrical associations of 'passion' in this play, and is in any case implausible in this scene, where Hamlet's action is above all impassioned. The line should be understood in the light of Hamlet's histrionic delivery of his advice to his mother. It says that he is at fault with regard to his delay in time and his weakness for theatricals.

He thinks both of himself and of others in terms of the theatre. The Ghost's reproachful gaze is warded off in these terms:

> Do not look upon me,
> Lest with this piteous action you convert
> My stern effects. Then what I have to do
> Will want true colour—tears perchance for blood.
> (127–30)

Hamlet returns here to the idea that his physical 'effects' are not entirely under his control, a thought which implicitly impugns his honour and which in itself would be enough to give the play a metaphysical dimension. At the same time the word 'colour' draws attention to the element of art required to master these 'effects'; the art being, of course, dramatic. The singular achievement of the first player is manifest in his ability to make his physical organs work as directed by the will: 'Look whe'er he has not turned his colour and has tears in's eyes' (II.2.515–16). The word is associated with another more complex piece of role-playing when Polonius hands Ophelia a book to read before her meeting with Hamlet, 'That show of such an exercise may colour/Your loneliness' (III.1.45). The two senses of 'colour', physical complexion and outward show, exemplified by these quotations are both at work in what Hamlet says of himself. His description of Claudius as 'a vice of kings . . . A king of shreds and patches', the latter perhaps alluding to the fool's motley, is, then, a natural extension of the consciousness of himself as playing a part implicit in the form of what Hamlet says as well as its content.

The form is conspicuously rhetorical from the very opening of the attack:

> Leave wringing of your hands. Peace, sit you down,
> And let me wring your heart . . . (34–5)

and this elaborate mode is maintained in the parallel construction of 'Such an act/That blurs. . . Calls. . . takes off. . . makes. . . O, such a deed as . . . plucks . . . ' and in the rhetorical device of contrasting the pictures of the Queen's two husbands, a device which is equally effective whether or not any pictures are visible. From this, Hamlet launches into a succession of rhetorical questions: 'Have you eyes? . . . Could you. . . batten on this moor? Ha, have you eyes? . . . what judgment/Would step from this to this? . . . What devil was't/That thus hath cozen'd you . . . ? O shame, where is thy blush?' The conspicuously artificial construction of what he says surely needs no further illustration. The Ghost's appearance does, indeed, put Hamlet off his stride, so that his speech becomes momentarily less deliberated in form, but he soon picks up the thread of rhetoric:

> It is not madness
> That I have utter'd. Bring me to the test,
> And I the matter will re-word, which madness
> Would gambol from. Mother, for love of grace,
> Lay not that flattering unction to your soul,
> That not your trespass but my madness speaks . . . (143–8)

The cadenced antithesis, so to speak, of 'trespass' and 'madness' marks Hamlet's resumption of his role. The colours of rhetoric are paradoxically an integral part of the prince's attempt to give what he has to do 'true colour'.

The superficial and willed nature of this colouring is suggested, along with its deep-rooted and personal quality, in those lines where Gertrude's shameful 'act'—one is inclined to wonder whether its very quality of being an action might not be its most shameful aspect

in the eyes of Hamlet—is denounced in terms not merely of doomsday but also of complexion:

> Heaven's face does glow
> O'er this solidity and compound mass
> With heated visage, as against the doom,
> Is thought-sick at the act. (48–51)

The 'colour' of a 'heated visage' shows blood, but 'the pale cast of
thought' is not far from these lines pregnant with contradiction.
Hamlet grandiloquently associates himself with heaven in his anger,
but his anger is self-destructive: the judgement of doomsday will
destroy the material universe, 'this solidity and compound mass',
but with it all faces that are capable of glowing. Hamlet's flesh is 'too
too solid' as well as 'sullied', and is part of the very mass that
judgement is passed upon even though he himself passes judgement
only on Claudius: his thought-sickness derives from his consciousness of this, that to be heaven's scourge and minister is to be punished
as well as to punish. If his face and heaven's face are alike, they are
alike in their material aspect[12] and heaven is merely part of the
physical universe, 'this brave o'erhanging firmament . . . a foul and
pestilent congregation of vapours' (II.2.300–3), all theological force
drained from it. The fire that glows within these sultry and menacing
lines is that sinister flame which burns in the lines with which
Hamlet prompts the first player to speak of Troy:

> Roasted in wrath and fire,
> And thus o'ersized with coagulate gore,
> With eyes like carbuncles, the hellish Pyrrhus
> Old grandsire Priam seeks (II.2.457–60)

The glow in heaven's face marks Hamlet out as liable, like Pyrrhus,
to the gods' indignation; shows him effortfully emulating the first
player's 'passion', searching for a 'true colour' for his inward nature;
and betrays him in his invocation of heaven as merely natural, a
sublunar being ultimately to suffer bodily destruction.

Excitements of my reason and my blood

Hamlet's dual role as the author and the actor of his own script gives
his words a treacherous quality. They are designed by someone who

has no clear conception of himself: of whether, for example, his nature is distinct from that of his father or not. His role-playing seems to satisfy a need in him not merely to keep others at a distance, in the capacity of an amazed audience, but also to discover himself deviously. The passage just discussed is an illustration of this, since it combines a vivid imagining of the shame to be felt by the righteous in the face of Gertrude's remarriage with Hamlet's own feelings of frustration and shame at the fact of his encumbered and divided life in the body. It is by no means the only example in the scene of Hamlet's way of talking about himself when he talks about his mother.

He speculates on her motives for abandoning his father for Claudius in terms which, similarly, apply to himself, and which also express that concern with the body and its ability to act independently of mind which surfaces in the phrase 'true colour' and in the doubt about what Hamlet was doing when he killed Polonius:

> You cannot call it love; for at your age
> The heyday in the blood is tame, it's humble,
> And waits upon the judgment, and what judgment
> Would step from this to this? Sense sure you have,
> Else could you not have motion; but sure that sense
> Is apoplex'd, for madness would not err,
> Nor sense to ecstasy was ne'er so thrall'd
> But it reserv'd some quantity of choice
> To serve in such a difference. (III.4.68–76)

The last lines of this passage have given editors great difficulty, often a sign that the language is ambiguous. This is obviously true of the word 'sense'. The range of meaning in this word, which can refer to bodily sensation or to a faculty of mind, has been glanced at earlier,[13] and it is plain that there is a shift from one aspect to another in the uses of it in lines 71–2. There are, however, two other words here to which a similar ambiguity attaches. A 'motion' may signify physical and observable movement, but not necessarily so. Shakespeare often uses it to describe an impulse within the mind, even an 'emotion'. Jenkins's citation of Aristotle cannot of itself delimit the meaning here. The word has been interpreted in either sense by commentators. 'Ecstasy' has, on the other hand, generally been glossed simply as 'madness'—Jenkins says 'state of hallucination' here, but glosses it 'madness' at line 140. This meaning is not clear-cut, however. The *OED* offers a general comment on the word's development from Greek:

> The classical senses of 'ἐκστασισ are 'insanity' and 'bewilder-ment'; but in late Greek the etymological meaning 'being put out of place' received another application, viz., 'withdrawal of the soul from the body, mystic or prophetic trance'; hence in later medical writers the word is used for 'trance', etc., generally. Both the classical and post-classical senses came into the modern languages, and in the present figurative uses they seem to be blended.

There seem, then, to be three meanings for the word hovering in Hamlet's use: a kind of bodily paralysis, madness (temporary loss of the reasoning power that commands the limbs), withdrawal of the soul from the body. The sentence in this passage is equivocally constructed. 'Ecstasy' may be a mere repetition of the idea of 'mad-ness' or it may be contrasted with it, implying a withdrawal of the soul rather than a confusion of the wits. Ophelia's account of Hamlet's visit to her, with Polonius's exclamation 'This is the very ecstasy of love', has already prepared us to receive the idea of the soul's separ-ation from the body.

These ambiguities make it very difficult to give the kind of clear paraphrase of the passage that editors prefer. It simply is not clear what Hamlet is trying to say, and this is so despite the apparently logical construction of his sentences. Nevertheless it is not a flaw in Shakespeare's art that Hamlet's thought is here obscure.[14] The mean-ingless repetition of '*reserv'd* some quantity of choice/*To serve*. . .' as much as tells us that Hamlet is meant to be seen as entangled in his own speech here. Furthermore, the subject-matter of the speech as it is announced in its key-words—'blood', 'judgement', 'sense', 'mad-ness', 'thrall'd', 'choice'—is sufficient explanation for his excitement and his oblique form of utterance. These words all stand for matters that concern and perplex him, though here he tries to cast them on his mother. The word 'ecstasy', the idea of 'madness', the idea of 'sense', do actually pass in this scene from being applied to Gertrude to sticking close to Hamlet, whose insistent denials—'I essentially am not in madness'—only confirm the force with which they stick. The change in Hamlet's tone from reproach of his mother to self-justification is not merely persuasive in dramatic terms: as a consequence of the Ghost's unexpected appearance it is also revelatory of the quality of Hamlet's reproach. In attacking his mother, Hamlet attacks the weak and 'feminine' part of himself, the part of him that does not share his father's 'nature', and which leaves him more than one 'drop of blood that's calm'. If he reproaches her for her lack of 'love' it is because his own love for his father may be questioned so long as Claudius lives. And so on.

A body possessed

Hamlet's 'rhapsody', then, depends on his being able to see Gertrude as someone existing in her own right, independent of him, who nevertheless stands for something in him. The body is referred to frequently in the closet scene not merely because Hamlet accuses Gertrude of allowing her 'reason' to be overruled by her sexual instinct, but because the body is what holds Gertrude and her son in a special relationship, one that Hamlet resents at the same time as he acknowledges it, and which at the start of the play leads him to regret that there is a 'canon 'gainst self-slaughter'. When Hamlet instructs his mother: 'Do not spread the compost on the weeds/To make them ranker', his words recall—and surely not by chance—the first soliloquy:

> Fie on't, ah fie, 'tis an unweeded garden
> That grows to seed; things rank and gross in nature
> Possess it merely.   (I.2.135–7)

The equivocal nature of Hamlet's response to the physical link of kinship with Gertrude is reflected in the way he mingles condemnation of the coming together of Claudius and his queen 'in the rank sweat of an enseamed bed' with turns of phrase, like those concerning 'sense', 'ecstasy' and 'motion', which open out into the mystery of mind and body relations and so tend to mitigate the offence he feels.

His mother's remarriage is 'such a deed/As from the body of contraction plucks/The very soul', and the words seem meant to damn; but the idea of body without soul in this play, spoken by this man, is disturbingly complex and thus reduces its force in simple attack, as here. Hamlet is too much concerned with bodies, too little concerned with souls; his own body seems to act without relation to mind and here he could be thinking of the debt of honour felt in his own body ('the body of contraction', engagement to his father's memory) and the general paralysis and incoherence registered there. His language in this scene is emphatically the language of sensation rather than that of reason:

> Eyes without feeling, feeling without sight,
> Ears without hands or eyes . . .

This bizarre and horrific imagining of a disordered body is followed by the evocation of heat and cold intensely felt, which, whilst it attributes force to sexual desire, also naturalizes it. It is no moral issue that fire burns:

> Rebellious hell,
> If thou can'st mutine in a matron's bones,
> To flaming youth let virtue be as wax
> And melt in her own fire; proclaim no shame
> When the compulsive ardour gives the charge,
> Since frost itself as actively doth burn
> And reason panders will.   (82–8)

Plainly, Hamlet's intention is to be ironic, but what is he being ironic about? The Riverside editors gloss: 'do not call it sin when the hot blood of youth is responsible for lechery, since here we see people of calmer age on fire for it', which makes good sense, but is startlingly different from what is actually said. Does 'frost' really mean, for example, 'people of calmer age'? Surely Hamlet has Gertrude specifically in mind, though we have difficulty in making the connection because Gertrude has seemed throughout a very unfrosty woman: he is here implying that she was a paragon of chastity in his father's lifetime, but the term he uses is in its absoluteness discomforting. He wants to be ironic about Gertrude, but as so often with Hamlet he falls into an extreme position, and his language betrays him. He wants to say something like 'The paragon of cold chastity now burns with all the fires of lust', but actually comes out with a truism: 'Frost burns'. It does. For an effective irony against his mother 'since' ought to mean 'now that'—'now that the frost itself blazes away like fire'—but the words which follow it do not allow any sense of novelty in the idea of frost-burn, and so it has to mean a flat 'because': 'because even frost can burn and cause the same pain as fire'. The result is not so much that irony leaks away from the sentence as that its object becomes, not Gertrude, but the whole world of sense where, come hot or cold, equally shameless acts must be suffered by those who, like the Queen, feel a 'compulsive ardour' and those who, like Hamlet, are all 'frost', cold in the performance of tasks which should fire them.[15] What comes through most forcefully is Hamlet's loathing for the body which ties him to his task of vengeance. Imaginatively he suffers that body as in a kind of fever, burning for the most part, and passing swiftly from 'fire' to 'frost'. (It is a sign of how little his mother understands him that her advice to him 'Upon the heat and flame of thy distemper/Sprinkle cool patience' sounds more likely to increase a fever than allay it.)

Our awareness that Hamlet's body weighs on him oppressively is enhanced not only by the sublime unconsciousness of any war between body and soul that allows the Queen to look into her very soul and see 'black and *grained* spots there' but also by the appearance of the Ghost. Its function is not merely to set the play back on the rails of plot; it is required as part of a family tableau, father and mother in their separate existences (he cannot make himself visible to her, she cannot see him—the symbolism is apt, unaffected and powerful), each deeply concerned in the life of the body (he cannot hold away from this world and his knowledge of it, she does not want to deny her desire for Claudius) before the tormented body-sense of their son. The First Quarto stage direction which puts the Ghost in its nightgown is appropriate because it is based on a sense of occasion inappropriate in any spirit truly divorced from the body. As for the Ghost's words, they show how concern for and knowledge of the body deflect its attention from its proper object:

> But look, amazement on thy mother sits.
> O, step between her and her fighting soul.
> Conceit in weakest bodies strongest works.　　　　　　　　(112–4)

The last line fits Hamlet far better than his mother, and it is no surprise that moments later *he* is the one whose 'ecstasy' is under discussion. There is potential comedy here, which is kept in check only by the poignancy and terror of Hamlet's own doubletalk, by the shock of the Ghost's own appearance, and by the intensity of concern shown by all three characters.

One of the effects of the Ghost's entry is, of course, to upstage Hamlet. Its appearance is a moment of 'theatre' sufficiently strong to

halt the prince halfway through his sentence. It is remarkable, therefore, that Hamlet's theatrical mode nevertheless triumphs in the
scene as a whole, and it is worth seeing how this is done: like
Gertrude, I think, the Ghost is defeated by its sense of guilt. Hamlet is
able to reassume the stage because the other two characters are
without the wish to compete.

The Queen's guilt is evident, though the significance of her not
conceding the substance of Hamlet's case is not generally recognized.
The Ghost's is given away in its demeanour. 'It steals away': we do
not need to remember Iago on Cassio, 'That he would steal away so
guilty-like' (*Othello* III.3.40) to get the force of that, but it may help.
Exeter attempts to *steal away* from the angry Queen Margaret in *3
Henry VI* (I.1.219), where also it is said that the King 'slily stole away
and left his men' (I.1.3); when Bertram tries to use it positively
(echoing Parolles) in *All's Well* (II.1.29,33) he is ludicrous. Only
Helena in the same play can use it with dignity—'For with the dark,
poor thief, I'll steal away' (3.2.129)—because her heroism consists in
humility and surviving the worst by facing it for what it is. Her
motives are clear: the Ghost's motives for stealing away are not.
Why does it not stay longer and speak more? The answer must surely
lie in what the Queen and Hamlet say after it has spoken. Two things
emerge in this: the unmanly disorder in Hamlet's physical person
('Forth at your eyes your spirits wildly peep') and the Queen's
inability to see the figure of the Ghost. If we view the ghost as a
devilish manifestation, both revelations may be regarded as satisfactory. Hamlet in his weakness is evidently nearer to destruction
than at the play's beginning, and the symbolic impact of the Queen's
failure to see the Ghost shows an enclosure in her own world which
seems likely to bring her harm. If, however, we regard the Ghost as
in some sense 'really' Hamlet's father, the effect is stronger and more
convincing: son and mother, by their different reactions, say that the
Ghost is out of place here. His concern for the life of the body,
whether his own ('All my smooth body') or that of others, is
shocking as well as pathetic; it is not proper in those who have no
bodies. The Ghost's stealing away signifies the shameful acknowledgement of this proposition by what was Hamlet's father. The
adverse comment on the artifice of 'honour' is apparent: the Ghost's
dramatic entry cannot by sustained; it has to crumble, and at last,
here, it does. Of course it would be more 'effective' for us not to see

the Ghost but only to hear him, but this 'effect' would be won at the cost of something vital to the play.

One phrase in what the Queen says seems to me especially pertinent to this. She says that her son's 'bedded hair, like life in excrements,/Start up and stand an end' (121–2)—a dishonouring action of the body, because uncontrolled. The simile 'like life in excrements' needs special consideration. *Excrement* is a word with two distinct etymologies, one based on the Latin *excrescere*, 'to grow out', which gives us the sense preferred by editors—Jenkins among them—of 'excrescence', used especially of hair, nails and feathers; the other based on the Latin *excernere*, 'to sift out', giving us meanings like 'lees' and 'faeces'. Because the etymologies are distinct the two forms of the word are kept separate in dictionaries, but it is unlikely that this can have been the case in life. I think it is fair to assume that one sense has been contaminated by another here, so that the Queen implies not merely 'as though hair had a life of its own' but 'as though there were life in what has been cast away' (*OED* cites 'certain excrements and outcasts of the world' from the 1560s). Hamlet does not just look as though he is seeing a ghost, he looks *like* the kind of ghost that comes back in its own body, as in 'The Wife of Usher's Well', and as, it was suggested by Hamlet himself (I.4.47ff.), might be the case with the Ghost that plagues him here. There is a double idea of illegitimate possession, Hamlet senior's Ghost assuming his cast-off body, and some form of 'life' that is not his own possessing Hamlet's hair. Hamlet might here say of his father,

> Thy natural magic and dire property
> On wholesome life usurps immediately.   (III.2.253–4)

And indeed, the Ghost is right from the start seen as a usurper:

> What art thou that usurp'st this time of night,
> Together with that fair and warlike form
> In which the majesty of buried Denmark
> Did sometimes march?   (I.1.49–52)

Horatio's intuition was correct; and Hamlet senior now may 'steal away' 'guilty-like' because his sense of honour has entailed a kind of usurpation of his son's life.

The actor who plays from thought

When Hamlet asserts that his body is ordered in normal fashion, then, he is not merely rejecting the suggestion of 'ecstasy'. He is maintaining his ability to act in his own person:

> My pulse as yours doth temperately keep time,
> And makes as healthful music.   (III.4.142–3)

No 'heyday in the blood' here; and for that reason the lines are moving, the body whose pulse is 'temperate' seeming to be especially vulnerable in this scene when consciousness of the body is, more often than not, feverish and oppressed. A moment of release is envisaged. Yet it is a false release. Neither Hamlet nor the Queen is in a situation where it would be natural for the pulse to beat in ordinary fashion. A proper sense of this incongruity modifies our sense of the lines as a whole.

But how should the actor express this incongruity? Should he intemperately shout out Shakespeare's lines, giving them the un-healthful music of the madness which the words deny? I think not. There is a change in the quality of Hamlet's speeches after the Ghost has left the stage, and it bears directly on what he says here. For although Hamlet continues to speak as an actor and in this way keeps the upper hand of the 'merely natural' Gertrude, his rhetoric does have a superficially more healthful music now. The units of sense within each speech are shorter, more manageable: they do not depend on the intense feeling which hangs clause after clause on to one conjunction, as we have seen in the scene's first part ('That blurs the grace . . .' and so on for six clauses and seven and a half lines, 'for at your age . . .' for four clauses in three lines, 'for madness would not err . . .' for another three clauses in three lines—these effects, of course, reinforcing that of the catalogue which arises from looking at this picture, and on this). There is a measure audible in Hamlet's words now:

> Confess yourself to heaven,
> Repent what's past, avoid what is to come;
> And do not spread the compost on the weeds
> To make them ranker.   (151–4)

It is even possible to speak of this in terms of balance. The speech is just as highly coloured and rhetorical as before, but now each sentence stops when its point is made:

> It will but skin and film the ulcerous place,
> Whiles rank corruption, mining all within,
> Infects unseen. (149–51)

Even if we consider these lines to be entirely directed outward to the Queen (and that is a difficult point of view to take), we must admit that there is no lingering on the nastiness beyond what is required to arouse repugnance. The 'music' is healthful, though its substance is not.

Control being the note of Hamlet's speech in the latter part of the scene, it would be a mistake, then, for him to speak of his temperate pulse without that control. The line preludes the disturbing and significant development in the scene, Hamlet's rededication to his part. In Diderot's 'Paradoxe sur le Comédien', two kinds of actor are distinguished. They correspond to the two kinds of acting we can witness here in Hamlet: from the 'players who play from the heart', says the first speaker in this classic dialogue,

> you must expect no unity. Their playing is alternately strong and feeble, fiery and cold, dull and sublime. Tomorrow they will miss the point they have excelled in today; and to make up for it they will excel in some passage where last time they failed. On the other hand, the actor who plays from thought, from study of human nature, from constant imitation of some ideal type, from imagination, from memory, will be one and the same at all performances, will be always at his best mark . . . [16]

Hamlet's changed style affirms his redefinition of himself as an actor.

However, this redefinition is not to be regarded as secure. His control is dangerously near slipping when he starts to talk about the King's sexual advances. This is hardly surprising. Nevertheless, the ironic tone and use of caricature maintain an effortful distance between him and his words here: he is able to bring this account of his loathed stepfather to his own conclusion. Much more perilous to his new-won poise is the moment when he comes to speak in praise of 'custom' to his mother. In I.4 he had sought to exorcise the 'habit' which he saw as a weakness in himself. But now 'custom', a 'monster . . . who all sense doth eat' (this phrase, of course, using the ambiguous quality of 'sense', meaning both 'which devours our decent feelings' and 'which is greedily incorporated in the life of our fleshly feeling') is also an 'angel',

> That to the use of actions fair and good
> . . . likewise gives a frock or livery
> That aptly is put on . . .
> For use almost can change the stamp of nature . . .
>
> (163ff.)

and that is what Hamlet, his 'nature' having once again failed him at the Ghost's appearance, needs most of all. Because a custom is a habit, and a habit is clothing ('frock or livery'), Hamlet speaks as though accustomization were an external and voluntary procedure —like acting. His leniency to his mother is in keeping, that is, with the new chance he is giving himself in acting 'from thought' rather than 'from the heart'. Its angelic quality is suspect, since it works from the outside in rather than as an essence, from the inside out; it represents a misapplication of 'thought' and a masking of his own problems from himself, as comparison with the passage in I.4 suggests. But the difficult moment passes: and he becomes more and more confident in the part he has to play.

> I must be cruel only to be kind.
> This bad begins, and worse remains behind.   (180–1)

The fact that Hamlet cannot bring himself to leave the stage when he has provided himself with a fine exit line illustrates the willed quality of his confidence, but does not undermine it. By the time he really is ready to go, the mask has been perfectly fashioned:

> Let it work;
> For 'tis the sport to have the enginer
> Hoist with his own petard, and't shall go hard
> But I will delve one yard below their mines
> And blow them at the moon.   (207–11)

The relation to life here is all attitude, all exterior, and nothing penetrates. The real Rosencrantz and Guildenstern are shockingly apart from the supposed mining operation; indeed, it is Hamlet who mines within his mask, and so 'infects unseen' Elsinore with the body of Polonius whom 'you shall nose . . . as you go up the stairs into the lobby' (IV.3.36–7).

The third act of *Hamlet* describes a sequence of events by which the prince is made into a deliberating actor. The final transformation is effected, paradoxically (and there is some symbolic appropriateness in this), at the moment of the Ghost's defeat; but whether it is motivated in Hamlet by desire to emulate his father or by mere self-despair this most gripping scene does not declare. That question leads us to Act Four.

10 Burlesque, parody and fugue

Breaking up

The seven scenes which in modern editions make up the fourth act of *Hamlet* do have a coherence of their own, although in this imperfect world, naturally, it is a disputed one. The third act has at its centre the play-within-the-play, Hamlet's spurious attempt to solve the problem posed him by the Ghost. In the two scenes following the performance of 'The Mousetrap' he is brought face to face with his own failure. He is unable to kill the King; he is unable to exercise authority over his mother. Yet he refuses to admit the failure that confronts him, and in so doing is overtaken by his madness. He goes to pieces. The fourth act mirrors this process in its accelerated rhythm and fantastic content. It too 'breaks up'.

The closet scene, though it lacks the great length of II.2 or III.3, is nevertheless a long one, the continuous nature of whose action is enhanced by the intensity of Hamlet's encounter with his mother. By contrast, the four scenes that follow are short—forty-five, thirty-one, sixty-eight and sixty-six lines successively, in contrast to the preceding two-hundred-and-seventeen. The contrast is not merely accidental. The brevity of these scenes establishes a restless stage rhythm; the audience sees the stage emptied and filled five times in an interval not much longer than the closet scene itself. It is as though Hamlet's interview results in a general restlessness in Elsinore. It certainly does so in him; the game of hide-and-seek which he plays with Rosencrantz and Guildenstern is a consequence of the scene with his mother in that it thrives on the nervous tension that led her to detect 'ecstasy' in him, as well as in that it serves to mitigate the aspect of deliberate threat to the King in his killing of Polonius. Hamlet leads the courtiers a dance, but the courtiers are representatives in this of the King: he is even more vitally concerned in Hamlet's actions than they are, and his impatience and flustered condition ('O Gertrude, come away . . . Come, Gertrude . . . O come away,/My soul is full of discord and dismay' (IV.1.28,38,44–5) find a physical equivalent in the anxious comings and goings of Rosencrantz and Guildenstern. Hamlet's removal from Elsinore does not end the turbulent sequence of the fourth act; his encounter with Fortinbras's captain, the only scene set beyond the confines of the court, 'breaks out' beyond the play's established compass at this point, and is followed by Laertes's threat to the King's security, where the play seems set to follow an altogether new line of narrative. The fourth act as a whole, then, reflects impatience, uncertainty and incoherence, and extravagance of mood stemming from Hamlet's madness but going beyond it. In this act, Hamlet's situation generalizes itself: he is caught in the same trap as the King, as Fortinbras and as Laertes.

In the first scene, for example, the King identifies himself with Hamlet at the very moment when he is working to put the greatest distance possible between him and his stepson. He says of Polonius's death to his Queen:

> Alas, how shall this bloody deed be answer'd?
> It will be laid to us, whose providence
> Should have kept short, restrain'd, and out of haunt
> This mad young man. But so much was our love,
> We would not understand what was most fit,
> But like the owner of a foul disease,
> To keep it from divulging, let it feed
> Even on the pith of life.   (16–23)

What is uncanny about these lines is our sense that in them the King is doing two things at once. At the more obvious level he is presenting a case to Gertrude for the action he has taken in regard to her son. He argues that, given equal opportunity, Hamlet could have killed him rather than Polonius. He might kill anyone, even his mother or his stepfather. Furthermore the two of them are endangered by what he has already done, because the responsibility for his deeds will be laid at *their* door. This is all justification for the plan to send Hamlet to England and for the haste with which it is to be executed; Gertrude's reply, dwelling on the pathos rather than the horror of her son's madness ('a weeps for what is done'), shows that some attempt to make the King's action palatable to her was necessary.

At another level, however, the King is talking with himself about his own guilt. The phrase with which he opens, 'O heavy deed', recalls directly the exclamation 'O heavy burden!' with which he concluded his first admission of guilt in the third act, and also the exclamations of his frustrated prayer: 'O wretched state! O bosom black as death!' The 'bloody deed' for which he has to answer now is the act by which he gained the crown; it was his love for Gertrude that was so great that he 'would not understand what was most fit', and he is 'like the owner of a foul disease' in that he cannot 'divulge' the secret of his guilt, which feeds on his very life. This secondary layer of meaning gives conviction to the first.

The two layers are not distinct from one another. Hamlet must at all times be to Claudius a visible reminder of the guilty means by which he gained the throne. This will be so whether or not the King believes Hamlet to have penetrated his secret. It would suit him better really to believe in Hamlet's madness, as this speech suggests, because then the prince might stand not only for the King's own guilt, but also for a possible escape from that guilt. Hamlet's madness might then signify for Claudius a 'disease' of his own, one which drove him to kill his brother, but which, as a disease, could exonerate him from blame. If Claudius were diseased, all that he need seek now is a 'cure' for his disease instead of the penitence and the forgiveness from heaven which were not forthcoming. The 'cure' is to be effected, he hopes, by Hamlet's death in England:

> Do it, England;
> For like the hectic in my blood he rages,
> And thou must cure me.   (IV.3.65–7)

For Claudius, the distinction between vehicle and tenor which resides in the single word 'like' is obliterated: Hamlet *is* the hectic in his blood; he *is* his foul disease. This failure on his part to respect logical categories is, however, itself a symptom of disease, 'the hectic', a fever that 'rages' in the blood and leads him not merely to act but also to think with a 'fiery quickness' (IV.3.43) that jumps over such distinctions.

Hamlet's madness is, then, the cause of the King's restlessness in two senses: in that it presents him, in the death of Polonius, with a practical and external problem; and in that it is a reflection of something within the King, the madness that led him to kill for the crown. This inner madness is ambiguous; as a disease of the body it may absolve the King from guilt, though as a disease of the soul it cannot. Claudius is caught up here in toils we have seen elsewhere, those of the mind–body relationship. His confusion is apparent in the way the 'foul disease' from which he suffers may be identified grammatically with 'our love' (IV.1.19)—an irony to which we must understand him oblivious. He is equally confused in the belief that Hamlet's death can 'cure' him—if Hamlet is in his blood, then Hamlet's death will be joined with his, as indeed is the case at the end of the play.

In all this the essential point is the association of the King's condition with Hamlet's madness, which puts them on a level— neither is perfectly in control of himself, both are victims of delusion, each is made a little less than himself in this approximation. Hamlet's case begins to generalize itself; Claudius shares with him his sense of the body as encumbrance and disease, his inner solitude (Gertrude cannot be imagined to understand the force of his utterance at all) and his uncertain understanding of his own situation as well as his 'madness'. The result is not, however, to assure us of an emergent 'meaning' in the play; rather, we are threatened by the encroachment of Hamlet's perplexities in the world of the Court, which threatens to break up, rather than to consolidate, as a desperate king attempts 'by desperate appliance' (IV.3.10) to cure his own disease.

The natural body

Gertrude describes Hamlet's madness to Claudius in terms of natural phenomena; he is

> Mad as the sea and wind, when both contend
> Which is the mightier. (IV.1.7–8)

The words concede the danger which he represents, but carry a mute plea: sea and wind cannot be blamed for the damage they cause, and neither should Hamlet. There is a similar appeal to the innocence of nature in her reply to the King's question 'Where is he gone?':

> To draw apart the body he hath killed,
> O'er whom—his very madness, like some ore
> Among a mineral of metals base,
> Shows itself pure—a weeps for what is done.
>
> (24–7)

His madness is seen not only as a phenomenon of nature, but as an attractive one. There is a suggestion here that good and evil are merely ways in which nature differentiates itself, for which the individual has no responsibility. Just as some metals are pure, others are base—there is no point in feeling that lead has something to answer for in not being gold. There is also a hint that nature may in some fashion be superior to distinctions of good and evil, since it establishes its own hierarchy, immediately recognized as right—the ore '*Shows itself* pure' by contrast to the 'metals base'. The antithesis of 'pure' and 'base' directs us towards the Queen's sense of class as the human aspect of nature's hierarchy, which is so powerful and so fundamental that even Hamlet's madness cannot outweigh the difference between him and those who are 'base'. His purity of blood is deemed to render him pure in other respects—'of unblemished character or nature; unstained or untainted with evil; guiltless, innocent' (*OED* s.v.5). Gertrude's words give Hamlet's tears a whole range of meaning—they demonstrate his guilelessness, but also a sensibility that distinguishes him from 'base' people; they are the token of repentance (in view of his madnesss and her metaphorical language, a spontaneous, unpremeditated, 'natural' repentance) and they represent his vulnerability.

The Queen's covert allusion to rank here is particularly appropriate, since Claudius is intent on being a king in words as well as deeds in this scene; the distinction he makes between 'you yourself' and 'us' (15) makes it clear that he is using the royal 'we' to refer to himself, and he makes much use of it. On the other hand, her appeal to nature in mitigation of her son is double-edged. It is uncomfortably like the manoeuvre performed by Claudius which substitutes a natural operation (cure) for a spiritual one (repentance), and yet it comes uncomfortably close to ascribing to Hamlet spiritual qualities of purity (that is, innocence) and penitence which Claudius wanted and of which he is still in need. No wonder that his reply to her is 'O Gertrude, come away'.

All that I have said here implies a complexity of feeling in the first scene of Act Four so great that an audience could hardly be expected to grasp it. It does not follow that since Shakespeare 'wrote for the theatre', this complexity should be considered redundant or somehow to be wished away. On the contrary—it makes a very positive contribution to the drama that we should be made aware that thoughts not immediately to be grasped lie within the words that Gertrude and the King speak, for by this means we feel with them in their distraction. The scene opens with the King's earnest entreaty:

There's matter in these sighs, these profound heaves,
You must translate. 'Tis fit we understand them.

Neither he nor Gertrude is able, however, fully to 'understand'. The 'matter' translated in their words remains obstinately reluctant to appear.

Claudius sees Gertrude as Ophelia saw Hamlet when he came to her 'with his doublet all unbrac'd' (II.1.78). Her 'profound heaves' are like her son's 'sigh so piteous and profound/That it did seem to shatter all his bulk' (II.1.94–5); they are tokens of a pain that is partly the pain of having a body at all, since it is so mysteriously and even obstructively related to spirit, and her description of Hamlet, 'Mad as the sea and wind, when both contend', translates the pain of her own sighs into an image of conflict within nature. The complexity and obliquity of the dialogue at this point in the play is mirrored in images of the necessary, encumbering and corrupting body and of a nature far from benign in her removal from the moral and spiritual.

The nature invoked by Claudius and Gertrude in the opening of the fourth act is one where sea and wind contend, where disease feeds 'even on the pith of life' and where the hierarchy of noble and base metals permits nevertheless of a juxtaposition so marked as to seem brutal (particularly when referred to the general tenor of the Queen's words). When Claudius wants to say that Hamlet must leave by the evening, his phrasing is ominous: 'The sun no sooner shall the mountains touch . . . ' By being delayed, the verb gets unexpected and inappropriate force, so that this sunset is a trial run for apocalypse, the sun's touching awkwardly close to collision. The suggestion here fits the King's last image in the scene of the world as a battlefield where 'poison'd shot', borne by a mere whisper, flies from one side of the earth to the other; Claudius speaks of 'woundless air' as though to assure himself that it cannot possibly be wounded, and the meaning 'as yet unwounded' lurks uncomfortably near.

This disturbed or disturbing nature is the complement to the diseased body attributed to himself by Claudius, and to Gertrude in the previous scene by her son (' . . . rank corruption, mining all within,/Infects unseen' III.4.150–1). As I have noted already, the Queen's sighs and heaves associate themselves readily with the natural strife between sea and wind which she likens to Hamlet's madness, and there is an obvious relation between her condition and Claudius's.

Hamlet has 'dragged' Polonius's body out of his mother's room, and Rosencrantz and Guildenstern are sent to find it: 'What have you done, my lord, with the dead body?' (IV.2.4). Hamlet answers them evasively and impertinently and likens their search to a game of hide-and-seek: 'Hide fox, and all after' (IV.2.30–31).[1] Claudius himself is led to take part in this game: 'Now Hamlet, where's Polonius? . . . Where is Polonius?' This elusive body concerns the King as much as the diseased body that he attributes to himself. One of Hamlet's jests encourages us to see the two bodies as equivalent:

Ros. My lord you must tell us where the body is, and go with us to the King.
Ham. The body is with the King, but the King is not with the body. The King is a thing—
Guil. A thing, my lord?
Ham. Of nothing . . .   (IV.2.25–30)

As Jenkins suggests, this must be an allusion to the King's two bodies, obscure because Hamlet is speaking as a madman, but menacing in its implications because it envisages the death of the King. 'The body is with the King': at any point in time, the King exists in the body of an individual. 'The King is not with the body': when the individual dies, the kingly office does not die with him, but continues. One implication of Hamlet's words is that the King has a body but that its mortality permits at any moment of his ceasing to be King and of someone else's taking over. The obscure fashion in which he speaks gives the words special resonance. The body is *too much* with the King, in his consciousness of the 'heavy burthen' of his guilt, in his sense of himself as diseased and seeking a desperate cure; but the King is not with his body—his thoughts put him at a remove from reality, he thinks that he can cure his illness by operating on Hamlet.

Polonius was killed by Hamlet in mistake for Claudius; Claudius recognizes that 'It had been so with us, had we been there'. Polonius's body in this sense substitutes for Claudius's: its elusiveness is an aspect of the King's equivocal relations with his own body. As his is corrupt with disease, that of Polonius will corrupt another way:

> if indeed you find him not within this month, you shall nose him
> as you go up the stairs into the lobby.   (IV.3.35–7)

Indeed, its elusiveness is part of its corruptibility:

> *Ham.* A man may fish with the worm that hath eat of a king, and eat
>   of the fish that hath fed of that worm.
> *King.* What dost thou mean by this?
> *Ham.* Nothing but to show you how a king may go a progress
>   through the guts of a beggar.

> (IV.3.27–31)

Hamlet evokes a world of constant change in which 'we fat all
creatures else to fat us, and we fat ourselves for maggots'. Polonius is
at supper 'not where he eats but where a is eaten'. Claudius feeds his
disease on his very life (IV.1.21–3); soon his disease will feed him to
the worms.

Hamlet's words serve as a commentary on the first three scenes of
Act Four, whose rapid action makes visible on the stage the mutability
of all earthly things, as the association of Claudius's disease with
Hamlet's madness, of Gertrude's sigh with Hamlet's, of Claudius's
body with Polonius's, makes it imaginatively real. Spenser's Mutability says of the four elements:

> Thus, all these fower (the which the ground-work bee
>   Of all the world and of all living wights)
>   To thousand sorts of *Change* we subject see:
>   Yet are they chang'd (by other wondrous slights)
>   Into themselues, and lose their natiue mights;
>   The Fire to Aire, and th'Ayre to Water sheere,
>   And Water into Earth: yet Water fights
>   With Fire, and Aire with Earth approaching neere:
> Yet all are in one body, and as one appeare.
> (*The Faerie Queene*, VII.vii.25)

The 'elements' of these scenes are all 'in one body'—that of Polonius;
are at strife with one another, like Gertrude's 'sea and wind'; and
change into each other (the dead body is 'compounded . . . with
dust, whereto 'tis kin'). The constant instability underlying the
world here displayed is caught in Hamlet's oxymoron 'The King is a
thing . . . of nothing'.[2]

There's matter in these sighs, these profound heaves,—
You must translate. 'Tis fit we understand them.

The point of these scenes is to show matter constantly translated and never understood. Neither Hamlet, Claudius nor Gertrude has a stable point of reference in the giddy changes rung here by Shakespeare on the 'matter' of the murder in the royal orchard.

The King, the prince and the old man

The body of the dead Polonius, then, is the focus for a world-view shared equally by Hamlet, his mother and his stepfather, but it has distinct meanings also for Hamlet and for Claudius. Hamlet discourses on it to the King, and what he says must partly be explained as said for effect—'a king may go a progress through the guts of a beggar'—and plainly includes a hint of menace. But at the same time it bears an obvious relation to Hamlet's own experience. The antithesis of king and beggar harks back to his first exchange with Rosencrantz and Guildenstern, for example: 'Then are our beggars bodies, and our monarchs and outstretched heroes the beggars' shadows' (II.2.263–4); it connects with the soliloquy 'O what a rogue and peasant slave am I!' and it reflects Hamlet's hesitation between the roles of man of honour and *honnête homme*. In other words, it expresses not only hostility to Claudius but an anxiety on Hamlet's part by now very familiar, an anxiety about his role in life.

The fact that he speaks with grotesque humour here should not be allowed to blind us to the element of self-reference in what he says. The humour too is characteristic. It is aggressive for all its grotesqueries: 'go a progress' splatters Claudius with contempt in the same way as Hamlet's imagining his own beard plucked off and blown in his face makes him contemptible. It is not, however, solely aggressive; it suggests an attempt at *contemptus mundi* of a vaguely Stoic kind, an erratic and impassioned burst for the dispassionate wisdom to which Hamlet has no real claim.

Corruption of the body blurs distinctions of rank. It does not necessarily invalidate them, but the element of covert threat to the King in what Hamlet says makes that possibility prominent. Indeed, all distinctions seem to break down in the face of death. Eating is normally considered to have the maintenance of the body as its chief end, but for Hamlet the body is maintained only in order that it should corrupt.

> We fat all creatures else to fat us, and we fat ourselves for maggots. Your fat king and your lean beggar is but variable service—two dishes, but to one table. That's the end.

Hamlet's repetition of the word 'fat' gives it a special force, perhaps to caricature the King physically or to suggest that he is slow-witted. Certainly it recalls 'the fat weed/That roots itself in ease on Lethe wharf' (I.5.32–3)[3] and the 'unweeded garden/That grows to seed', possessed by 'things rank and gross in nature'. It recalls, in other words, the world as it is seen by the self-condemning Hamlet at the very beginning of the play, and in the midst of the activity of Act Four reminds us that his case has advanced little, that the activity on his part is spurious. The grossness of the world is Hamlet's burden, and remains so even when Polonius's body is safely stowed.

The King's burden is his guilt, of which he hopes to be rid in ridding himself of Hamlet. We know this to be a false hope, and its falsity is given partial expression by Hamlet's revelation of the whereabouts of the body. Even with Hamlet gone, the smell (of something 'rotten in the state of Denmark' I.4.90) will remain.

The King's guilt leads him to see himself as suffering from a 'foul disease', one which has grown 'desperate'; he is well on the way to smelling too. Indeed, he smells already: 'O, my offence is rank, it smells to heaven . . . ' (III.3.36). His concern for Polonius's body need not be seen exclusively as an attempt to anticipate and placate the wrath of Laertes but as something more, a concern to deal with the bad smell of his own life by acting in a Christian manner ('bring the body/Into the chapel'). Just as he sees Hamlet as the 'hectic' in his blood, putting on to his nephew the blame for his troubles which properly belongs to himself, so, by a similar process of displacement, the burial of Polonius is to be a burial of his 'offence'. The body of Polonius, 'The unseen good old man', as Gertrude calls him, is also symbolically for the King the 'body of sin':

> Know ye not, that so many of us as were baptized into Jesus Christ, were baptized into his death;
>   Therefore wee are buryed with him by baptisme into death, that like as Christ was raised up from the dead by the glorie of the Father: even so wee also should walke in newnesse of life.

For if we have bene planted together in the likenesse of his death: wee shal be also in the likenesse of his resurrection:

Knowing this, that our old man is crucified with him, that the bodie of sinne might be destroyed, that henceforth we should not serve sinne.

There is a parodic relationship between this text from Romans (vi.3–6) and the King's behaviour. It seems strained at first. But on the one hand the text is undeniably of importance in the *Henry IV* plays,[4] so that there is no implausibility in Shakespeare's making use of it again, and on the other, immediately prior to the death of Polonius the King is seen attempting to pray to heaven for forgiveness, so that we not only look at his 'disease' as a spiritual sickness but also have in mind the proper method to deal with it. His desperation has all the marks of a spiritual crisis too—it could be the despair integral to Puritan 'conversion'; what happens is that instead of turning his back on his sin and turning towards God, the King puts off the burden of his sin partly on to Hamlet and partly on to Polonius. He hopes to achieve by this sleight 'newnesse of life', thinking that once Hamlet, the second of his two sin-carriers, is dead, his 'joys' will begin. The passage from St Paul reveals the motivation of the King's insistence on retrieving Polonius's body, and shows how decisively he has abandoned the attempt to reconcile himself with his God which preceded the death of the 'old man'.

The King projects his guilt on to the body of Polonius as Hamlet does his sense of dishonour; but whereas the guilt belongs to an essentially religious scheme of 'offence', 'mercy', 'pardon' and 'repentance' (III.3.36ff.), Hamlet's nausea is the individual expression of feelings rooted in the social domain of kings and beggars, which is naturally bounded by death—'That's the end'. The two kinds of meaning which either character associates with the dead courtier's body are in conflict, and rehearse at their level the conflict within nature as it is perceived by Gertrude and the King. This conflict is also, of course, the conflict inseparable from honour, and is aptly represented in the opposite interpretations to which the body of the old stickler for honour gives rise. It may not be irrelevant to this that what leads Claudius to think that he can put himself at ease by dismissing Hamlet is the value he places on the crown, which has already held him back from full repentance. He identifies himself so fully with the role of king—'our majesty and skill' (IV.1.31) and

'Our sovereign process' (IV.3.66) are representative self-references
—that it is unthinkable for him that he should give it up. But it is not
so for the audience, for whom the gap between the King's appearance
(or 'countenance', IV.2.14) and the reality of his conscience becomes
more and more noticeable. There is, for example, potential comedy
in the King's grumbling that the 'multitude' is so enamoured of
Hamlet that they will only sympathize with him if he is punished,
being quite indifferent to what he is being punished for, since his
own situation is much the same; he is so much in love with himself
that he resents the trouble he is put to without weighing the 'offence'
which is the cause of that trouble. The comedy is, however, less than
genial, as Claudius's later lapse into the first person singular makes
clear:

> And, England, if my love thou hold'st at aught—
> As my great power thereof may give thee sense,
> Since yet thy cicatrice looks raw and red
> After the Danish sword, and thy free awe
> Pays homage to us . . .   (IV.3.61–5)

The reality of Claudius is a love that expresses itself in power, whose
'sense' is the rawness of a wound, and whose freedom is an enforced
homage: but it is also a hold on 'greatness', a defence of the 'effects' of
his murder, a satisfaction with the outward signs of 'honour' that his
lavish use of the royal 'we' suggests. Lying behind the opposed
views of Polonius's body which we may associate with Claudius and
Hamlet there is another which they hold in common—the mysterious
entanglement of man's pursuit of honour with the body.

The extravaganza of mind

A consecutive line-by-line account of the fourth act of *Hamlet* does
not give the best view of it. The effect of the rapid action at its start
should be that of a hasty passage on thin ice. The commentator can
choose to emphasize the speed of action and scamper over the scenes
himself—neither Dover Wilson nor Eleanor Prosser has much to say
about them at all—or he can try, as I have, to show where the sense of
menace in them comes from. What is marvellous in Shakespeare's art
is that his effects are based in a comprehensive imagination of people,
the way they live and the way they think; he gives us all the elements

beneath the surface that make the ice treacherous, and still keeps the action just as fast as he needs it to be.

This fourth act is an extravaganza; no direct course of events is followed in it. In its first three scenes a host of meanings coalesce about the body of Polonius, unexpected perspectives are opened up and disappear; they are a fantasia on a ground-bass, characterized by Hamlet's 'lawless' 'liberty' (IV.1.8,14). The last three scenes suggest extravaganza by another means: Ophelia's madness parallels Hamlet's but also shows it up, and Laertes innocently parodies the role of unquestioning avenger. The note is one of quasi-parody. Hamlet's meeting with Fortinbras's captain is a moment of transition between these two aspects of the act, its transitional character reinforced by its being a chance meeting of two expeditions bound in utterly different directions. This is, of course, only how the scene looks in the Second Quarto—all we get elsewhere is the eight lines in which Fortinbras sends his captain to the 'rendezvous' appointed with Claudius: Hamlet and his soliloquy are missing. The brief form of the scene increases the pace of the first half of the fourth act, gives emphasis to its heterogeneous nature, and makes the contrast between the extended Laertes-Ophelia scenes and what precedes them more marked. The *inclusion* of Hamlet's soliloquy, on the other hand, makes explicit the play's continuing concern with honour and does so in a form, a fantasia, appropriate to this part of the play. The extravaganza here is one of mind, playing with the themes of its meditation.

Eleanor Prosser, remarking that 'at this point in the play, the soliloquy is as irrelevant as the situation', has suggested that it is

> possible that Shakespeare originally intended the entire scene for earlier in the play (probably before the mouse-trap), that he realized it was redundant, tentatively shifted it to its present position, but ultimately cut it for the stage version.[5]

This will be found more plausible by those who see the play simply as developing a story in action: the conception of drama underlying this book is more complex. At any rate, the soliloquy's quality of 'redundancy' fits it well for a place in the eccentric design of the fourth act.

Prosser finds that ' "To be or not to be" and "How all occasions" exactly parallel each other in the issues debated and the decision reached',[6] but the impartial reader or spectator is more likely to be impressed by the similarity of the use to which Fortinbras is here put with that to which the player is put at the end of Act Two. In both cases Hamlet is egging himself on to action by contrasting his situation with another man's. The difference—and this applies just as much to 'To be or not to be' as it does to 'O what a rogue and peasant slave'—is one of tone. The self-caricature of the second act, the Roman yearnings of the third, are absent. Despite its sanguinary close, the soliloquy has something dreamlike about it, at times even complacent:

> How all occasions do inform against me,
> And spur my dull revenge. What is a man
> If his chief good and market of his time
> Be but to sleep and feed? a beast, no more.   (IV.4.32–5)

Hamlet is obviously not seriously worried by the possibility that he is 'a beast, no more'; he makes no particular application, but goes on arguing at the general level—'Sure he that made *us* with such large discourse . . . ', happily attributing 'capability and godlike reason' to himself among others.

The occasion informs against him by showing Fortinbras's ability to act in a bad cause at a time when Hamlet is (or has been?) incapable of acting in a cause that is 'good'. This simple contrast is, however, complicated by the admiration Hamlet feels for the man who is to receive his 'dying voice'. 'Examples gross as earth exhort me', but when it comes to the point Fortinbras turns out not to be gross at all but

>   a delicate and tender prince,
> Whose spirit with divine ambition puff'd
> Makes mouths at the invisible event,
> Exposing what is mortal and unsure
> To all that fortune, death, and danger dare,
> Even for an egg shell.   (48–53)

How does 'divine ambition' differ from 'godlike reason' in the valuation placed upon it? This weakening of the contrast Hamlet wishes to make finds its explanation in the single line 'Exposing what is mortal and unsure', which evokes not only the uncertainty of the sublunar world, but Hamlet's sense that he is vulnerable and in

the very simplest sense, unsure of himself: 'I do not know/Why yet I
live to say, "This thing's to do" '—these touching monosyllables
incorporate a real bafflement, one which is the condition of Hamlet's
life, not merely a local perplexity. It underlies his attitude to Fortinbras, whom he wishes to contrast unfavourably with himself.
Fortinbras is going to war about an 'eggshell', and his men will die
'for a fantasy and trick of fame', but Hamlet is spurred on to action
by a 'great argument'—'a father kill'd, a mother stain'd'. When he
tries to sum the difference up, however, Hamlet is betrayed by his
own form of words:

> Rightly to be great
> Is not to stir without great argument,
> But greatly to find quarrel in a straw
> When honour's at the stake.   (53–6)

We have already heard him describe Fortinbras's cause as 'the question
of this straw', one in which, by the captain's account, honour alone is
at stake: the 'little patch of ground' disputed 'hath in it no profit but
the name'. It is natural therefore to interpret Hamlet's lines as a
non sequitur, saying that the right way to be 'great' is not to behave
like Fortinbras, but to behave like Fortinbras.[7] The contradiction
seems to express Hamlet's state of mind perfectly, and to explain the
violent reaction by which he falls into the language of a man who
wants to make our flesh creep:

> O, from this time forth
> My thoughts be bloody or be nothing worth.   (65–6)

There is a resemblance to 'To be or not to be' here, since that
soliloquy also shows its speaker in confusion. Whereas the earlier
speech is that of a man straining to find a role on which to model his
own behaviour, here he is involved in the pretence that he knows
what his role should be; hence the dreamlike way in which he
stumbles upon his own deficiency: 'I do not know/Why yet I live to
say "this thing's to do" '. The trouble is that Hamlet has got used to
not knowing. There is no urgency any more in his interior debate;
even the attempt to import it fails: 'from this time forth/My *thoughts*
be bloody . . . ' Thoughts, not deeds: the prince leaves the stage to
hurry on the journey which takes him day by day and hour by hour

further from the man he claims he should kill. The vagary of Act Four continues.

Or does it? Emrys Jones has argued that this scene is not the middle of the fourth act, but the last scene of the first part of the play normally equivalent to the first three acts of modern editions.[8] There is no division of the play into acts and scenes beyond II.2 in the First Folio, and there is none at all in the Quartos, so that the conventional arrangement of editors is based on guesswork and tradition. Jones argues that IV.4 parallels V.2, in that Fortinbras figures in both—the extended form of IV.4 opposes him to Hamlet as he is clearly opposed in the play's last scene. There would be an obvious and satisfactory symmetry in concluding both halves of the play with a Fortinbras scene. As I have noted earlier, the case is strengthened by the absence of any clear indication of a break in the action between III.4 and IV.1 in the early texts (though the absence is more marked in the First Quarto and Folio). Jones's argument seems too damaging to my own account of the conventional fourth act not to be mentioned and in some fashion answered.

And yet where so much is speculative—was there an interval in the Elizabethan playhouse?—I need not pursue the matter too fiercely. The counter-argument turns on the unemphatic nature of this Fortinbras scene in its short form and the diminished symmetry produced by the inclusion of Hamlet's soliloquy, and it might be supported by the considerations that the proportions between the two halves of the play produced by breaking at this point would be uncomfortably exaggerated, and that a scene so much concerned with movement and transition is well suited to the role I have ascribed to it in the economy of the conventional Act Four. There is something more important than reaching a decision in this ill-defined controversy, and that is to grasp the shifty nature of the scene itself and the loose relationship with what leads into and away from it that permits it to be seen as having the force of a bridge-passage *or* that of a conclusion. It is precisely this ambiguous quality that places it appropriately in the extravaganza described in this chapter.

Metamorphoses

Ophelia, in the next scene, 'Spurns enviously at straws, speaks things in doubt/That carry but half sense'. The connection with what precedes it may be loose, but it is certainly there. Her madness shares something with the sanity of Fortinbras and Hamlet or, more to the point, their sanity shares with her madness:

> Her speech is nothing,
> Yet the unshaped use of it doth move
> The hearers to collection. They aim at it,
> And botch the words up fit to their own thoughts,
> Which, as her winks and nods and gestures yield them,
> Indeed would make one think there might be thought,
> Though nothing sure, yet much unhappily. (IV.5.7–13)

She has become a kind of dumb-show; her body is the ambiguous medium for thought, which is both 'much' and 'nothing'. The echoes here are ominous: over some distance the figure she presents looks back to that of the ungartered Hamlet, but closer at hand the gentleman's description of her chimes with Hamlet's last line 'My thoughts be bloody or be nothing worth', retrospectively giving his 'nothing' a cheerless sound, and linking it too with his gibe at the King, who is 'a thing . . . of nothing'. In Ophelia we are to see the changes produced by Hamlet's actions, but not only that; we are to see also the osmotic process of interchange between personalities and situations that obstructs Hamlet's search for an identity, but which also gives it urgency. This general principle of social osmosis is illustrated in Horatio, whose advice to the Queen, nakedly pruden-tial, aligns him temporarily with the King and his brisk despatch of his 'dangerous' stepson (IV.3.2):

> 'Twere good she were spoken with, for she may strew
> Dangerous conjectures in ill-breeding minds. (IV.5.14–15)

(In the Folio, this speech is given to the Queen—but the point about osmosis stands.) Osmosis is most prominent in Ophelia's uncertain references to Hamlet and her father. Andrew Gurr remarks that

> Her conflation of love for her father and her lover, victim and murderer, expresses the tangled weave she has been innocently trapped in.[9]

That is so, but the matter does not end there. Ophelia's songs are ominous with regard to Hamlet's journey: 'He is dead and gone, lady,/He is dead and gone', but they also give a strange twist to the

quality of her love for her father. She sings about an unnamed man
who may stand in her mind at various times for the father or the
lover or both: 'How should I your true-love know/From another
one?' The two figures merge; they have both been loved, and both
have failed her. Hence the moment of rebellion when she sings that
'his' shroud 'bewept to the ground did *not* go/With true-love
showers'. The 'not' 'violates both the metre and the expected sense'
as Jenkins says, but, as he goes on to say, may be explained in terms
both of her father's 'hugger-mugger' burial and of her feelings about
Hamlet. The second song is likewise ambiguous in its reference, a
complaint against father and lover, though there is no mystery about
the 'he' intended. It may be a satire on her father, since Hamlet never
in fact touched her, or it may be a vindication of his point of
view—Hamlet would have tumbled her if her father had not prevented it. It may also attack a male conspiracy in which the father's
warning puts the onus on his daughter to resist what he is quite
happy to accept as a fact of nature—'Young men will do't if they
come to't'. It may reflect on her change from sanity to insanity—loss
of maidenhood would have been better than loss of sanity.

Once again, interpretation should not rest heavily upon what she
says. It is more important that we register the wide terms of reference
for her words than that we define them clearly. In between the two
songs there comes a brief passage of prose, which in its allusion to
change at a general level gives the essence of what we are to understand:

> They say the owl was a baker's daughter. Lord, we know what we
> are, but know not what we may be. God be at your table.   (42–4)

The story of the baker's daughter who was ungenerous to Jesus has
little relevance to Ophelia's plight except that it is about transformation, something which may overtake anyone. 'What we may be' is
what the future holds (as in 1 John 3:2, to which it alludes, with
irony) not some existing potential in ourselves to be realized by our
own efforts; and what the future holds is, king or beggar, to be
served to one table—'not where he eats, but where a is eaten'; 'God
be at your table.'

Eleanor Prosser has said that 'there is nothing grotesque in
Ophelia's madness, nothing that would alienate the audience';[10] this
accords with the way the part is usually performed, but nevertheless

blunts the point of what Shakespeare has written. We sympathize with Ophelia—the grotesque does not exclude such sympathy—but it is an excess of sympathy if we lose the sense that here Ophelia is a type as well as an individual—a type of change that thrusts itself on to people whether they will or no, change that threatens and diminishes them. The description of her 'winks and nods and gestures' (which should be incorporated in the stage performance) distances us from her, in its grotesquerie, so that this typical aspect of her may be perceived; the conflation of father and lover in her wanderings is not solely pathetic in effect but points to this change in her at the same time as what she says (and sings) implies the malleability of *all* phenomena in individual experience. The grotesque—a style in the visual arts associated with the fantastic combination of natural forms, human, animal and vegetable—appropriately evokes the universal tendency of existing systems of order to dissolve, a tendency from which not even kings and their dynasties are free.[11] Indeed, I have already pointed to the way—earlier in this act—Claudius and his queen are drawn to thoughts of a mutable sublunary world. Claudius is pointedly associated with the grotesquerie of Ophelia's madness too: his innocent exclamations ('How do you, pretty lady?', 'Pretty Ophelia') are themselves subject retrospectively to change by the wrongness of his comment on her when she is gone: 'O, this is the poison of deep grief . . . '. The word 'poison' reveals him as characteristically forgetful of his own crime (this forgetfulness being, of course, the reason that his guilt when felt is felt so strongly, as well as the cause of its indirectly forcing itself upon his speech as it does here); just as characteristically, he is taken up with himself so that his account of Ophelia's suffering drifts naturally, but to him imperceptibly, into the catalogue of his own woes:

> O my dear Gertrude, this,
> Like to a murd'ring-piece, in many places
> Gives me superfluous death. (94–6)

'*Superfluous* death': the irony is savage, but the phrase reverberates beyond the King's self, linking up with an abundance of change that threatens every individual; change suggested by all the movement, by much of the imagery and by the madness of Ophelia in this act.

Shapes and tricks

I have already used the scenes in which Laertes is won over by the King to plan vengeance on Hamlet to illustrate principles of honour-conduct in the play. But that discussion deliberately put on one side the question of the light in which these scenes, dramatically, are presented. Evidently they do not function thematically in any simple sense to remind the audience that this is a play one of whose principal concerns is honour. The return of Laertes is presented to us under specific poetic and dramatic auspices which radically affect our view of him. Ophelia's madness does not exist in relation to him solely as another motivating force for his revenge; it cannot do so, for it is Polonius and his family, not simply Laertes, who are identified with the cause of formal honour, and the madness of Ophelia must for this reason be seen as a consequence of her father and her brother's both sticking so rigidly to that cause. Besides motivating further her brother's pursuit of vengeance, therefore, Ophelia's insanity questions the wholesomeness of its principles, and does so in the typically concrete terms of Shakespearean poetic drama—consider, for example, the contrast between his exaggerated language and the infinitely more pathetic popular speech of Ophelia's ballads, pathetic even in their declination from traditional themes to an obscure figuring-forth of her own distress.[12]

Moreover, Ophelia's madness is seen in the light of Hamlet's, hers being as it were a pure madness whilst his is adulterated by the possibility that it has in part the rational motive of warding off the King's suspicions. This contrast between the insane characters does not, however, serve to show up the falsity of any diagnosis that Hamlet is mad: it cannot do so, since his conduct cannot be rationalized in its entirety, a fact which may be helpfully embodied for us in the ambiguities of the line 'Excitements of my reason and my blood' in the soliloquy immediately preceding the discovery that Ophelia's wits have turned.[13] The point of the parallel between Ophelia and Hamlet in madness would seem rather to be that her madness evokes the pathos that Hamlet's crazy callousness and the early rapidity of action forbade us: the pity we feel for her reflects back on him. It might be argued that her confusion of father and lover mitigates his confusion of Polonius with the King, which it mirrors, but this would be to strain too hard for a point which has no dramatic or poetic emphasis. On the other hand, her confusion does associate itself with suggestions throughout the fourth act of a menacing tendency to change in the order of things, and this general tendency certainly does attract sympathy to the prince, with the result that initially, at any rate, the returning Laertes has our interest in himself rather than as someone with overwhelming reasons to be drawn to revenge.

Laertes, in any case, figures the very destructive force which the Queen imagined at work in Hamlet, which haunts the King's imagination and whose effects are seen in Ophelia:

> The ocean, overpeering of his list,
> Eats not the flats with more impetuous haste
> Than young Laertes, in a riotous head,
> O'erbears your officers. The rabble call him lord,
> And as the world were now but to begin,
> Antiquity forgot, custom not known—
> The ratifiers and props of every word—
> They cry, 'Choose we! Laertes shall be king!   (IV.5.99–106)

Sea and flats here substitute for the sea and wind of Hamlet's madness in Gertrude's account: Laertes himself represents the force of madness, here universalized to the chaos that ruled when the world was 'but to begin'. The adherence to principles of honour about which he makes so much noise, 'That drop of blood that's calm proclaims me bastard', and so on, consequently appears as a force for disorder in a fundamental sense, even though we understand its absoluteness to derive precisely from the need for order, recognized in Laertes's resentment of his father's 'means of death, his obscure funeral' (210).

Indeed, the contradictions in the action reveal themselves at this point in the play most violently, as the unconditional commitment to his cause of the youthful Laertes is nevertheless qualified by the King's soft words. There is comedy in this, of course. Howard Jacobson, for example, has stressed the ludicrous nature of Gertrude's protecting her husband from the young rebel ('Let him go, Gertrude . . . ') and how this reflects on his grandiose claim that there is a 'divinity doth hedge a king'.[14] The touches of the comic are, however, blended to grotesque effect: they exist in a context of indecorum which we register as such because it has defined the mood

of the play since the interruption of 'The Mousetrap'. The King's
assumption of his own dignity, as here or at the opening of the fourth
act, answers to the general offence to decorum which, however, he
can do nothing to control. No sooner has he packed the 'mad young
man' off to England than he is faced by a mad young woman, with a
dangerous and ill-tempered brother. His dignity fails to impose itself
upon this disturbed scene: he wins Laertes over only by a sacrifice of
part of what he has paid for so dearly, allowing himself to be judged
(or at least offering so to allow himself, still a notable abdication) as
though he were Laertes's equal. But then, since the prayer scene, we
have understood that Claudius is insecure in the possession of those
dignities which nevertheless he cannot give up—'like a man to
double business bound' (III.3.41) he functions properly neither as
man or king. The 'comedy' of his encounter with the rebellious
Laertes has its roots in his own bad faith, and its frenzy is that of the
collapsing world of the fourth act in its entirety. Our consciousness
of these aspects of the action counterpoises the comic here and
might, were it not for the re-entry of Ophelia, take the grotesque as
far as horror.

Ophelia's return makes pathos, not horror, the dominant effect,
and once again it is a grotesque pathos. The incongruous exclamation 'Fare you well, my dove', following on 'They bore him bare-
fac'd on the bier', suggests that once again she has her lover as well as
or rather than her father in mind, and Laertes's reaction consequently
would seem inappropriate whatever we felt about revenge, since he
is still thinking of Polonius:

> Hadst thou thy wits and didst persuade revenge,
> It could not move thus.   (IV.5.167–8)

Laertes thinks he sees what has happened to his sister, but he does
not; he merely settles more firmly into the role he has chosen for
himself. The three lines added in the Folio text to his first reaction on
seeing Ophelia emphasize the failure truly to respond on his part
since, as Jenkins points out, they apply equally well to the consequences of Hamlet's departure as to those of Polonius's death.
Laertes, however, grasps only one half of the truth: he is diminished
by the inability to mean what he so beautifully says:

Nature is fine in love, and where 'tis fine
It sends some precious instance of itself
After the thing it loves. (161–3)

When Ophelia leaves the stage, having distributed her posies, it is as though she had never appeared for the second time. The King resumes his mollification of Laertes, and he, a little less certainly perhaps, reiterates the belief that something must be done about his father's death. This ready forgetting of what we have just seen is partly its justification; it is a *lack* in the King and Laertes that appears here. But the exposure of this lack is not the only reason for Ophelia's return, which also keeps alive the sense of general instability infecting the whole of the act so far and most brilliantly realized in its poetic and dramatic form.

It seems to have been Shakespeare's original intention to reverse the tendency to chaos in the characters' imagination and experience by introducing the news of Hamlet's return in a very positive fashion; the first Quarto's version of this scene is quite different from any other. It puts its emphasis on certainties—not merely the certainty that the Queen is guiltless of complicity in her husband's murder, but certainty as a form of thought and speech. The positive note is struck in its very first line: 'Madam, your son is safe arriv'de in *Denmarke* . . .' and it is sustained by the clarity of Horatio's appointment to meet Hamlet 'on the east side of the Cittie/To morrow morning' and his firm reply when the Queen expresses anxiety that her son, once returned to court, may 'Faile in that he goes about'; 'Madam, never make doubt of that . . .' It is impossible to tell how much this scene may owe to the earlier play on which Shakespeare based his work, and so our confidence in identifying Shakespeare's intentions here must be qualified; what does emerge clearly is the difference between the First Quarto version of the scene and the one which we all know as part of the received text, based on the Second Quarto and First Folio.

In this scene a gentleman informs Horatio that some sailors wish to speak with him, they enter, Horatio receives the letter from Hamlet and reads it. The circumstances of Hamlet's escape are given distinctly and fully, as they are not in the First Quarto:

Ere we were two days old at sea, a pirate of very warlike appointment gave us chase. Finding ourselves too slow of sail, we put on a
compelled valour, and in the grapple I boarded them. On the
instant they got clear of our ship, so I alone became their prisoner.

(IV.6.15–20)

If we wanted an image of the mutability that rules in human affairs,
this would be it: that of the prince on his way to death who courage-
ously takes a risk, loses it and yet in consequence gains his life and
liberty. Shakespeare emphasizes the rapidity of events—'Ere we
were two days old at sea', 'on the instant'—and the comparatively
simple form of his sentences accords with this, effect following cause
with expressive immediacy.

The passage stands out clearly in its context of uncertainty, to
which it is bound thematically—and naturally. 'I have words to
speak in thine ear will make thee dumb . . .': the uncertainty lies not
so much in what Hamlet has to say as in what Horatio will think of it
and what Hamlet will do about it. It develops the caution of the sailor
who presents the letter to Horatio: 'If your name be Horatio, as I am
let to know it is'. The visible intermediaries, the caution, the intima-
tion of horrors to come, all combine to make our sense of the fickle
state of things in Elsinore more acute. The note of confidence sounds
clearly in this scene only once, but it is significantly put in the mouth
of one whose place is not the court:

1. Sailor   God bless you, sir.
Hor.   Let him bless thee too
1. Sailor   A shall, sir, and please him.

Thus the scene is in one sense climactic: Hamlet's adventure realizes
at the level of plot much of what has been intimated more deviously
in stage movement and in words earlier in the act. In another sense,
however, it redefines and redirects the action, by focusing on the
court of Elsinore and what is to happen there, and it opens up the
possibility of something more purposeful than the *ad hoc* fixing and
temporizing at which we find the King still at work in the last scene
of Act Four. And indeed, spurred on by the arrival of his stepson, the
King himself is induced to think further ahead than we have seen him
do before. His dialogue with Laertes is directed by the news of
Hamlet's return to long-term planning, to precisions and to un-
attractive clarities:

Hamlet, return'd, shall know you are come home,
We'll put on those shall praise your excellence,
And set a double varnish on the fame
The Frenchman gave you, bring you, in fine, together,
And wager o'er your heads. He, being remiss,
Most generous, and free from all contriving,
Will not peruse the foils . . .   (IV.7.129–35)

The King's fluency serves in lieu of varnish: what is proposed is
shameful, but his glib and oily art denies shame occasion to appear by
running so easily through the details of what is to be done. This
glibness itself has to do with the King's vision of the world as
inherently unsteady:

> nothing is at a like goodness still,
> For goodness, growing to a pleurisy,
> Dies in his own too-much. That we would do,
> We should do when we would: for this 'would' changes
> And hath abatements and delays as many
> As there are tongues, are hands, are accidents . . . (115–20)

What suggests that this is the King's vision, and not simply something designed to work his purpose with Laertes, is not merely its
congruence with so much else in the fourth act but also the way in
which the King's use of 'we' characteristically allows him to talk of
himself without declaring that he is doing so. He speaks of 'goodness', we may assume, to make Laertes more at home with the evil he
intends. The argument is that good intentions can by their very
quantity stifle themselves: Laertes should therefore act now that
Hamlet's return presents him with the chance. Claudius invokes the
terms of good and evil: he had done this before, and most powerfully, in the prayer scene. That was a case of missed opportunity: he
wanted to repent, and he should have done so, but he did not. 'This
"would" changes':

> And then this 'should' is like a spendthrift sigh
> That hurts by easing.   (122–3)

He hurts himself by handling the ethical categories of good and evil
to which, since his failure to repent, he feels he has no claim. The
'ease' that he seeks is the entirely secular freedom from worry that
the death of Hamlet may bring. It may be also that his words suggest

some sort of relief is afforded him by the mere contemplation and
naming of 'goodness' and what he 'should' have done, and that the
hurt is that the relief is only momentary. What does emerge is the
complex and shifting motivation of the move towards a fixed plan to
dispose of Hamlet. The King has earlier in the scene said of the
Norman gentleman Lamord that

> So far he topp'd my thought,
> That I in forgery of shapes and tricks
> Come short of what he did.   (87–9)

No doubt 'forgery' does have the primary sense of 'mere imagining',
but it also had a strong association with the idea of fraud by the time
Hamlet was written. That association is present in the word 'tricks',
of course, and also in 'shapes', because to disguise oneself was to put
on someone else's 'shape'; it is hard therefore not to conclude that the
King declares in this line the duplicitous nature so painfully bared
also in the lines just considered.

The King, however, 'in forgery of shapes and tricks', *comes short* of
Lamord: the gentlemanly business of managing a horse is, *pace*
Sidney and the *Apologie*, also rendered suspect by the double meaning,
and so the whole business of the honour-transaction planned by
Claudius and Laertes is made out to be disreputable. The course of
action charted so firmly by the end of the scene is, then, presented to
us as charted through very muddy waters indeed, and charted by one
whose firmness is founded on a sense of his own spendthrift's lack.

The effect ought to be one of repulsion. Certainly there are few
more shocking lines in Shakespeare than Laertes's reply to the question 'What would you undertake/To show yourself indeed your
father's son . . . ?': 'To cut his throat i'th'church'. What mitigates the
shock is our sense that Laertes is being manipulated, and is too
innocent to perceive it; we do not have grounds to believe he fully
understands what he is saying. Like the King, too, he is driven on by
a kind of desperation, the need to do something, which the last
episode of the act brings forcibly home to us. The point of the
Queen's beautiful description of Ophelia's death is not to distance us
from all that has gone by, but silently to plead for the terrible
confusions of the two men. Ophelia 'fell in the weeping brook' in
consequence of her own harmlessness, making 'fantastic garlands'
and attempting to hang her 'crownet weeds' (the phrase implies

devaluation of the 'crownet' of honour) on a willow-tree. The Queen makes her speech a lament for pastoral innocence, recalling the flower-catalogue of classical elegy, and attributing a perfect natural harmony to the dead girl:

> Her clothes spread wide,
> And mermaid-like awhile they bore her up,
> Which time she chanted snatches of old lauds,
> As one incapable of her own distress,
> Or like a creature native and indued
> Unto that element. (174–9)

The speech acts as a powerful reminder of the inharmonious actuality of the King's negotiation with Laertes, its bad faith and shameful ironies ('No place indeed should murder sanctuarize,/ Revenge should have no bounds', for example). Ophelia in death is mermaid-like, and this implies her having found the place intended her by nature. In the world of the men, Lamord

> to such wondrous doing brought his horse
> As had he been incorps'd and demi-natur'd
> With the brave beast,

but this strikes them as 'witchcraft', not nature, a matter of 'shapes and tricks'. Their world of strenuous, fraudulent activity is the opposite of her passivity and helplessness. She is 'incapable of her own distress'; they are not. The extravaganza of the fourth act comes to rest on this grim opposition between an aware and suicidal passivity and the desperately fraudulent, almost monstrous, but finally all too human strivings of those whom the world possesses. Somewhere between these opposites, it would seem, Hamlet must discover his own nature. The question is how far his own pursuit of honour will enable him to do better than the men who plot against him.

11 Graveyard thoughts

Adam was a gentleman

It is quite usual to feel that Hamlet, on his return to Denmark, has changed. Dover Wilson is only one of many to put the feeling into words, but he is unusually frank about his motives:

> Hamlet returns from his voyage a changed man, with an air of self-possession greater than at any other time of the play . . . The real source of the change is, of course, a technical one. The requirements of tragic drama compel his creator to win back our respect for him before the end . . . Hamlet, we feel, is himself, or almost himself; and we begin to hope once again, though because he is the hero of a tragedy we know that our hope is vain.[1]

To this we might reply that Shakespeare was happily unfamiliar with 'the requirements of tragic drama' and certainly not to be compelled by them. Aristotle did not have for him the power which he has exercised over his more learned readers, and he wrote for audiences whose interest was plainly more in story than in genre. He was content to exploit the ambiguities of form which these conditions permitted, most notably in *King Lear* and *Cymbeline*, but not least significantly in *Hamlet* itself where, as I have tried to show, the relationship of sympathy to horror aroused by the prince is very complex and not to be swept into the basket of tragic principles. The change in Hamlet, in so far as there is one at the beginning of the fifth act, has to be considered in the light of the text itself, rather than in that of some theory designed to turn Shakespeare into Sophocles. He will surely do very well as he is.

Let us suppose, without speculating on his motives, that Shakespeare did want us to register a change in Hamlet at this point. He could have introduced this 'new' man in many ways—for example, with the lines which in fact open the play's last scene, in which Hamlet describes his escape from the pirates and his despatch of Rosencrantz and Guildenstern. This would have brought us up to date with the story and would have lent a greater air of purposefulness to the 'self-possession' Dover Wilson notes, a quality the presence of which we might even be inclined to doubt in Hamlet's fanciful elaborations upon the fate of 'my Lord Such-a-one' and 'my Lady Worm'. But Shakespeare did not write the scene this way. Instead, he chose to delay Hamlet's entry with Horatio, beginning this new phase in the story with sixty lines of chat between one grave-digger and another. It would be surprising if this arrangement of the scene had nothing to do with the 'new' face Hamlet is to put on.

Granville-Barker felt that these clowns had to be 'kept in their place' lest the coarseness of their humour and the 'guffaws' to which it can give rise 'fatally break the finer threads of implication and allusion by which the continuity of cause and effect—in this subsidiary story of Hamlet, Ophelia, and Laertes—is sustained'.[2] But Granville-Barker too was possessed by the idea that the tragic experience in Shakespeare should be in the good old Aristotelian mould. It seems clear that a change of tone from the high rhetoric of Laertes, the King and the Queen to the popular and conventionally 'low' idiom of the grave-diggers was intended. We are miles away here from the pretensions, the ambitions and the constraining artifice of court life in Elsinore. It would not, even, feel wrong if the effect of the grave-diggers' dialogue were faintly disruptive. In the last three scenes 'coarseness' and the mob both threaten to break down the conventions of the court, and here they may fulfil that function, symbolically at least. At the same time, the play does not endorse revolution—Shakespeare is not Marx *avant la lettre*—and so some discretion is needed in the presentation of the scene. It all depends on how the grave-diggers are imagined. Eleanor Prosser writes of 'the idiotic nonsense of a witty old rascal and a country bumpkin'[3] and the description accords well with Granville-Barker's determination to keep such characters down. The grave-diggers do not have to be played like this, though, and their idiocy is strictly limited by Shakespeare's own text.

Of course the opening remark is well in the tradition of mis-terming clowns like Dogberry and Elbow: 'Is she to be buried in Christian burial when she wilfully seeks her own salvation?' But the joke is a shrewd one at the expense of dogmatic Christianity as well as the striving society which cannot simply accept the salvation which will be freely given; and because these clowns are not seen doing anything foolish—unlike Dogberry and Elbow, they are quite equal to their work and know the ins and outs of it—this shrewdness rubs off on them. Their chaff has a common sense to it that makes 'idiotic nonsense' a less than adequate description. It has a point for them and a point for us.

As far as they are concerned, their idle talk makes a team, of them. Because it is all related to their work it confirms their identity as workmates, men happy in their work and even proud of it—that is the point of the riddle about building strong: the houses a grave-maker makes last till doomsday. Theirs is a privileged point of view on life and death, and enables them to see some things at least very clearly indeed: 'If this had not been a gentlewoman, she should have been buried out o' Christian burial'. The mock-solemn discussion of the point of law, 'if I drown myself wittingly, it argues an act . . . ', is not a country bumpkin's hash of how the gentlefolk decide things in court, it is that pretence of stupidity which has for so long been the working man's protection from the wrath of his 'betters' that it is now habitual. It is not genuine stupidity: beneath it all he knows 'the truth on't' and needs not mince the matter with his equal.

Adam was a gentleman; he bore arms and used them for digging. The nobility of labour has never been so completely or unearnestly expressed as in this clown's teasing variation on a time-honoured theme. 'When Adam delved and Eve span, who was then a gentle-man?' No grudge is expressed, but the criticism of the social order is comprehensive. These men really do 'grunt and sweat under a weary life'—at least, it does not seem to afford opportunity for doing much else—and the behaviour of the gentry, with their claims to an honour, which is distinct from the simple doing well that was within Adam's reach, and is so still for the poorest man, looks odd enough. They do not build houses at all, they are upstarts (not 'ancient gentlemen') and they manipulate the law in their own interests. If Hamlet is a changed man, then our perspective on him will be a new one, too—new and potentially critical; but it is very different from that imagined by Eleanor Prosser, who suggests that the effect of the grave-diggers' dialogue is to make us aware, upon Hamlet's entry, 'of the ultimate insignificance of even the most agonizing struggles of any single human being, for death will come, but life will go on'.[4] She too yearns for an Aristotelian catharsis, and in its interest perceives wider horizons than Shakespeare actually presents us with.

A courteous and casual eye

When Hamlet enters, his first words establish his distance from the grave-diggers. 'Has this fellow no feeling of his business? a sings in grave-making.' Given the frankly disenchanted view of 'great folk' which we have just been offered, 'this fellow' comes out with an unpleasantly squeamish air, particularly as the preceding dialogue establishes that the grave-digger does have a 'feeling of his business'. Horatio's reply shows an equal insensitivity to the point in question: 'Custom hath made it in him a property of easiness'. If the grave-digger can get on with his work so blithely it is not, however, that he is merely inured to it. He considers, for example, the circumstances in which Ophelia dies not out of any apparent liking for scandal but because the grave he digs is *his* grave, and the digging of it *his* service for her, 'rest her soul'. Hamlet is, then, offensively wide of the mark when he complacently agrees with his companion: ' 'Tis e'en so, the hand of little employment hath the daintier sense.'

Looked at in the light of the scene's first sixty lines, Hamlet *is* changed, but it goes against the spirit of Shakespeare's text to feel that he is changed for the better. Modern commentators do so nevertheless, because a 'better' Hamlet is more suitable as a tragic hero. Granville-Barker's characterization of Hamlet in the latter part of the play is perhaps one of the most interesting, because he does at least recognize that such an interpretation puts a strain on the text:

> When he returns he is 'sane' again; the inner strife is ended. Upon what terms? They show in his placid philosophizings beside the forgotten Ophelia's grave. His power to suffer for his mother's sin has thinned out to the sentiment of 'Alas, poor Yorick!' And when we hear of the lethal trick he has played upon his one-time comrades, his enemy's ignorant instruments, and that it comes not near his conscience, plainly he no longer lacks nerve to deal with that enemy himself . . . So here is a Hamlet fit at last for his task. But in the conversion much that seemed lovely in his nature has perished, failing under the test to which he had to put it. Yet though the physical man issues from the trial sorely strained, and the mind is hardened, the spirit is still not debased. Its nobility shines through the apology to Laertes for the 'madness' which has been 'poor Hamlet's enemy'. Let the terrible task be but fulfilled, there is promise of a Hamlet at peace, and the better a man for his

ordeal. But that cannot be. The penalty of things done in that 'sore distraction' must be paid.[5]

Plainly Granville-Barker would have been happier if he had not had to concede the thinned-out quality, the diminution of Hamlet in the last two scenes. But he saw—and was too honest a critic not to record it—that Hamlet condemns himself in his condescending reference to the grave-digger's song—'Had he no feeling either, who could turn his back upon the havoc he had made? It is he that is digging his grave'—and that this unfeeling quality permits Hamlet to go on 'to sentimentalize over Yorick'.[6]

Other critics smooth the scene out in the interests of a balanced, or reconciled, or at last truly philosophical prince. He shows, we are told, 'the composure of a man who has at last seen death, his own, and that of all mankind, in true perspective'.[7] Another critic writes: 'Assured, collected, indifferent to old debates and even, when the time comes, to his own person, the Hamlet of these final scenes has never been so princely'.[8] His collectedness is to be distinguished clearly, says this same writer, from 'the grave-digger's gross inurement'. It is: but if the grave-digger is, as I suggest, not so much 'gross' as Tolstoyan in his simplicity, his honesty and his trust, Hamlet's refurbished princeliness may still be a doubtful blessing.

'That skull had a tongue in it, and could sing once': Hamlet thinks it very insensitive of the clown to sing as he digs his grave, but it is the prince who expresses an idle resentment of the very fact of death. It is idle because it is not regret for a particular loss, nor the wish to accommodate knowledge of death to knowledge of life that Hamlet expresses; it is the speech of someone who will not let bygones be bygones, who will not let the dead bury the dead, and who will not, either, take stock of the living in relation to the dead and in particular of his own responsibility for the grave above which he stands (he needs only to ask for whom it is intended):

> How the knave jowls it to th' ground, as if 'twere Cain's jaw-bone, that did the first murder. This might be the pate of a politician which this ass now o'er offices, one that would circumvent God, might it not?   (V.1.76–80)

This is certainly high and mighty, in its attitude to the politician as much as to 'the knave', 'this ass'. There is plenty of contempt in tone, but it does not define itself as a religious *contemptus mundi*. Eleanor

Prosser is not by any means, however, the only writer to argue that in this speech and those that follow we are offered a meditation upon death that is religious in substance and to be discussed in terms of great profundity. She quotes extensively from the English version of Luis de Granada's *Of Prayer and Meditation* (earliest known edition 1582) in order to make her case, even suggesting that the book may have had a 'direct influence', whatever that might be, on *Hamlet*. Her parallels do not amount to much, however—for example:

> Then the gravemaker taketh the spade, and pykeaxe into his hande ['a pickaxe and a spade, a spade'] and beginneth to tumble downe bones upon bones, and to tread downe the earth verie harde upon him. ['Did these bones cost no more than breeding, but to play at loggets with 'em?']⁹

But even more to the point, the tone is quite different. Luis quite lacks the supercilious humour of 'to play at loggets with 'em'—he is unconcerned to make himself audible in what he says; but Hamlet, whatever else he is doing, is intent on letting Hamlet be heard. Shakespeare makes the point by having him every now and then turn in a perfunctory way to Horatio for confirmation. It is not that he has expressed any doubt. Shakespeare could well have let Horatio withdraw whilst Hamlet meditated in earnest: he is present because Hamlet is not in earnest. It is quite unnecessary to argue whether or not graveyard meditation in itself would be morbid, therefore; what needs to be done is to determine the direction in which Hamlet's own words point.

They point surely to this world, but not to the other; their contempt for my lord and my lady, for the politician and the lawyer, is unbalanced by any expression of faith in God. Howard Jacobson is right to say that 'it is with the courteous and casual eye of the aristocrat that he notices' what he notices here.¹⁰ The tone is worldly, and the humour is that of a master of the world ('Here's fine revolution and we had the trick to see't'—but in the presence of the grave-digger this master looks smaller to us than he does to himself. His superiority is not really so superior.

Yet what he says is designed to reinforce his own sense of that. The politician, my lord, my lady, the lawyer, people who were looked up to, who were clever and had tricks in plenty, nevertheless could not protect themselves from being knocked about by the 'dirty shovel' of 'this mad knave'. They are all 'sheep and calves' because they sought assurance in their tricks, as the lawyer in his parchment, and the assurance was useless. Hamlet, at least, knows better than that; his assurance has other foundations. What they are is to appear later. For the time being it is enough that we see the contrast between the aristocrat and the labourer, between the man whose bones ache at the thought that his breeding may not be sufficiently fine to escape burial in the common graveyard and the man who works there and sings in his work. The contrast makes it clear that the change in Hamlet is, as Granville-Barker says, a hardening, a decisive adoption of the aristocratic role. And the significance of that, in the light of Hamlet's personal dilemma, is not encouraging for its outcome.

Lying in the grave

'I will speak to this fellow.' Only 'great folk' can indulge their whims with such freedom. All the world is Hamlet's oyster, or at least that is what his poise would seem to imply. Certainly he treats each one of its inhabitants as his inferior. 'Whose grave's this, sirrah?' Hamlet consistently addresses the grave-digger with the 'thou' of master to servant and receives the 'you' of respect in return.

'He discusses death and decay philosophically and calmly . . . '[11] not quite. He keeps his distance from whatever it is he is dealing with now, from the clown by the correctness of the chosen pronoun and other things, from the subject of death by his playing on words ('Will his vouchers vouch him no more of his purchases . . . ?' and so on) and from death itself by the display of the 'daintier sense' that belongs to 'the hand of little employment' ('And smelt so? Pah!'— putting down the skull). He puts on a display of sang-froid, that of the aristocrat, because this is the role to which he is now and at last committed. There is, however, an element of bravado, and hence of the spurious, about this display: he need not pursue the topic of death so hard. Is he, despite himself, obsessed with death? Or is he trying to show himself just how 'noble' in bearing he can be? We are entitled to suspect both motives at work.

The grave-digger does not give Hamlet an easy triumph. His gormlessness is only apparent: he can argue briskly enough in the defensive fashion of his class, and the wisdom of acceptance of death underlies all he says. When he tells Hamlet that the grave he is digging is his own, he does not mean only that he is the one who has made it, but that the grave is meant for him too; no man can escape it. And the ballad that he sings in it, to the disgust of Hamlet, is about the appropriateness of death:

> O a pit of clay for to be made
> For such a guest is meet. (94–5)

The song is printed in *Tottel's Miscellany* as 'The Aged Lover renounceth Love' (by Lord Vaux, and according to Gascoigne, written by him on his deathbed) and it seems that either it passed, as such songs do, into the popular repertoire,[12] or Shakespeare saw the congruence between it and the folk wisdom to be expressed by the clown. (Dover Wilson, in his New Cambridge edition, remarks merely that the poem 'seems to us absurd enough in itself'.) Perhaps it is worth noting that 'such a guest' is a phrase that can also flash out of the song at Hamlet himself.

If so, he rejects it, as he rejects what the grave-digger says. The grave is the property of its maker, according to Hamlet, only in the sense that he deserves it for lying about whose body is to rest in it ('I think it be thine indeed, for thou liest in't'). But the grave-digger is not to be put out in this fashion; he is not lying in the grave, he is standing in it, and he knows that it is paradoxical of him to maintain that someone else's grave is also his own, but the paradox is true; Hamlet, therefore, is the liar. He is careful, though, not to give the lie direct ('you lie out on't sir, and therefore 'tis not yours. For my part, I do not lie in't, yet it is mine'). It is not profitable to follow the quibbles here much further; the important thing is to note the prominence given to lying. The lie is bitterly resented by persons of honour; giving the lie 'deserves stabbing' says Raleigh in his poem, 'The Lie'. Only the inferior rank of the clown permits him to be so downright; it would be degrading for Hamlet to take offence. On the other hand, the exchange reminds us of two kinds of uprightness, that of the self-conscious scorner of other men's faults, and that of the man whose body is perpendicular to the earth, standing, not lying on it. It is the latter virtue (if it may be so termed, and he would, I think, encourage us so to term it) that the grave-digger presents, and it is his faith in the value of life itself that permits his triumph over Hamlet: ' 'Tis a quick lie, sir, 'twill away again from me to you'. Life implies movement and change and sets up the conditions for even the quibbling the two of them have enjoyed. 'Quickness' is all, for the grave-digger; his profession gives him a special insight into it, and its predominant value for him is expressed in his reluctance to term the dead Ophelia a woman, 'one that was a woman, sir; but, rest her soul, she's dead'. The speed and humour of the dialogue here is fully expressive of the values he champions.

Hamlet is not, of course, put out by any of this, but his reaction is scarcely genial:

> How absolute the knave is. We must speak by the card or equivo-cation will undo us. By the Lord, Horatio, this three years I have took note of it, the age is grown so picked that the toe of the peasant comes so near the heel of the courtier he galls his kibe.
>
> (133–8)

If he did not say that the sore was on the courtier's heel, one would swear that it was on his own. He has been praised here for at last noticing the world around him, but it is open to question whether he is not just indulging his fancy for the part of nobleman to the extreme, boosting his ego by doing it well. It is impossible, of course, to say whether or not this man, with his own love for 'equivocation', does or does not resent the grave-digger's wit, but the way in which he pursues the business, dangerous for the clown, of young Hamlet's madness and its causes keeps the question very open. The grave-digger's contortions here are very much of a self-protective kind.

As for Hamlet: how do his thoughts develop? Forced to abandon his questioning of the grave-digger about his own alleged madness, he comes out abruptly with: 'How long will a man lie i'th' earth ere he rot?' Nothing prompts it, unless it be the clown's reference to 'our last King Hamlet' a few lines earlier. It comes out of Hamlet's complete relaxation, perhaps, if we can believe in that; if not, then from the obsession and the fear which the aristocrat's mask would subdue. The grave-digger's reply, at any rate, takes Hamlet in a safe direction, to the world of the common life and of the tanner, of whom he knows so little that he must ask why *his* body should take longer to rot than anyone else's.

Now Yorick's skull is turned up, and Hamlet is off on another track. It is striking that in this scene, as in the second act, he is shown once again static on stage, whilst things happen to him. The only difference lies in the fixity of his pose amongst the graves. Dover Wilson, like Granville-Barker, detects a pinch of sentimentality in the Yorick speech. If that connotes self-regard, then he is surely right.[13] The form of what Hamlet says may belong to the tradition of *ubi sunt*, but the feeling is personal. 'Where be your gibes now, your gambols, your songs, your flashes of merriment, that were wont to set the table on a roar?' This is not merely a tribute to the power of death, or a vivid scrap of memory—it is a lament for a savour gone out of Hamlet's own life, and perhaps expresses abhorrence not merely for the mortal body but for the 'jest' and 'fancy' with which Hamlet himself cloaked his disgust.[14] It is hard to feel, as he tells us of his gorge rising, that he is calm and philosophical here. That is why his allegation of the smell that clings to the skull strikes people as morbid, as well as a natural reaction.

'To what *base* uses we may return, Horatio!' He might regard Alexander's fate, reduced to stopping a bunghole, with equanimity, but it does not seem so. Even Alexander's dust is 'noble' for Hamlet, and its fate therefore shameful. It is the contrast between imperious Caesar and the hole he stops, rather than the universal fate of death, that Hamlet underlines; and it is ominously in keeping with his distaste for the sullied flesh generally. There is nothing new in it. All that is new is that his fantasies of sharing in the life of 'patient merit' are gone. In him 'honour' has vanquished 'honesty'.

Different from us

Hamlet's encounter with the grave-digger is dramatic in conception: it is a revelation to us of the 'new', exclusively aristocratic Hamlet, and its development is by way of confrontation, one in which the prince does not come off as well as he might or ought. The focus is upon Hamlet, not his meditations; and just as it would be unsatisfactory to sum the scene up as 'comic relief' so it is to think of it as 'a tableau', presenting 'the idea of melancholy in its Aristotelian sense, and of the melancholic as one whose solitude and alienation are bound up with unusual gifts for contemplation'. The dramatic impact of the scene is *not* to characterize Hamlet as 'a thinker' or to make us see that 'his sensibility is far superior to that of anybody else in the play'—or if it is the latter, it is with the qualification that 'superior' refers to class and bearing but has no moral virtue.[15]

On the other hand, though I have emphasized the critical light in which Hamlet is here displayed, the limits of this criticism must by understood. On the stage Hamlet is placed physically above the grave-digger in his grave, and all of him is exposed. The physical image is one of the vulnerability of Hamlet's station, and can by itself provoke a measure of sympathy for him. That sympathy is reinforced by the grave-digger's genial want of resentment at the 'great folk'; his strength is in his understanding of his job and the pride he takes in it. Indeed, where Hamlet seems anxious, self-conscious as ever, in the newly chosen role of imperturbable aristocrat, the grave-digger is strikingly at ease, well able to get the better of the tragic hero—and this contrast works in favour of the prince, because he is liable to threat, liable to the vicissitudes to which Caesar and Alexander were subject, and does not like it. 'He hath bore me on his back a thousand times, and now—how abhorr'd in my imagination it is'—these words have even a fated ring, as though to say how hard it is to be born a prince, that even the gratitude you ought to feel for the servants who do all they can for you comes, in the end, in spite of oneself or not at all. The effect of the contrast with the clown is, then, not merely criticism; instead we are left to feel that 'The rich are different from us'—or at least that princes are. They may have money and class, but class does make life difficult for them:

> O that that earth which kept the world in awe
> Should patch a wall t'expel the winter's flaw.

(208–9)

In describing the historical Caesar as 'that earth which kept the world in awe' Hamlet even shows his own awareness of the vanity of human pretensions. But he does not abandon them.

On stage again

What follows is another specimen of that drama-within-the-drama of which *Hamlet* makes such a speciality. The King and Queen, with Laertes and others, enter behind the coffin of Ophelia, and the prince becomes a spectator. He is himself impressed by the theatrical quality of what he sees. It is a rite, and the manner of its performance, not the fate of poor Ophelia's soul, is the subject of discussion. There is a natural progression from the discontent Laertes expresses at the manner of his sister's burial to the outward expression of feeling in his leap into her grave:

> What is he whose grief
> Bears such an emphasis, whose phrase of sorrow
> Conjures the wand'ring stars and makes them stand
> Like wonder-wounded hearers? (247–50)

'Emphasis' and 'phrase' are both terms associated with rhetoric: but one went to *hear* a play, and wonder was aroused by tragedy as well as oration. The gesture whereby Hamlet reveals himself—'This is I,/Hamlet the Dane!' seeems to spring from the theatrical implications of the preceding lines rather than from what is strictly rhetorical in them. Certainly, 'Nay, and thou'lt mouth,/I'll rant as well as thou' has more to do with the Globe theatre than the Roman law-court.

The maimed rites for Ophelia are a form of theatre not just because in them the outward act is to convey an inner (and religious) meaning, but because their maiming betrays an intention to qualify that meaning. They are to say something about Ophelia, and even more about the King's attitude to her death.

'I have little doubt that the real origin of these "maiméd rites" was theatrical convenience. Shakespeare needed a funeral, but elaborate ceremonial, such as was customary at Elizabethan court burials, would have involved singing men and boys and have taken time.'[16] Whatever the exigencies of the company for which Shakespeare wrote, Dover Wilson is surely wrong: the offence to honour which is implied by the reduced scale of the funeral is a prime motive in Laertes's behaviour here and is, of course, thematically linked in most intimate fashion with the rest of the play.

Why then did Dover Wilson resort to the desperate expedient of 'theatrical convenience' to explain the peculiar nature of the obsequies? What did he feel needed explaining? The answer must be that he felt that, whether or not it was thematically appropriate, the funeral was not practically justified in terms of the story. There seems no need to treat as a suicide someone who has merely fallen into the river and drowned. As we have seen, the Queen's account of the matter is ambiguous; it does not make it clear whether Ophelia willed her death or not. It leaves us free, in fact, to be suspicious about these maimed rites, and to share in Laertes's indignation. The Priest says:

> Her death was doubtful;
> And but that great command o'ersways the order,
> She should in ground unsanctified been lodg'd
> Till the last trumpet . . .   (227–30)

The grave-digger's assumption that she is being given Christian
burial at the behest of 'great folk' is proved to be right.

There can be no doubt that the 'great command' comes from the
King. It is plainly not ecclesiastical, and Laertes, the remaining
member of the family, obviously could not force the issue. But the
King, we might expect, would take his wife's view of the death: he
would not have it branded as suicide—unless it were in his interest to
do so. And it is. The King has good reasons to reduce the scale of the
funeral, considering that 'the people muddied,/Thick and unwholesome in their thoughts and whispers/For good Polonius' death'
(IV.5.81–3) are all on Laertes's side, and Ophelia's death can only be
another spur to them to revolt. The 'maimed rites' are then politically
contrived, a means to master a difficult situation for the King, whose
presence with the Queen is not the least remarkable aspect of the
funeral, plainly a sop for Laertes who, in the face of their condescen-
sion, really has no one to complain about but Hamlet:

>   O, treble woe
> Fall ten times treble on that cursed head
> Whose wicked deed thy most ingenious sense
> Depriv'd thee of.   (239–42)

The staging here is expert and effective.

'That is Laertes, a very noble youth. Mark', says Hamlet to himself
or to Horatio. The suggestion is, I suppose, that his identity may be a
clue to that of the person 'of some estate' whose funeral this is. In
view of Laertes's own preoccupation with correct form, however, as
well as Hamlet's own newly aristocratic bearing, 'a very noble
youth' is a significant description, showing the way Hamlet's mind
is moving now ('I ought to be rather nobler still than this very noble
youth'), as well as the direction in which ours should move. Laertes's
nobility does not preclude feeling, and a real tenderness can be
granted him in the lines 'Lay her i'th' earth/And from her fair and
unpolluted flesh/May violets spring'. Nevertheless, the care with
which Laertes stresses Ophelia's virginity may be interpreted as
exercised on behalf of her good name and the family's. Hamlet's

'wicked deed' was abandoning Ophelia, so that she went out of her mind, deprived of her 'ingenious sense'. Harold Jenkins glosses 'ingenious' as 'mentally alert' but in the sixteenth and seventeenth centuries the word was often confused with 'ingenuous', meaning 'pure' as well as 'well-born'. Its combination with 'sense', together with the fluid syntax permitted by postponing the verb, allows us to register the 'wicked deed' as a seduction which her well-born innocence foiled, and the abandonment as something just about as disgraceful as seduction would have been. Laertes should have mixed feelings about the 'virgin crants' which the poor dead girl has been allowed.

In all this there is a challenge to Hamlet's own sense of honour. As an aristocrat he has to assert his status as of higher degree than Laertes's. Does he leap into the grave after his rival? Dover Wilson, Granville-Barker and Prosser are all sure he does not,[17] because it would ruin the effect of 'This is I,/Hamlet the Dane'. Eleanor Prosser writes:

> . . . I take the statement to be Hamlet's conscious assertion not only of his royal dignity but also of his sanity. The power of the assertion is destroyed by a grotesque jump down to Laertes' level in the trap. The line requires a positive movement, with Hamlet stepping forward to declare himself.[18]

But with these words Hamlet enters the drama he has just been watching: as we have seen, it is a shabby drama of political manipulation. His assertion of royal dignity (which may not necessarily extend to challenging the King himself) is addressed specifically to Laertes, and in a context of 'honour', the aristocratic value to which by his new pose Hamlet implicitly commits himself. It has, therefore, something about it of the gentlefolk's pathetic vulnerability as it looks viewed from the grave-digger's place in life. This is the strange way men dedicated to the definition of themselves merely in terms of rank do behave, and it is grotesque as well as marvellous. (It is still grotesque even if Hamlet and Laertes only grapple at the grave's edge.) It is a far more strained reading than mine that sees *politics* as Hamlet's concern at this moment in the play, or thinks that his sanity is affirmed in 'Woo't weep, woo't fight, woo't fast, woo't tear thyself?'.[19] The Queen's conclusion—'This is mere madness'–is reasonable, and though we might maintain that her son's behaviour

here is merely a specimen of the 'antic disposition' put on for the
occasion, the usual difficulty remains of showing that it must be so
when little if any hint is given of his looking beyond the present
moment in the play.

But, it might be said, Hamlet does show control here. 'It is a
Hamlet now royally master of himself indeed', says Granville-
Barker '. . . who can sustain the onslaught with the mettled steadi-
ness'[20] of

> Thou pray'st not well.
> I prithee take thy fingers from my throat,
> For though I am not splenative and rash,
> Yet have I in me something dangerous,
> Which let thy wiseness fear.   (252–6)

Certainly there is resolution and deliberation here; but it is focused
within narrow confines, on Laertes, and it is in the same trammelling
aristocratic mould which has been Hamlet's since the opening of the
scene. There is no opening out to the presence of the King or of his
mother; Hamlet is knit up entirely to 'outface' (his own word)
Laertes. There is something 'dangerous' about him, he says. It is a
threat—but it is also an assertion, for 'danger' at this time still means
the 'power of a lord or master' and 'dangerous' has the sense 'difficult
to please', that is, showing the 'daintier sense' of the nobleman. His
speech is full of the drollery of someone for whom nothing can be
granted seriousness: 'Why, I will fight with him upon this theme/
Until my eyelids will no longer wag'. Life is beneath him, a mere
wagging of the eyelids.

If this is impressive it is so because, for once, Hamlet is playing his
part without the kind of self-involvement obvious, for example, in
the scenes with Ophelia and his mother. But it is a 'part' that he plays.
Dover Wilson speaks of the 'essential nobility' revealed in him in this
scene,[21] but 'nobility', like 'superiority', is an equivocal term, and it is
this quality of it that is reflected in Hamlet's odd appeal to Laertes:

> What is the reason that you use me thus?
> I lov'd you ever. But it is no matter.   (284–5)

It is, after all, Hamlet who has been treating Laertes in questionable
fashion rather than the other way round. It is twenty lines and more
since the two of them were separated, and Laertes has since then not

said a word, whilst Hamlet has ranted to his heart's content.

Even before his exit from the funeral, he regains control, asking Laertes the cause of his violence. 'But it is no matter'. From the aspect of eternity, even agonizing squabbles are of passing concern.[22]

One must protest that the violence has been Hamlet's, intruding on Ophelia's funeral, challenging the bereaved brother with his 'What is he . . . ?' and subjecting him to ignominy in his speech ('Dost come here to whine . . . ?'). The sublime note which Prosser discerns here really is not possible. It is contradicted by the very next lines, which mark his exit:

Let Hercules himself do what he may,
The cat will mew, and dog will have his day.

Unable to make plain to those around him 'the truth of this tragic discord between will and deed', says Granville-Barker, Hamlet 'flings them instead, for their satisfaction, a jingling reassurance of his "madness" '.[23] But it cannot be that, for the dog who has his day is plainly Laertes, the man to whom we are urged to think Hamlet here behaves well! (Dover Wilson's New Cambridge note, which makes Laertes out to be Hercules and Hamlet to be the dog—which Jenkins accepts as offering a second meaning—is surely wrong, since the reading goes against the very grain of Hamlet's assertion of superiority to Laertes.)[24] Hamlet leaves the stage perhaps in the calm of aristocratic superciliousness, but certainly not with all passion spent. The 'new' Hamlet is just as terrifying a phenomenon as the 'old'.

12 Heaven ordinant

Providence

Commenting on the change in Hamlet following his adventures at sea, as Dover Wilson, Granville-Barker and so many others have done after him, Bradley notes three things: a new 'consciousness of power', 'a slight thinning of the dark cloud of melancholy' and 'a sense in Hamlet that he is in the hands of Providence':

> This had, indeed, already shown itself at the death of Polonius, and perhaps at Hamlet's farewell to the King, but the idea seems now to be constantly present in his mind. 'There's a divinity that shapes our ends,' he declares to Horatio . . . How was he able, Horatio asks, to seal the substituted commission?
>
> Why, even in that was heaven ordinant, Hamlet answers; he had his father's signet in his purse. And though he has a presentiment of evil about the fencing-match he refuses to yield to it: 'we defy augury: there is special providence in the fall of a sparrow . . . the readiness is all.'[1]

Looking at the graveyard scene in isolation it was not difficult for me to argue against all those critics who see a radical change in Hamlet on his return to Denmark, and to put forward the view that all we find in him is an intensification of one aspect of his behaviour with which we are already familiar, his assumption of aristocratic superiority. But, as the example of Bradley shows, it is not customary to consider the scene in this way; in the light of Hamlet's allusions to Providence it looks rather different. It will be no surprise, however, that very different interpretations of Hamlet's relationship to Providence have been offered. Bradley, for example, is sceptical whether there has been 'any material change in [Hamlet's] general condition, or the formation of any effective resolution to fulfil the appointed duty', and finds in him 'that kind of religious resolution which . . . really deserves the name of fatalism rather than that of faith in Providence, because it is not united to any determination to do what is believed to be the will of Providence'.[2] This is not very flattering to Hamlet, and it does not ascribe much of a Christian message to the play. On the other hand, critics like H.D.F. Kitto, Irving Ribner or Maynard Mack,[3] by stressing the element of reckless courage in Hamlet as it appears in his account of how Rosencrantz and Guildenstern were despatched, are able to present the prince as God's commendably active partner, no mere passive instrument. The presence in the play of references to Providence does not of itself simplify the business of what the whole thing is about.

'These passages strike us more when put together thus than when they come upon us at intervals in reading the play', remarked Bradley.[4] Indeed they do. When we look at them in this way it is also striking that, after all, they do not all come from the last act, that is, following Hamlet's return. He refers to God's continuous watch over and care for human affairs twice before he sets out for England. Possibily not enough importance has been attached to the fact that his first such reference comes at the end of the scene where at last things have become serious for Hamlet, that is, when he has killed Polonius. We have to consider the possibility that Hamlet's characterization of himself there as 'heaven's scourge and minister' is aimed at mitigating the sense of guilt incurred for the old man's death.

At first, this idea may seem implausible. Hamlet hardly seems to feel guilt at all about what he has done: 'For this same lord,/I do repent'. When 'same' is 'appended redundantly to a demonstrative', says the *Oxford English Dictionary* (s.v.5), it usually expresses 'some degree of irritation, or contempt, sometimes playful familiarity'; contempt seems nearest the mark here, and Granville-Barker rightly comments on Hamlet's cruelty in this speech.[5] Repentance is not to be expressed in this offhand manner; at least, we cannot credit it as repentance if there is no more to go on than this. And yet what Hamlet says shows him to acknowledge that there is something to repent of; his expression of contempt is bravado, like a child's saying he is sorry as insolently as he dares. It is legitimate, I think, to see some uneasiness beneath the callous exterior and to find that uneasiness continued in the lines which attempt an unapologetic apology for the unrepentant tones in which the prince announced his repentance:

> but heaven hath pleas'd it so,
> To punish me with this and this with me,

That I must be their scourge and minister.

                                                    (III.4.173–5)

The announcement is a characteristically enigmatic piece of
Hamlet-talk. If it is difficult to understand, that is surely because it is
the utterance of someone who distrusts even his own intuition, and is
consequently evasive at the most fundamental level of language.
What is meant by 'heaven'? Does Hamlet mean the Ghost, or God
using the Ghost as his instrument, or God without reference to the
Ghost at all? What is 'this'? Is it the dead Polonius, who has certainly
been punished and whom Hamlet, against all the evidence, now
claims to be a cause of grief to him, or is 'this' the fact 'that I must be
their scourge and minister'? Does Hamlet really feel punished? It is
surely very possible that he evokes the feeling in order not to face the
guilt which in so far as he is able he would deny, guilt for Polonius's
death. When he says that he is heaven's 'scourge and minister' he
produces a phrase fully expressive of the confusion in him. Commentators generally explain that a 'scourge' is 'a wicked man used by
God to punish wickedness in others, damning himself in the process'[6] and this meaning is obviously pertinent. On the other hand, so
are the literal senses of the instrument and the man who wields it; as
the latter Hamlet knows what he is doing, as the former he does not.
The phrase exculpates him for the murder of Polonius in two ways,
by saying that he did not know what he was doing, and also that
what he did was what he knew (or knows) God wanted him to do.
The figurative sense of 'scourge' is surely secondary and, as it were,
accidental. The lines are eerie in effect not because they manifest
Hamlet's powerful faith in Providence and his resignation to a role
appointed him by God, but because they show him using ideas of
God's purpose to plaster over his own bad faith.

The bad faith appears more openly in the soon-succeeding lines
where he talks about Rosencrantz and Guildenstern:[7]

                     they must sweep my way
And marshal me to knavery. Let it work;
For 'tis the sport to have the enginer
Hoist with his own petard, and't shall go hard
But I will delve one yard below their mines
And blow them at the moon.   (III.4.206–11)

The double meaning of 'knavery', which can signify either the King's plot or some plot yet to be devised by Hamlet, sits uncomfortably with those interpretations that take Hamlet's characterization of himself as a minister of heaven in good faith. The prince's confidence in his insight into divine purpose is uncomfortably close (thanks to its callousness and its ambiguous stance in regard to the dead Polonius) to his confidence in his ability to provide for the destruction of others. This should be borne in mind later when considering the proximity in Hamlet's account of his voyage of his mention of 'heaven ordinant' and 'royal knavery'.

Hamlet's second allusion to divine interest in his affairs left Bradley, very reasonably, uncertain what to make of it. Speaking of the King's secret purposes, the prince says 'I see a cherub that sees them' (IV.3.51). According to the Riverside editors this means 'heaven sees them', but they are plainly wrong. There is nothing overweening about their gloss, whereas the line itself hints at something of that kind. Jenkins describes the line as 'A hint that Hamlet perceives more than the King supposes' It goes further however. The repetition of 'see' implies that Hamlet has a God's-eye-view of the cherub, or at least that he is used to taking a privileged vantage-point where divine purposes are concerned. It is difficult to argue positively that Hamlet is now showing bad faith. He is speaking in a mad fashion, and one of the privileges of insanity may be to see more keenly into human affairs, perhaps so keenly as to see how they relate to God's own business. In so far as Hamlet is pretending to be mad, he here produces a 'mad' remark; in so far as he is mad, it is mad. Only in so far as we suspect that he is sane and not speaking entirely for effect can we call his good faith in doubt. But if he were sane, would he claim the sort of knowledge that he does claim here? The line is capable of producing a ripple of anxiety in the reader or audience, just enough to remind us that heaven is a dangerous topic for Hamlet, one that may be and is associated in him with an ugly and self-justifying arrogance.

Since the graveyard scene is one in which this arrogance is made the focus for our attention, it would not be surprising to find there a trace of it in regard to God's affairs. Just a trace may indeed be found when Hamlet is brooding on the graveyard relics, skull by skull: 'This might be the pate of a politician which this ass [the gravedigger] now o'er-offices, one that would circumvent God, might it not?' (V.1.78–80) The assurance with which the prince speaks of God implies that for his part he has no need or wish to escape divine scrutiny. The context—Ophelia's open grave, the religious common sense of the so-much-condescended-to grave-digger—suggests the opposite. It is with all this in mind that one should come to the last scene. Hamlet's plausibility as a conscious agent of Providence is here stretched to the utmost, particularly in the account of his escape from the trap set for him in England by the King.

An ambiguous revelation

Hamlet's story of his sea-adventures is oddly placed in the play. It would surely have been more natural to have introduced it earlier on, when their outcome was fresher in our minds. It would have been simple to arrange for Hamlet to retail his escape to Horatio at the beginning of the graveyard scene. As it is, it would be difficult to believe that Hamlet could have waited so long to tell it, or Horatio to hear it, if the story were not in itself so engrossing. It is only when we consider the play from the point of view of its author that the scene starts to look rather arbitrarily placed at the opening of the play's final movement. What purpose is served by this positioning?

The narrative is certainly not postponed in order to whet our appetite for it. In the first place, Hamlet's letter to Horatio in IV.6 gives us a quite sufficient explanation of his reappearance in Denmark ('a pirate of very warlike appointment gave us chase', and so on), and in the second, although that letter suggests that Hamlet has more to tell Horatio than the letter contains, the words in which the suggestion is made are such as to allay our curiosity rather than to make it keener: 'I have words to speak in thine ear will make thee dumb'. It is surely natural to suppose that what Hamlet has in mind is his discovery of the King's plot to have him killed when he arrived in England; but we know all about that. There is nothing for us to look forward to in the promise of blood-curdling news for Horatio. Indeed, were we to be awaiting from the prince a further account of the escape, the effect of the graveyard scene, where we wait for Hamlet to discover that he has been standing above the grave of Ophelia, would be diminished; two kinds of interest would compete with each other to the detriment of both.

In the First Quarto, the scene in which Hamlet describes his adventures to Horatio is, of course, not present. It would be redundant, since the letter which Horatio receives and retails to Gertrude is circumstantial enough to record that 'by great chance' Hamlet 'had his fathers Seale' and so was able to arrange for Rosencrantz and Guildenstern 'without discoverie' the fate which his stepfather had planned for him. The contrast of this version with that of the Second Quarto and the Folio emphasizes the deliberate quality of having Hamlet tell Horatio about his escape at the very start of the last scene. This later placing has a double effect. Firstly, it means that we do not learn that Hamlet has sent Rosencrantz and Guildenstern to their death until after the graveyard scene. Hamlet's dangerous quality is emphasized just before the fencing-match. Secondly, we learn that Hamlet believes God to be on his side, and to sanction his killing. His father's seal, which was the means of murdering the two courtiers, was not in his purse on board ship 'by great chance', as Horatio puts it in the First Quarto, but, in Hamlet's view, because 'even in that was heaven ordinant'. It looks as though Shakespeare wanted us to see Hamlet just before the catastrophe as someone believing himself licensed by God to kill. It is, to say the least, an ambiguous revelation.

Dark backward

However, an important function of Hamlet's narrative is to present him as very much the same person he has been throughout the play, not in that it shows him to be changeable and indecisive still, for it does not, but in that the various aspects which he shows here are recognizably connected with ones we have already seen. This function is given more emphasis by the fact that we already know the story in its broad outlines, that Hamlet was the only prisoner taken by the pirates and that Rosencrantz and Guildenstern 'hold their course for England' (IV.6.25). The story itself, that is to say, is a rehearsal of familiar material, except in regard to Hamlet's belief about his help from God; even the news that Rosencrantz and Guildenstern 'go to't' is linked—in the Second Quarto and its followers, but not in the Folio text—with what we already know, Hamlet's intention to 'delve one yard below their mines/And blow them at the moon' (III.4.210–11). This speech requires a characteristic movement of mind in its hearer or reader, a reference back to what has already been seen and heard, which must keep pace with the impetuous forward movement of the speech itself.

'Sir, in my heart there was a kind of fighting/That would not let me sleep'. The mood of excitement that this suggests is the one already described by Gertrude as a 'lawless fit' in which her son was 'Mad as the sea and wind when both contend/Which is the mightier' (IV.1.7–8). The same idea of the strife within the person, and one that is a threat to its existence, occurs in the Ghost's plea to Hamlet on Gertrude's behalf in the closet scene:

> O, step between her and her fighting soul.
> Conceit in weakest bodies strongest works.
> Speak to her, Hamlet.   (III.4.113–15)

The opening of Hamlet's narrative is ominously coloured by these two earlier versions of the same idea. Here it is given characteristically physical emphasis by Hamlet himself. His body-consciousness reflects his concern with a dilemma of honour, and it is no less characteristically focused here on the heart, the seat of all noble passions and the most susceptible of all Hamlet's organs.

'Methought I lay/Worse than the mutines in the bilboes.' By his comparison, Hamlet identifies himself with the lowest form of life on the ship that is imaginable; his discomfort makes him inferior even to the men on board in chains. The comparison is ostensibly restricted to his uncomfortable restlessness, but pushes out beyond such limits. To find 'a kind of fighting' in his heart gives Hamlet good reason for classing himself amongst his inferiors. To acknowledge the possibility of unmasterable conflict (not passion) within the heart would be to lose caste; it would be alien to aristocratic self-sufficiency and self-definition. Actually to suffer it, then, would be extreme degradation, something far worse than the sense that 'Denmark's a prison' (II.2.243) to which Hamlet gave voice half-mockingly and not without deprecation in talking to the courtiers. But 'the bilboes' are not simply the fetters worn by low-class people; they belong here specifically to 'mutines', that is, to those who have attempted rebellion against authority. Hamlet himself is subject to an authority against which he feels drawn to rebel; the impotence of that feeling is expressed in the way he puts himself amongst those who have failed in rebellion even before his act of mutiny, the despatching of Rosencrantz and Guildenstern, is performed. The word 'mutine' has been used before in the play and with a significantly equivocal effect:

> Rebellious hell,
> If thou can'st mutine in a matron's bones,
> To flaming youth let virtue be as wax
> And melt in her own fire . . .   (III.4.82–5)

Might it not be a similarly hellish prompting now that makes Hamlet feel 'Worse than the mutines in the bilboes'?

Certainly his words at this point direct us to think of the closet scene as well as of what happened on board the ship. 'Rashly—/And prais'd be rashness for it' recalls two earlier moments in the play, the first when he spoke the improbable words to Laertes 'though I am not splenative and rash'—evidently spoken with sang-froid and as part of a threat (V.1.254)—and the second the exchange with his mother at the death of Polonius: 'O, what a rash and bloody deed is this!' and its rebuttal 'Thou wretched, rash, intruding fool, farewell' (III.4.27,31). These are not auspicious overtones for the word's appearance here, especially as the Queen's judgement that Polonius's murder was 'rash' is right. It is hard to believe that that 'indiscretion' served anyone well, and a similar reservation with regard to Hamlet's action in the narrative seems to be invoked by Shakespeare's choice of word. (Indeed, since 'rashness' connotes youthful vigour as well as foolish haste, and is associated with 'indiscretion', the satisfaction Hamlet takes in his rashness suggests that he has become more like the person he was imagined to be by Polonius and Laertes in the first act, a person whose 'nature crescent' makes 'unmaster'd importunity' likely in him (I.3.11,32).)

> Rashly—
> And prais'd be rashness for it: let us know
> Our indiscretion sometime serves us well
> When our deep plots do pall; and that should learn us
> There's a divinity that shapes our ends,
> Rough-hew them how we will—   (V.2.6–11)

This is only the beginning of a long sentence almost twenty lines in length, most artfully developed in order to end with the revelation that 'My head should be struck off'. In speaking of rashness and indiscretion, Hamlet is conspicuously calm. It is again the sang-froid

of his encounter with Laertes. As there, he establishes by style his
distance from the events he describes. Don Juan might retail a
conquest in the same detached manner (and might also invoke, with
a little thrill of blasphemy, 'a divinity that shapes our ends'). 'Let us
know . . . '. Who are 'we'? Is it Hamlet and Horatio? If so, the
companion is invoked rather as a member of the congregation,
privileged to be granted such insight as Hamlet can offer. Or is
Hamlet again using his royal 'we'? It would suit his present mood of
superiority to circumstance, the mood of the graveyard enlarged and
exalted, very well. As for the 'divinity that shapes our ends', the tone
of the line is not inevitably blasphemous. Hamlet might be thought
really to evince a religious humility that contrasts the unsuccess of
'our deep plots' with the might of the unseen Creator. Man proposes,
God disposes. This is, however, a superficial reading, for Hamlet can
lay claim to no 'deep plots' of his own. His rashness is a release from
thought which, he says, was justified by its bringing about what
thought could not achieve; and it is this justification of his mindless
action that matters, rather than any affirmation of faith in a Christian
Providence. The outcome of his rashness should tell us what it was
Hamlet had previously been plotting without success. It cannot have
been his escape from the ship, since that has nothing to do with the
business of the seal immediately ensuing on the rashness in whose
praise he speaks; it might have been knowledge of the contents of the
packet, but it does not appear that 'deep plots' would have seemed
necessary even to Hamlet to gain this; it seems most likely, then, that
Hamlet is claiming that he had considered deeply how to score off
Rosencrantz and Guildenstern and perhaps, through them, the King.
Both these claims must be spurious, because a little thought shows
that nothing is served by their death but Hamlet's irrational dislike of
them. It will not matter to the King whether or not they live when
they get to England if they have failed to secure the death of Hamlet.
The prince himself admits their secondary importance when he later
explains that they are themselves to blame for their death because
they got in the way between him and the King. In the light of all this,
'deep plots' looks like a phrase designed to make Hamlet's vacilla-
tions sound impressive.[8]

It might be objected, of course, that at the moment he mentions
these plots we do not know what the outcome of his rashness will be,
and that consequently the arguments here fail to take into account

the effect of what Hamlet says in the theatre, where we are not supposed to be in possession of facts before they are revealed. Even looked at in this way, however, the passage is suspect as an expression of Christian faith. The idea that God oversees the affairs of men is, of course, unexceptionable, but linking it to the praise of rashness is decidedly questionable. Does it follow from God's continual and invincible care for man that men ought to behave irrationally in order that divine Providence should manifest itself more clearly? That would be a strange doctrine, and only Hamlet's qualification— 'Our indiscretion *sometime* serves us well'—saves him from it. We are required to judge from the event whether rashness has served him well in this instance. If the bad aura of the word 'rashness' itself is not enough to make us wary here, then Hamlet's own qualification should be. It should in any case be noted that 'a divinity' can mean either 'a God' or 'a godlike power'—that is, that it shares with the line 'I see a cherub that sees them' a nuance of hubris.

Perhaps the word 'nuance' needs special emphasis. What the reader or audience should register is not that Hamlet is speaking out of sinful pride when he justifies his rashness by God's Providence, but that in his excitement he leaves himself open to the charge of speaking in that way, and that it might be possible for the charge to be sustained. His excitement is a mitigating circumstance, though it is hardly possible for us to say how far it would in fact mitigate any sinfulness there might be in what he says. What it does do is make it doubtful how far Hamlet is aware of all that what he is saying means, a familiar state of affairs as far as the prince is concerned. Hamlet's excitement is not simply a matter of the past events on the ship; it is also part of the telling of those events in the present, manifest most obviously in the syncopated rhythm as well as the diction of his speech. The rhythm is one of heavy but unexpected stresses, often clashing: 'Úp fröm mÿ cábiň, 'tǒ fińd oút them, hád mÿ děsiře,/ Fíngěr'd thěir páckět. . . ' 'Tǒ miňe own róom ǎgáin . . . ' Verbs are given great emphasis. An incongruous sexual suggestiveness in the words used by Hamlet at once reinforces our sense of his excitement and distances us and him from it. 'Grop'd I to find out them', by inverting verb and subject, not only gives the verb prominence but nudges the subject on towards 'them' who are no sooner encountered than he has had his desire in 'fingering' their packet. Drolly and mockingly, Hamlet attributes to himself a masculine activity exercised

upon the feminine passive of Rosencrantz and Guildenstern (who
'did make love to this employment'); the mockery insulates Hamlet
from any possible charge of self-admiration by making fun of
his rash action, at the same time as it evokes the excitingly in-
discreet qualities of it. The sexual double entendre, used both to
contain and to express the excitement of the deed, calls up the
ambiguous force with which at the end of the second act Hamlet
compared himself to 'a very drab,/A scullion', as well as the
equivocal element in his intemperate outbursts on sex to Ophelia and
his mother. What is new is that the element of containment and
control predominates over that of emotion expressed—the double
entendre is, as the sentence develops, brought in line with the simpler
irony of 'No, not to stay the grinding of the axe' and the speaker's
excitement is finally identified not with the act of unsealing 'the
grand commission', but with his indignation at the treachery of his
stepfather.

At any rate—and paradoxical though it may seem—aristocratic
poise turns out to be the outstanding feature of Hamlet's narrative,
and the audacious and dramatic treatment of his excursion to the
place where the courtiers lay is of a piece with the confident handling
of the sentence and its story. Hamlet makes so bold, 'My fears
forgetting manners, to unseal/Their grand commission'. The allusion
to manners comes from someone who feel himself above manners,
an aristocrat who calls a spade a spade and who, if a man has
whor'd his mother, says so in plain English. But language is his
servant, not his master; that is implicit in all he says. He stands above
and apart from language and at that distance shapes his utterance:

> I found, Horatio—
> Ah, royal knavery!—an exact command,
> Larded with many several sorts of reasons
> Importing Denmark's health, and England's too,
> With ho! such bugs and goblins in my life,
> That on the supervise, no leisure bated,
> No, not to stay the grinding of the axe,
> My head should be struck off.   (18–25)

'An exact command that my head should be struck off' would have
gone to the point too fast for Hamlet: it might have seemed that he
was anxious to impart his information. So he spins his sentence out,

but with an air of casualness lest too much art be visible. Even his
bravado must be lightly worn. Was the Ghost a 'goblin damn'd'
(I.4.40) or not? Was he frightening? Nothing is admitted in 'With ho!
such bugs and goblins' but a becoming indifference to Hamlet's own
case. Granville-Barker speaks of a 'grim enjoyment of the business'
manifest in the elaboration of this speech.[9] That is to take it very
much as Hamlet wants Horatio to take it, with the qualification that
'grim' is a little too intense. But it becomes us in the audience to see
that Hamlet does compose his speech with a view to how it sounds,
perhaps to himself as well as to his companion.

As the story unfolds the note of amused detachment appears more
and more clearly, taking us further and further from the passing
disquiet that the reference to the 'divinity that shapes our ends' might
have caused. This detachment is not by any means a religious detachment. It belongs to an aristocrat who can mock the manners of an
inferior world. One sentence takes off the flowery language of official
communiqués ('peace should still her wheaten garland wear') and
most carefully takes off *from* it, in order to come to rest on the baldly
shocking phrase 'Not shriving-time allow'd'. Hamlet plays a brutal
comedy with language in this sentence; its brutality is part of the
account he has to settle where Rosencrantz and Guildenstern are
concerned. In another sentence he turns upon himself the weapon of
drama which he had tried to use against the King: 'Or I could make a
prologue to my brains,/They had begun the play'; his aristocratic
strength shows in his not remarking on this reversal, just as his
nobility of bearing lies in his having transcended all gentility—the
gentility, for example, of thinking it 'A baseness to write fair'. He is
happy to acknowledge not that he did 'Yeoman's service', but that
his skill in writing could do it for him. This poise seems meant to tell
us, and the speaker himself, that he is indeed a mighty opposite to the
King. It does not follow, of course, that he is one; indeed the
occasions with which the narrative presents us of linking this Hamlet
with the one we have seen already make it seem unlikely that he is
doing much more here than cheering himself up.

Excuses

There is little in Hamlet's account of his escape to suggest that it is a
'new' prince who is offering it. The common notion that he has been

spiritually reborn derives from a not very scrupulous consideration of his allusions to Providence. Irving Ribner, for example, tells us that 'faith in the providence of God' is 'the principal mark' of Hamlet's 'regeneration':

> He has escaped from the death awaiting him in England not only through his own ingenuity, but also through a series of semi-miraculous accidents without which his most careful plans would have come to nought. It is clear to the new Hamlet whom we meet in the final act that heaven has preserved him, that his own valour could serve him only when supported by divine purpose. This Hamlet affirms for Horatio . . . [10]

The train of argument is obviously confused: Hamlet's ingenuity secures the death of Rosencrantz and Guildenstern, not his own escape, and the description of the accidents associated with the escape and their murder as 'semi-miraculous' begs the question of what there is that is at all miraculous about them. When is a fortunate accident not 'semi-miraculous'? As for the clarity with which Hamlet sees heaven to have preserved him, heaven was ordinant, according to him, not in the encounter with the pirates but in the provision of his father's seal in his purse. It could be argued that the seal enabled Hamlet's tampering with the 'grand commission' to go undetected, and so contributed to his escape as well as to the demise of its bearers; but the point is theoretical, since Hamlet himself describes his action as a response to theirs: '*They* had begun the play./*I* sat me down . . .' He might feel bound to thank God for the answer he was able to produce, not— from anything that appears in his words—for his preservation.

The death of Rosencrantz and Guildenstern is important to Shakespeare. He does not bring it to our attention only here at the beginning of the last scene; he also introduces ambassadors from England at its end, whose only function apart from that of filling the stage is to announce that it has been brought about. It is, then, not a matter to be passed over in silence.

H.D.F. Kitto's interpretation attempts to establish the reasonableness of Hamlet's turning the tables on the two courtiers. He quotes the prince's account of it:

Why, man, they did make love to this employment.
They are not near my conscience. Their defeat
Doth by their own insinuation grow.
'Tis dangerous when the baser nature comes
Between the pass and fell incensed points
Of mighty opposites.   (57–62)

And on this he remarks:

> This is not Hamlet trying to exculpate himself. Shakespeare is not
> interested in that kind of thing here. He is saying: 'This is what
> happens in life, when foolish men allow themselves to be used by
> such as Claudius, and to get themselves involved in desperate
> affairs like these.' To prove that this is what he meant, we may
> once more reflect what Horatio might have said, and then listen to
> what he does say:
>   Why, what a King is this!
> How could Shakespeare more decisively draw our attention away
> from a nice and private appraisal of Hamlet's character, as expressed
> in this affair, and direct it to the philosophic or 'religious' frame-
> work in which it is set? Horatio says just what Laertes says later:
> 'The King! the King's to blame.'[11]

Horatio's remark shows him not so much as having something to
say about the King, as *not* saying anything about Hamlet. His brief
comments in this long dialogue suggest self-restraint and submission
rather than the arbitrating force which Kitto attributes to him here.
What he says does not, in any case, incline us to think about the
'philosophic or "religious" framework' because Hamlet is so very
positively inclined to be unphilosophical. 'Does it not, think thee,
stand *me* now upon . . . ' says Hamlet in reply to Horatio; he is
concerned not with philosophy, but as usual, with himself and his
dilemma. But fairness requires that the whole of this next speech be
quoted, for Hamlet certainly does say quite a lot about the sort of
king that Claudius is:

> Does it not, think thee, stand me now upon—
> He that hath kill'd my king and whor'd my mother,
> Popp'd in between th'election and my hopes,
> Thrown out his angle for my proper life

And with such coz'nage—is't not perfect conscience
To quit him with this arm? And is't not to be damn'd,
To let this canker of our nature come
In further evil?   (63–70)

The control manifest in the opening long sentence of Hamlet's narrative is missing here. The hostile account of Claudius slips in parenthetically, and its grammatical relation to the body of the sentence is not firmly secured. It is as though the thought of what now stands upon Hamlet to do is in some way unwelcome to him, inducing the vilification of Claudius as a simple diversion only later to be brought, in a fashion, into the structure of the sentence by linking 'he' with 'him' when Hamlet has recovered nerve and can face the thought of quitting 'him' with 'this arm'. It is consistent with the immediate context that after justifying his dismissal of Rosencrantz and Guildenstern Hamlet should seek to justify what he contemplates with regard to the King, and it is consistent in the larger perspective of the play that he should fuel his own righteousness by thinking what a 'bloody bawdy villain' Claudius is (II.2.576). Where such an interpretation is plausible, rather more is needed to prove Kitto's point than he has actually provided.

He does, it is true, rely also on the assumption that Hamlet is regenerate in the play's last act. The difficulties to which this assumption gives rise are by no means confined to whatever my commentary so far may have suggested in the way of objection. Eleanor Prosser, who works very hard indeed to see an ethically acceptable Hamlet in the final scene, finds it impossible nevertheless to excuse his treatment of Rosencrantz and Guildenstern.

The trouble lies not merely in the events described but in the way Hamlet describes them. The shocking phrase 'Not shriving-time allow'd' shocks Prosser; it fits too well with what the 'old' Hamlet had promised:

His malice has led him far beyond the needs of self-protection. In blowing his two old friends at the moon, he has acted exactly as he vowed he would act. He has, moreover, accomplished the same fate he intended for Claudius by damning his assumed enemies to Hell.[12]

Nor can she accept that there is a distinction to be made between the Hamlet of the voyage and the Hamlet who has been 'forced to admit the facts of mortality'[13] in the graveyard:

> In the first place, Hamlet's conviction that 'heaven [was] ordinant' in providing him the means for killing implies that he believes divine will favoured the revenge. Moreover, the obvious satisfaction with which he now reports his trick seems to indicate that he has not been purged in any way.[14]

Furthermore, says Prosser, Hamlet's prospective justification of the killing of the King ('. . . is't not perfect conscience?') shows very much the same quality of vindictiveness. She is unable to breathe easily until she gets to 'It will be short; the interim's mine . . ', where we do, it seems, 'hear again the tones of the Hamlet who emerged from the graveyard . . .'. The flash of the 'old' Hamlet is left behind, and though the 'loose ends' which are associated with it are 'not incidental to the main theme but crucial to interpretation' she can offer no better explanation than that 'Shakespeare did not finish polishing the play'. Evidently she thinks it possible that Hamlet's narrative derives from the ur-*Hamlet* and that it would have been removed if the poet had had time to review his play as a whole. The play's great length suggests that Shakespeare in fact had good time to write it; there is no textual support for the idea that the last act incorporates imperfect revision, and the only revision needed was omission of lines 1–74 (as in the First Quarto) and lines 372–7 (which in the First Quarto say nothing of Rosencrantz and Guildenstern); Prosser's suggestion has, therefore, little *prima facie* plausibility. In any case, how could matter 'crucial' to interpretation go unrevised? Later, she describes these difficulties as 'minor in light of the play as a whole'[15]—'crucial' seems nearer the mark. Hamlet's lordly dismissal of Rosencrantz and Guildenstern only reveals what his dialogue with the grave-digger implied—an overweening sense of his own superiority.

Horatio's role in all this is, as I have noted, subdued. 'That is most certain'; 'Is't possible?'; 'I beseech you'; 'Ay, good my lord'—these nondescript utterances fix our attention firmly on Hamlet. Two of his lines throw light on our reaction to what Hamlet says. When he musingly exclaims 'So Guildenstern and Rosencrantz go to't', he betrays uneasiness by going back to the point when Hamlet had

finished with it. That is why Kitto has to defend the prince from a
charge of 'self-exculpation'. And when Hamlet asks him.

> is't not to be damn'd,
> To let this canker of our nature come
> In further evil?   (68–70)

Horatio does not reply, but shows himself still to be thinking of the
consequences of the trick played on the unfortunate courtiers:

> It must be shortly known to him from England
> What is the issue of the business there.   (71–2)

To this Hamlet replies, but in such a way as to turn his face from the
nature of that 'issue':

> It will be short. The interim is mine,
> And a man's life's no more than to say 'one'.   (73–4)

What this means is in dispute. The Riverside editors take it as saying
that killing a man takes no longer than saying 'one', but Prosser
thinks that 'both context and tone imply that he does not mean to use
the brief time to strike down Claudius' (230). Jenkins takes up a
midway position. 'To the hint that he has only a short time in which
to act Hamlet retorts that man's whole life is short.' It is possible to
agree with both Jenkins and the Riverside editors and yet to feel that
Prosser's response to the tone is accurate. The terseness here is
affected, not characteristic and not lucid; it is characteristic only as a
piece of play-acting, in which Hamlet pretends to have made up his
mind without showing that he has done so. He goes on immediately
to talk of Laertes. Prosser thinks that this shows him intent on
forgiveness and reconciliation, but 'by the image of my cause I
see/The portraiture of his' (77–8) makes it clear that he is also
thinking, as usual ineffectually, about revenge. Altogether his reply
to Horatio is uncomfortable. In so far as his friend implies that he
should do something soon, Hamlet poses nobly but, by implication,
indecisively; and in so far as Horatio has the deaths of Rosencrantz
and Guildenstern in mind, Hamlet simply refuses to consider them.

Hamlet's account of his escape draws attention further to his
adoption of the aristocratic role and its fundamental relation to his
dilemma by suggesting its connection with earlier aspects of his

behaviour. At the same time, it shows him to be evasive of his responsibility for an action at once unnecessary and ethically indefensible. His evasiveness takes the form of bravado, but also that of invoking ideas of divine sanction for what he has done; these ideas cannot be justified in any conventional view of Providence. It remains to be seen whether Hamlet's view of his place in the divine scheme of things is unconventional.

Dieu et mon droit

It is significant that Hamlet's allusions to Providence come in the later part of the play. Three of the five occur in the last scene. All come when Hamlet has abandoned toying with the role of 'honest' man which is so important, for example, in 'To be or not to be'. They all tend to magnify his part in human affairs, or are compatible with an enlarged sense of his own importance. They are associated with his newly acquired and self-conscious aristocratic bearing.

The association is natural, since God has traditionally been considered to uphold the cause of honour; most obviously in the judicial combat, where the victor is the man with divine backing. The hierarchy of honour—seen from the point of view of its principal exponents—is, then, established by God himself. Pitt-Rivers observes that 'The superb mottoes of the aristocracy of Europe rub in the point: *Roi ne puis, duc ne daigne, Rohan suis*, or prouder still: *Despúes de Dios, la Casa de Quiros*'.[16] The motto associated with the English coat of arms is in this category: *Dieu et mon droit*. God is given precedence, but only just. Does God determine what I may do, or do I judge what is fitting for God? When Henry VIII retained the title of Defender of the Faith, bestowed on him by the Pope, he asserted an essentially aristocratic intimacy with God's affairs. The rather more thrusting motto of the Sardis of Ferrara, *Deus et ego*, only takes the English device one stage further in frankness. The word which goes with the Scottish coat of arms leaves God out of it altogether, but appropriates his wrath: *Nemo me impune lacessit*, 'No one harms me unpunished'. We can see that Elizabeth I and James I had an interest in maintaining solidarity with God and in representing themselves as the means by which honour was to be distributed throughout the kingdom; establishment of their authority over the heralds and attempts to bolster the Earl Marshal's office helped further this aim.

We can also see that pride of rank made it difficult to accept that the divine sanction of one's honourable status came through the monarch only—hence the challenges to royal authority such as Essex's knighting of his own men, or the incessant bickering about duelling in the reign of James I. Hamlet's claim that heaven was ordinant in his affairs recalls the motto of the Ducs de Grammont, *Dei gratia sum id quod sum* (not so very different from what Woodward calls 'the haughty *Lo soy que soy*' which it replaced). One might also cite the punning *Deus dedit* of the Deodati of Lucca. The coincidence of Hamlet's redefinition of himself as an aristocrat with his sense of divine favour of some kind may be seen as no coincidence at all, but a natural consequence of his concern for personal honour. Furthermore,

> seen from the individual's point of view, to have recourse to justice is to abnegate one's claim to settle one's debts of honour for oneself, the only way in which they can be settled. When challenged to fight, it is not honourable to demand police protection. Therefore, while the sovereign is the 'fount of honour' in one sense, he is also the enemy of honour in another, since he claims to arbitrate in regard to it. He takes over the functions of the Divinity thanks to his sacred character. The change from the period when the law prescribed the judicial combat to that when the duel was made illegal corresponds to an extension of the competence of the state in judicial matters. Yet no man of honour, least of all an aristocrat, was prepared to remit to the courts the settlement of his affairs of honour. Hence the inefficacy of the legislation against duelling.[17]

Hamlet was written at a time when the claims of personal honour were far from regulated by common law, and it exploits the excited feelings which honour might arouse by intensifying the conflict between honour and honesty, by emphasizing both the power and the savagery of the desire for revenge, as well as by depicting the 'fount of honour' as itself a muddied source. The 'sacred character' of Claudius as King can certainly be questioned, particularly in the light of his attempted prayer, and this is one reason why we cannot reject outright the notion that, after all, Hamlet is the sacred one, even if tainted—he might in this respect be like Richard II. That king, however, expected too much of heaven:

For every man that Bolingbroke hath press'd
To lift shrewd steel against our golden crown,
God for his Richard hath in heavenly pay
A glorious angel: then if angels fight,
Weak men must fall . . .   (*Richard II* III.2.58–62)

Hamlet's own ambiguous appeals to heaven reflect a conventional concept of divine sanction similarly pressed to unconventional extremes. The dominant function of the scene with Horatio at the opening of V.2 is to show him exposed in his extreme position.

13 Hamlet's end

Osric

When he wrote *Hamlet* Shakespeare was retelling an old story whose most exciting features were to be retained—the Ghost, the prince's mad talk, probably the play-within-the-play and the fatal catastrophe. There is no reason to think that he was trying at the same time to create an Elizabethan discussion-drama in which the hazards and rewards of the pursuit of honour were the subject for debate. Shakespeare's play has unity by virtue of its dealing with honour, but honour is not its central concern. What interests Shakespeare is Hamlet and his fate. No character is made a privileged spokesman on the subject of honour, and when the opportunity arises of criticizing the idea, it is not taken; in the graveyard scene and Hamlet's account of the sea-voyage, for example, attention is fixed on Hamlet and the person he is rather than on some abstract principle thought to be determining his conduct. In both these cases Hamlet speaks theatrically, as someone presenting himself to the world; the element of rant, the element of self-justification, works to remind us that there is more to Hamlet than is allowed expression by him in any one speech. He cannot be summed up. Because the sense of honour is intimately related to the sense of identity it provides Shakespeare with a means of entry to states of mind whose complexity defies articulation, but we are never allowed to feel that Hamlet realizes his identity completely in any one expression of concern for honour. This does not only protect him from the most severe of our criticisms—for example, when he adopts the man-of-the-world bravado of 'Why, man, they did make love to this employment . . .' (V.2.57), where the contempt or impatience in 'man' stands for something not to be grasped even by Horatio—but also keeps us intent on what happens next, since there is always something more of Hamlet to come.

Hamlet's fate is to drive himself into a situation from which he cannot escape, to die and leave behind the sense that there was more to him than he was able to get into his life. His fate is ironic, because in accomplishing his task of revenge he seems to fulfil himself as a man of honour; and yet it is pathetic, because he never completely identifies himself with the cause of honour. (The 'rashness' which inspires his discovery of the King's treachery and his answer to it is associated with the qualities of honourable youth but also with the madness that disfigures honour as much as it dissimulates it. The same ambiguous quality is attached to the assent Hamlet gives to the fencing-match.)

Irony and pathos are the qualities which Shakespeare evokes at the end of the play, and he does so by building on the extremity of Hamlet's position in the story of his escape as it is offered to Horatio. Hamlet does not retreat from this position, and yet circumstance and his own temperament reveal it to be other than it first appears. Although his narrative is climactic in its revelation of how far Hamlet will go in the cultivation of his aristocratic stance, it is introductory to the whole scene, because it fails to exhaust the nervous energy expended in its telling, and this naturally seeks further release. The contrast between the narrative itself and the uncontrolled violence of his ensuing outburst against Claudius, 'He that hath kill'd my king and whor'd my mother', warns us that the lull of 'It will be short. The interim is mine' is based on no settled resolution. Osric's entry provides welcome distraction for the prince, and the opportunity to work off more of his unsatisfied aggressiveness.

Hamlet treats Osric much as he has already treated Polonius, Rosencrantz and Guildenstern. The juxtaposition of this scene of rough humour with the story of how Hamlet dealt with his fellow-voyagers to England suggests the force of his hostility not to the King but to the court. It is a hostility that may be interpreted either as the reflection of true honour on false (Osric is only a jumped-up landowner) or as revulsion from the society that sustains the sense of honour that is driving Hamlet further and further into the role of his opposite, a Laertes. His insistence that Osric should put his hat back on his head recalls the 'courtesy . . . not of the right breed' (III.2.305–6) shown to Rosencrantz and Guildenstern after 'The Mousetrap' was broken up, particularly the pressing upon Guildenstern of the recorders; and his production of Osric's assent to contradictory accounts of the weather echoes the business with Polonius about the cloud which is shaped like a camel, a weasel and a whale (III.2.367ff.). These reminiscences give the scene a typical quality, suggesting that

Hamlet's loathing for court life goes deeper than his new-found attitude of nobler-than-thou; and consequently they soften our response to Hamlet's narrative, whose assertions of divine interest in the prince's personal affairs now seem merely an extension of that loathing, something which he does not understand himself and which leads him to strike out wherever and however he can at the court ethic of subservience (which is nevertheless, and paradoxically, inseparable from the ideal of honour he appears to be intent on maintaining).

Hamlet's attack on Osric is out of proportion, just because Osric is only a pretext. His speech is indeed affected, but his little conceit 'the card or calendar of gentry', with its ensuing pun 'the continent of what part a gentleman would see', unnecessary ornament that it is, does not warrant the rebuke administered by Hamlet in his reply. He parodies an involved syntax and an *outré* vocabulary; Osric's sentences are straightforward in construction and his vocabulary not so very extraordinary. Beside Hamlet's satiric 'definement', 'inventorially', 'dozy', 'of great article', Osric's 'differences' looks quite harmless. Osric is fulsome and in his fulsomeness strains to be courtly: 'very dear to fancy, very responsive to the hilts, most delicate carriages, and of very liberal conceit' shows this, where 'responsive' for 'matching' and 'carriages' for 'hangers' are marks of strain; but the overall effect is of surfeit, as earlier with his description of Laertes.

Hamlet does not parody Osric. He invokes Osric's ideal of courtliness to annihilate him; he demonstrates that what Osric admires is despised by the prince to whom he defers. He does this for one of two reasons suggested by the text (characteristically neither one excludes the other). First, he despises Osric for his lack of wit and possession of wealth. Second, he disdains the deference which Osric offers him; external honours are of no concern to him. In deploying his superior wit against Osric Hamlet makes two contradictory assertions: that he is indifferent to honour and that he is so far superior in honour to Osric that he can without loss of it feign indifference to it.

Eleanor Prosser finds Hamlet to be 'the epitome of princely graciousness' in his exchange with Osric, but she has private reasons for doing so: 'The leisurely parenthesis of relaxed fun conveys Hamlet's new serenity and poise in a way that the Graveyard Scene could not'.[1] Poise hardly seems to be the mark of Hamlet's performance here, using a steam-roller to crack a nut. She says that he exhibits 'wit without bitterness, satire without malice', but overlooks the wilful quality in this exercise of Hamlet's wit, which appears as no over-flow of genial spirits ready to play with equal pleasure, let us say, upon Horatio as upon Osric but as a weapon to hold Osric off and isolate the prince with his friend.

Like Hamlet's tone, the isolation is ambivalent. On the one hand it betokens Hamlet's holding himself in readiness. There is a powerful contrast between the wild sea-adventure and the encounter with the empty-headed 'water-fly' Osric which Hamlet reinforces by his disdain; the implication is that *he* belongs in the world of action. Yet he hardly gets closer to it by establishing a distance between himself and, of all people, Osric. There is an uneasy hint that in concerning himself so much with Osric, even if it is to separate himself from him, Hamlet is displaying something less than the readiness which, we are soon to learn, is 'all'. It is this ambivalent quality that colours the prince's acceptance of the King's plan:

> Sir, I will walk here in the hall. If it please his Majesty, it is the breathing time of day with me. Let the foils be brought, the gentleman willing, and the King hold his purpose, I will win for him and I can . . .   (170–4)

This reads just as well if it is taken to express want of alacrity as if it were sang-froid or courtly indifference; and indeed Hamlet's pre-vious quibble 'How if I answer no?', though hardly meant to imply reluctance, does stress the negative rather than the positive qualities of his response.

As Prosser says, this scene is no 'irrelevant bit of comic relief'. It develops the high aristocratic tone of the preceding dialogue with Horatio and reintroduces a sense of uncertainty in Hamlet which the excited heroics of his narrative had seemed to exclude. Further, it confirms our sense of him as someone who does not quite fit the courtly ideals for which he would seem to believe himself made. Finally, it reveals in him an aggressive restlessness that he feels it right to expend on even such an unworthy object as Osric. The fate of Rosencrantz and Guildenstern can hardly be forgotten, but our consciousness of it is modified by an awareness that, willy-nilly,

Hamlet may have prepared in his unknowingness and confusion a similar fate for himself.

The sparrow

Hamlet's encounter with Osric is used by Shakespeare to announce the imminence of the fencing-match and artfully to postpone it, but it also serves as a bridge between his references to Providence in the narrative to Horatio and the last reference to 'special providence in the fall of a sparrow'. Bradley's suspicion that Hamlet indulges in fatalism[2] can hardly be based on the earlier references because these are associated with actions for which Hamlet evidently takes responsibility; it derives from the speech with which Hamlet prefaces the entry of the King and his court. The second half of the scene, in which Hamlet is killed, is introduced to us under the auspices of his belief in 'special providence'; the first half of the scene, however, shows us that Hamlet's understanding of Providence is as uncertain as his adherence to the principle of honour. Hamlet, approaching the moment of his own trial, describes Osric as one

> of the same bevy that I know the drossy age dotes on—only got the tune of the time, and out of an habit of encounter, a kind of yeasty collection, which carries them through and through the most profound and winnowed opinions; and do but blow them to their trial, the bubbles are out. (185–91)

Hamlet's judgement on Osric is that he lives only by externals; our judgement on Hamlet's adherence to an internal principle of noble— that is, honourable—conduct must take into account the instability of his own notion that God has a special care for him, an instability that veers from rashness to fatalism within two hundred lines.

When the Lord enters to announce the imminent arrival of the King and Queen, and to confirm Hamlet's readiness for the match, Hamlet assures him:

> I am constant to my purposes, they follow the King's pleasure. If his fitness speaks, mine is ready. Now or whensoever, provided I be so able as now. (197–9)

It has become usual to follow the interpretation of Walker, first offered in 1860, and find double entendre in 'purposes' and 'pleasure', so that Hamlet says at one level that he stands by what he told Osric and will act as the King wishes, but at another that he is constant in his resolve to overcome his mighty opposite and to despatch him whilst he is indulging himself, 'With all his crimes broad blown' (III.3.81), 'Not shriving-time allow'd' (V.2.47). This is hardly an interpretation suitable for those who believe Hamlet to be someone whose actions are sanctified by Providential care, and it is no surprise that Eleanor Prosser pays it no attention. Rightly; not because it presents Hamlet in a bad light, as an unChristian avenger, but because it clashes with his innocent reply to Horatio's observation 'You will lose, my lord': 'I do not think so . . . I shall win at the odds'. This shows him to be without suspicion about the match; he is saying that, with the advantage allowed him (Laertes must put himself at least three rounds, or 'passes', ahead) , he will win. If he suspected the match, he would not think of winning in terms of the odds; if he does not suspect the match there is no reason to find double entendre in the earlier speech.[3]

One might feel, of course, that Hamlet *ought* to be suspicious—that is another matter. If he really believed the King to be determined in his enmity, then indeed he ought to consider whether there might not be more to the proposed wager than meets the eye. His gentlemanly superciliousness should not rule out the possibility of spotting foul play. Superciliousness, however, would be carried too far if we understood Hamlet to mean by 'I shall win at the odds' that as an agent of Providence he must win—this would carry him too far in the direction of overconfidence for the following lines, 'Thou wouldst not think how ill all's here about my heart' to be pathetic, and they must be so, for they are connected with a fear that after all he may not be the man of honour that by his pose he suggests himself to be: 'it is such a kind of gain-giving, as would perhaps trouble a woman'. There is nothing conventionally noble in a man's being troubled in a womanly way.

This disturbance of the heart looks back to the 'kind of fighting' in it that preluded the discovery of the royal commission on board ship; it augurs more deaths. But it also looks back to the problematic nature of the body–soul relationship as Hamlet has experienced it since the beginning of the play. It is not helpful, therefore, to consider it, as Fredson Bowers does, as akin to the protagonist's dismissal or misunderstanding of an omen in Greek tragedy (Bowers cites, as an analogue, Agamemnon's failure to heed the prophecy of Cassandra). Shakespeare's tragedy depicts a more complex, if no less passionate, human nature than the Greeks'. Hamlet continues to be a mystery to himself, and his allusions to Providence do not clarify or resolve that mystery.

Bowers inteprets the play in terms of a simplistic Christianity that accepts Hamlet's actions as undertaken in a truly Christian spirit:

> The point of the catastrophe is Hamlet's death-in-victory with its reconciliation and Divine acceptance of the penalty he must pay for his tragic error [killing Polonius]. It follows that the faults that blinded the classical protagonist to his last chance to escape must be taken as virtues in Hamlet that demonstrate the clearing of his understanding as manifested by his refusal to evade the required payment for his past error.[4]

Putting on one side both the question of the extent to which Hamlet recognizes himself in error with respect to Polonius (or Rosencrantz and Guildenstern, whose deaths should be associated with his) and also that of whether or no Hamlet displays the virtue of generosity in failing to reckon with Laertes's possible villainy, we may still ask where exactly it is that Hamlet discovers that a payment is required of him. It is not here:

> . . . We defy augury. There is special providence in the fall of a sparrow. If it be now, 'tis not to come; if it be not to come, it will be now; if it be not now, yet it will come. The readiness is all. Since no man, of aught he leaves, knows aught, what is't to leave betimes? Let be.   (215–20)

'We defy augury' has Roman rather than Christian associations: it was Caesar who, despite the warning of the augurers, would go to the Senate on the Ides of March, and died for it (*Julius Caesar*, II.2.37–45). Hamlet's resignation to the inevitable is well in accord with his propensity for Roman attitudes. He combines the superiority of the Roman philosopher who has the strength to raise himself above the accidents of life with that of the man of honour who, on the *Deus et ego* principle, has special relations with his Maker.

The reference to 'special providence' and the fall of a sparrow is undeniably Christian, but it does not follow that it is profoundly so. Indeed, Hamlet is at least unorthodox in associating the text in

Matthew with the idea of 'special providence'. It is properly used to illustrate the general workings of it:

> He doth not instance Gods providence in the Prophets or famous men; lest they or we should think God onely took care for the excellent, but not for us; but in sparrows, little birds, of small price and accompt.[5]

'Special providence' is distinct from general in the fashion described here by George Hakewill:

> The Providence of God no doubt extends it selfe to all his workes both great and small, there is not a Lilly growes in the field, nor a haire falls from our heads, nor a sparrow lights on the ground without the Divine Providence; yet may it not be denyed but that it extends to some in a more speciall manner then to others, as namely to his *Church* in a more speciall manner than to other men, and to men in a more speciall manner then to unreasonable creatures . . . Thus also his providence reacheth both to generalls and individualls, but to generalls more especially (because they more immediately conduce to the perfection of the world, and consequently to the advancement of his honour) but to the individualls in relation to their generalls.[6]

Hakewill's examples of 'special providence' are of classes of being, men in comparison with 'unreasonable creatures' (this example figures in the *Summa Theologica* of Aquinas) and the Church in comparison with men; but he allowed for its operation where individuals were concerned—God's Providence was at work when Augustus Caesar assumed control of the Roman Empire 'that hee might thorow the world settle an universall peace, when the *Prince of Peace* was to bee borne in it . . . '[7] Hamlet's case can hardly be compared with that of Augustus, however.

The notion that God's Providence concerns itself extensively with the affairs of individuals or of the communities to which they belong seems to be Calvinist. In the *Christian Institutes* (I.xvii.4.8) Calvin makes it clear, for example, that good and bad harvests represent different kinds of judgement on the harvesters. Keith Thomas has noticed the tendency in Elizabethan England to interpret everyday calamities—gales, fires, outbreaks of plague—in these terms.[8] Hamlet's belief that in the least disaster—the fall of a sparrow, even—the hand of God is to be seen smacks, however incongruously it may seem to us, of this popular Calvinism, and not of its most attractive qualities. To extend 'special providence' as far as the fall of a sparrow is dangerously to restrict the freedom of the will (as some commentators on the verse in Matthew evidently saw) and to subject the world to a fate such as the Stoic philosophers described and from which Calvin had some trouble in distinguishing his own brand of providence.[9] Hamlet has a personal interest in rendering the exercise of his own will superfluous, and his adoption of Roman attitudes ('My fate cries out . . . ' (I.4.81)) is already adumbrated in the allusion to augury. As for describing himself as a 'sparrow' (if indeed he does, and is not referring contemptuously to the 'lecherous' King), that is part of the aristocratic refusal to make much of himself.

If it be now, 'tis not to come; if it be not to come, it will be now; if it be not now, yet it will come—the readiness is all.

There is nothing in these words that cannot be reconciled with a Christian acceptance of the conditions of a particular life. But there is nothing in them either to make a conventional Christian interpretation inevitable or necessary. 'The readiness is all' has been linked with Edgar's 'Ripeness is all' in *Lear* and with the Christian texts associated with it,[10] but the context hardly urges us to do so. Whose readiness for what is meant? Is 'it' Hamlet's own death or that of the King? Does Hamlet have a premonition of the death which is 'ready' for him? These questions are unanswerable, and their obstinacy makes of the whole utterance something characteristically equivocal, and Hamlet-like. Christian patience in any case sounds very different from the nigh-impenetrable rigmarole of this: 'Since no man, of aught he leaves, knows what is't to leave betimes, let be.' Even allowing for the light cast by Jenkins's fine emendation, the addition of the second 'aught' in 'Since no man of aught he leaves, knows aught, what is't to leave betimes?', one may still feel that Hamlet's juggling repetition of 'leaves' and 'aught' creates a suggestion of justifiable anxiety rather than of Christian patience, and that this colours 'let be' with a deep nullness of feeling as well as with positive resignation or fatalism. The man who imagined this Hamlet and who wrote the words that he speaks was the inventor of Lear's

I will do such things—
What they are yet I know not, but they shall be
The terrors of the earth!   (*King Lear*, II.4.280–2)

Like Lear, Hamlet is pathetic and appalling.

Capitulation

The last scene of *Hamlet* divides in two, the first half quiet and almost domestic, the second a matter of trumpets, drums and ordnance. Shakespeare manages his first half so that the prince reaches a sort of crisis in his attempts at self-definition. Identifying himself as in some special relation to God, he manages at the same time to divest that special relationship of meaning; assuming the indifference to omen that has already characterized, in Shakespearean tragedy, the bold Roman Cassius and his proud victim Julius Caesar, he nevertheless speaks in tones which Bradley described accurately as those of 'sad or indifferent self-abandonment' to 'Fate'. Our sense of these contradictory elements fighting, as it were, within the speech which heralds the King's entry makes of the public half of the scene a test. The contest is not simply between Hamlet and Laertes; that is overshadowed by the promise of a resolution of Hamlet's own nature in his dealings with the entire court of Elsinore, reassembled for the first time on stage since the play-within-the-play.

Shakespeare makes Hamlet capitulate to the idea of honour and the gentlemanly straightaway. Dover Wilson is enthralled by the generosity of Hamlet's response to the King's request that he should be reconciled with Laertes,[11] but it is surely not by chance that his own speech puts the emphasis on madness, and in an equivocal fashion which suggests, without affirming it, that he is still mad:

Was't Hamlet wrong'd Laertes? Never Hamlet.
If Hamlet from himself be ta'en away,
And when he's not himself does wrong Laertes,
Then Hamlet does it not, Hamlet denies it.
What does it then? His madness. If't be so,
Hamlet is of the faction that is wrong'd;
His madness is poor Hamlet's enemy.   (229–35)

The present tense here has more than a conditional force, and the insistent repetition of the third-person 'Hamlet' also does its bit to give the speech an air of the insane. Dr Johnson was offended by Hamlet's excusing himself with a lie, but the speech itself suggests that there is no lie and that Hamlet really is to some extent crazy, a possibility that Johnson could not entertain because of the offence to decorum. Dover Wilson, of course, takes this speech to show that Hamlet *has been* mad, but is not so when he makes his apology. The trouble is that the speech is rather stronger than this would suggest; its repeated words (not merely 'Hamlet' but 'himself', 'wrong', 'does', 'then', 'madness') get in each other's way, as though the speaker himself is not clear what it is he is saying, and this awkwardness takes away from the handsomeness of the apology and increases the degree of its distraction. Nor is there any reason why the audience should stick with Dover Wilson in assuming that Hamlet's madness figured only in the death of Polonius (Jenkins adds the scene at Ophelia's grave); its quality of shiftily existing in the apology itself would prompt us to suppose, if we have not already done so, that madness had something to do with that other 'rash and bloody deed', the sending of Rosencrantz and Guildenstern to their death. This in its turn should lead us to question the sanity of Hamlet's assertions of his God-protected status.

However, the dramatic point is not merely to show us a Hamlet who exists on the margin of sanity, or who sits on the fence between it and its opposite. The speech has a larger reference to the gentlemanly ideal to which he is capitulating:

> Let my disclaiming from a purpos'd evil
> Free me so far in your most generous thoughts,
> That I have shot my arrow o'er the house
> And hurt my brother.   (241–4)

The 'brother' here is at once Laertes and Hamlet himself (since 'Hamlet is of the faction that is wronged'); the qualities of the 'honourable' Laertes have, as we know from the graveyard scene, been appropriated by Hamlet. But if so, a curious light is cast on the self-division in the preceding lines. Is Hamlet's 'madness' his Hamlet-half, and 'Hamlet' his Laertes-half? Or should it be put the other way round? Is it the pursuit of a Laertesian honour that has led him to wrong Laertes? It would not be the first time that 'generous' —that is, well-born, aristocratic—thoughts had led to disaster.

These questions are not likely to be formulated by the conscious mind during a performance of the play. But their force will be registered all the same, because the audience has before it the two opposite but equal figures, Hamlet and Laertes, about to fight but here locked in a contest of 'generosity', a contest in which it is impossible to name a victor since the doubt of Hamlet's sanity makes it questionable how far he is qualified to behave nobly. The paradoxes of the situation and its foundation in paradox, specifically the paradox of honour which is at once an internal and an external attribute, are reinforced by Laertes's reply:

> I am satisfied in nature,
> Whose motive in this case should stir me most
> To my revenge; but in my terms of honour
> I stand aloof, and will no reconcilement
> Till by some elder masters of known honour
> I have a voice and precedent of peace
> To keep my name ungor'd. But till that time
> I do receive your offer'd love like love
> And will not wrong it.   (240–8)

On the face of it, this is reasonable: Laertes says that he accepts Hamlet's apology as far as he is personally concerned, but that as far as his 'name' is concerned he will have to take advice. The problem, not put by him in words, must be Hamlet's supposed return to sanity. Women and children, the aged and the mad are all beyond the resentment of honour, which has to do with status amongst one's peers;[12] Hamlet therefore did nothing in his madness that Laertes could resent. But Laertes might now be censured for accepting too readily Hamlet's assertion that he has been mad. Hamlet now being sane, and Laertes having been injured by the death of his father and sister, Laertes ought perhaps now to resent what *then* he could not. These are matters on which Laertes might properly take advice; in so doing, he would act as a loyal subject of Elizabeth or James I was urged to act in putting his case before the Earl Marshal rather than settling his score privately.

Laertes's good faith can be questioned, however, just as much as Hamlet's. Laertes is agent in the King's plot against Hamlet and he is using talk of honour to promote that plot, which is of a kind unlikely to meet with the approval of an Earl Marshal, since its justification depends on the doubtful premise that means are not to be considered in maintaining a 'name ungor'd'. Furthermore, the antithesis of nature and honour ('satisfied in nature . . . but in my terms of honour . . . '), though not irresolvable, points to an internal contradiction in the claims of honour to be based on nature. Steevens thought the speech 'a piece of satire on fantastical honour',[13] which is to go too far, but does illustrate the force of the contradiction. It adds to our sense of the two opponents in the fencing-match as defining themselves by conventions which desperately wring only apparent sense out of confusion of ideas and feelings and, because in this they are alike, of them as pathetically in the grip of a larger force, which is neither that of heaven nor that of the King's malign intention towards Hamlet but rather that of the society in whose conventional structure the yearnings of people for personal and social stability are accommodated imperfectly. The sense is of a society in which everything fits, but in which nothing fits as it should. Laertes's phrase 'receive your offer'd love like love' perfectly captures the spirit of a generosity trammelled by the very forms designed to express it, as does Hamlet's

> I'll be your foil, Laertes; in mine ignorance
> Your skill shall like a star i'th' darkest night
> Stick fiery off indeed (252–4)

which by the invocation of his own 'ignorance' reminds us of the intentions which Laertes has concealed from him and so gives an air of his being pathetically rash in 'freely' embracing Laertes's love and 'frankly' playing with him; the ambivalent quality of these words relating, of course, to that in 'generous' a few lines earlier, and to the generosity by which Hamlet here calls Laertes a 'star' in comparison with himself. 'I'll be your foil' contains a pun which must escape Hamlet but not his audience; he will be the instrument of Laertes's revenge in the fencing-match, achieving honour in his own—but also, from one point of view, in its own—destruction. This star shines in Hamlet's speech 'Brief as the lightning in the collied night' of *Midsummer Night's Dream* (I.1.145),

> too rash, too unadvis'd, too sudden,
> Too like the lightning, which doth cease to be
> Ere one can say 'It lightens.' (*Romeo and Juliet*, II.2.118–20)

The reconciliation of Hamlet and Laertes is not mutual and it must be fragile: Shakespeare's poetry exquisitely expresses the pathos and the precariousness of Hamlet's situation and, in placing him along with Laertes as mastered by the conventions which he seeks to use, makes his capitulation to the gentlemanly role less damning than we might have expected. (The quality of its mitigation is intensified by the reflection that, in imitating Laertes's pursuit of honour as it appears to him, Hamlet seeks to act; it is the attempt to make something of himself that leaves him open to the charge of taking the soft option, accepting the public valuation of honour as true.)

The fight

The reconciliation of Hamlet with Laertes is a characteristically masterly piece of Shakespearean drama. It is not properly a reconciliation at all; it invokes both honour and madness in doubtful terms, so that motivation is obscured, and it calls in question values of prime importance to characters in the play. Yet it maintains dramatic tension by these means. In particular, it constitutes one of those reversals of expectation on which the drama thrives. When the court enters to see the match between Hamlet and Laertes, the prince has been brought to a point where his definition of himself as a man of truly honourable and aristocratic bearing must be tested. Will it prove adequate to the threat posed by Laertes and the King? Immediately it appears that it will not, for it is his faith in the social values of honour ('pardon't as you are a gentleman', he says) that leaves him the dupe of Laertes, at the mercy of his poisoned rapier. At the same time it is made clear that in compensation for this Hamlet is no nearer to understanding himself. His apology to Laertes shows little awareness of the wrong that has been done by him, and the words with which Hamlet excuses himself do not suggest that he has considered seriously, as he should have, whether or not he was responsible for his actions. Indeed, he addresses himself so completely to the present occasion, and with so little regard for the past, that we could be excused for thinking of him here as a monster of egotism. And yet we do not. The uncertain motivation on either side of the reconciliation puts the two parties to it on an equal footing. The two opponents in the fencing-match reflect each other; they reflect the divisions in themselves; and those divisions are seen to reflect divisions in the values of their society as a whole. Because both young men are trying to live according to those imperfect values, at least part of the blame for the wrong they do may be put on the society that nurtures the values by which they live. Hamlet and Laertes are in this way protected from the full weight of our opprobrium. Indeed, if anything, they call upon our sympathy, because we feel them to be hampered by the code they wish to respect. The star to which Hamlet compares Laertes shines all the brighter because it is independent of the sky that surrounds it. It stands for a clarity and 'fiery' energy of being quite alien to the existence of either principal in the minor ritual of court life that is the fencing-match, a match stage-managed on either side by the King. Hamlet's reiterated emphasis on freedom ('*Free* me so far in your most generous thoughts'; 'I embrace it *freely*,/And will this brothers' wager *frankly* play') has about it a pathos akin to that of the star, a pathos which not even our knowledge of the *un*generous behaviour of Laertes can counteract. Is not he as much as Hamlet caught in the toils of 'honour'?

Furthermore, the device of making each character reflect the other, which here means far more than simply allowing us to see that both are sons of murdered fathers, draws our attention away from individual character to the situation in which he is placed. This can be brought out if we compare this scene with that of the play-within-the-play. The comparison is one suggested by the text itself, not only because the two scenes stand out as large court occasions but also because in both scenes certain characters 'play' whilst others watch. The difference between the two occasions is marked, however, in that the players of 'The Mousetrap' come to the court from outside and, in what the Player King has to say about 'honour', subject its values to a healthy, if fruitless, critique, whilst the 'players' of the fencing-match are of the court itself, and their actions are determined by those notions of honour which the players would have criticized. This is summed up in the different part played by the King in either scene. During 'The Mousetrap' he has little to say: it is his business simply to be a spectator. But the fencing-match is not only his private contrivance to rid himself of Hamlet; it is also a public statement of his faith in the gentlemanly way of life. *He* is a 'player' too, not as a combatant, but as a gambler, and acts as a kind of master of ceremonies:

Set me the stoups of wine upon that table.
If Hamlet give the first or second hit,

Or quit in answer of the third exchange,
Let all the battlements their ordnance fire . . .

(264–7)

The fencing-match is 'his', far more emphatically and intimately than 'The Mousetrap' was Hamlet's, and its not altogether spurious courtesy and ceremony, overlaying malice and what else, shadowy and alarming, accurately reflect the horror and confusion of his own character.

Claudius is a king and not a king; he has a right to his throne and no right to it; he does not quite fit it. Neither Hamlet's apology nor Laertes's conditional acceptance of it quite fits the context of honourable aspiration. This idea may be extended to the fencing-match itself, which is not quite a duel but is so close to it as to be mistaken for one. The rapier is useless except as an instrument of honour in the duel. But the duel is an activity which the monarch must not sanction. Hence the fencing-match celebrates a form of courtliness that can be approved only so long as it does not realize itself in the activity which is its *raison d'être*. James I, of course, managed to disapprove publicly of the duel and to tolerate duellists in his court. Claudius's attitude has something of the same ambivalence. Even if it were not the instrument of Laertes's revenge, the fencing-match would consequently have the character of a *duel held in check*—the closest that the court could come to celebrating what officially it must disapprove, the quarrel of honour. Laertes's merely conditional acceptance of Hamlet's apology

Till by some elder masters of known honour
I have a voice and precedent to peace

is a forceful reminder of the doubtful status of 'honour' at court, with its implication that he may still seek 'revenge'.

But of course he actually *is* seeking revenge—the matter of honour which, for the time being at least, he appears to waive in fact governs his action here. We might say that for Laertes the fencing-match *is* a duel, a contest arising from an affront to his honour, and offering him the appropriate satisfaction of *la lessive du sang*, except that by fixing the odds he destroys the fundamental premise of the single combat; that the disputed matter is referred to the arbitration of God. For Hamlet, on the other hand, the match is—on the surface at least—merely the exhibition of skill proposed to him by Osric on the

King's behalf. And yet for him too it is something different; his imagining earlier in the scene 'the pass and fell incensed points/Of mighty opposites' evokes a scene of duelling, and his later 'gain-giving' anticipates a mortal consequence to his encounter with Laertes which would not be possible if it were merely an exhibition match. Hamlet's apprehensions encourage us to regard it as a duel.

But it is not one. Zitner examines sensitively the ethos of duelling as it appears in Vincentio Saviola's *Practise* of 1595, but relates it too directly to the matter of Shakespeare's play:

> In Hamlet's self-conception, in his efforts to free himself from passion, in his speculation on man and men, in his final accord with providence, one discerns, I think, Saviola's ideal figure, the gentleman duellist who may combat lawfully.[14]

It is nearer the truth to say that in Hamlet we see someone haunted by these ideals rather than someone who achieves them. He commands pathos rather than admiration precisely because he does not see how close the match is to being a duel. Nothing quite fits. His 'ignorance' is not merely a lack of skill in comparison with Laertes; it is a fundamental misconception of what is involved in the match between them. He just does not know what is going on. His being able to imagine Laertes as a star, when in fact his rival is working covertly against him, reflects back on Hamlet and makes *him* star-like in being possessed of a sensibility that so clearly distinguishes him from all those about him. At the same time, this quality stands out by being inappropriate to the occasion; it does not fit.

The mistakes which accompany the contest are, then, a making manifest of the incoherence which shapes it. An almost-King, an almost-reconciliation and an almost-duel naturally conspire together to produce 'accidental judgements, casual slaughters'. Hamlet wins the first two rounds; the Queen drinks the poison intended for her son; Laertes wounds the Prince but drops his foil and gets Hamlet's in return; Laertes recognizes his own 'treachery' and the King's guilt; Hamlet wounds the King and has him drink off the poisoned cup. This concentration of events satisfactorily releases the tension built up in the preparation for the duel, and the confusion produced on stage is a physical counterpart for the entangled motives underlying the fencing-match which give rise to it. The sudden spate of appar-ently random action also complements the sequence in Act Four.

There, the haphazard development of the action and random pacing of scenes related to the madness attributed to Hamlet; here the quality of violent and imperfectly directed deeds is related not to the prince alone, but to the court world he inhabits and to whose ethic he attempts to adapt himself. In exhibiting the fullest range of connections between Hamlet's aspirations and personal dilemma on the one hand and the aspirations and imperfections of the court on the other, the sequence of accidental and unexpected deaths with which the play ends justifies itself as a conclusion to the dramatic poem that is *Hamlet* as well as to the story on which the poem is based.

Hamlet's fate—and the King's

Hamlet at last kills the King; the end, sought by his father's ghost and so much debated by him, is achieved. But what are we to make of the fact? Are we to understand that after all Hamlet was, as he maintained, subject to a 'special providence' that might justify the slaughter? Or is it more proper to conclude with Norman Council that the act endorses an almost Roman fatalism?

> No man can know anything about this life, about the connection between this life and 'providence', or about the life to come . . . there is no answer to Hamlet's 'To be or not to be'. Since both conditions are inscrutable, since the conventional forms of behaviour required by obedience, honour and love are untrustworthy guides in this world, and since assigning value to a cause in order to salvage honour from life provides a merely apparent and transitory solution, there remains only the fatalistic 'readiness' to meet whatever circumstances 'outrageous fortune' or 'the divinity that shapes our ends' might provide.[15]

Is Stephen Booth's view that the play yields 'an impossible coherence of truths that are both undeniably incompatible and undeniably coexistent'[16] to be preferred to either of these? The 'impossible coherence' of Hamlet's killing Claudius would, I suppose, rest in its being the unallowable deed of a revenger *and* an act of justice—'He is justly served', as Laertes says.

One way of answering these questions is to consider the meaning of Hamlet's act in relation to what he has previously said about himself as 'scourge and minister' of the heavens. The King's death is of a kind to suggest that Providence ('special' Providence) is at work in it.

> God hath marked all great sins with some signal and express judgments, and hath transmitted the records of them, or represented them before our eyes . . . and that being sufficient to affright us from those crimes, God hath not thought it expedient to do the same things to all persons in the same cases, having to all persons produced instances and examples of fear by fewer accidents, sufficient to restrain us, but not enough to pass sentence upon the changes of Divine providence.[17]

Jeremy Taylor here shows himself well enough aware of the danger men run in too readily interpreting events as declaring a divine judgement. But in his *Life of Christ* he goes on to except certain cases from this general scepticism:

> If the crime and the punishment be symbolical, and have proportion and correspondence of parts, the hand of God strikes the man, but holds up one finger to point at the sin . . . That blasphemer, whose tongue was presently struck with an ulcerous tumour, with his tongue declared the glories of God and his own shame . . . And that famous person, and of excellent learning, Giacchettus of Geneva, being by his wife found dead in the unlawful embraces of a stranger woman, who also died at the same instant, left an excellent example of God's anger upon the crime, and an evidence that he was then judged for his intemperate lust.[18]

The King's death by poison who had gained his throne by poison obviously falls into the category described by Taylor. ' . . . When a sin infers the judgment with a legible character and a prompt signification, not to understand God's choice is next to stupidity or carelessness'[19]; Hamlet himself points out the 'legible character' of the King's reward for sin in his punning cry 'Is thy union here?', the 'union' being at once the poison by which the King sought to end his rival's life, and the poisoned affection that led him to kill his brother and take his brother's wife for his own. It seems then that we are to acknowledge, after all, a 'special Providence' in the fall of Claudius, the lecherous sparrow, and this might incline us to revise our opinion of Hamlet's claims that a divine interest was particularly concerned in his affairs.

To give way to this inclination would surely be wrong. The objections to Hamlet's account of his own situation remain, and are reinforced if we care to look elsewhere in Jeremy Taylor; for he warns us 'that we do not judge of our final condition by any discourses of our own, relying upon God's secret counsels and predestination of eternity'.[20]

Yet the main consideration should be simply that we are not encouraged to *think* about divine justice once justice has been effected. Hamlet says nothing to suggest that he sees heaven as ordinant in what he has just done; he does not mention heaven or its ruler. Instead, Hamlet remains fixed in the world of honour and its vindication. He is concerned above all for his 'name', and it is on this account that he begs Horatio to 'report me and my cause aright'. At the moment of death he is still thinking of the need for his story to be told correctly. Fortinbras must be informed not only of Hamlet's 'dying voice' on his behalf but also of 'th'occurrents more and less/Which have solicited—the rest is silence'. Hamlet's honour, not his relation to his mother, is what Hamlet dwells on after the death of Claudius.

All the same, it does not follow that Shakespeare presents us with Stephen Booth's 'impossible coherence' in thus making the agent of special providence indifferent to the forces he has served. Providence may work through individuals, but it is no necessary part of its working that the individual should be conscious of it. The 'coherence' of divine purpose and unconscious instrument is quite possible. Yet it is also disquieting, because the contrast between God's power and man's weakness is such a large one. Hamlet has hesitated and prevaricated so long about the possibility and meaning of action that when divine judgement comes with completeness and apparent immediacy it seems as though the condition upon which Hamlet acts may in some way not be fair. This seeming is so much a matter of what is unstated here that, of course, it cannot be suggested that Shakespeare's play directs itself against orthodox Christian feeling at this point; but the possibility that we might revolt against it is allowed for in what he offers.

Equally, Christian feeling may be reinforced by an access of sympathy for Hamlet in his inability to root his life in something more certain than the secular 'honour' that now, we might say, obsesses him. That honour's instability is given us here in a detail

noted by Booth,[21] the way in which we move from the Christian
death of Laertes, with its exchange of forgiveness ('Mine and my
father's death come not upon thee,/Nor thine on me'—'Heaven
make thee free of it') to the Christian invocation of angels for the
dead Hamlet by Horatio through the '*Roman*' gesture by which
Horatio offers suicide and Hamlet describes death (not salvation) as
'felicity'. This fluctuation in the values to which the characters
subscribe is fully expressive in the play's own terms.

Hamlet's fate is, then, to be an exemplar of human weakness,
despite and because of his attempted self-dedication to honour. The
extent to which his weakness is culpable is, however, not to be
judged by men. Taylor says of God's 'peremptory, final unalterable
decree' that he keeps it

> in the cabinets of the eternal ages, never to be unlocked, till the
> Angel of the Covenant shall declare the unalterable, universal
> sentence.[22]

It is certainly not revealed in Shakespeare's play.

And yet, in its last movements, Hamlet is presented to us not
merely as a self-deceiver, but as vulnerably open and 'generous' (the
word, which Hamlet applies to Laertes, significantly belongs to the
honour-constellation, as it is rooted in ideas of race and heredity as
well as of the freedom which, in the last use of the word 'free' in the
play (V.2.337), turns out—definitively as it were—to be an attribute
at the disposal of heaven). Eleanor Prosser notes that 'Shakespeare
does everything in his power to make Hamlet's killing of both
Laertes and Claudius as sympathetic as possible'.[23] In a general way
she is surely right. Furthermore, our sympathy for Hamlet is maintained even in the last moments when honour is his principal concern.

There are at least two reasons why this should be so. The first is
that he reverts to the image of himself as an actor, but this time the
self-disgust and contempt for the stage of Act Two are missing;
instead the idea is used to establish a common identity between
Hamlet and his fellow-men. The use of the word 'audience' directs
his appeal beyond his own world, the court of Elsinore, to the world
in which we ourselves live, the world of Shakespeare's audience:

> You that look pale and tremble at this chance,
> That are but mutes or audience to this act . . . (339–40)

This access of consciousness, though it is allowed for in the sense of honour, is nevertheless something new in Hamlet. There is a gracious acknowledgement of dependence on us to sustain his honour; it seems here, for the first time, a truly social virtue. There is no mockery either in Hamlet's last characterization of himself as a 'player'; we have a sense of his perfoming for us, for our instruction and our pleasure. If we are so thrilled by events as to 'look pale and tremble' it is a reminder of our complicity in the weakness he manifests—we too are 'guilty creatures sitting at a play' (II.2.585); are weak enough to take pleasure in mortality and the merely mortal.

The second reason why Hamlet holds our sympathy at the play's end is that he, who has been so loquacious—and especially about his own affairs—has at last the sense to see that *his* talking is not going to make anything better: 'O I could tell you—/But let it be' (342–3). To be understood, he needs to be explained: but even at the end he cannot explain himself. What warms us to him here is the dawning on him of a sense that this is so.

Most royal

It seems that by altogether unconventional means *Hamlet* the play endorses conventional wisdom—the power of God, the weakness of man; but on the one hand we come to this wisdom by such a devious and in itself engrossing route that it strikes us with the force of novelty, and on the other it is so presented that it appears not as a final truth, but as the instigation of further thought. Horatio demands of Fortinbras 'What is it you would see?/If aught of woe or wonder, cease your search'. The woe and the wonder are indeed inseparable, because Hamlet's death and the King's call in question the obscure relationship between human aspiration and potentiality and the actually efficacious and immediate divine order which is superior to them. God is at once remote, in his apparent indifference to Hamlet's anxious, self-suspecting, self-deceiving, play-long sifting of motives, and near, in the judgement of the King and in the sudden reversal of so many human expectations.

The questions that are raised by the outcome of the fencing-match are not, however, exclusively or even predominantly theological. Metaphysics merely enlarges the play's human perspectives, a chief point of reference in which is the idea of honour upheld, at what cost, by the prince. The questions cluster here: 'Now cracks a noble heart. Good night, sweet prince . . . '. Horatio's affirmation is at once bold and uncertain in meaning. Hamlet's heart was noble, in that the blood of a nobleman beat there and he aspired to vindicate that nobility in his conduct, but whether much ethical force resided in the nobility he achieved is not easily determined. The 'heart' here is both physical and spiritual, and Horatio's meaning hovers uneasily between the two categories. Was Hamlet a 'sweet prince'? His conduct in general, as we have seen it, hardly justifies the epithet. Yet at his worst Hamlet's foulness is mitigated by the obscurity of the surrounding world, by the trick language has of conspiring with his evasiveness, and by the angle from which we are encouraged to view it. In the frankness with which he speaks to Laertes following his own prevaricating apology, there is something of a child's guilelessness for which the description 'sweet' is not inappropriate; and so his bearing in the last moments may give an unexpected but convincing force to the insipid adjective. Equally, it may strike us as insipid.[24] But in the light of what has happened it is unlikely to strike us as a savage irony by which a monster of egotism is presented to the world as other than he is. The whole force of the questionable quality at the close of the play is to commend to us a spirit of charity: 'And flights of angels sing thee to thy rest'. The prayer is fitting to anyone in the weakness of mortality.

It is sometimes suggested that the arrival of Fortinbras at the moment Hamlet dies is an ironic comment upon the action as a whole—after all the suffering, Prince Stupid ascends the throne with an inappropriately conventional tribute to Hamlet of military honours. Something of this may appear in Eleanor Prosser's depressed account of the final state of affairs:

> I, for one, see no hope for Denmark in the fact that Fortinbras is now at the helm. His past actions give little assurance that he will be a temperate and judicious ruler who seeks only peace and stability . . . flushed with victory, he re-enters Denmark like a conquering hero . . . He is acting not like a privileged guest in Denmark but like its sovereign . . . According to early exposition in the play, he has no rights . . . Order has been restored, but not by a figure representing the rule of reason and integrity. A strong man has taken over.[25]

But surely this is too depressed. Hamlet's 'dying voice' gives Fortinbras's role enough authority for us not to question his rights closely: what matters is that Fortinbras enters as it were with Hamlet's blessing, and acts with Horatio in honouring him in death. The fate of Denmark is not allowed much attention; the fate of the Danish Court, as a thing of the past, is. Fortinbras's claim to the throne is advanced modestly and made subordinate to his grief, and Horatio emphatically associates it with Hamlet's wishes:

Fort. For me, with sorrow I embrace my fortune.
    I have some rights of memory in this kingdom,
    Which now to claim my vantage doth invite me.
Hor. Of that I shall have also cause to speak,
    And from his mouth whose voice will draw on more. (393–7)

Howard Jacobson, noting 'the odd inappropriateness of Hamlet's funeral', nevertheless gets the closing moments in better proportion:

> We do not feel that Fortinbras has made some telling error, or that the soldier's music and the rites of war either serve Hamlet too generously, or pay him scant respect. Do we not feel, rather, that while everything that is passing before us is not exquisitely right, it is perfectly satisfactory?[26]

I think that this is right, but that it is so because Fortinbras enforces a proper circumspection concerning the very idea of honour. What strikes him when he enters is not simply that a pile of bodies faces him, but that these bodies are those of 'princes'. His words here are the key to what remains of the play:

> This quarry cries on havoc. O proud Death,
> What feast is toward in thine eternal cell,
> That thou so many princes at a shot
> So bloodily hast strook?   (369–72)

He imagines death as preying on princes, who are the substance not of an everday meal but of a 'feast' where especially dainty meats will be served. The implication is that their titles make them vulnerable, because desirable. At the same time, however, death is himself a prince, 'proud' in that he has a sense of himself preventing him from doing what he considers to be beneath him; his 'feast' is a feast of intimates, doing them honour by offering them more than the show of brotherhood, and his 'cell' is the private room set apart for them. Fortinbras's words betray a lively sense of the impropriety of death married to a deep belief that honour and the hierarchy of rank are sustained from beyond the grave. This ambiguous feeling, expressed in terms of high decorum but not to be dismissed as merely conventional, explains the resolute conventionality with which the matter of Hamlet's death is treated. The 'noblest' are to be summoned to hear its circumstances, and Hamlet is deemed 'likely, had he been put on,/To have prov'd most royal'. This is not a statement to which we are required to put a label of 'true' or 'false'; it is rather a way of dealing with what has happened. The ambiguity in the word 'royal' might at an earlier stage in the play have proved an embarrassment, like that in 'great' pursued by Hamlet so anxiously following his encounter with Fortinbras's captain on the way to Poland; but here its ambiguity is a blessing, since it keeps at bay the question implied by Fortinbras's first horrified reaction to the 'quarry' of 'princes', questions given an added force by the news that Rosencrantz and Guildenstern too are dead, as though great men had an affinity with death not only in themselves but in their dealings with others. It seems better to promote the merely conventional idea of honour as a military virtue, a reflection of the qualities that make a good soldier, than to enquire, as Hamlet did, too closely into its real substance. The merely wishful aspect of Fortinbras's action is clearly expressed in his words 'Such a sight as this/Becomes the field, but here shows much amiss' (406–7). That is his tribute to the fashion in which, at the court of Elsinore, things do not fit, but it is made with a sense of what is fitting.

Conclusion

Hamlet is a play idiosyncratically constructed, but it does all hang together. Its five acts correspond to five distinct stages in a single action. In the first act, the Ghost's appearance precipitates a flurry of activity culminating in Hamlet's interview with it and his promise to 'remember'. The second act reverses the apparent purposefulness of the drama, replacing it with an evasive preoccupation with accident. The third act pursues a delusively purposeful action, the staging of the play-within-the-play and its consequences. This act passes over ambiguously into the fourth, where all strength of purpose is dissipated in Hamlet's madness and its oblique representation in the madness of Ophelia and her brother's fury. Finally, the last act resumes the clarity of movement that was the mark of the first, Hamlet in this act at last modelling his behaviour more or less on the pattern implied by the Ghost's demand.

Formally, then, the play is founded upon the protagonist's evasion of the task imposed on him: the middle three acts set this evasion forth, and do so in terms at once surprising and convincing. The nervous vitality and refinement of Shakespeare's writing play a very large part in giving the action plausibility; but they also work to call up sympathy for a principal character many of whose actions are repugnant by suggesting how far the very conditions of his life hamper him in choosing what he will do with it. At the beginning of the play, Hamlet is trying to hold himself apart from the Court: he wants to be pure spirit. At the end of the play, Hamlet's body lies with those of King, Queen and Laertes. 'Is thy union here?' Hamlet's is; the last scene shows, above all, the social setting as a circumscription on his action now willingly embraced.

Hamlet, then, is a play about trammelled freedom, and honour has a natural bearing on this theme, for it signifies something that is at once inalienable from the individual and yet the creation of a community. Honour rests in your own self, your intentions, your sense of what is your due, and yet it is a matter of outward show, of your place in the social order, too. Shakespeare exploits this equivocal nature of honour to the utmost in his play without, however, advocating any one version of it. *Hamlet* seems to me entirely characteristic of Shakespeare's art in the emphasis placed in the end on a sympathetic view of aberrant human nature rather than on a final judgement.

Such a study as this implies, of course, that we need to know more about honour in sixteenth- and seventeenth-century England and its relation to the plays of Shakespeare. It has a bearing on most of them, and a significant bearing on many. My own guess is that there, as here, the fascination which it exercised on Shakespeare will prove to lie in the very unseizable quality of the concept, a quality which so aptly defines the outlines of Shakespearean charity.

In *Njal's Saga* there is an extraordinary moment when, after the fight at Rang River where he has just killed four or five men, his personal enemies, Gunnar of Hlidarend is congratulated on the revenge he has achieved, and replies: 'But I wish I knew . . . whether I am any the less manly than other men, for being so much more reluctant to kill than other men are'.[1] That doubt is a doubt about honour: having done all that is supposed to be 'manly', Gunnar still wonders whether really he is 'manly'. Such doubts relate to a fundamental uncertainty in the conditions of self-knowledge and self-definition, an uncertainty to which Shakespeare returns again and again in his tragedies. Hamlet's honour, like that of Othello or Coriolanus, is only the point at which that uncertainty becomes visible to the protagonist.

Notes

Introduction

1 Ed. Harold Jenkins, 1982.
2 E.g., Jeremy Treglown, 'Shakespeare's "Macbeth": Davenant, Verdi, Stoppard and the question of theatrical text', *English*, xxix, 1980, pp. 95–114.
3 William Empson, '*Hamlet* when new', *Sewanee Review*, lxi, 1953, p. 41.
4 A point made to me forcefully by Professor Stephen Orgel.
5 '. . . it is a multi-faceted notion . . . it is this which gives it its essential character and function and which also makes it so paradoxical in usage' (Julian Pitt-Rivers, *The Fate of Shechem, or the politics of sex*, 1977, p. viii).
6 'Where the action is' in his *Interaction Ritual* (1972), pp. 142–270.

1 Honour and the Polonius household

1 Paul Siegel, 'Shakespeare and the neo-chivalric cult of honor', *Shakespeare in his time and ours* (Notre Dame, Indiana, 1968), pp. 122–62; Alice Shalvi, *The relationship of Renaissance concepts of honour to Shakespeare's problem plays* (Salzburg Studies in English Literature, Jacobean Drama Studies VII, Salzburg, 1972); Norman Council, *When honour's at the stake* (1973). Bertram Joseph, *Conscience and the King: A study of Hamlet* (1953) also gives the subject careful attention.
2 *Shakespeare and the Renaissance concept of honour* (Princeton, 1960), p.448.
3 See F.R. Bryson, *The point of honor in sixteenth-century Italy: An aspect of the life of the gentleman* (Chicago, 1935).
4 J. Pitt-Rivers *The Fate of Shechem*, p.9.
5 See the book by Pitt-Rivers cited above, n. 4, and other works by him; J.G. Peristiany (ed.), *Honour and shame: The values of Mediterranean society* (1965), which was the original place of publication for Pitt-Rivers's important essay, 'Honour and social status', reprinted in *The Fate of Shechem*; J.K. Campbell, *Honour, family and patronage: A study of institutions and moral values in a Greek mountain community* (1964).
6 Mervyn James, *English politics and the concept of honour 1485—1642 (Past and Present*, supplement 3, 1978).
7 Julio Carlo Baroja, 'Honour and shame: A historical account of several conflicts', in Peristiany (ed.) *Honour and shame*, p. 89, to which this paragraph continues to refer.
8 Lawrence Stone, *The crisis of the aristocracy 1558—1641* (1965), pp. 233–4.
9 James, *English politics*, p.5.

10   James, pp. 22–8; p.49.
11   Baroja, in Peristiany, pp. 98–100.
12   J.E. Neale, *Queen Elizabeth I* (1934; 1961), p. 80; *Dictionary of National Biography*, s.v. 'Pickering, Sir William'.
13   Thomas Randolph to Sir Nicholas Throgmorton, 31 March 1565, quoted in Neville Williams, *Thomas Howard, Fourth Duke of Norfolk* (1964), p. 91.
14   Neale, *Queen Elizabeth*, p. 147; on the use of colours and costume in factional struggles of this kind see Jacques Heers, *Parties and political life in the medieval west*, trs. David Nicholas (Amsterdam, 1977), pp. 286–90.
15   Neale, pp. 146–7.
16   Robert Baldick, *The duel* (1965), pp. 18–19, has a brief account.
17   This account is based on that in the *Dictionary of National Biography* and on Robert Lacey's *Robert, Earl of Essex: An Elizabethan Icarus* (1971).
18   On Lord Bourgh, see W.R., *The most horrible and tragicall murther of . . . John Lord Bourgh* (1591).
19   These are quotations from the letter from Essex to Lord Willoughby, 4 January 1598–9; *Historic Manuscripts Commission* (Salisbury, 9, 1902), pp. 9–11.
20   Lacey, *Robert, Earl of Essex*, p. 156.
21   S.P. Zitner, 'Hamlet, duellist', *University of Toronto Quarterly*, xxix, 1969, is good on the rapier and the meaning of the duel.
22   Stone, *The crisis of the aristocracy*, p.245. This paragraph is largely indebted to his discussion.
23   Eleanor Prosser, *Hamlet and revenge,* 2nd edn (Stanford, California, 1971), p. 14, n. 40.
24   See *A Publication of His Maties Edict . . . against Private Combats and Combatants*, 1613; *The Charge of Sir Francis Bacon touching Duells*, 1614; and Stone, p. 248.
25   See Natalie Zemon Davies, 'The reason of misrule: Youth groups and charivaris in sixteenth-century France', *Past and Present* 50, February 1971, pp. 41–75; E.P. Thompson, ' "Rough Music": le charivari anglais',
     Annales, xxvii, 1972, pp. 285–312; Claude Gauvard and Altan Gokalp, 'Les conduites de bruit et leur signification à la fin du Moyen Age: le charivari', *Annales*, xxix, 1974, pp. 693–704.
26   Elizabeth M. Brennan, University of London unpublished Ph.D thesis, 1958, 'The concept of revenge for honour in English fiction and drama between 1580 and 1640', p. 105.
27   s.v. 'Honor', *International Encyclopaedia of the Social Sciences*, ed. David L.
     Sills, VI (New York, 1968), p. 504.
28   *The Riverside Shakespeare*, ed. G. Blakemore Evans (Boston, Mass., 1974).
29   The line is present only in F1; its ambiguity only enhances the force of the speech as a whole.
30   F1's reading, 'sanctity', takes up the effort underlying 'temple' at l.12;

'safety' relates more obviously to Laertes's sense of a body under threat. Jenkins adopts Theobald's emendation 'sanity', finding 'safety' to be metrically unsatisfactory, and 'sanctity' to be of doubtful sense. The metrical objection is not, however, sound; compare the octosyllabic line at 100 in the same scene.

31 F1's reading, 'peculiar Sect and force', once again reinforces the sense of Hamlet as set apart by rank and power.

32 *The Fate of Shechem*, pp. 22, 11.

33 *On Hamlet* (1948), p. 51: 'it would have been so normal to them [the audience] that this may well be the reason why Shakespeare did not make it plainer . . . '

34 *The Fate of Shechem*, p. 23.

35 See G.R. Waggoner, '*Timon of Athens* and the Jacobean duel', *Shakespeare Quarterly*, xvi, 1965, p. 307, n. 22.

36 Georg Simmel, 'The web of group-affiliations', trs. Reinhard Bendix, in '*Conflict*' and '*The web of group-affiliations*' (Glencoe, Ill., 1955), p. 163. Simmel's *Soziologie*, from which this is translated, was first published in Leipzig in 1908. The bracketed words are supplied by the translator.

37 Siegel, p. 132, n. 15.

38 This is what makes it appropriate that the King should emphasize to Laertes that his fencing had been admired by a Frenchman: 'The scrimers of their nation/He swore had neither motion, guard, nor eye/If you oppos'd them' (IV.7.99–101).

39 *The Fate of Shechem*, pp. 4–5, quoting what Théophile Gautier, in *Le Capitaine Fracasse*, describes as a Spanish saying.

40 *The Fate of Shechem*, p.1.

41 *A publication of His Ma*^ties *Edict*, pp. 5–6. On the Earl Marshal and his Court of Honour, see G.D. Squibb, *The High Court of Chivalry: A study of the Civil Law of England*, 1959, pp. 29–46.

42 Shalvi, *The relationship of Renaissance concepts of honour*, p. 328, n. 19.

43 *The Fate of Shechem*, p. 7.

44 'The duel of honor . . . was fought in private, often without witnesses, not to decide the justice of a case, for the offence was usually open, but to preserve honor from injury' Ruth Kelso, *The Doctrine of the English gentleman in the sixteenth century*, University of Illinois Studies in Language and Literature, xiv, 1–2 (Urbana, Ill., 1929), p.100.

45 In the Overbury case, the prosecution 'declared that murder was the most horrible of all crimes and of all murders that by poisoning the most detestable . . .' F.T. Bowers, *Elizabethan Revenge Tragedy* (1940), p. 26.

46 The conflict between sets of ideal rules, for example the moral code of the Christian and the conventions governing resentment and satisfaction for slighted honour, means that the vocabulary of 'rules' and 'codes' is generally too rigid to describe accurately what happens when a particular individual is concerned for his honour.

47 *The Fate of Shechem*, p. 1.

48 *The Fate of Shechem*, pp. 37, 40.

2 Hamlet, body and soul

1 *Shakespearean criticism*, ed. T.M. Raysor, 2nd edn (1960), I, p. 19.
2 S. Booth, 'On the value of *Hamlet*', *Reinterpretations of Elizabethan Drama*, ed. Norman Rabkin (New York, 1969), pp. 139, 175.
3 Recently, for example, by Martin Scofield, *The Ghosts of Hamlet: The play and modern writers* (1980), pp. 183–5.
4 Nicholas Brooke, *Shakespeare's early tragedies* (1968), p. 173.
5 Reuben Brower, *Hero and saint: Shakespeare and the Graeco-Roman tradition* (1971), p. 280.
6 H.A. Mason, 'The Ghost in *Hamlet*', *Cambridge Quarterly*, iii, 1968, pp. 133, 134.
7 Torquato Tasso, *Discourses on the heroic poem*, trs. Mariella Cavalchini and Irene Samuel (1973), p. 142, and on repetition, p. 150.
8 William Segar, *Honor Military and Civill . . .* (1602), p. 116.
9 It is possible that 'prick'd on' qualifies 'our last King' rather than 'Fortinbras' in I.1.80–84, but in any case the pride of one seeks to rival the pride of the other. The basis in honour of the combat between Hamlet senior and 'ambitious Norway' is even clearer in Belleforest's version of the story, which Shakespeare may have used.
10 J. Pitt-Rivers, *The Fate of Shechem*, p.1.
11 John Dover Wilson, *What happens in 'Hamlet'*, 3rd edn, (1935; 1951), p. 55.
12 Robert H. West, *Shakespeare and the outer mystery* (Lexington, Ky, 1968), pp. 56–68.
13 E. Prosser, *Hamlet and revenge*, p. 143.
14 Prosser, p. 107.
15 Prosser, p. 132.
16 Jenkins avoids this question by quoting from a poem in Tottel's *Miscellany*: 'Wherefore with Paul let all men wish, and pray To be *dissolv'd* of this *foul fleshy* mass'; he also cites the quotation from St Paul in the Homily on the Fear of Death: 'St Paul himself declareth *the desire* of his heart, which was *to be dissolved* and loosed from his body . . .' Hamlet does not speak of his flesh as 'foul' but 'sullied', implying a specific act of sullying; and his toying with the idea of suicide confirms that he is reacting to that specific act. The context makes it unlikely that it could be original sin and man's first disobedience that are referred to here.
17 Prosser, p. 126.
18 Prosser, pp. 126–7, n. 23.
19 Cf. Bertram Joseph, *Conscience and the King*, p.46.
20 William Empson, 'Mine eyes dazzle', review of Clifford Leech, '*The Duchess of Malfi*', *Essays in Criticism*, xiv, 1964, pp. 80–86, rejects the view that an audience would instantly condemn the remarriage of a widow.
21 *The Fate of Shechem*, p. 23.
22 *The Fate of Shechem*, p. 44.
23 J.C. Baroja, 'Honour and shame', in *Honour and shame*, p.86.

24 *Honour and shame*, p. 118. Violet Alford, 'Rough music or charivari', *Folklore*, lxx, 1959, pp.505–18, describes the persistence of the English charivari in relation to wife-beating; earlier it had been directed against irregular forms of sexuality, as elsewhere in Europe.

25 Frank W. Wadsworth, 'Webster's *Duchess of Malfi* in the light of some contemporary ideas on marriage and remarriage', *Philological Quarterly*, xxxv, 1956, pp. 395–407, makes the point forcefully.

26 E.P. Thompson, ' "Rough music": Le charivari anglais', *Annales*, xxvii, 1972, pp. 295–6.

27 Robert Burton, *The Anatomy of Melancholy*, I.ii.1.ii: ed. Holbrook Jackson (1932; 1948), I, p.200.

28 Mary Douglas, *Purity and danger: An analysis of concepts of pollution and taboo* (1966), p.102.

29 'Of prognostications', *Essays* I.11, trs. John Florio, ed. J.I.M. Stewart (1931), I. p.44.

30 *The Anatomy of Melancholy*, I.i.2.iii; I, p. 148.

3 Hamlet and the Ghost

1 H. Granville-Barker, *Prefaces to Shakespeare* (1958), I. p.58

2 Q2 reads 'eale'. The Riverside note suggests that there is a pun on 'evil', an emendation suggested by Keightley in 1867, and 'eale' (meaning 'yeast'). This yoking of moral and physical substance accords very well with the present discussion. As Jenkins point out, however, there are difficulties in accepting 'eale' as the 'hypothetical variant' of a dialectal form (*yele*).

3 H.A. Mason, 'The Ghost in *Hamlet*', *Cambridge Quarterly*, iii, 1968, pp. 141, 144.

4 E. Prosser, *Hamlet and revenge*, pp. 139–43.

5 Prosser, p. 140.

6 *The Anatomy of Melancholy*, I.i.2.iv; I, p. 153.

7 W. Empson, '*Hamlet* when new', p. 21.

8 On the relation between honour and the sacred, see J. Pitt-Rivers, *The Fate of Shechem*, p. 13, and *Mana*, (1974) his inaugural lecture at the London School of Economics.

4 Hamlet's weakness

1 Cf. Zvi Jagendorf, ' "Fingers on your lips, I pray": On silence in *Hamlet*,' *English*, xxvii, 1978, pp. 121–8.

2 B.G. Lyons, *Voices of melancholy* (1971), p. 81.

3 Ibid.

4 J. Pitt-Rivers, *The Fate of Shechem*, pp. 12–13.

5 *The Fate of Shechem*, p.14.

6 *The Anatomy of Melancholy*, I.ii.5.i; I, p. 376.

7 *The Anatomy of Melancholy*, I.i.2.iv; I, p. 153.

8   H. Granville-Barker, *Prefaces to Shakespeare*, I, p. 69.
9   *Prefaces to Shakespeare*, I, p. 75.
10 Mark Rose, *Shakespearean design* (Cambridge, Mass., 1972; 1974), p. 107.
11 E.g., J. Dover Wilson, *What happens in 'Hamlet'*, p. 124; H.D.F. Kitto, *Form and meaning in drama* (1956; 1960), p. 292; Andrew Gurr, *Hamlet and the distracted globe* (1978), p. 32.
12 Cf. Emrys Jones, *Scenic form in Shakespeare* (1971), pp. 78–81.
13 Lyons, *Voices of melancholy*, pp. 93–4.
14 Lyons, p. 93.
15 Often quoted: e.g., J. Dover Wilson, p. 97.
16 William Empson, *Seven types of ambiguity*, 3rd edn, (1953), pp. 90–101.
17 Dover Wilson, p. 211 and n.

5   Hamlet and his inferiors

1   E. Prosser, *Hamlet and revenge*, p. 159.
2   Q2 reads 'wand', which modern editors expand to 'wann'd'; F1 reads 'warm'd', which looks like an attempt to avoid the difficulty inherent in the use of 'wan' as a verb.
3   F1 reads 'scullion', which brings out the class element clearly. Q2 'stallion' follows naturally from 'whore' and 'drab' and implies an animal that 'services' other animals. Class is, then, implicit in either reading.
4   See Harold Skulsky, *Spirits finely touched: The testing of value and integrity in four Shakespearean plays* (Athens, Ga, 1976), pp. 15–50; originally ' "I know my course": Hamlet's confidence', *PMLA*, lxxxix, 1974, pp. 477–86.
5   Harry Levin, *The question of Hamlet* (New York, 1959; 1970), p. 27.
6   Levin, p. 156.
7   William Empson, '*Hamlet* when new', pp. 39–40, 189.
8   S.P. Zitner, 'Hamlet, duellist', *Univ. of Toronto Quarterly*, xxxix, 1969, p. 9.
9   William Empson, *The structure of complex words* (1951), p. 215; the earlier quotations in this paragraph will be found there on pp. 202 and 186.
10 Morris Palmer Tilley, *A dictionary of proverbs in the sixteenth and seventeenth centuries* (Ann Arbor, Michigan, 1950), H 539, 542.
11 J. Pitt-Rivers, *The Fate of Shechem*, p. 31.
12 Tilley, *A dictionary of proverbs*, H 582, 577–8.
13 Empson, '*Hamlet* when new', p. 191.
14 Francis Fergusson, *The idea of a theater* (Princeton, 1949), pp. 112–15.
15 Herbert Howarth, *The tiger's heart* (1970), is suggestive of the general pertinence of Shakespeare's claim to honour to his own plays.

6 Hamlet's being

1 ' "To be or not to be: that is the question" surely implies another question. This is true whether (a) one accents "that", implying the rejection of a preceding question; (b) one accents "is", reaffirming the proposition after a previous doubt; (c) renders "that is" as a spondee, thus more subtly reaffirming the question after a doubt,' Ralph Berry, ' "To say one": An essay on *Hamlet*', *Shakespeare Survey* 28, 1975, p. 108. Berry does not consider the nature of the supplanted question.

2 W. Empson, '*Hamlet* when new', p. 186.

3 Marjorie B. Garber, *Dream in Shakespeare* (New Haven, Conn., 1974), p. 105.

4 Harry Levin, *The Question of Hamlet*, p. 68.

5 '*Hamlet* when new', p. 186. Harold Jenkins ('Hamlet and Ophelia', *Proc. of the British Academy*, xlix, 1963) notes, in addition, that in its present position the dialogue complements that with Gertrude in III.4.

6 Levin, p. 69 and diagram, p. 167.

7 W. Segar, *Honor Military and Civill*, p. 113. Compare Segar's use of 'nature' here with the Ghost's emphasis on nature and unnatural conduct in its plea to Hamlet in I.5.

8 Nigel Alexander, *Poison, play and duel* (1971), p. 73.

9 T.S. Eliot, 'Shakespeare and the Stoicism of Seneca', *Selected Essays* (1951), pp. 129, 130–31.

10 T.W. Baldwin, *Small Latine and lesse Greeke* (Urbana, Ill., 1944), II, p. 603ff., argues that 'To be or not to be' alludes to Cicero's *Tusculan Disputations*. He is too positive. Doubtless Cicero is in the background with Seneca; but I am not attempting to expound sources.

11 I use the Loeb edition of the *Epistulae Morales*, with translation by Richard M. Gummere (1917–25; 1953) and of the *Moral Essays*, with translation by John W. Basore (1928–35; 1958). As a slight indication of the currency of the Senecan ideas discussed, when a passage cited is to be found in the *Flores Lucii Annei Senecae* of Erasmus (Antwerp, 1539), the fact is signalized by: (E). References for the paragraph in question are as follows: *Ad Lucilium* XXIV.24 (E)—the italics are mine; *Ad Lucilium* LXXVII.9; *De Providentia* IV. 13–15 (E); *Ad Lucilium* LXXXII. 17; *De Providentia* VI.9.

12 For example, *De Constantia* V.3: 'ubi iam virtus honestumque est' ('where virtue and honesty already are'). These generalizations are based on *L. Annaei Senecae, Operum Moralium Concordantia*, ed. P. Grimal (Paris, 1965–70).

13 Contrast *De Providentia* III.14: 'Graue est a deterioribus honore anteiri? Vatinio [Cato] postferatur' (following Grimal's punctuation)—'is it hard to be overtaken by inferiors in seeking office? Let him be defeated by a Cato'—with *De Clementia* I.ii.1: 'sicut medicinae apud aegros usus, etiam apud sanos honor est, ita clementiam quamuis poena digni inuocent, etiam innocentes colunt', where there is no irony: 'as medicine is

used by the sick, yet is held in honour by the healthy, so with mercy—though it is those who deserve punishment that invoke it, yet even the guiltless cherish it'.

14 *De Providentia* V.4.

15 In other words, OED's 'free', sense 3, 'Noble, honourable, of gentle birth and breeding' and sense 4, 'in regard to character and conduct: noble, honourable, generous, magnanimous' are prominent. If the phrase is taken to establish a distinction, I suggest that 'free' has a colouring from OED's sense 2, 'enjoying civil liberty: existing under a government which is not arbitrary or despotic, and does not encroach on individual rights', thus connecting with Hamlet's feelings about 'honest' men: one might compare Seneca's use of 'liber', and the hero's use of 'liberté' in Laforgue's 'Hamlet'.

16 T.S. Eliot, *Selected Essays*, p. 139

17 *Ad Lucilium* LXXXII. 15–16, 23. Virtue is 'straightforward and peremptory' (22).

18 *Ad Lucilium* CII. 21–2.

19 *Ad Lucilium* XLI.3 (E). In *The Workes both Morrall and Natural[of] Lucius Annaeus Seneca* (1614), the translator, Lodge, exclaims of this, 'Oh excellent and deep Epistle!'.

20 *Ad Lucilium* XI. 1–2, 6 (E); cf. *Hamlet*, I.4.23 ff.

21 *Ad Lucilium* CII.1

22 OED s.v. 'their', sense 4.

23 Levin, *The question of Hamlet*, p. 71.

24 Cf. my earlier suggestion that Hamlet's melancholy might in some sense be *cause* of the Ghost's appearance.

25 These paradigms do not originate in Stoic philosophy, but are prominent within it: see J.Jacquot, ' "Le Théâtre du Monde" de Shakespeare à Calderon', *Revue de Littérature Comparée*, xxxi, 1957, pp. 341–72.

26 L.C. Knights, 'An approach to "Hamlet" ' (1960), '*Some Shakespearean themes' and 'An approach to "Hamlet"* ' (Penguin Books, 1966), p. 210.

27 J. Pitt-Rivers, *The Fate of Shechem*, pp. 7, 10, 13.

7 Hamlet and Ophelia

1 M. Rose, *Shakespearean design*, p. 111.

2 OED, 'plaster', *v*, sense 2.

3 H. Jenkins, 'Hamlet and Ophelia', p. 140.

4 J. Dover Wilson, *What happens in 'Hamlet'*, p. 130, cited by Jenkins, *supra*.

5 E. Prosser, *Hamlet and revenge*, p. 175.

6 L.C. Knights, '*Some Shakespearean themes' and 'An approach to "Hamlet"* ' ', pp. 184, 190, 191, 192. See also G. Wilson Knight, 'The embassy of death: An essay on *Hamlet*', *The Wheel of Fire*, 4th edn, revised and enlarged (1949; 1960), pp. 17–46, and H.D.F. Kitto, *Form and meaning in drama* (1956; 1960), pp. 246–337.

7 Knights, pp. 196–7.

8 Knights, p. 211.
9 W. Segar, *Honor Military and Civill*, p. 122, allows that 'A scholler also having taken degrees of schoole, was not denied the title of Gentrie', but the emphasis in most Elizabethan writing on the subject is on honour as a military or aristocratic attribute.
10 H. Jenkins, 'Hamlet and the fishmonger', *Deutsche Shakespeare-Gesellschaft West Jahrbuch* 1975, p. 119; cf. Jenkins, p. 151.
11 'Hamlet and the fishmonger', pp. 120, 118. In the introduction to his edition of *Hamlet*, Jenkins does not speak of 'obsession' here, but he still interprets the exchanges with Polonius at II.2.171 ff. and 399 ff. as foreshadowing that with Ophelia in III.1.
12 Jenkins puts the case for Ophelia's innocence incontrovertibly, I think, in 'Hamlet and Ophelia'.
13 Cf. John Bayley, *The uses of division* (1976), of *Hamlet* in general: 'we may feel behind the brilliance of the action, and its power to absorb us, there is nothing really there at all' (p. 187)—a view modified later in the book and in his *Shakespeare and tragedy* (1980).
14 Jenkins, 'Hamlet and Ophelia', p. 143.
15 Harold Goddard, *The meaning of Shakespeare* (Chicago, 1951), p. 357.
16 Abraham Cowley, 'Inconstancy', *Poems*, ed. A.R. Waller (1905), p. 74.
17 Cf. Jean Rousset, '*L'intérieur et l'extérieur: Essai sur la poésie et sur le théâtre au XVIIe siècle* (Paris, 1968), pp. 73 ff., 128 ff.
18 *Elizabethan lyrics*, ed. Norman Ault (1925; 1966), p. 181.
19 J.C. Baroja, 'Honour and shame', in *Honour and Shame*, ed. J.G. Peristiany, p. 110.
20 J. Pitt-Rivers, *The Fate of Shechem*, p. 11: the reference is to the play by Tirso de Molina.
21 W. Empson, '*Hamlet* when new', pp. 187–8.

8 Hamlet's theatre

1 Jenkins omits the final 'sir'—presumably on the grounds that it is one of F1's 'playhouse additions to the dialogue' (*Hamlet*, ed. H. Jenkins, p. 75, and see pp. 62–3). Significantly, he does not argue the particular case.
2 F1 reads 'my choice', graphically indicating a man divided inside himself.
3 *Hamlet*. ed. Bernard Lott (New Swan Shakespeare: Advanced series, 1960), p. 108.
4 F1's reading 'my' for 'thy' at line 79 makes Horatio merely Hamlet's puppet: 'with the very comment of *my* soul/Observe my uncle'.
5 W.W. Greg, 'Enter Ghost', *Modern Language Review*, xiv, 1919, pp. 362–3. I owe this reference to Jenkins.
6 Cf. H. Skulsky, *Spirits finely touched*, as cited at chapter 5, n. 4.
7 W.W. Robson, *Did the King see the dumbshow?* (Edinburgh, 1975), p. 9. The reference to the 'duel' is on p. 14. This inaugural lecture is also printed in *Cambridge Quarterly*, vi, 1975, pp. 303–25.

8   Robson, p. 6.
9   Robson, pp. 8–9.
10 W. Empson, '*Hamlet* when new', pp. 36–7.
11 Jenkins offers a similar gloss.
12 M.C. Bradbrook, *Shakespeare the craftsman* (1969), p. 129, followed by Nigel Alexander, *Poison, play and duel*.
13 *Hamlet*, ed. J. Dover Wilson (New Cambridge Shakespeare, 1934), p. 208.
14 Jenkins refers us to 'in the full bent' (II.2.30), which he glosses by reference to 'the utmost to which a bow may be drawn', but *OED* gives no warrant for this sense to be found here.
15 E. Prosser, *Hamlet and revenge*, pp. 183–4.

9 Claudius and Gertrude

1   F1 reads 'dangerous' for 'near us' at III.3.6 and 'Lunacies' for 'brows' at line 7. These readings emphasize an awareness of Hamlet's madness at the expense of ideas that he may be ambitious, and so confirm the general sense of Claudius as straightforwardly businesslike here.
2   W. Empson, '*Hamlet* when new', p. 21.
3   Wilbur Sanders and Howard Jacobson, *Shakespeare's magnanimity* (1978), p. 34.
4   This is F1's reading; Q2 'showe' is weak and does not connect as 'shove' does with the idea of movement in 'currents'.
5   J.Pitt-Rivers, *The Fate of Shechem*, pp. 5, 6.
6   *The Fate of Shechem*, p. 3.
7   J. Pitt-Rivers, *Mana*, p. 8.
8   Cf. *The Fate of Shechem*, p. 7, quoted p. 29.
9   *The Fate of Shechem*, p. 2.
10 E. Prosser, *Hamlet and revenge*, 2nd edn, p. 193.
11 Ibid.
12 F1's version of these lines is interesting:

> Heavens face doth glow,
> Yea this solidity and compound masse,
> With tristful visage as against the doome,
> s thought-sicke at the act.

.e punctuation leaves it in doubt whether 'Heavens face' and 'this ▪idity and . . . masse' are distinct or identical, an ambiguity reinforc-▪g the interpretation here. 'Tristful' has surprising psychological force ▪ the heated circumstances of the speech. It is a nice point whether F1 ere offers a better reading than Q2. Jenkins in fact reads 'tristful', ▪hough sticking in general to Q2.
▪f. also William Empson, ' "Sense" in *Measure for Measure*', *The structure ▪of complex words*, pp. 270–88.

14 However, the omission of ll.71–6, 'Sense . . . difference', from F1 may indicate authorial dissatisfaction with these lines, which have no equivalent in Q1,

15 F1 reads 'As reason panders will', at l.88. It is good because it links physical and moral spheres more tightly than in Q2.

16 Tr. Walter Herries Pollock, in Denis Diderot and William Archer, *'The Paradox of Acting' and 'Masks and Faces'* (Dramabooks, New York, 1957), p. 15.

10 Burlesque, parody and fugue

1 Jenkins omits these words, only found in F1, on the grounds that they 'have a subtle incongruity' that makes them likely to be an actor's interpolation.

2 J. Dover Wilson, in his edition of the play for the New Cambridge Shakespeare, finds an allusion here to Psalm cxliv.4. This adds a further refinement to Hamlet's riposte.

3 The F1 reading 'rots' is weaker, but still appropriate.

4 Cf. D.J. Palmer, 'Casting off the old man: History and St Paul in *Henry IV*', *Critical Quarterly*, xii, 1970, pp. 267–83.

5 E. Prosser, *Hamlet and revenge*, 2nd edn, p. 208.

6 *Hamlet and revenge*, p. 209.

7 Jenkins removes the *non sequitur* by assuming that Shakespeare here writes negligently, meaning to say that greatness is *not* 'not to stir without great argument'. This is a desperate thesis for an editor to advance.

8 Emrys Jones, *Scenic form in Shakespeare* (1971), pp. 78–81.

9 Andrew Gurr, *Hamlet and the distracted globe* (1978), p. 104.

10 E. Prosser, *Hamlet and revenge*, p.213.

11 Cf. Mikhail Bakhtin, *Rabelais and his world*, trs. Hélène Iswolsky (Cambridge, Mass., 1968), pp.24–52 and *passim*.

12 Viktor Shklovsky has applied his notion of *ostranenie*—'defamiliarization' or 'making strange'—to Ophelia's use of folk-song: see 'O Gekube', *Teatr'*, 1958, 5, pp.63–8.

13 See chapter 9, pp. 197–200.

14 W. Sanders and H. Jacobson, *Shakespeare's magnanimity*, pp. 23–4.

11 Graveyard thoughts

1 J. Dover Wilson, *What happens in 'Hamlet'*, 3rd edn, pp. 266–7.

2 H. Granville-Barker, *Prefaces to Shakespeare*, pp. 136–7, n.17.

3 E. Prosser, *Hamlet and revenge*, 2nd edn, p. 220.

4 Ibid.

5 Granville-Barker, *Prefaces to Shakespeare*, p. 250.

6 *Prefaces to Shakespeare*, p. 136.

7   Prosser, *Hamlet and revenge*, p. 226.
8   W. Sanders and H, Jacobson, *Shakespeare's magnanimity*, p. 54.
9   *Hamlet and revenge*, pp. 223, 224, following the lead given by Louis Martz, *The poetry of meditation* (New Haven, Conn., 1954).
10 Sanders and Jacobson, *Shakespeare's magnanimity*, p. 54.
11 K. Sagar, '*Hamlet*', p. 58.
12 *Tottel's Miscellany (1557–87)*, ed. Hyder E. Rollins, revised edition (1928; 1965), II, p. 285.
13 '[Hamlet] has become a sentimentalist in his last phase', *What happens in 'Hamlet'*, p. 268.
14 '. . . the scene is a comment, visual and verbal, on the whole "antic disposition". Melancholy meditation is now explicitly harmonized with the world that gives rise to it' (B. Gellert Lyons, *Voices of melancholy*, p. 105).
15 Lyons, *Voices of melancholy*, pp. 99–100, 104.
16 *What happens in 'Hamlet'*, p. 295.
17 Harold Jenkins does not commit himself on the matter of the author's intention.
18 *Hamlet and revenge*, p. 227.
19 J.K. Walton, 'The structure of *Hamlet*', *Hamlet* (Stratford-upon-Avon Studies 5, 1963), p. 84, argues most fully that Hamlet does not leap into the grave; Nigel Alexander finds Hamlet's counter-rant shows him coming 'to terms with . . . aggressive and sexual complications . . .', *Poison, play and duel*, p. 168; many critics want the action to validate Hamlet's claim to royalty in 'This is I,/Hamlet the Dane'.
20 H. Granville-Barker, *Prefaces to Shakespeare*, p. 139.
21 *What happens in 'Hamlet'*, p. 271.
22 *Hamlet and revenge*, p. 227.
23 *Prefaces to Shakespeare*, p. 140.
24 Cf. the discussion of Hercules in the play, Lyons, *Voices of melancholy*, pp. 107–9. According to Mrs Lyons, 'Hamlet's comparisons of himself with Hercules . . . characterize his heroic role as well as his ambivalence about assuming it.' She thinks the cat and dog to be generally symbolic of the melancholic's world.

12 Heaven ordinant

1   A.C. Bradley, *Shakespearean tragedy*, 2nd edn (1905; 1952), p. 144.
2   Bradley, *Shakespearean tragedy*, pp. 144–5.
3   For Kitto and Ribner, see below, notes 11 and 10; Maynard Mack, 'The world of *Hamlet*', *Yale Review*, xli, 1952, pp. 502–23.
4   Bradley, p. 144.
5   H. Granville-Barker, *Prefaces to Shakespeare*, p. 107.
6   *Hamlet*, ed. Bernard Lott, p. 144.
7   These are omitted from the Folio text; Q1, from a point equivalent to III.4.138, ends the scene briskly, and has no reference to the two

courtiers. Hamlet's self-characterization as 'minister and scourge' is also lacking in Q1. Folio's omission provides for greater surprise and, with that, shock, when Hamlet announces the trick he has played on Rosencrantz and Guildenstern.

8   The Folio reading is 'deare plots', emphasizing Hamlet's view of himself as cherishing, rather than profoundly meditating, them. The variant does not substantially affect the argument here.

9   *Prefaces to Shakespeare*, p. 142.

10   Irving Ribner, *Patterns in Shakespearian tragedy* (1960; 1971), p. 80.

11   H.D.F. Kitto, *Form and meaning in drama* (1956; 1960), p. 325.

12   E. Prosser, *Hamlet and revenge*, p. 227.

13   N. Alexander, *Poison, play and duel*, p. 164.

14   *Hamlet and revenge*, p.229.

15   *Hamlet and revenge*, p. 230, the source of other quotations from Prosser in this paragraph.

16   J. Pitt-Rivers, *The Fate of Shechem*, p. 3. Mottoes cited come from Jacopo Gelli, *Divise-Motti e Imprese di Famiglie e Personaggi Italiani*, 2nd edn, (Milan, 1928); R.Pinches, *Elvin's Handbook of Mottoes revised* (1971); and John Woodward, *A treatise on heraldry British and foreign*, 2 vols, (1896), pp. 378–92.

17   *The Fate of Shechem*, p. 9.

13   Hamlet's end

1   E. Prosser, *Hamlet and revenge*, p. 231.

2   A.C. Bradley, *Shakespearean tragedy*, 2nd edn, p. 145.

3   There is no reason to suppose that Hamlet is not being frank with Horatio.

4   'The moment of final suspense in *Hamlet*: "We defy augury" ', *Shakespeare 1564—1964*, ed. Edward A. Bloom (Providence, RI, 1964), p. 54.

5   John Downame, *Annotations upon all the Books of the Old and New Testament*, 2nd edn (1651; 1657), on Matt. 10:29.

6   George Hakewill, *Apologie or Declaration of the Power and Providence of God*, 3rd edn (1635), Lib. V, p. 23. The book was first published in 1627, but the fifth and sixth books are later additions, each with its own pagination.

7   Hakewill, Lib. IV, p. 507.

8   Keith Thomas, *Religion and the decline of magic* (1971), p. 84 and elsewhere.

9   *A Harmonie upon the three Evangelists . . . with the Commentary of M. John Calvine* (1584), pp. 282–3.

10   E.g., Harry Levin, *The question of Hamlet*, p. 101; J.V. Cunningham, *Tradition and poetic structure* (Denver, 1960), pp. 136–40; Prosser, *Hamlet and revenge*, pp. 282–3.

11   J. Dover Wilson, *What happens in 'Hamlet'*, pp. 274–5.

12   J.Pitt-Rivers, *The Fate of Shechem*, pp. 7–8.

13 Variorum *Hamlet*, ed. H.H. Furness (1877; 1918), pp. 7–8.
14 S.P. Zitner, 'Hamlet, duellist', pp. 8–9.
15 N. Council, *When honour's at the stake*, p. 110.
16 S. Booth, 'On the value of *Hamlet*', p. 171.
17 *The Whole Works of the Right Rev. Jeremy Taylor,* ed. Reginald Heber, 15 vols, (1839), III, p. 328.
18 *The Whole Works*, III, p. 228.
19 *The Whole Works,* III, p. 230.
20 *The Whole Works*, III, p. 175.
21 Booth, 'On the value of *Hamlet*', p. 155.
22 *The Whole Works*, III, p. 177.
23 Prosser, *Hamlet and revenge*, p. 236.
24 A.L. French, *Shakespeare and the critics* (1972), pp. 56–7, argues vigorously the inappropriateness of the epithet 'sweet' as a sign of the play's weakness.
25 Prosser, pp. 239–40.
26 W. Sanders and H. Jacobson, *Shakespeare's magnanimity*, p. 56.

Conclusion

1 *Njal's Saga*, translated by Magnus Magnusson and Hermann Palsson (Penguin Books, 1960), p. 135.

Index

This index is made up of proper names and a few select topics. A reference to page number and note identifies a specific quotation on the page indicated. Page numbers in italics refer to the concluding section of notes. Peers are indexed by title, not by family name.